Modern Studies in European Law

Recent titles in this series:

Private Autonomy in EU Internal Market Law:
Parameters of its Protection and Limitation
Rufat Babayev

'ree Movement and Welfare Access in the European Union:
-Balancing Conflicting Interests in Citizenship Jurisprudence
Victoria Hooton

and Investment Treaty-Making Post-Lisbon: Moving Beyond Mixity
Gesa Kübek

The Normative Foundations for EU Criminal Justice:
Powers, Limits and Justifications
Jacob Öberg

ıbourhood Law: Wider Europe and the Extended EU's Legal Space
Alessandro Petti

The Dynamics of Powers in the European Union
by Christina Eckes, Päivi Leino-Sandberg and Anna W Ghavanin

: European Convention on Human Rights and Private Law:
Comparative Perspectives from South-Eastern Europe
Edited by Mateja Durovic and Cristina Poncibò

Judging Composite Decision-Making:
The Transformation of European Administrative Law
Filipe Brito Bastos

EU Diplomacy in Multilateral Fora
Edited by Christine Kaddous and Frank Hoffmeister

The Market Citizenship Illusion:
Free Movement Rights for Atypical Workers
Alice Welsh

Actors and Roles in EU Disability Law
Edited by Delia Ferri and Eva S Krolla

The Impact of War (in Ukraine) on the EU
ited by Inge Govaere, Sacha Garben and Eleanor Spaventa

:an Judiciary: A Community of Law and a Community of Judges
dited by Alejandro Saiz Arnaiz and Joan Solanes Mullor

sus over Liberal Democracy: Insights from European Judges
ımona Coman, Viktor Kazai, Leonardo Puleo and Andrew Bradley

For the complete list of titles in this series
loomsbury.com/uk/series/modern-studies-in-european-law/

DISSENSUS OVER LIBE

This book explores what judges do and how t growing dissensus over liberal democracy.

Focusing on the European landscape, it their roles when judicial independence and features interviews with judges from variou courts, complemented by a series of acad tionship between law and politics in times c narrative reveals unique personal experienc role of the judiciary and the rule of law in th the book engages with these issues through ute to broader debates beyond Europe and t

Volume 134 in the Series Mod

T

Ed

S

Dissensus over Liberal Democracy

Insights from European Judges

Edited by
Ramona Coman
Viktor Kazai
Leonardo Puleo
and
Andrew Bradley

•HART•
OXFORD • LONDON • NEW YORK • NEW DELHI • SYDNEY

HART PUBLISHING
Bloomsbury Publishing Plc
Kemp House, Chawley Park, Cumnor Hill, Oxford, OX2 9PH, UK
1385 Broadway, New York, NY 10018, USA
Bloomsbury Publishing Ireland Limited, 29 Earlsfort Terrace, Dublin 2, D02 AY28, Ireland

HART PUBLISHING, the Hart/Stag logo, BLOOMSBURY and the Diana logo are trademarks of Bloomsbury Publishing Plc

First published in Great Britain 2025

A catalogue record for this book is available from the British Library.

A catalogue record for this book is available from the Library of Congress.

ISBN: HB: 978-1-50998-500-5
ePDF: 978-1-50998-502-9
ePub: 978-1-50998-501-2

Typeset by Compuscript Ltd, Shannon

For product safety related questions contact productsafety@bloomsbury.com

To find out more about our authors and books visit www.hartpublishing.co.uk. Here you will find extracts, author information, details of forthcoming events and the option to sign up for our newsletters.

This publication received funding from the European Union's Horizon Europe research and innovation programme under the Call HORIZON-C12-2021-DEMOCRACY-01 as part of the research project RED-SPINEL, Grant agreement n°101061621.

Co-funded by the European Union

The **RED-SPINEL** – ***R****espond to* ***E****merging* ***D****issensus:* ***S****upranational* ***I****nstruments and* ***N****orms of* ***E****uropean* ***L****iberal* ***D****emocracy* – Project is funded by the European Union (EU) through Horizon Europe, and is executed under the authority of the European Research Executive Agency (REA) of the European Commission. Coordinated by Ramona Coman as Principal Investigator (PI), the Project started in the autumn of 2022 at the Institut d'études européennes of the Université libre de Bruxelles and runs till the first quarter of 2026. **RED-SPINEL** seeks to shed light on the growing dissensus surrounding liberal democracy and the rule of law within and beyond the EU. The project examines how policy instruments and legal mechanisms at the EU level have evolved in response to dissensus surrounding liberal democracy and its constitutive dimensions. **RED-SPINEL** brings together academics and researchers from seven universities – Université libre de Bruxelles (ULB, BE), Universiteit van Amsterdam (UvA, NL), Libera Università Internazionale Degli Studi Sociali Luiss Guido Carli (Luiss, IT), Universitatea Babeș-Bolyai (UBB, RO), University of Warwick (UoW, UK), Uniwersytet Mikołaja Kopernika w Toruniu (NCU, PL), and l'École des Hautes Études Commerciales HEC Paris (HEC, FR); and four nonacademic institutions – Peace Action Training and Research Institute (PATRIR, RO), Milieu Consulting (MILIEU, BE), Magyar Helsinki Bizottság / Hungarian Helsinki Committee (HHC, HU), and Stichting Nederlands Instituut voor Internationale Betrekkingen (Clingendael, NL).

ACKNOWLEDGEMENTS

This book idea originated from the JUSTICE research project,[1] which examined how governmental measures restricting judicial independence led to judicial mobilisations in Poland, Romania, and Hungary. Building on the initial research findings and within the framework of the Horizon Europe RED-SPINEL project we sought to further explore the role of judges in the context of the growing dissensus over liberal democracy. Our aim is to move beyond the debates centred on Central and Eastern Europe, which have often drawn media attention, and to examine how the dismantlement of the core pillars of liberal democracy are perceived, understood, experienced, and responded to by judges in other European national contexts as well. In other words, the motivation is to understand how judges perceive their roles when democracy and its core values are under strain.

As co-editors of this volume, since April 2024 we have been meeting with 18 judges from various Member States of the European Union and European countries, each with experience at different levels of jurisdiction. Some have been actively engaged in defending democracy and the rule of law in their countries, while others have taken a more reserved stance. We express our sincere appreciation for their time, their engagement, and the exchanges that greatly enhanced this project.

We are grateful to Sinéad Moloney and Sasha Jawed from Hart Publishing for giving us the opportunity to publish this book. We hope it will be a valuable read not only for the academic community, but also for judges, political and social actors, and citizens alike. We extend our gratitude to Lisa Conant (University of Denver), Gábor Halmai (EUI), Agnieszka Kubal (Oxford University), Katarína Šipulová (Masaryk University) and Tommaso Pavone (University of Toronto), who kindly agreed to comment on some of these interviews in light of their research work. Thanks are also due to Joanna Britton for her careful proofreading of the manuscript.

A heartfelt thank you to Yavuz Aydin, a Turkish judge and political refugee who, as he himself states in this book, 'went to bed a judge and woke up a terrorist' in his own country. Despite these circumstances, he has played a crucial role in helping us connect with numerous European judges, allowing us to gain valuable insights into how dissensus over liberal democracy is understood, perceived, and debated within this professional milieu and across various national contexts.

Ramona Coman, Viktor Kazai, Leonardo Puleo and Andrew Bradley
Brussels, 9 January 2025

[1] The project 'Judicial (in)dependence: political, social and legal support and resistance(s) in Hungary, Poland and Romania (JUSTICE)' – coordinated by Ramona Coman with Leonardo Puleo as post-doctoral researcher (December 2020–December 2023) received funding from the *Fonds de la Recherche Scientifique* (FNRS), Belgium.

TABLE OF CONTENTS

PART II
INSIGHTS FROM SOUTHERN EUROPEAN JUDGES

PART III
INSIGHTS FROM CENTRAL AND EASTERN EUROPEAN JUDGES

PART IV
INSIGHTS FROM NEIGHBOURING EUROPEAN COUNTRIES

PART V
ACADEMIC DEBATES

ABOUT THE CO-EDITORS

Ramona Coman is a professor in political science at the Université libre de Bruxelles and Emeritus President of the *Institut d'études européennes*. She is the author of *The Politics of the Rule of Law in the EU Polity: Actors, Tools and Challenges* (Palgrave 2022), *Réformer la justice dans un pays post-communiste. Le cas de la Roumanie* (Editions de l'Université de Bruxelles) and the co-editor of *Politics and Governance in the Post-Crisis European Union* (Cambridge University Press, 2020). Coman teaches courses on Decision-Making in the EU, the Rule of Law and Mutual Trust in Global and European Governance as well the PhD Seminar on Theory, Research and Methods in Political Science. Since 2023, she is a visiting professor at the College of Europe in Bruges. As of October 2022, she is the Principal Investigator of the Horizon Europe project 'Respond to Emerging Dissensus: Supranational Instruments and Norms of European Democracy' (RED-SPINEL, 2022–2026) and the academic coordinator of the Marie Sklodowska Curie Joint Doctorate Network GEM-DIAMOND, which both examine the growing dissensus over liberal democracy and its implications for the EU's capacity to act in its internal and external policies.

Viktor Kazai is a lawyer specialised in comparative constitutional law and EU law with a doctoral degree from Central European University (Vienna). Most recently, he joined Université libre de Bruxelles, *Institut d'études européennes* – (Belgium) as a post-doctoral researcher in the RED-SPINEL project and supported the work of the Berlin-based NGO, Civil Liberties Union for Europe as a senior rule of law expert. In addition to his participation in international research projects focusing on the European rule of law crisis (RECONNECT, RED-SPINEL), he has been involved in human rights litigation as a legal advisor, most importantly before the European Court of Human Rights, and has been collaborating with human rights NGOs. Viktor Kazai has published in several reputable law journals, including the *Hague Journal on the Rule of law*, *The Theory and Practice and Legislation*, *Jus Politicum* and *Annuaire international de justice constitutionnelle*. His first monograph titled *The Equilibrium of Parliamentary Law-making Comparative Perspectives on the Role of Courts in a Democracy* was published by Routledge in 2024.

Leonardo Puleo is a postdoctoral researcher at the University College Dublin and a research fellow at the Institut d'études européennes (IEE) of the Université Libre de Bruxelles (ULB). He obtained his PhD in June 2021 from the Sant'Anna School of Advanced Studies and the University of Florence, with a dissertation on challenger parties in Europe. In December 2021, he joined the IEE/ULB to contribute as post-doctoral researcher to the PDR project JUSTICE, coordinated by Ramona Coman, which examined judges' mobilisation, opposition, and resistance against the erosion of the rule of law and democratic backsliding in Central and Eastern European countries. Currently, his research agenda focuses on party competition, with a focus on the spreading of illiberal ideas and the challenges against liberal democracy. His work has been published in several peer-reviewed journals, including *West European Politics, Political Studies, Party Politics*, and *Democratization*.

Andrew Bradley is a member of the IEE-ULB RED-SPINEL Project Management Team since November 2023. He served previously as Chief of Staff in the Office of the Secretary-General of the Organisation of African, Caribbean and Pacific States (OACPS) during the period 2020 to August 2023. Andrew headed the Office of the International Institute for Democracy and Electoral Assistance (International IDEA) to the European Union (EU) in Brussels from 2012 to 2018. He was also stationed at the Headquarters of International IDEA in Stockholm, Sweden where he led the Global Programmes Division of the Institute during the period 2010–2011. Andrew served as the Assistant Secretary-General for Political Affairs and Human Development of the African, Caribbean and Pacific (ACP Group) of States from 2005 to 2010. Prior to that, he served as a diplomat in South African Embassies and Missions in Canada, Switzerland and Belgium. Andrew authored and contributed to numerous articles and publications, and his academic qualifications include graduate and post-graduate degrees and diplomas in Political Sciences, Strategic Studies, International Marketing and International Politics.

LIST OF CONTRIBUTORS

Benedetta Arrighini, PhD student in European law at the Université libre de Bruxelles, FGV Direito Rio, and Luiss University in Rome

Yavuz Aydin, former Turkish judge, founder of *Justice for Rule of Law*

András Bálint Baka, former President of the Supreme Court of Hungary

Lars Bay Larsen, former Vice-President of the Court of Justice of the European Union

Dragana Boljević, judge at the Supreme Court of Serbia

Manuela Cadelli, judge at the Namur Court of First Instance, Belgium

Dragoş Călin, judge at the Bucharest Court of Appeals, Romania

Lisa Conant, professor of political science at the University of Denver, USA

Monika Frąckowiak, judge at the District Court in Poznań, Poland

Dieter Grimm, former judge at the Federal Constitutional Court of Germany

Gábor Halmai, professor of law at the European University Institute, Italy

Javier Hernández García, judge at the Supreme Court of Spain

Małgorzata Maria Gersdorf, professor at the University of Warsaw and former President of the Supreme Court of Poland

Mariarosaria Guglielmi, President of MEDEL and European Delegated Prosecutor, Italy

Agnieszka Kubal, associate professor at the Centre for Socio-Legal Studies (CSLS), Law Faculty and a Research Fellow at Green Templeton College, United Kingdom

Zdeněk Kühn, judge at the Czech Constitutional Court, Czechia

Giulia La Torre García, Marie Sklodowska-Curie doctoral fellow with the Université de Genève and the Université libre de Bruxelles

José Igreja Matos, President of the Court of Appeal of Porto, Portugal

Tamás Matusik, judge, former President of the National Judicial Council, Hungary

Tommaso Pavone, assistant professor of European Politics at the University of Toronto, Canada

Luca Perilli, judge at the Specialised Section for International Protection of the Court of Catania, Italy

Katarína Šipulová, Co-director of the Judicial Studies Institute, Law Faculty, Masaryk University, and a ReConstitution Scholar (2024–2025)

Kees Sterk, judge at the District Court of Breda, the Netherlands

Andrea Titz, judge, Vice-President of the Traunstein Regional Court, Germany

Christopher Vajda, former judge of the United Kingdom and Northern Ireland at the Court of Justice of the European Union

ABOUT THE CONTRIBUTORS

Benedetta Arrighini is a MSCA Ph.D. Fellow (GEM-DIAMOND Joint Doctorate Network) in International and European Law at the Université libre de Bruxelles, FGV Direito Rio, and Luiss University in Rome. Her research focuses on EU-Mercosur relations in criminal matters and their impact on the rule of law, adopting a comparative regionalism and interregionalism approach. She examines the EU-Mercosur cooperation beyond trade, with a strong emphasis on fundamental rights. Her academic and professional interests include criminal law, European criminal law, and international criminal law, with a particular focus on the impact of criminal law on fundamental rights. Arrighini holds a Master's degree in Law from the University of Trento and an LL.M. from the College of Europe in Bruges. She is also a qualified lawyer in Italy.

Yavuz Aydin served as a justice counsellor at the Permanent Delegation of Turkey to the EU (Brussels) from 2011 to 2014. However, in July 2016, while working as a judge in Turkey he was dismissed by the government as part of a crackdown following the attempted coup of the same year. He was among the 4,500 Turkish judges purged by President Erdogan. Aydin graduated from Ankara University Law Faculty and obtained his first Master's degree in EU Law and European Human Rights Law from Exeter University (UK). In 2018, Aydin has been granted political asylum in Romania. He now resides in Belgium where he obtained his second Master's degree in Interdisciplinary EU Studies from the *Institut d'études européennes* of the *Université libre de Bruxelles*. He is a Rule of Law laureate of Iustitia 2021 awards and continues his advocacy for democracy and judicial independence through the NGO Justice for Rule of Law.

András Bálint Baka is a Hungarian lawyer and university professor who holds a PhD in Legal and Political Science. From 1990 to 1998, he was the Director General of the Hungarian School of Public Administration. For 11 months in 1990 and 1991, Baka served as Member of Parliament (without party membership) in the parliamentary group of the Hungarian Democratic Forum. In 1991, he was elected to the European Court of Human Rights (ECtHR) as a judge in respect of Hungary, a position he held until 2008. In 2009, Baka was elected President of the Supreme Court of Hungary for a six-year term, but he was removed from office in 2011. In 2016, the ECtHR found in *Baka v Hungary* that the termination of his mandate was a violation of the European Convention on Human Rights (ECHR). Until his recent retirement, Baka served as Chamber President of the Supreme Court. He served as the Deputy President of the Administrative Tribunal of the Council of Europe from 2018 until 2024.

Dragana Boljević has been a judge since 1988, initially handling civil cases in the Belgrade Fifth Municipal Court then District Court from 2002, and later in the Belgrade Court of Appeal from 2013. Since 2021, she has served as a judge of the Supreme Court of Serbia. Throughout her career, Boljević has held numerous institutional roles: President of the working groups of the National Judicial Reform Commission for the Guidelines for Judicial Laws (2006–2007) and for drafting the law on the High Judicial Council (2007); member of the Serbian Justice Ministry's working groups and member of the National Parliament's Constitutional Committee working group. Boljević has been a member of the Judges' Association of Serbia (JAS) since its establishment in 1997 and served as JAS President from 2006 to 2019. After 2019, she assumed the role of JAS Honorary President and spokesperson. At the international level, Boljević served as the General Secretary of the *Magistrats Européens pour la Democratie et les Libertés* (MEDEL). In 2007, she was awarded Person of the Year in the Rule of Law by Organisation for Security and Co-operation in Europe (OSCE).

Lars Bay Larsen studied at the Københavns Universitet (University of Copenhagen, Denmark). He graduated with a BA degree in political science in 1976, and then returned to study at the same university in 1978, this time enrolling in the Faculty of Law, where he obtained a complete law degree in 1983. After graduation, he was appointed as an official at the Danish Ministry of Justice where he worked from 1983 to 1985. From 1985 to 1986, he was Head of Section at the *Advokatsamfund* (Danish Bar Association). After returning to the Danish Ministry of Justice, he served successively as Head of Section from 1986 to 1991, Head of Division from 1991 to 1995, Head of the Police Department from 1995 to 1999, and Head of the Law Department from 2000 to 2003. He was also Representative of the Kingdom of Denmark on the K4 Committee from 1995 to 2000, the Schengen Central Group from 1996 to 1998, and the Europol Management Board from 1998 to 2000. He was called to the Bar in Denmark in 1991 and, in 2003, the focus of his career turned to the judiciary when he joined the Højesteret (Supreme Court of Denmark) where he served as a judge until 2006. Bay Larsen's career also illustrates the valuable complementarity between practice and teaching, since he was a lecturer (1984–1991) – and then associate professor (1991–1996) in family law at the Københavns Universitet. Since 2008, he has been a lecturer in European criminal law at the University of Luxembourg. Bay Larsen has been a Judge at the Court of the European Union since 11 January 2006. He was later elected by his peers to the position of President of Chamber and performed that function for two successive terms (9 October 2012–8 October 2018). From 8 October 2021 to 7 October 2024, when he retired, he was the elected Vice-President of the Court of Justice.

Manuela Cadelli has been a judge at the Namur Court of First Instance in Belgium since 1999 and she has also been President of the *Association syndicale des magistrats* since 2013. She is the author of several books, including *Radicaliser la justice, projet pour la démocratie* (Editions SAMSA 2018).

Dragoş Călin is a judge at the Bucharest Court of Appeals (since April 2009). He is a trainer in EU law at the National Institute of Magistracy, Bucharest (since 2006), and an Associate Researcher at the Institute for Legal Research of the Romanian Academy Centre for European Legal Studies (since 2010). Dragoş Călin is a founding member and

Co-President of the Romanian Judges' Forum Association (since 2007), Director of the Romanian Judges' Forum Review (since 2009), Vice-President of the European Group of Magistrates for Mediation (GEMME) (May 2010–May 2012), founding member (2009) and Vice-President of the International Conference for Mediation and Justice (2012–2016), member of the Association of European Magistrates for Human Rights (since 2011), member of the Franco-Romanian Lawyers Association (since 2009), and a member of the Association of Magistrates of the European Union (since 2007). Dragoş Călin holds a PhD in law (University of Bucharest, Faculty of Law) with a dissertation entitled *The Dialogue between Constitutional Courts and the Court of Justice of the European Union* (2018). He graduated from the Faculty of Law of the University of Bucharest in 1998 and from the National Institute of Magistracy in 2003. Dragoş Călin is the author of over 200 books and articles in the field of law.

Lisa Conant is professor of political science at the University of Denver, Faculty affiliate of the Sie Center for International Security and Diplomacy, and core faculty of the Institute for Comparative and Regional Studies. She specialises in the politics of European legal integration, exploring the impact of judgments by the Court of Justice of the European Union and European Court of Human Rights, the Europeanisation and globalisation of national courts, transformations in European citizenship, Brexit, and the relationship between legal mobilisation and human rights protection in Europe. Conant teaches courses on European politics, international law and human rights, the European Union, and the politics of immigration and citizenship. She has engaged in extensive archival and interview-based research across Europe through doctoral and postdoctoral fellowships at the Free University of Berlin and the European University Institute in Florence, and she regularly returns to Europe for ongoing research. Conant has a Ph.D., Political Science, University of Washington (1998) and is affiliated at the American Political Science Association, Council for European Studies, European Union Studies Association and the Law and Society Association.

Monika Frąckowiak was appointed a judge in 2007 in the civil department of the District Court in Poznań, Poland. Since 2016, Frąckowiak has been representing Iustitia at international meetings, especially with European Union institutions. From December 2017 to 2022, Frąckowiak was also a member of the Board of MEDEL, and since December 2022, she has been the Vice-President of MEDEL.

Małgorzata Maria Gersdorf graduated with honours from the Faculty of Law and Administration at the University of Warsaw in 1975. From 1991 to 2004, she was a member of the Supreme Court's Office for Studies and Analysis (formerly the Judiciary Office). Then, until 2005, she served as the Supreme Court's general counsel. On 15 July 2008, Małgorzata Maria Gersdorf was appointed by the President of the Republic of Poland to serve as a judge on the Supreme Court. She has received numerous awards, including the *Standing in the Name of the Principles* Award from the Movement of Citizens of the Republic of Poland (8 January 2019). This distinction is awarded to members of the legal profession, including judges, prosecutors and lawyers, who uphold the independence of the courts. Gersdorf also received the *Award of Devoted Optimists* from the magazine *Anoche Tuve Un Sueño* under the auspices of UNESCO (23 April 2019), a distinction for individuals and institutions whose work promotes ethical, philosophical, economic, scientific and cultural values to build a better future for coming generations. Gersdorf has also received the Theodor Heuss Prize (11 May 2019) for exemplary fortitude, clarity and civil courage in defending the conditions necessary for a constitutional democracy; the Bonn International Democracy Prize (8 November 2019) for her commitment to an independent judiciary, her strong support for the separation of powers and opposition to attempts by the Polish executive branch to exert political influence on the judiciary, and her defence of democracy and the rule of law in Poland; the Kant-Weltbürger-Preises Award (30 October 2021) at the conference *Europa Wertgemeinschaft verteidigen und starken!* Protecting and strengthening the European community of values in Freiburg; and the Gez Medal (2021, presented in March 2022) for those fighting for freedom and democracy.

Dieter Grimm is a German legal scholar (born 11 May 1937 in Kassel) and former member of the Federal Constitutional Court of Germany. In 1957, he began studying law and political science in Frankfurt. After passing the First State Examination in 1962, he studied at the Sorbonne in Paris and then at Harvard University, earning an LLM degree in 1965. He returned to Germany and passed the Second State Law Examination in 1967. Grimm worked as researcher at the Max Planck Institute for European Legal History headed by Helmut Coing in Frankfurt. He wrote a doctoral dissertation on the French legal scholar Léon Duguit and was awarded a doctoral degree for his thesis *Solidarity as a Legal Principle*. He remained at the Institute and contributed to Coing's Handbook of Sources and Literature of Recent European Private Law History. In 1979, he habilitated at the University of Frankfurt with the thesis *Constitution and Private Law in the Nineteenth Century*. From 1979 to 1999, Grimm was a professor at the University of Bielefeld. He focused on the origins and functionalities of modern constitutions and published important essays in 'Law and State of Civil Society' (1987), 'Constitutional History of Germany' (1988) and 'The Future of the Constitution' (1991). In 1987, at the suggestion of the Social Democratic Party of Germany (SPD), Grimm was elected by the Bundesrat to the First Senate of the Federal Constitutional Court, and he served there from 1987 to 1999. In this role, Grimm was responsible, in particular, for cases concerning freedom of expression, freedom of broadcasting and the press, freedom of assembly and association, general personality rights, data protection law and competition law. He played a key role in preparing groundbreaking decisions as a rapporteur in these areas. In 2000, Grimm joined the Wissenschaftskolleg zu Berlin as a Permanent Fellow and moved to the Humboldt University of Berlin, where he became emeritus in 2005. He served as Rector of the Wissenschaftskolleg from 2001 to 2007 and continued his teaching career as a visiting professor at Yale Law School from 2002 to 2017. Among his most important publications are *Sovereignty* (2009; English edition 2015), *The Future of the Constitution* (2012), *Europe yes – but which one?* (2016; English edition 2017), *Constitutionalism. Past – Present – Future* (2016; paperback 2019) and *Constitutional Adjudication* (2021; English version 2024).

Mariarosaria Guglielmi has been a European Delegated Prosecutor since 2021, based in Rome. From October 2015 to April 2021, she worked as a prosecutor at the Rome First Instance Court, specialising in economic crimes and judicial cooperation in criminal matters. From September 2007 to October 2015, Guglielmi was seconded to the secretariat of the Superior Council of the Judiciary (*Consiglio Superiore della Magistratura*), where she supported different commissions, including those dealing with the regular professional evaluations of judges and prosecutors, the selection and evaluation of judicial and prosecutorial candidates for managerial positions, and international relations. Guglielmi actively participated in judicial associations and served as General Secretary of Magistratura Democratica, the Italian association of judges and prosecutors, from 2016 to 2021. Internationally, she has been the President of MEDEL (*Magistrats Européens pour la Démocratie et les Libertés*) since December 2022, having previously served as its Vice-President since 2017. Additionally, she is a member of the editorial board of the journal *Questione Giustizia* and has authored numerous articles on topics related to rule of law, self-government, and judicial and prosecutorial independence.

Gábor Halmai is professor emeritus and scientific director of the project TRust, Independence, Impartiality and Accountability of Legal Professionals under the EU Charter – part 2 (TRIIAL 2) in the Center for Judicial Cooperation of the Robert Schuman Centre for Advanced Studies. Between 2016 and 2022 he was Professor and Chair of Comparative Constitutional Law at the Law Department of the European University Institute (EUI). He served as Director of Graduate Studies at the Law Department from 2017 till 2021. His primary research interests are comparative and European constitutional law. Halmai joined the EUI in 2016 after a teaching and research career (at the Eötvös Loránd University in Hungary, at the Princeton University in the USA, at the European Master's Program in Human Rights and Democratization in Italy) as well as years of professional career as chief advisor to the President of the Hungarian Constitutional Court, member of the EU Fundamental Rights Agency's Management Board and numerous other civic activities. Halmai is founder and editor-in-chief of Fundamentum, the Hungarian human right quarterly, and Member of the Scientific Advisory Board of the European Yearbook on Human Rights, and of the Review of Constitutionalism and Constitutional Change (RC3). Halmai's recent research focuses on illiberal constitutional theories and developments in East-Central Europe.

Javier Hernández García is a law graduate from the Autonomous University of Madrid. He was admitted to the judicial profession in Spain in 1989. Javier Hernández García was an investigating judge until 1996, when he was transferred to the Tarragona Provincial Court, where he sat as a judge until January 2020. After a brief period at the Criminal Division of the High Court of Justice of Catalonia, since November 2020 Javier Hernández García has been serving on the Criminal Division of the Spanish Supreme Court.

Agnieszka Kubal is Associate Professor at the Centre for Socio-Legal Studies (CSLS), Law Faculty and a Research Fellow at Green Templeton College. Kubal completed her DPhil at the University of Oxford (2011). Upon post-doctoral spells at the International Migration Institute (Oxford), CSLS (Oxford) and Davis Centre for Russian and Eurasian Studies (Harvard), she was based at the School of Slavonic and East European Studies (SSEES) at UCL, where she held an Associate Professorship in Sociology. Kubal is an interdisciplinary socio-legal scholar with area studies interest in Central Eastern Europe and Russia. She is the author of two monographs, *Socio-legal Integration. Polish post-2004 EU Enlargement Migrants in the UK* (2012, Ashgate/ Routledge) and *Immigration and Refugee Law in Russia. Socio-Legal Perspectives* (2019, Cambridge

University Press). Kubal is currently working on a co-authored monograph entitled *Who are the humans behind Human Rights in Eastern Europe and Russia? Historical and Comparative Perspectives* (under contract with UCL Press). She is currently a Principal Investigator on an UKRI/ERC Starting Grant (2022–2027) 'Who are the humans behind Human Rights in Eastern Europe and Russia?' (HuRiEE).

Zdeněk Kühn graduated from the Faculty of Law of Charles University in Prague (1997 Mgr., 2000 JUDr., 2001 Ph.D.) and the University of Michigan Law School, Ann Arbor, USA (LL.M. in 2002, S.J.D. in 2006). Since 1997, he has been teaching jurisprudence at his alma mater in Prague, where he became a Docent (associate professor) in 2006 and was appointed Professor of Jurisprudence in 2018. Kühn also lectures at many foreign universities, both in Europe (e.g. faculties of law in Toulouse, Zagreb, etc), in the USA (eg Cornell University, University of South Carolina, University of San Francisco, etc) and in Israel (Bar Ilan University). His first steps in the legal profession led to advocacy. From 1997 to 2001, he worked as a legal trainee (articled clerk) in Prague, and he passed his bar exam in 2000. During his studies in the USA, he actively participated as an expert in Czech and Czechoslovak law in several important cases, eg in the Assicurazioni Generali SpA Holocaust Insurance Litigation from 2002 to 2004. After returning to the Czech Republic, he was a law clerk at the Constitutional Court for three years from 2004. In 2008, Kühn was appointed judge of the Supreme Administrative Court after having been appointed an *ad hoc* judge of the European Court of Human Rights the year before. In addition to his academic work, he regularly gives lectures to judges and other practitioners at home and abroad. He was also a European Bank for Reconstruction and Development expert in support of legal and constitutional reform in Moldova (including repeated expert visits to Chisinau (2011–2015) and an EBRD expert in support of legal and constitutional reform in Albania (2012). He is the author of several monographs on the judiciary and judicial interpretation of law, and several hundred articles published in English, Arabic, Russian, Bulgarian, and Chinese. He has also contributed to several commentaries on Czech Bill of Rights, the Code of Procedure before Administrative Courts, Antidiscrimination Law etc. On 19 December 2023, President Petr Pavel appointed Kühn a Judge of the Czech Constitutional Court.

Giulia La Torre García is a Marie Sklodowska-Curie doctoral fellow with the Université de Genève and the Université libre de Bruxelles. She holds a Master's degree in European Law from the Université libre de Bruxelles and a double Bachelor's degree in Law and Political Science from the University of Valencia. During her undergraduate studies, Giulia La Torre García spent an Erasmus year at the Karl-Franzens Universität Graz, where she began to specialise in EU law. She is a qualified lawyer at the Spanish Bar Association and acquired legal experience in the Labour and Criminal Law Departments of various law firms. Her broader research interests lie in the fields of EU law, constitutional law and legal theory, with a focus on the interplay between national constitutionalism, general principles of EU law, and legal reasoning in the Court of Justice of the EU.

José Igreja Matos has served as a judge since 1990 and presently holds the position of President of the Court of Appeal of Porto, Portugal, elected by his peers. Throughout his career, Judge Igreja Matos has held significant roles both nationally and internationally. He served as President of the European Association of Judges from 2016 to 2021 and subsequently, from 2021 to 2023, he led the International Association of Judges, the largest organisation of judges globally, representing national associations of judges or similar bodies from 92 countries. Currently, he holds the position of Vice-President of the Consultative Council of European Judges within the Council of Europe. Judge Igreja Matos has been a member of the Advisory Board of the United Nations Judicial Integrity Network and has participated in expert missions across various regions of the world, from Myanmar to Serbia, and from the United Kingdom to Mongolia. He has been selected to participate in numerous study visits by prestigious institutions such as the UN, Council of Europe, OECD, OSCE, EU, and IBA. In addition to his judicial duties, Judge Igreja Matos has been invited by judiciaries and academic institutions worldwide to deliver numerous lectures, conferences, and training sessions. Judge Igreja Matos has been actively involved in supporting human rights causes, from advocating for Judge Afiuni's case in Venezuela to aiding in the repatriation of women judges from Afghanistan amidst Taliban violence. Judge Matos has been a prominent figure in events advocating for judicial independence and rule of law in Europe, including participation in the European Parliament and the PACE conferences. Igreja Matos writing has been published in various reviews, including *EU Law Live*, *Verfassungblog*, and several national and international periodicals. Judge Matos has authored and co-authored more than a dozen books on a range of judicial topics, particularly focusing on judicial independence, human rights, and civil law procedure. Judge Matos has also served as the Director of the judicial magazine, *Julgar*, for over four years and is an associate investigator at the University of Coimbra.

Tamás Matusik graduated from Pázmány Péter Catholic University (Budapest) in 2004. Since then, he has held various positions in the judiciary. Matusik started as a trainee judge at the Metropolitan Court in Budapest and later passed the bar exam in 2008. After working as an assistant judge he was appointed as a judge in 2009 and has been serving as an investigative judge at the Central District Court of Buda since then. In 2014, Matusik served as Head of the International Relations Department of the National Office for the Judiciary as a seconded judge. Since 2015, Matusik has been the Head of the Investigative Judge Department of the Central District Court of Buda. Matusik became a Member of the National Judicial Council in 2018, where he also served as the international representative of the Council. On 7 June 2023, he was elected President of the National Judicial Council. In addition to his judicial duties, Judge Matusik has authored several journal articles on investigative judicial proceedings, the protection of fundamental rights, the pre-trial detention, and alien policy custody. He is also known for giving lectures at conferences, judicial trainings and LLM (Master of Law) courses.

Tommaso Pavone is Assistant Professor of European Politics in the Department of Political Science at the University of Toronto in its St. George Campus, where he is also Director of the Centre for the Study of France and the Francophone World (CEFMF), an Associate Graduate Faculty member of the Centre for European and Eurasian Studies (CEES), as well as Visiting Researcher at the ARENA Center for European Studies at the University of Oslo. In 2024, Pavone received the Carolina de Miguel

Moyer Young Scholar Award, which recognises the scholar under age 40 'who is judged to have made (through a body of publications) the most significant contribution to the interdisciplinary study of Europe.' Pavone's research and teaching interests span comparative politics, law and society, and judicial politics, focussing on Europe and the European Union and traces how interactions between lawyers, courts, and policymakers impact political development, social change, and the rule of law. His latest book with Cambridge University Press – *The Ghostwriters: Lawyers and the Politics Behind the Judicial Construction of Europe* – has been praised as 'the most important book on European legal integration in decades' and has won seven major awards from the American Political Science Association (APSA), the Law and Society Association (LSA), the European Union Studies Association (EUSA), and the American Society of International Law (ASIL).

Luca Perilli has been a judge in Italy since 1995, with experience in criminal, civil, and asylum law. He is currently a judge at the Specialised Section for International Protection of the Court of Catania, Italy. Since January 2016, Perilli has served as the Italian Contact Point of the Courts and Tribunals Network of the European Union Agency for Asylum (EUAA). He is a member of the Judicial Experts' Pool of the Agency and has been a trainer for judges in several national and international training courses on asylum law. In 2021, he was reporter on judicial independence and access to justice in Turkey for the Turkey Tribunal, an international people's Tribunal. From January 2016 to January 2020, he was a member of the Board of Directors of the Italian School for the Judiciary (SSM), and from November 2016 to January 2020 he was also a member of the European Judicial Training Network (EJTN) Steering Committee and Chair of the EJTN Judicial Training Methods (JTM) Working Group. Among his many other international achievements, he served as an independent expert from 2008 to 2017 in 26 peer-based missions organised by the European Commission (EC) in (potential) candidate countries to the EU, including Albania, Croatia, North Macedonia, Montenegro, Serbia, Turkey (and Tunisia) to assess whether national legislation and its application complied with EU standards. In addition, from 2008 to 2019, Perilli acted as the independent expert of the Council of Europe for several activities and projects on the rule of law and human rights, including, most notably, the 2014 report on the Individual Application to the Constitutional Court of Turkey for the protection of fundamental rights. Since 2005, Perilli has been a speaker at several international conferences about topics including human rights, the rule of law, asylum law, effectiveness, and quality of justice, organised, among others, by the European Commission, the Council of Europe, the European Union Agency for Fundamental Rights, the European University Institute (EUI), and the EJTN. He is the President of the Association Justice for Rule of Law, based in Belgium, and a member of various international and Italian associations in the field of justice.

Katarína Šipulová is the Co-director of the Judicial Studies Institute, Law Faculty, Masaryk University at Brno. She earned her PhD in European Studies at the Faculty of Social Studies, Masaryk University, and an MSt degree in Socio-Legal Research at the University of Oxford. Apart from the academic work, Šipulová held a position as the head of the analytical department at the Supreme Court of the Czech Republic and provided consultation to both Supreme and Constitutional Court of the

Czech Republic, Czech Ministry of Justice and Slovak Ministry of Finances, mostly in projects targeting the rule of law or international commitments. She regularly taught courses 'Human Rights, Democracy and Constitutionalism' and 'Transitional Justice and Democratization' at the Faculty of Social Studies, Masaryk University. Šipulová provides advice and consultation for the Czech Supreme Court, Czech Ministry of Justice, and Slovak Ministry of Finances. She is a member of the Committee for Fundamental Rights and Prevention of Discrimination of the Czech Republic's government Council for Human Rights, and also a member of the Steering Committee of the Law and Courts Group in the European Consortium for Political Science. Šipulová's research activities are centred on courts, judicial independence, transitional justice and democratisation of the Central and Eastern European countries.

Kees Sterk is a senior judge in the Netherlands with more than 30 years of experience in the field of civil and criminal law. His extensive experience includes serving as a judge in the District Court of Breda, the Court of Appeal of 's-Hertogenbosch, the Supreme Court of the Netherlands and the District Court of Zeeland-West-Brabant. From 2013 to 2020, he was Vice-President of the Council for the Judiciary. In 2013, Sterk joined the European Network of Councils for the Judiciary (ENCJ) as part of the project on Independence and Accountability and became the Chair of the project in 2016. In 2018, he was elected President of the ENCJ. During his presidency, the Polish Council for the Judiciary was suspended as a member because it was not independent from the Polish executive branch. Sterk studied law at Tilburg University, where he defended his PhD thesis on the subject of danger in tort law, comparing French, Swiss and Dutch law. Since 2020, he has been a part-time Professor of Administration of European Justice at Maastricht University. His expertise includes the application of European law, including the European Convention on Human Rights, in Dutch case law, especially with regard to the institutional entrenchment of the core values of the judiciary in the Member States of the European Union. His 2023 inaugural speech concerned the selection and appointment of judges in European law. In 2022, he wrote a paper on the culture of accountability for Councils for the Judiciary for the Organization for Security and Co-operation in Europe (OSCE). In January 2022, Sterk joined the Netherlands Helsinki Committee (NHC). He served as Chair of the Review Committee, reviewing the Bosnian and Herzegovinian Council for the Judiciary in 2023. He was also a member of the Organisation for Economic Cooperation and Development (OECD) team that reviewed the Ukrainian judiciary in 2024. He regularly delivers lectures to Central-European judges on various subjects relating to judicial independence.

Andrea Titz is a prominent German judge who currently serves as the Vice-President of the Traunstein Regional Court, a position she has held since 1 February 2020. In 2022, she was also elected to the role of Co-Chair of the German Association of Judges. Titz began her career in 1995, when she joined the Traunstein public prosecutor's office. Over the years, she has held various positions. She became a judge in the local courts of Mühldorf am Inn and Altötting in 2002 and later moved to the Munich II public prosecutor's office. As the spokesperson for the Munich Higher Regional Court, she was actively involved in high-profile cases such as the tax trial against Uli Hoeneß, the former manager of FC Bayern Munich, and the National Socialist Underground

(NSU) and bribery trials. Titz has also been an active member of judicial associations and has held various positions including Deputy Chair of the Presidium of the German Association of Judges and Chair of the Bavarian Association of Judges. Her election as Co-Chair of the German Association of Judges on 29 April 2022 was a recognition of her contributions to the legal field.

Christopher Vajda was the judge representing the United Kingdom and Northern Ireland at the Court of Justice of the European Union (CJEU) from 2012 until the United Kingdom left the EU in 2020. He was called to the Bar of England and Wales in 1979 and was appointed a King's Counsel (KC) in 1997. Vajda practiced at Monckton Chambers until 2012 and then again from 2020. He is a member of the Luxembourg Bar, a visiting professor at the College of Europe in Bruges, at Luxembourg University and at King's College, London.

LIST OF ABBREVIATIONS

AEAJ	Association of European Administrative Judges
AfD	*Alternative für Deutschland* (Alternative for Germany)
AFJR	*Asociația Forumul Judecătorilor din România* (Romanian Judges' Association Forum)
ANM	*Associazione Nazionale Magistrati* (National Association of Magistrates), Italy
ASM	*Association Syndicale des Magistrats* (Magistrates' Trade Union Association), Belgium
CCEJ	Consultative Council of European Judges, Council of Europe
CEE	Central and Eastern Europe
CEPEJ	*Commission européenne pour l'efficacité de la justice* (European Commission for the Efficiency of Justice), Council of Europe
CJEU	Court of Justice of the European Union
CoE	Council of Europe
CVM	Cooperation and Verification Mechanism
EAJ	European Association of Judges
EAW	European Arrest Warrant
ECHR	European Convention on Human Rights
ECtHR	European Court of Human Rights
EEC	European Economic Community
EJTN	European Judicial Training Network
ENCJ	European Network of Councils for the Judiciary
EP	European Parliament
EU	European Union
FdI	*Fratelli d'Italia* (Brothers of Italy)
Fedasil	Federal Agency for the Reception of Asylum Seekers, Belgium

Fidesz	*Magyar Polgári Szövetség* (Hungarian Civic Alliance)
FPÖ	*Freiheitliche Partei Österreichs* (Freedom Party of Austria)
IAJ	International Association of Judges
JAS	*Drustvo sudija Srbije* (Judges' Association of Serbia)
KRS	*Krajowa Rada Sądownictwa* (Polish Council for the Judiciary)
MABIE	*Magyar Bírói Egyesület* (Hungarian Association of Judges)
MEDEL	*Magistrats Européens pour la Démocratie et les Libertés* (European Judges for Democracy and Liberty)
NVA	*Nieuw-Vlaamse Alliantie* (the New Flemish Alliance), Belgium
OBH	*Országos Bírósági Hivatal* (National Office for the Judiciary), Hungary
OBT	*Országos Bírói Tanács* (National Judicial Council), Hungary
PiS	*Prawo i Sprawiedliwość* (Law and Justice), Poland
RN	*Rassemblement national* (National Rally), France
TEU	Treaty on European Union
UNHCR	United Nations High Commissioner for Human Rights
UNJR	*Uniunea Naţională a Judecătorilor din România* (Romanian National Union of Judges)

1

How do Judges Conceive their Roles in a Context of Growing Dissensus over Liberal Democracy – And why do Narratives Matter?

RAMONA COMAN

Introduction

Democracy is under challenge in various parts of the world, and the European Union (EU) is no longer an exception in this respect.[1] A vast literature has emerged in recent years explaining how democracy is being eroded or even dying[2] not by *coups d'état*, but by electoral ballot, whether free or not. The cases of Poland and Hungary have been among the most debated in Europe and have received international attention, particularly since the 2010s when the Hungarian Fidesz (*Magyar Polgári Szövetség*, Hungarian Civic Alliance) and the Polish PiS (*Prawo i Sprawiedliwość*, Law and Justice) governments began challenging the core institutional pillars of liberal democracy – and, more specifically, its liberal tradition, including the rule of law, the separation of powers, and fundamental rights. Judges and judicial institutions are at the centre of a wider phenomenon.[3] In both countries, albeit in different ways, governments limited the power of the courts and the independence of judges; they transformed judicial institutions from the top,[4] dismissing or replacing judges, despite domestic contestation

[1] TA Börzel, T Risse, SB Anderson and JA Garrison (eds), *Polarization and Deep Contestations. The Liberal Script in the United States* (Oxford, Oxford University Press, 2024).

[2] S Levitsky and D Ziblatt, *How Democracies Die* (New York, Crown, 2018); W Sadurski, 'How Democracy Dies (in Poland): A Case Study of Anti-Constitutional Populist Backsliding' (2018) 18/01. Sydney Law School Research Paper, www.ssrn.com/abstract=3103491.

[3] A Sajó, *Ruling by Cheating: Governance in Illiberal Democracy* (Cambridge, Cambridge University Press, 2020) 292.

[4] W Sadurski, *Poland's Constitutional Breakdown* (Oxford, Oxford University Press, 2019); B Bugaric and T Ginsburg, 'The Assault on Post-Communist Courts' (2016) 27 *Journal of Democracy* 69; L Gamboa, B García-Holgado and E González-Ocantos, 'Courts against Backsliding: Lessons from Latin America' (2024) 46 *Law & Policy* 358.

and European and international criticism. On the one hand, within the judiciary, there is growing concern not only over increasing political interference in judicial matters or political attacks but also on pathways towards autocratisation. On the other hand, within society, the image of the justice system is not always positive,[5] especially in countries where there is a prevailing sense that citizens are dissatisfied with the idea of justice per se.

Poland and Hungary are not isolated cases, even if in these contexts the transformations have been the most visible and radical.[6] European and international institutions and organisations have reported and documented various ways in which political institutions sanction or harass judges and interfere within the exercise of judging.[7] In recent decades there have been concerns regarding several EU Member States, as illustrated by various reports issued by the European Commission, not only about countries that have recently joined the EU, but also 'old' or 'older' Member States. In some cases, these revolve around the efficiency of the justice systems.[8] In others, there are inherent political tensions over the judicial appointment process and judicial independence, which is a *sine qua non* condition for countries to join the EU. In yet other cases, what is at stake is the gradual dismantlement of core pillars of liberal democracy, and this puts strain on the very values on which the EU is founded, such as the respect for human dignity, freedom, democracy, equality, the rule of law, and respect for human rights, including the rights of persons belonging to minorities, as enshrined in Article 2 of the Treaty on European Union (TEU).

Dissensus over liberal democracy has taken many forms over the decades both at the domestic and supranational/international levels. Despite the diversity of definitions,[9] it is commonly accepted that liberal democracy brings together two traditions: the democratic tradition based on equality and popular sovereignty and the liberal tradition based on the rule of law, respect for human rights and individual liberties. While liberal democracy has always been contested, in recent years, the most outspoken and virulent criticism has come from populist and radical right parties (see chapter 2). Through abusive constitutionalism,[10] constitutional coups,[11] or abuse of the constitution[12] in some political regimes, populist governments have changed the rules of the polity to centralise power, strengthen the role of the executive, and limit the independence of institutions such as courts and central banks, and these acts have

[5] According to the 2024 Flash Eurobarometer, EU citizens rate the justice system in their countries in terms of independence of courts and judges as 'good' and 'very good' (11%), 'fairly good' (41%) and 'fairly' or 'very bad' (37%). Flash Eurobarometer 540, 'Perceived Independence of the National Justice Systems in the EU among the General Public' (2024) www.europa.eu/eurobarometer/surveys/detail/3193, 6.

[6] D Giannoulopoulos and Y McDermott (eds), *Judicial Independence Under Threat* (The British Academy by Oxford University Press, 2022).

[7] United Nations General Assembly, Report by D Garcia-Sayan, 2022.

[8] R Coman, *The Politics of the Rule of Law in the EU Polity. Actors, Tools and Challenges* (Cham, Palgrave, 2022) 109.

[9] W Merkel, 'Embedded and Defective Democracies' (2004) 11 *Democratization* 33.

[10] M Krygier, 'Rule of Law (and Rechtsstaat)' in JR Silkenat, JE Hickey and PD Barenboim (eds), *The Legal Doctrines of the Rule of Law and the Legal State (Rechtsstaat)* (Cham, Springer, 2014) 45.

[11] Sadurski (n 4).

[12] P Blokker, *New Democracies in Crisis? A Comparative Constitutional Study of the Czech Republic, Hungary, Poland, Romania and Slovakia* (Milton Park, Routledge, 2014).

significant implications for both politics and policies.[13] Beyond this trend towards autocratisation, the values and institutions of liberal democracy have given rise to growing dissensus more generally. This phenomenon extends beyond the role of judges and their independence per se; it concerns their function in upholding the rules of the polity and fundamental values, as well as their position within the broader political regime (see chapter 3).

Against this backdrop, this book explores what judges do and how they perceive their role in a context not only where their independence is being debated or undermined, but also at a time when other fundamental values are under strain at both the national and European levels. This book is not about how judges think, in the sense of how they decide cases and what explains their decisions.[14] It is more about how judges conceive their roles in a context of growing dissensus over liberal democracy. The subject becomes all the more important amid the rise to power of political parties, in Europe and beyond, which view judicial independence, alongside other independent institutions, as obstacles to the expression of the people's will.

To address this question, the book invites readers to approach this topic from the actors' point of view. It brings together 18 interviews with judges from various European states (both Member and non-Member States of the EU) and levels of jurisdictions. Some of the judges interviewed served at the Court of Justice of the EU (CJEU) and the European Court of Human Rights (ECtHR). Some are constitutional or supreme court judges, others lower court judges from various legal fields, and prosecutors. Some of these judges have been active leaders of their professional associations at the national or international and European levels, or both. Some are known for their academic publications or their public statements.[15] Others are recognised for their institutional positions and the reports they have produced for regional and international organisations on the independence of judges. Others have gained recognition through their actions in the public sphere, being actively involved in defending the rule of law and their independence in their country through various *répertoires d'action*.

In the quest to better understand this phenomenon, the book includes 18 interviews with (by alphabetical order): Yavuz Aydin (former Turkish judge, founder of Justice for Rule of Law), András Bálint Baka (former President of the Supreme Court of Hungary), Dragana Boljević (judge at the Supreme Court of Serbia), Lars Bay Larsen (former Vice-President of the Court of Justice of the European Union), Manuela Cadelli (judge at the Namur Court of First Instance in Belgium), Dragoş Călin (judge at the Bucharest Court of Appeals, Romania), Monika Frąckowiak (judge at the District Court in Poznań, Poland), Dieter Grimm (former member of the Federal Constitutional Court of Germany), Mariarosaria Guglielmi (president of MEDEL and Italian prosecutor), Javier Hernández García (judge at the Supreme Court of Spain), Małgorzata Maria Gersdorf (former President of the Supreme Court of Poland), Zdeněk Kühn (judge of the Czech Constitutional Court,

[13] R Coman and C Volintiru, 'Anti-liberal Ideas and Institutional Change in Central and Eastern Europe' (2021) 24 *European Politics and Society* 5.

[14] RA Posner, *How Judges Think* (Cambridge, Harvard University Press, 2010).

[15] Some of their publications are mentioned in the biographical notes.

Czechia), José Igreja Matos (President of the Court of Appeal of Porto, Portugal), Tamás Matusik (former President of the National Judicial Council, Hungary), Luca Perilli (chair of the Trento Migration Court, Italy), Kees Sterk (judge at the District Court of Breda, the Netherlands), Andrea Titz (judge, Vice-President of the Traunstein Regional Court, Germany) and Christopher Vajda (former judge of the United Kingdom and Northern Ireland at the Court of Justice of the European Union).

Although the choice of these 18 judges does not ensure a full representation of domestic situations, nonetheless we sought to cover a range of national contexts, including, for example where judges had been imprisoned and others gone into exile, as in Turkey; and countries which experienced a coup on the judiciary followed by a process of 're-electing' all judges, like in Serbia. Within the EU, in recent years, judges have been harassed, dismissed, or subject to disciplinary sanctions in Hungary, Romania, and Poland, with Czechia representing an exception to this trend. The book also features judges from Southern European countries such as Portugal, Spain and Italy, all three having introduced major reforms to strengthen the independence of the judiciary in the 1980s and 1990s,[16] often with mixed results and remaining high levels of tension between politics and the judiciary. Ultimately, the independence of the judiciary is not only under threat in recent democracies. Other national contexts are included such as Belgium, Denmark, Germany, the Netherlands, countries where radical right parties won recent elections or are gaining electoral support. The case of the United Kingdom (UK) has proved particularly interesting in the context of Brexit, as there too different questions arise concerning the relationship between political and legal constitutionalism.

Narratives Matter

Using this book to give judges a voice is arguably already a way of taking a stand in itself. 'At the risk of being accused of exaggerated sympathy', to use Bruno Latour's words, this may also may create the impression that the authors are trying to idealise the role of judges in democracy or glorify their actions.[17] Yet the focus on judges' insights is not new to the social sciences or legal studies[18] nor to cultural and artistic milieus. The courage and wisdom of judges as well as times where judges have betrayed justice have

[16] C Guarnieri and P Pederzoli, *La puissance de juger* (Paris, Editions Michalon, 1996) 178; C Guarnieri, 'The Judiciary in the Italian Political Crisis' (1997) 20 *West European Politics* 157, 158; P Magalhaes, C Guarnieri and Yorgos Kaminis, 'Democratic Consolidation, Judicial Reform and the Judicialisation of Politics in Southern Europe' in R Gunther, N Diamandouros and D Sotiropoulos (eds), *Democracy and the State in the New Southern Europe* (Oxford, Oxford University Press, 2006); J-L Briquet, 'Juges rouges ou Mains propres ?' (2002) 15 *Critique internationale* 45; J-L Briquet, 'La crise politique en Italie. Les analyses de la science politique italienne' (1995) 8 *Revue française de science politique* 127; C Vigour, 'Réformer la justice en Europe. Analyse comparée des cas de la Belgique, de la France et de l'Italie' (2004) *Droit et société* 291.

[17] B Latour, *La fabrique du droit. Une ethnographie du Conseil d'État* (Paris, La Découverte, 1999).

[18] Posner (n 14).

given rise to various fictional books,[19] movies[20] featuring real or fictional judges, as well as documentaries.[21] Nonetheless, as Graver put it, 'judges with a name and biography are notably absent in legal scholarship.'[22] While Graver addressed this research gap in *Valiant Judges, Iniquitous Law. Thirteen Stories of Heroes of the Law* through a series of judicial biographies, our book seeks to contribute to this question from a different perspective.

Rather than reconstructing the biographies of judges, the aim of the interviews we conducted was to focus on judges' reflections on the current European and global transformations challenging not only democracy but also their profession. The 18 interviews represent 18 different narratives with personal feelings, emotions, and ethical dilemmas. As Judge Bay Larsen put it, 'we are each a product of our personality, of our experiences, and what we have studied' (chapter 4). The interviews are meant to offer insights into actors' perceptions and the roles judges envision for themselves as both individual and collective actors in the relationship between law, politics, and society. The aim is not to depict an objective response to the main question of the book but to give a voice to the subjectivity of the actors and their reflexivity. Through these 18 interviews the book seeks to reflect the pluralism that characterises the profession regarding important questions related to the independence of judges and their roles in relations to politics and society.

Such narratives matter for researchers, both for scholars in political science and in the sociology of law. They provide a rich source of information about how people make sense of reality.[23] The question of judges think and how they present facts and events to give meaning to their roles and action becomes important as this provides a sense of the narrators' ideas 'both in relation to others and in the specific context of their described behaviour'.[24] It contributes to a process of problem definition and often have both empirical and moral dimensions.[25] Narratives help us understand not only people's personal and professional trajectories, but also the personal and professional motivations behind their behaviour. Narratives are also important in providing both individuals and collectives with a sense of purpose and place.[26] In an interview, the narrator become the centre of the narrative, as in an autobiographical *récit*. Narratives are key to understanding the role of actors in specific contexts

[19] F Kafka, *The Trial* (I Parry trans, Penguin Group, 2019).

[20] *Giovanni Falcone* (1993) is biographical film directed by Giuseppe Ferrara. It is the story of the anti-mafia judges pool established in the 1980s at the Palermo Courthouse in Sicily, Italy. *RBG* (2018) was a film directed and produced by Betsy West and Julie Cohen. It retraces Justice Ruth Bader Ginsburg's journey to the Supreme Court in the United States of America. For other examples of movies featuring real judges, see Duke Law, Bolch Judicial Institute, www.judicialstudies.duke.edu/2021/12/watch-these-10-movies-shows-featuring-real-judges/.

[21] For example, the documentary Judges Under Pressure (2021) – produced by Director Kacper Lisowski and Producer Iwona Harris – follows the Polish Judge Igor Tuleya, the face of the protest movement in Poland. The synopsis is available at: ff.hrw.org/film/judges-under-pressure/.

[22] HP Graver, *Valiant Judges, Iniquitous Law. Thirteen Stories of Heroes of the Law* (London, Routledge, 2024) 1.

[23] M Patterson and K Renwick Monroe, 'Narrative in Political Science' (1998) 1 *Annual Review of Political Science* 315.

[24] Patterson and Renwick Monroe (n 23).

[25] DA Stone, 'Causal Stories and the Formation of Policy Agenda' (1989) 104 *Political Science Quarterly* 281.

[26] Patterson and Renwick Monroe (n 23) 321.

and, as stated in the first pages of the introduction, what judges think and what legitimises action or inaction. They allow researchers to make sense of why and how judges interact and how these interactions determine outcomes, be they concrete action or inaction, and how these lead to the emergence of new fields of power through socialisation in national and transnational milieus. Through narratives, actors construct individual and collective identities, both national and European. As Somers and Gibson underlined, trying to understand how people act to change their world requires us to understand how people understand themselves, whether as autonomous or more conforming actors[27] (for example, regarding whether or not should they speak out).

The interviews[28] present various realities reflecting judges' personal opinions. Yet, they are unified by a set of common questions that the co-editors proposed for discussion. Without seeking to force excessive cohesion on the narratives, to ensure coherence, all interviews were organised in three parts.

The first part covered background questions, ie the professional, academic, and personal trajectory of judges and their motivations to pursue this career path. As the chapters illustrate, some always wanted to become judges, some came from families of lawyers. Others found their calling later in life and were the first in their families to pursue university studies. They all have many years of experience as judges or prosecutors in different jurisdictions and all are involved in forms of European or international forms of judicial cooperation.

The second part covered questions about the current state of democracy in Europe and about judicial independence. Emphasis was put on threats to liberal democracy, the erosion of judicial independence, and the implications for judges and citizens alike.

The third part focused on the role of judges in protecting democracy and judicial independence, as well as on the relationship between law and politics. Attention was devoted to the individual and collective actions judges take to defend their independence in general, in particular the values of liberal democracy. The concluding questions concern the role of the EU in safeguarding the rule of law in general, and common values. The interview guide was generally followed closely although the interviewers often let the interviews evolve naturally in order to let the judges present their narrative.

About the Structure of the Book

The book is organised in five main Parts.

In the first two chapters, two of the co-editors attempt to problematise this phenomenon. In chapter 2, Leonardo Puleo examines the emerging dissensus over liberal

[27] MR Somers and GD Gibson, 'Reclaiming the Epistemological "Other": Narrative and the Social Constitution of Identity' in C Calhoun (ed), *Social Theory and the Politics of Identity* (Oxford, Blackwell, 1994) 35.

[28] The interviews were conducted in person or remotely. Interviews lasted minimum one hour. Discussions sometimes lasted longer. One judge responded to our question in writing. Some of the interviews were conducted in the national language of the judge and then translated into English.

democracy from a political science perspective, exploring the ideological foundations of contemporary illiberalism, the spread of illiberal practices, as well as the illiberal contagion among European citizens. In chapter 3, Viktor Kazai, takes on a legal perspective to focus on the role of judges in political regimes, the ideal of judicial independence and its challenges.

The interviews are organised geographically presenting insights from judges from Western and Northern Europe (Part I), Southern Europe (Part II), Central and Eastern Europe (Part III), and non-EU European countries (Part IV). It is naturally impossible to summarise all aspects of the interviews here. They go (far) beyond the questions proposed for discussion, although the titles of the chapters – which are quotes from the interviews – reflect one main idea, representative of the questions: How do judges conceive their roles and what is at stake?

In Part I, in chapter 4, drawing on his experience as a Danish judge at the CJEU Lars Bay Larsen illustrates the interplay not only between national and European law but also between the Court of Justice of the European Union and the European Court of Human Rights, while comparing the CJEU to the American Supreme Court. Referring to the current challenges faced by judges, he argues that this is not a situation that can be remedied by judges only; the judges, national and European alike, must obviously fully respect the limitations for judges. In chapter 5, sharing her experience as a Belgian judge and as former President of the *Association Syndicale des Magistrats*, Judge Manuela Cadelli embraces a *longe durée* perspective to frame the role of judges in a wider historical and philosophical context. She reflects not only on the role of judges and their relation to power, but also on the notion of activism and on its significance in democratic regimes in a context of the resurgence of the 'penal populist', which seeks to designate an enemy as 'the migrant, the delinquent, the poor, the demonstrator, etc'. Drawing on his experience as a judge at the German Constitutional Court, Dieter Grimm in chapter 6 reflects on the legal reasoning and the purpose of the law, emphasising that 'consensus-building and reconciling different opinions is … an important part of a judge's work'. He reflects on the state of democracy in Europe, paying particular attention to Germany and the challenge of a populist party – *Alternative für Deutschland* (AfD, Alternative for Germany) – but also considers to how to strengthen democracy at the EU level, echoing his own academic work. In chapter 7, Dutch Judge Kees Sterk, former President of the European Network of Councils for the Judiciary (ENCJ), highlights the importance of trust in judicial institutions, while sharing his personal experience in pan-European institutional and non-institutional cooperations with judges from various EU and non-EU Member States. He reflects on the interplay between law and politics and, more specifically, on areas of law that have given rise to political dissensus in recent years, illustrating the implications for judges of vague laws. In chapter 8, German Judge Andrea Titz, former President of the Bavarian Association of Judges, discusses the implications of the rise of populist parties for the judiciary. She reflects on how law is created and emphasises that the application of the law 'cannot be separated from its origins and moral implication'. In chapter 9, Christopher Vajda, former British judge at the CJEU, raises a broader question, inviting us to reflect on the co-existence of courts and legislators in this context of growing dissensus. He traces this debate back to the tensions between governments and courts on fundamental rights and same-sex marriages in the 2000s.

In Part II, the narratives of the Italian, Spanish and Portuguese judges illustrate how past experiences and the memories of fascist eras have shaped not only judges' role but also their motivation to enter the profession, as well as considering how current political developments continue to challenge this role.

In chapter 10, Mariarosaria Guglielmi, European delegated Italian prosecutor and President of MEDEL (*Magistrats Européens pour la Démocratie et les LIbertés*), delves into the Italian case showing how the politically motivated attacks on individual judges and prosecutors have 'old roots' in the country and how the judiciary is witnessing a 'crisis of distrust', in a context in which some political actors have argued that judges 'take decisions against the government'. In chapter 11, Portuguese Judge José Igreja Matos, Vice-President of the International Association of Judges (IAS), highlights that the state of democracy is a subject of debate for judges and that his experience in Latin America helped him to understand 'the present European challenges'. While not all the cases brought to court lead to conflicts, some have the potential to do so, particularly 'cases that deal with challenges for modern societies such as abortion, discrimination against minorities, and the use of technology'. He reflects on the judicial culture and the role of judges when democracy is under strain, arguing that judges must decide with their consciences, with the sole comfort of the law. In chapter 12, Italian Judge Luca Perilli sheds light on the tensions that can arise between judges and political actors across different fields of law, with migration being just one example. He also examines the clash between domestic rules and norms and rights protected by European treaties and international conventions, arguing that being a judge today 'is a very difficult and challenging tasks' which requires 'high professional and ethical skills'. In chapter 13, Javier Hernández García, a judge at the Supreme Court of Spain, examines the importance of the connection between EU and national law. He discusses the rule of judges, arguing that they do not have a 'carte blanche to take a proactive stance on any and all political initiatives'. Judges, he contends, 'must exercise particular caution when engaging in public acts of protest'.

In Part III, the book presents Central and Eastern European (CEE) narratives about the role of judges in general and more particularly in the context of the disputed measures concerning the independence of the judiciary that were adopted by the Hungarian Fidesz, the Polish PiS, and Romanian Social Democrat governments. Most of the judges in this part hold strong opinions about the state of democracy in their countries. In chapter 14, Judge András Baka – whose mandate as President of the Supreme Court of Hungary was 'prematurely and illegally terminated' by the Fidesz overvehement – asserts that his country 'has shifted away from being a democracy'. Judge Baka recalls the context and the manner in which the end of his term of office took place and, more broadly, the changes introduced by the government which affect both the justice system and democracy as a whole. He argues that 'the interpretation of legal rules is the primary tool with which the judiciary can uphold democracy'.

In chapter 15, Judge Dragoş Călin, co-President of the Romanian Judges' Association Forum, reflects on indirect transformation of the Romanian judiciary, from inside, 'using a part of the judiciary'. Judge Călin uses his personal experience to illustrate how judicial instruments 'like the Judicial Inspectorate can be used to intimidate the judges who still resist'. In chapter 16, drawing on her personal experience Polish Judge Monika

Frąckowiak, member of the Board of MEDEL, asserts that 'judges cannot speak only through their judgments', arguing that they need 'to be active and open to society' while at the same time is difficult to find a balance between being 'simply a judge and being an activist', since, for Frąckowiak, 'a judge should always be limited by the position they hold'. In chapter 17, Małgorzata Maria Gersdorf, former First President of the Supreme Court of Poland, tells how she was able to serve until the end of her term despite attempts to remove her from office. She argues that, in the current context, the very status of a judge requires deep reflection – not only in Poland but across Europe. In chapter 18, Zdeněk Kühn, Constitutional Court judge in Czechia, situates the role of judges in a broader reflection, arguing that it is 'dangerous' to concentrate too much attention on constitutional court judges, as 'the sole guardian of liberal democracy'. Judges, in his view, should not 'intensify' culture wars. However, as stated in chapter 19 by Tamás Matusik, a Hungarian judge and former president of the Hungarian National Judicial Council, 'when judges' independence and integrity are called into question, they must be prepared to respond'.

Part IV concludes the series of interviews with two narratives from the perspective of two non-EU Member States judges who are, however, both integrated into the European formal and informal networks of judges. In chapter 20, former Turkish judge Yavuz Aydin shares his poignant story of bravery in the face of persecution by the Turkish regime, distilling through his experience a sense of hope about how judges and citizens might resist autocrats. In chapter 21, Serbian Judge Dragana Boljević discusses her perception of how EU institutions use the topic of judicial independence in accession countries opportunistically, with a tendency to 'manipulate their demands for the independence of the judiciary whenever there is a deadlock in some other domain'.

To conclude, in Part V, five academics were invited to provide commentaries on a selected number of interviews and in so doing to reflect on how to make sense of these narratives as researchers. The focus on judges' narratives might be of interest to different fields of research – political science, law, the sociology of law or socio-legal studies, and European studies to mention a few. The commentaries are provided by scholars who share a common interest in courts, judges and their relationship with both politics and society, yet they examine the situation through different conceptual tools and from different angles. Each commentary situates the interviews analysed in their field of research while underlining some new avenues for research.

In chapter 22, Lisa Conant – whose research primarily examines the impact of judgments by the Court of Justice of the European Union[29] and the European Court of Human Rights – discusses the material from the perspective of comparative constitutional law and politics, considering how to cultivate a balance between democratic accountability and legal constitutionalism in the growing context of dissensus over liberal democracy. She argues that improving 'democratic accountability may be a more effective way to fortify liberal democracies than relying on dominant models of legal constitutionalism'.

[29] L Conant, *Justice Contained: Law and Politics in the European Union* (Ithaca, NY, Cornell University Press, 2002).

In chapter 23, Gábor Halmai – a scholar in Comparative and European Constitutional law[30] – engages in a comparative exercise, trying to explain why judges' actions have taken different forms in Germany, Italy, and Hungary with a focus on the structural (political power relations) and institutional (appointment procedure, jurisdiction, etc) factors conditioning judicial resilience. Like Lisa Conant who emphasises the importance of democratic accountability, Halmai highlights the significance of 'a constitutional culture in which the people understand the importance of judicial independence'.

In chapter 24, Agnieszka Kubal, whose research deals with human rights mobilisation in Eastern Europe and Russia,[31] examines the strategies employed by judges to safeguard their independence. She argues that, in a context of democratic backsliding, judges have increasingly turned to international apex courts, marking a shift away from the traditional approach of legal formalism. She devotes particular attention to the concept of dual legalism, 'which forces judges to confront ethical dilemmas'.

In chapter 25, Tommaso Pavone, a researcher focusing on the politics behind the legal construction of Europe and the role of Euro-lawyers,[32] reflects on the strategies used by judges to defend their independence. Pavone argues that the EU's response to the rule of law crisis in some Member States has 'catalysed a mechanism of judge-driven legal mobilisation that is novel to the post-war Europe', spurring judges to mobilise European law in their action. Contrasting the findings of this book with his own interviews with Euro-lawyers, he concludes that in this context of democratic backsliding even more than lawyers, judges are at the '*avant garde* of this legal mobilisation'. But at the same time, 'judges' opposition to backsliding governments also risks going too far and becoming counterproductive'.

In chapter 26, Katarína Šipulová draws on her research interest in judicial resistance[33] to examine the limits of judicial activism in the face of democratic decline. She suggests that the interviews in this book show that some judges 'embraced activism and resistance as a necessary defence against political encroachment', while others 'expressed scepticism both towards the glorified alliance with supranational institutions' and towards the 'normative heroisation of the judiciary'. Šipulová's question is: Can courts effectively safeguard democracy without becoming too political? Like Gábor Halmai, she concludes that 'judicial independence cannot survive on institutional safeguards alone. Judicial culture might be one of the variables impacting effectiveness of existing institutions'.

In chapter 27, I reflect on how these interviews can inform new avenues of research to better understand the interplay between political and legal constitutionalism, as well as the role of judges in political regimes. I argue that the interviews reveal new developments in the interactions between law and politics, as well as in relation to the willingness of several judges to strengthen the bonds between law and society. From a more theoretical point of view, I argue that judges' responses to the rule of

[30] G Halmai, *Perspectives on Global Constitutionalism* (The Hague, Eleven International Publishing, 2014).

[31] A Kubal, *Immigration and Refugee Law in Russia* (Cambridge, Cambridge University Press, 2019).

[32] T Pavone, *The Ghostwriters: Lawyers and the Politics Behind the Judicial Construction of Europe* (Cambridge, Cambridge University Press, 2022).

[33] K Šipulová, 'The Light and the Dark Side of Judicial Resistance' (2024) 47 *Law & Policy* 1.

law crisis in EU Member States and beyond have not only intensified top-down and bottom-up forms of Europeanisation but also strengthened mechanisms of horizontal Europeanisation. The latter have given rise to different 'outcomes' such as ethics for judges, a sense of collective identity as European judges, and bonds of solidarity – important factors in the emergence of a judicial culture.

In chapter 28, Andrew Bradley provides key takeaways from the interviews and commentaries of this volume on how to safeguard the independence of the judiciary and to ensure the optimum functioning of the judicial system at the national and supranational levels.

The ideas gathered in this book mark the beginning of a broader pan-European reflection, which is undeniably relevant today. This book may therefore interest a variety of audiences: judges and their professional associations; academics and researchers; but also the wider public eager to understand how judges perceive the major challenges of our time, as well as their roles in politics and society.

2

Illiberalism on Trial: Ideational Boundaries, Institutional Practices, and Public Diffusion

LEONARDO PULEO

Introduction

In their classic volume on authoritarian transition, Juan José Linz and Alfred Stepan suggested that one of the requisites for full democratic consolidation is the absence of contestation over the democratic nature of the political regime.[1] Democracy is thus consolidated when it becomes 'the only game in town, when no one can imagine acting outside democratic institutions'.[2] Over the last decade, however, the hegemony of liberal democracy seems to have waned; and today every reliable democracy index indicates that democracies are in retreat – both in absolute number and in terms of quality.[3] Europe is no exception to this trend.[4] In the past decade, the emergence of rule of law crises within the EU[5] has led to a decline in the protection of fundamental rights, minority rights, and judicial independence in several countries. This decline has often been accompanied by instances of executive aggrandizement at the expense of other constitutional powers.[6]

[1] J Linz and A Stephan, eds., *The Breakdown of Democratic Regimes: An Introduction* (Baltimore, The Johns Hopkins University Press, 1978).

[2] A Przeworski, *Democracy and the Market: Political and Economic Reforms in Eastern Europe and Latin America* (Cambridge, Cambridge University Press, 1991) 26.

[3] A Lührmann and SI Lindberg, 'A Third Wave of Autocratization is Here: What is New about it?' (2019) 26 *Democratization* 1095; A Schafer and M Zurn, *Democratic Regression. The Political Causes of Authoritarian Populism* (Cambridge, Polity Press, 2024).

[4] Most recent index on the state and quality of democracy reveals sever regression in the European region. See *V-Dem, Democracy Report 2024: Democracy Winning and Losing at the Ballot*. University of Gothenburg: V-Dem Institut; *Freedom House Dataset*, available at: www.v-dem.net/documents/43/v-dem_dr2024_lowres.pdf.

[5] R Coman, *The Politics of the Rule of Law in the EU Polity: Actors, Tools and Challenges* (Cham, Springer Nature, 2022).

[6] N Bermeo, 'On Democratic Backsliding' (2016) 27 *Journal of Democracy* 57.

It is important to recall that democracy has always been an 'essentially contested' concept,[7] often influenced by various ideological traditions.[8] Similarly, democracy and liberalism were not always inherently interconnected; their explicit union – and subsequent global expansion – are a relatively recent development, started in the nineteenth century, decisively driven by post-World War II constitutionalism,[9] and achieving its peak of ideological dominance after the end of the Cold War.[10]

Although the presence of actors contesting liberal democracy and its tenets within the European political systems is not in itself a new phenomenon, both the electoral rise of illiberal actors and the mainstreaming of illiberal narratives have reached unprecedented levels. The contemporary public sphere is witnessing the increase of dissensus over liberal democracy[11] supported either by political entrepreneurs[12] or networks of intellectuals, think tanks, associations, and civil society organisations with illiberal sensibilities.[13] While democracy *per se* is rarely the explicit target of contestation – and illiberal leaders often employ democratic rhetoric to demand greater adherence to the *will of the people* – the liberal guarantees embedded within democratic principles since the end of World War II are increasingly under attack.

The Ideational Boundaries of Contemporary Illiberalism

The origins of the term 'illiberal democracy' can be traced back to an influential 1997 article in which Fareed Zakaria used the phrase to describe those political regimes holding elections with some degree of competitiveness – albeit not free or fair – while systematically violating fundamental rights and the separation of powers.[14]

Viktor Orbán's (in)famous 2014 speech in Băile Tuşnad marked a turning point, presenting the illiberal state as a desirable political model.[15] Since then, illiberalism

[7] WB Gallie, 'Essentially Contested Concepts' (1956) 56 *Proceedings of the Aristotelian Society* 167; D Collier, D Hidalgo and O Maciuceanu, 'Essentially Contested Concepts: Debates and Applications' (2006) 11 *Journal of Political Ideologies* 211.

[8] M Freeden, 'Democracy Dis-integrated: The Current Conceptual Confusion' (2020) 25 *Journal of Political Ideologies* 1.

[9] N Bobbio, *Liberalism e Democrazia* (Roma, Franco Angeli, 1988); M Plattner, 'From Liberalism to Liberal Democracy' (1999) 10 *Journal of Democracy* 121.

[10] F Fukuyama, *The End of History and the Last Man* (London, Penguin, 1993).

[11] R Coman and N Brack, 'Dissensus over Liberal Democracy: Concept-Building and Typology' (forthcoming) *European Political Science*.

[12] S Engler, T Gessler, T Abou Chadi and L Leemann, 'Democracy Challenged: How Parties Politicize Different Democratic Principles' (2023) 30 *Journal of European Public Policy* 1961; G Piccolino and L Puleo, 'Ideological Drivers of Participatory Democracy in Europe: Disentangling the Different Approaches of Populism and Post-materialist Politics' (2024) 23 *European Political Science* 115.

[13] R Coman, E Paulis, L Puleo and N Trino, 'Building and Legitimizing an Illiberal Transnational Field: Illiberal Think Tanks' Struggle for Cultural Hegemony in Poland and Hungary' (forthcoming) *European Political Science;* K Bluhm and M Varga, *New Conservatives in Russia and East Central Europe* (London, Routledge, 2019).

[14] F Zakaria, 'The Rise of Illiberal Democracy' (1997) 76 *Foreign Affairs* 22.

[15] V Orbán, *Prime Minister Viktor Orbán's Speech at the 25th Bálványos Summer Free University and Student Camp*, available at: www.2015-2019.kormany.hu/en/the-prime-minister/the-prime-minister-s-speeches/prime-minister-viktor-orban-s-speech-at-the-25th-balvanyos-summer-free-university-and-student-camp.

and illiberal democracy have become 'mobilizing buzzwords',[16] signalling a rejection of political values perceived as being imposed by the West – such as minority rights, cosmopolitanism, LGBTQI+ rights, gender and reproductive rights, and inclusive approaches to migration; – while simultaneously promoting conservative cultural values, organicist interpretations of *the nation*, and hostility toward non-majoritarian institutions designed to limit executive power.[17]

The difficulties in delineating the boundaries of contemporary illiberalism are intertwined with the multifaceted nature of its opposite: liberalism – a concept which encompasses a plurality of ideological stances – some of which may even be conflicting. In addressing illiberalism, we should avoid the mistake of treating liberalism as an axiomatic concept with inherently positive connotations.[18] As several scholars have argued,[19] the notion of liberalism as an uninterrupted march toward the expansion of rights is ahistorical. In the nineteenth century, liberal intellectuals were able to oscillate between endorsing the diffusion of political rights – for men – in Europe and supporting colonialism and slavery elsewhere.[20] Contemporary 'really existing liberalism' may range from defending the independence of judicial institutions and protecting individual self-expression in the face of oppressive power to endorsing policies that fuel rampant inequalities, such as the hyper-deregulation of financial markets and the privatisation of public services.[21] As a leading scholar on liberalism has aptly asked: 'Of what exactly is illiberalism supposed to be the opposite?'[22]

In the light of such varieties of liberalism, contemporary illiberalism can be understood as a plurality of reactive stances against 'today's liberalism in all its varied scripts – political, economic, cultural, geopolitical, civilisational – often in the name of democratic principles and by winning popular support'.[23] Therefore, most ideational approaches to contemporary illiberalism tend to conflate the concept with ethno-nationalism and anti-globalism,[24] as well as with patriarchal, anti-feminist, and anti-LGBTQI+ values.[25] A more parsimonious approach has recently been proposed by Zsolt Enyedi, who defines illiberalism as the ideational opposition to the principles

[16] A Buzogány, 'Illiberal Democracy in Hungary: Authoritarian Diffusion or Domestic Causation?' (2017) 24 *Democratization* 1307.

[17] H Canihac, 'Illiberal, Anti-liberal or Post-liberal Democracy? Conceptualizing the Relationship between Populism and Political Liberalism' (2022) 4 *Political Research Exchange* 1; JT Kauth and D King, 'Illiberalism' (2020) 61 *European Journal of Sociology* 365; M Laruelle, 'Illiberalism: A Conceptual Introduction' (2022) 38 *East European Politic* 303; R Coman and C Volintiru, 'Anti-liberal Ideas and Institutional Change in Central and Eastern Europe' (2023) 24 *European Politics and Society* 5.

[18] A Mondon, 'I Was Gonna Fight Fascism … The Need for a Critical Approach to Illiberalism' (2024) 4 *Journal of Illiberalism Studies* 9.

[19] D Losurdo, *Controstoria del liberalismo* (Bari-Roma, Laterza, 2005), H Rosenblatt, *The Lost History of Liberalism: From Ancient Rome to the Twenty-first Century* (Princeton, Princeton University Press, 2018).

[20] Losurdo (n 19).

[21] A Mondon, 'Really Existing Liberalism, the Bulwark Fantasy, and the Enabling of Reactionary, Far Right Politics' (2024) *Constellations* (advance online publication).

[22] Rosenblatt (n 19).

[23] Laruelle (n 17).

[24] R Smilova, 'The Ideational Core of Democratic Illiberalism' in A Sajó, R Uitz and S Holmes (eds), *Routledge Handbook of Illiberalism* (New York, Routledge, 2021) 193.

[25] P Guasti and L Bustikova, 'Varieties of Illiberal Backlash in Central Europe' (2023) 70 *Problems of Post-Communism* 130.

of liberal democracy.[26] If liberal democracy is a political system designed to constrain the manoeuvrability of political leaders, ensure equal treatment for all citizens, and promote pluralism, then illiberalism refers to political projects aimed at increasing power concentration, fostering a partisan state, and creating a closed society.

The illiberal preference for unbounded government power directly clashes with the rule of law, which serves as an antidote against uncontrolled and unrestricted power.[27] Far-right and populist parties – such us Fidesz in Hungary, PiS in Poland, Brothers of Italy (*Fratelli d'Italia*, FdI) in Italy, the Freedom Party of Austria (*Freiheitliche Partei Österreichs*, FPÖ) in Austria, Alternative for Germany (*Alternative für Deutschland*, AfD) in Germany, and the National Rally (RN – *Rassemblement national*) in France – are frequently implicated in fostering contemporary illiberalism. From the supply side of political competition, it is evident that some features of contemporary illiberalism – such as the rejection of cosmopolitanism and open society, as well as the opposition against cultural, social and ethnical minorities – align closely with right-wing ideologies.[28] Furthermore, the populist framing of politics as a dichotomous moral opposition between *the people* and *the elite* serves to legitimise hostility toward elites and non-majoritarian institutions such as constitutional courts, judicial councils and other independent institutions that are designed to protect minorities from the arbitrariness of government power.[29]

The Illiberal Playbook: The Judiciary at the Forefront

When illiberal forces gain control of national cabinets, they invariably employ abrasive rhetoric targeting judicial independence, particularly when the judiciary challenges their political goals. This appears to be the case, for example, with the current FdI-led government in Italy[30] and was also evident during Berlusconi's previous governments.[31] However, with robust institutional support, as seen in Hungary[32] and Poland,[33] illiberal parties have gone further, systematically taking over independent institutions and dismantling judicial independence. More broadly, comparative studies reveal that far-right populist parties in government have a detrimental impact on the quality of democracy, particularly on indicators such as checks on government power, freedom of expression, fundamental rights, and civil liberties.[34]

[26] Z Enyedi, 'Concept and Varieties of Illiberalism' (2024) 12 *Politics and Government* 1.

[27] M Krygier, 'Illiberalism and the Rule of Law' in Sajó, Uitz and Holmes (n 24).

[28] M Plattner, 'Illiberal Democracy and the Struggle on the Right" (2019) 30 *Journal of Democracy* 5; Engler, Gessler, Abou Chadi and Leemann (n 12).

[29] J-W Muller, *What is Populism?* (Philadelphia, University of Pennsylvania Press, 2016).

[30] G Baldini, 'From "Anomaly" to "Laboratory"? Fratelli d'Italia, Illiberalism and the Study of Right-Wing Parties in Western Europe' (2024) 22 *Political Studies Review* 402.

[31] C Dallara, 'Powerful Resistance Against a Long-running Personal Crusade: The Impact of Silvio Berlusconi on the Italian Judicial System' (2015) 20 *Modern Italy* 59.

[32] M Bánkúti, G Halmai and KL Scheppele, 'Hungary's Illiberal Turn: Disabling the Constitution' (2012) 23 *Journal of Democracy* 138.

[33] W Sadurski, *Poland's Constitutional Breakdown* (Oxford, Oxford University Press, 2019).

[34] D Vittori, 'Threat or Corrective? Assessing the Impact of Populist Parties in Government on the Qualities of Democracy: A 19-Country Comparison' (2022) 57 *Government and Opposition* 589.

Over the past few decades, various aspects of judicial independence have come under threat in several European countries. One major concern is the erosion of judicial self-governance, coupled with the politicisation of judicial appointments and promotions, including those to apex courts and leadership positions. Additionally, mechanisms of judicial accountability – such as disciplinary procedures and ethical regulations – are increasingly being weaponised for political purposes. In several EU countries, judges also contend with inadequate remuneration and insufficient judicial funding, which can undermine their ability to perform their duties effectively. Furthermore, judges' freedom of expression and right to private life have been frequently curtailed through political attacks, smear campaigns, and other coercive measures.

In this context, it is crucial to understand the agency of illiberal challengers in attacking and ultimately dismantling independent liberal-democratic institutions. This process can follow an 'illiberal playbook', a strategic set of tactics used by political entrepreneurs to erode democracy.[35] As noted by Ramona Coman and Clara Volintiru, illiberal narratives drive systemic changes that reshape politics, policy, and polity.[36] First, illiberal leaders employ cultural policies and abrasive rhetoric to disrupt the existing liberal consensus. For far-right leaders this often involves promoting ultra-conservative values – for example by restricting abortion rights or opposing LGBTQI+ rights – or advancing revisionist historical narratives, including relativising the crimes of Nazi-fascism. Second, illiberal actors sometimes take actions that violate national, EU, or international laws, curtailing the independence of the judiciary, media, and other democratic institutions. While legally risky, these moves are seen as necessary to consolidate domestic political control. Finally, illiberal challengers frequently operate in a grey zone, bending existing rules without outright violating them. This allows them to expand executive control over multiple branches of government, undermine judicial independence, and restrict the manoeuvring space of political opponents.

Poland and Hungary provide clear examples of how the illiberal playbook is enacted, revealing several affinities. In both countries, illiberal governments have worked systematically to exert control over civil society, by creating and supporting a network of loyal research institutions, universities, and civil society organisation that contribute to the cultural transformation.[37] Additionally, both governments have implemented policies aimed at eliminating resistance from independent institutions, with a particular focus on the judiciary. In Hungary, starting in 2010, the government implemented both constitutional reforms and ordinary legislation to weaken the autonomy of the Constitutional Court while simultaneously strengthening its control over ordinary courts.[38] In Poland, PiS's through ordinary legislation and illegal acts progressively assumed the control of

[35] ALP Pirro, B Stanley, 'Forging, Bending, and Breaking: Enacting the "Illiberal Playbook" in Hungary and Poland' (2022) 20 *Perspectives on Politics* 86.

[36] Coman and Volintiru (n 17).

[37] A Pető, 'Current Comment: The Illiberal Academic Authority. An Oxymoron?' (2021) 44 *Ber. Wissenschaftsgesch* 461; Coman, Paulis, Puleo and Trino (n 13); Bluhm and Varga (n 13); S Bill, 'PiS's Strategies of Elite Replacement' (2022) 36 *East European Politics and Societies* 118; V Behr, 'Towards a Transnational and Social History of Anti-Liberalism. Insights from the Trajectory of Ryszard Legutko' (2023) 24 *European Politics and Society* 22.

[38] Bánkúti, Halmai and Scheppele (n 32); G Halmai, 'The Coup Against Constitutional Democracy. The Case of Hungary' in M Graber, S Levinson and M Tushnet (eds), *Constitutional Democracy in Crisis?* (Oxford, Oxford University Press, 2018) 243.

the Constitutional Tribunal,[39] the National Council of the Judiciary (*Krajowa Rada Sądownictwa*, KRS),[40] and the Supreme Court,[41] increasing the disciplinary control over judges contesting the capture of the judiciary.[42]

Drawing on the Hungarian and Polish experiences, it is indeed possible to sketch a vast arsenal of court-curbing practices against constitutional principles, which have often been implemented by both Fidesz and PiS in their efforts to seize power by (i) manipulating the composition and capturing the presidency of the court, (ii) limiting the court's jurisdiction, (iii) restricting the court's freedom of decision-making, and (iv) refusing to comply with and implement constitutional rulings.[43] Similarly, a comparative analysis of court-packing practices reveals how illiberal governments can resort to a broad range of strategies to achieve (a) the expansion of the court – aimed at diluting dissenting voices, (b) the emptying of the court – to remove dissent, or (c) the swapping of court members – replacing dissenting judges with loyal ones.[44] While court-curbing measures are not extraordinary, they become particularly dangerous in the hands of illiberal leaders. Systematic court curbing can be a part of broader efforts to dismantle checks and balances, undermining democratic foundations.[45]

It is tempting to see the problem of illiberalism as being confined to CEE countries, and consider Western European countries as more insulated from illiberal challenges. However, even though the process of backsliding observed in Hungary and Poland has no direct parallel in Western Europe, several illiberal trends which stretch and put pressure on both the judiciary and political systems can be identified. In Italy, after courts blocked the deportation process at a detention hub facility built in Albania for migrants awaiting the outcome of their application for international protection, the government and the minister of justice vehemently attacked Italian judges in the media. France has witnessed a dramatic increase in Emmanuel Macron's use of emergency powers and attempts to criminalise reporters filming police repression during protests and strikes. In the UK, Boris Johnson's cabinet suspended Parliament during the Brexit crisis in 2019 and approved the 2022 Nationality and Borders Act, which threatens citizenship rights and asylum protections. In Austria, Sebastian Kurz's media manipulation and attempts to undermine judicial independence were prominent before he was indicted. In Greece, under Kyriakos Mitsotakis, a decline in press freedom and threats to academic freedoms have been recorded. Some of these examples are drawn from a recent article by Giorgos

[39] Sadurski (n 33).

[40] K Kovács and KL Scheppele, 'The Fragility of an Independent Judiciary: Lessons from Hungary and Poland–and the European Union' (2018) 51 *Communist and Post-Communist Studies* 189.

[41] JE Moliterno and P Čuroš, 'Recent Attacks on Judicial Independence: The Vulgar, the Systemic, and the Insidious' (2021) 22 *German Law Journal* 1159.

[42] Kovács, and Scheppele (n 40); Sadurski (n 33); Moliterno and Čuroš (n 41); L Pech and KL Scheppele, 'Illiberalism Within: Rule of Law Backsliding in the EU' (2017) 19 *Cambridge Yearbook of European Legal Studies* 3; KL Scheppele, 'Autocratic Legalism' (2018) 85 *The University of Chicago Law Review* 545.

[43] V Kazai, 'Constitutional Adjudication under Political Pressure – Judicial Review in Illiberal Political Regimes', paper presented at ICON-S CEE conference held in Prague in 2019, 5.

[44] D Kosař and K Šipulová, 'Comparative Court-Packing' (2023) 21 *International Journal of Constitutional Law* 80.

[45] B Bugaric and T Ginsburg, 'The Assault on Postcommunist Courts' (2016) 27 *Journal of Democracy* 69; Z Kühn, 'The Judiciary in Illiberal States' (2021) 22 *German Law Journal* 1231; M Wyrzykowski and M Ziółkowski, 'Illiberal Constitutionalism and the Judiciary' in Sajó, Uitz and Holmes (n 24).

Katsambekis,[46] highlighting the mainstreaming of illiberal and authoritarian practices. They underscore the need for caution in limiting our analysis to the far-right alone, suggesting we should instead focus on the reasons why citizens refrain from sanctioning the violation of democratic and liberal norms through elections.

Seeking Signs of Normative Backlash across the Citizenry

When examining citizens' support for liberal democracy in Europe, the picture might appear slightly improved. While some studies suggest a generational detachment from liberal democracies amongst younger cohorts,[47] others argue that these findings partially cherry-pick results.[48] The most up-to-date and reliable analyses of democratic support in Europe, however, indicate a remarkable pattern of stability.[49] Democracy still remains by far the most preferred political regime among Europeans. Most importantly, data from the European Values Survey reveal consistent patterns of stability since the 1980s.

However, when charting attitudes about the extent to which citizens like a strong leader 'who does not have to bother with parliament and elections', then we witness dramatic increases, especially in Italy, Spain, and Slovakia.[50] This raises a critical question: who are those citizens attracted to the idea of a leader potentially bending liberal rules?

At the individual level, studies have explored the relationship between party affiliation and preferences for a strong leader. Unsurprisingly, far-right voters are more likely to express high levels of support for strong leaders.[51] Moreover, far-right voters not only exhibit a stronger preference for authoritarian leadership but also demonstrate less support for defending free speech, judicial independence, and free media – especially when their preferred parties are in government.[52]

At first glance, one might be tempted to attribute the problem exclusively to the far-right *milieu*, suggesting that the broader European citizenry – apart from the far-right – is immune to illiberal temptations. However, this interpretation would be misleading.

[46] G Katsambekis, 'Mainstreaming Authoritarianism' (2023) 94 *The Political Quarterly* 428.

[47] RS Foa and Y Mounk, 'The Danger of Deconsolidation: The Democratic Disconnect' (2016) 27 *Journal of Democracy* 5; RS Foa and Y Mounk. 'The Signs of Deconsolidation' (2017) 28 *Journal of Democracy* 5.

[48] P Norris, 'Is Western Democracy Backsliding? Diagnosing the Risks' (2017) *Journal of Democracy*, Online exchange on 'Democratic Deconsolidation', available at www.journalofdemocracy.org/wp-content/uploads/2018/12/Journal-of-Democracy-Web-Exchange-Norris_0.pdf.

[49] A Wuttke, K Gavras and H Schoen, 'Have Europeans Grown Tired of Democracy? New Evidence from Eighteen Consolidated Democracies, 1981–2018' (2020) 52 *British Journal of Political Science* 416.

[50] Wuttke, Gavras and Schoen (n 49).

[51] T Donovan, 'Authoritarian Attitudes and Support for Radical Right Populists' (2019) 29 *Journal of Elections, Public Opinion and Parties* 448; A Malka, Y Lelkes, BN Bakker and E Spivack, 'Who Is Open to Authoritarian Governance within Western Democracies?' (2022) 20 *Perspectives on Politics* 807.

[52] W van der Brug, S Popa, SB Hobolt and H Schmitt, 'Democratic Support, Populism, and the Incumbency Effect' (2021) 32 *Journal of Democracy* 131.

A recent wave of experimental studies has investigated the extent to which voters punish candidates who engage in democratic or liberal transgressions.[53] These experiments asked respondents to choose between pairs of fictional candidates with varying characteristics, such as age, gender, party affiliation, ideology, policy preferences, and behaviours. The findings reveal that respondents consistently prioritise co-partisanship[54] or alignment with policy preferences;[55] even when their preferred candidates engage in illiberal and undemocratic actions such as suggesting that 'court rulings can be ignored' or that it is 'acceptable to harass journalists'.[56]

This results in a puzzling contradiction: while most European and US citizens profess strong support for liberal democracy, they often fail to electorally punish candidates who pose explicit threats to it. One potential explanation is that citizens prioritise partisanship or policy outcomes such as tax cuts or increased public spending over democratic principles. However, a more concerning interpretation suggests that citizens may exhibit biases in recognising undemocratic or illiberal behaviours when such behaviours are committed by their co-partisans. An important study by Suthan Krishnarajan reveals that, despite a solid understanding of democracy and a general attachment to liberal principles, citizens hold perceptual biases in identifying undemocratic behaviours. In experimental settings, participants tended to evaluate a democratic action committed by an opposing politician as less democratic than an undemocratic action by a co-partisan.[57]

Conclusions

The chapter has provided some theoretical coordinates on the rise of contemporary illiberalism by disentangling its ideational nature, discussing its practices, and assessing its diffusion among the general public.

Despite being often associated with the far-right, I have suggested that it would be overly optimistic to view contemporary illiberalism as being confined to a specific party family. Far-right rhetoric has permeated mainstream politics, demonstrating its influence on the entire political agenda.[58] In parallel, illiberal practices have moved from the fringe to the core of European polities, threatening inter-institutional accountability

[53] GMH Graham and W Svolik, 'Democracy in America? Partisanship, Polarization, and the Robustness of Support for Democracy in the United States' (2020) 114 *American Political Science Review* 392; M Lewandowsky and M Jankowski, 'Sympathy for the Devil? Voter Support for Illiberal Politicians' (2023) 15 *European Political Science Review* 39; KVS Frederiksen, 'Do Partisanship and Policy Agreement Make Citizens Tolerate Undemocratic Behavior?' (2024) 86 *Journal of Politics* 766.

[54] Graham and Svolik (n 53).

[55] Lewandowsky and Jankowski (n 53); Frederiksen (n 53).

[56] Frederiksen (n 53).

[57] S Krishnarajan, 'Rationalizing Democracy: The Perceptual Bias and (Un)Democratic Behavior' (2023) 117 *American Political Science Review* 474.

[58] T Akkerman, S de Lange and M Rooduijn (eds), *Radical Right-Wing Populist Parties in Western Europe: Into the Mainstream?* (London, Routledge, 2016); A Mondon and A Winter, *Reactionary Democracy: How Racism and the Populist Far Right became Mainstream* (London, Verso, 2020).

as well as the rights of all political, social, cultural, or ethnic minorities, increasing the dissensus over liberal democracy.[59]

A further source of concern is the entanglement between illiberal claims and partisan competition. Political elites may actively cultivate polarising tendencies, dividing society into two opposing camps: those who support and those who oppose.[60] This primary conflict may originate from support for or opposition to a personalistic leader such as Donald Trump but such divisions can quickly conflate with other cross-cutting societal cleavages. This dynamic transforms the defence of liberal and democratic norms into a partisan struggle. Indeed, the US case vividly illustrates how not only Democrats, but also Republican supporters perceive their rivals' victory as an existential threat to democracy.[61]

In contexts where political elites call for a restriction of rights and launch attacks on institutions that are supposed to limit the arbitrariness of their power by upholding the law, the judiciary is placed under explicit and increasing pressure. First, judges are increasingly called upon to evaluate the conformity of illiberal legislation with national, EU, and international laws, particularly in cultural (eg migration, reproductive and gender rights, LGBTQI+ issues) and administrative policies. This process of constitutional review often triggers political and delegitimising attacks by politicians in the media, contributing to the erosion of the judiciary's autonomy. Second, the judiciary itself is a primary target of the illiberal agenda. As discussed, illiberal leaders almost inevitably move to undermine judicial independence, seeking to establish direct control over the courts to secure their legislation and eliminate institutional opposition. This dual challenge places judges at the centre of debates on the dissensus over liberal democracy. Judges' public and private choices may end up legitimising illiberal leaders, while their acts of opposition and resistance may contribute to slowing down autocratisation by defending judicial independence and raising public awareness of the transformations implemented by illiberal governments.

[59] Coman and Brack (n 11).

[60] J McCoy and M Somer, 'Toward a Theory of Pernicious Polarization and How It Harms Democracies: Comparative Evidence and Possible Remedies' (2018) 68 *The ANNALS of the American Academy of Political and Social Science* 234.

[61] J Kingzette, JN Druckman, S Klar, Y Krupnikov, M Levendusky and JB Ryan, 'How Affective Polarization Undermines Support for Democratic Norms' (2021) 85 *Public Opinion Quarterly* 663.

3

The Essence of Judicial Independence: The Autonomous Interpretation of the Law

VIKTOR KAZAI

Introduction

'It is emphatically the province and duty of the Judicial Department to say what the law is.'[1] So wrote Chief Justice Marshall in the majority opinion of *Marbury v Madison*. This quote captures the essence of the judiciary's role according to the separation of powers principle.[2] Although the interpretation and application of the law may not seem a remarkable authority at first glance, this is a significant tool for the judiciary, enabling it to monitor and check the power of the political branches. According to the rule of law, actions by individuals and legal entities, including state organs, must adhere to the law, while the judiciary is responsible for enforcing this principle through the adjudication of legal disputes.[3] However, increasing reliance on the judiciary to decide public policy issues and resolve political conflicts[4] puts the courts in a delicate position. Political actors, particularly those in the governing majority, may become frustrated by the judiciary's autonomous interpretation and application of the law, which can sometimes conflict with their political agendas. This dynamic often leads political actors to attempt to restrict judicial independence. Yet, even authoritarian regimes do not go as far as to eliminate the judiciary from the constitutional structure.[5] Rather, governing majorities employ various strategies to influence judicial decision-making and limit or even undermine the judiciary's authority while maintaining an appearance of constitutional legitimacy.

[1] *Marbury v Madison*, 5 US 137, 177 (1803).

[2] JS Martinez, 'Horizontal Structuring' in A Sajó and M Rosenfeld (eds), *The Oxford Handbook of Comparative Constitutional Law* (Oxford, Oxford University Press, 2012).

[3] A Bedner, 'An Elementary Approach to the Rule of Law' (2010) 2 *Hague Journal on the Rule of Law* 48, 58–60, 67–69.

[4] R Hirschl, 'The Judicialization of Politics' in RE Goodin (ed), *The Oxford Handbook of Political Science* (Oxford and New York, Oxford University Press, 2011).

[5] See eg T Ginsburg and T Moustafa, *Rule by Law: The Politics of Courts in Authoritarian Regimes* (Cambridge, Cambridge University Press, 2008).

This chapter provides a preliminary overview of the interviews included in this volume with a focus on the judges' insights into the autonomous interpretation of the law as the essential role of the judicial branch. The text addresses the courts' vulnerability to the influence of the political branches and explores the various angles of judicial independence. The chapter concludes with the observation that the ultimate guarantee of the judiciary's independence is the constitutional culture, whether or not political actors and wider society respect judicial independence and are committed to upholding it.

The Role of the Judiciary in the Separation of Powers

The independence of the judiciary as a separate branch of government with its own distinct constitutional function is a relatively recent development that emerged in Europe and North America during the eighteenth century. The division of the legislative, executive, and judicial functions of the state evolved as a response to specific issues within Western societies and reflected the demand for certain values to be incorporated into governmental structures and processes.[6] By now it is generally accepted that the different branches of power in a modern constitutional democracy have a distinct core function. Sajó and Uitz summarise this idea succinctly as follows: 'the legislature legislates, the executive executes the laws, and the judiciary administers justice'.[7]

Many interviews in the volume reflect this understanding of the principle of the separation of powers and the judiciary's role within this. This is most clearly articulated by Baka (chapter 14) who notes that: 'Among the different branches of power, the parliament is responsible for establishing the framework of the state and, of course, the judiciary, while the government's role is to execute laws and decisions. By contrast, the judiciary has the authority to interpret legal measures, which is an effective tool: it has power over the meaning of the law.' In a similar vein, albeit in the context of the European Union, Vajda also emphasises the clear distinction between the role of EU legislators – who are responsible for making laws through a democratic process – and that of the CJEU, whose task is to ensure that laws are applied and upheld. 'The Court is there to decide legal disputes according to [EU law]. But the Court does not enter the political arena. It is independent of politics. Its sole role is to rule on the interpretation and legality of the law' (chapter 9).

Autonomous Interpretation of the Law as the Core of the Judicial Function

The administration of justice, as the key characteristic of the judicial function, consists of interpreting the law to adjudicate cases. In their interviews, many judges emphasise

[6] MJC Vile, *Constitutionalism and the Separation of Powers*, 2nd edn (Indianapolis, Liberty Fund, 1998) 23.
[7] A Sajó and R Uitz, *Constitution of Freedom. An Introduction to Legal Constitutionalism* (Oxford, Oxford University Press, 2017) 130.

that the interpretation of the law and its application is not necessarily a lonely exercise. Judges share this responsibility with their colleagues, as highlighted by Grimm, who stresses that judicial decision-making is a collaborative process: 'Consensus-building and reconciling different opinions is … an important part of a judge's work' (chapter 6). Sterk (chapter 7) pointed to the vital role of judicial dialogue between lower instance courts and national apex courts, describing how this allows judges to interpret and apply the law while incorporating established legal precedents, thus promoting a flexible approach to achieving justice. In his interview, Larsen (chapter 4) remarks that the CJEU's work to guarantee the uniform interpretation and application of EU law is often reactive, responding to cases referred to by national courts rather than leading the agenda on legal issues. Hernández García (chapter 13) brings attention to the fact that judges may disagree on various interpretations, reflecting the complexities of legal adjudication. He emphasises, in particular, the challenges posed by the supremacy of EU law to the relationship between national courts and the CJEU. Disagreement among judges, however, may not always be visible to the public because, for example, dissenting opinions are not permitted at the CJEU as noted by Vajda (chapter 9) and Hernández García (chapter 13).

We can discern from many interviews that the interpretation of the law serves as a powerful tool in the hands of the judiciary for several reasons. First, it plays a crucial role in shaping the meaning of the law, a point emphasised by both Vajda (chapter 9) and Perilli (chapter 12), who note the significant influence of the CJEU in developing essential principles of EU law, such as direct effect, primacy, and fundamental rights. Second, judicial interpretation can lead to the invalidation or disapplication of laws when these do not comply with the constitution, international law, or EU legislation. Perilli highlights how judges are required to navigate the intricate relationships between the various sources of law, sometimes needing to disapply national laws that conflict with EU regulations. Finally, the power of judicial interpretation manifests in the decisions that judges make, which serve to exercise control over the political branches, ensure legality, and uphold the rights and freedoms of individuals. Cadelli (chapter 5) emphasises that the essence of judicial work lies in rendering timely and reasoned decisions that maintain constitutional authority and protect public interest. This sentiment is echoed by Guglielmi (chapter 10), who asserts that judges must impartially guarantee rights and freedoms, reiterating the critical function of the judiciary as a counterbalance to governmental power.

The Fragility of Courts in the System of Checks and Balances

The judicial interpretation of the law can be a powerful tool for maintaining constitutional democracy, as long as the system of checks and balances works well and there is widespread respect for judicial independence. Grimm notes that during his tenure at the Federal Constitutional Court of Germany, he experienced no political interference or pressure, even amid significant criticism of unpopular decisions (chapter 6). In contrast, Baka notes that during his time as Chief Justice in Hungary, he faced severe political attacks following Fidesz's rise to power in 2010 due to his criticism of the government's judicial reform plans (chapter 14). The case of Baka (chapter 14) is a good example of what happens when the 'social consensus' on judicial independence (chapter 8) fades. In this situation, also mentioned by Judge Titz (chapter 8) and Aydin (chapter 20), judges can easily find themselves exposed to political interference as part of the 'least dangerous' or weakest branch of power which has 'no influence over either the sword or the purse; no direction either of the strength or of the wealth of the society; and can take no active resolution whatever.'[8]

Even in reasonably well-established democracies, politicians often capitalise on the vulnerability of courts to implement their own political agenda without any control, while also blaming judges for unsolved political issues. Hernández García (chapter 13) notes that the politicisation of justice often stems from a crisis in representative democracy. He explains that when polarised parliaments fail to reach consensus, unresolved conflicts can end up in the judiciary, and if politicians are dissatisfied by the outcome, they may delegitimise the courts by framing judicial decisions as politically motivated, thereby compromising the integrity of the judicial system. The situation is arguably worse in countries experiencing democratic backsliding. As Perilli points out (chapter 12), judges are a primary target of autocrats because they safeguard individual rights and uphold judicial independence, obstructing the emergence of authoritarian regimes. Perilli notes: 'The disapplication of the national law or its interpretation in line with supranational principles might not meet the expectations of the political majority and it might lead to political pressure or even attacks on the judiciary' (chapter 12). In a similar vein, Călin observes that 'Autocratisation occurs when political leaders in government reduce the capacity of other branches of the state to check their powers' (chapter 15).

In sum, despite their important role in maintaining constitutional democracy, courts remain fragile within the checks and balances system and are vulnerable to uncontrolled political majorities. In the literature, Issacharoff notes that '[c]ourts are at their strongest when there is uncertainty among political rivals for power, and at their most precarious when all institutional levers are under the control of a single dominant party.'[9] In her interview, Gersdorf captures this precarious situation: 'The guarantees of the tripartite division of power are too weak in the face of a genuinely unchecked executive power, which is becoming increasingly widespread. … In countries that have moved away from democracy, judges are sometimes pitted against all other organs of the state, along with the entire state propaganda apparatus and power of repression' (chapter 17).

The Dimensions of Judicial Independence

In order to protect courts from undue interference and to guarantee their essential role in enforcing the rule of law and fundamental rights, the principle of judicial

[8] A Hamilton, 'Federalist no 78 (1788)' in GW Carey and J McClellan (eds), *The Federalist* (Indianapolis, Liberty Fund, c2001) 402.

[9] S Issacharoff, *Fragile Democracies. Contested Power in the Era of Constitutional Court* (Cambridge, Cambridge University Press, 2015) 273.

independence is enshrined in various legal instruments, not only in domestic law but also in international and EU law. Most importantly, in the Council of Europe, the principle of judicial independence is protected by the European Convention on Human Rights (1950) as well as other soft law instruments.[10] Compliance with these standards is overseen by the Venice Commission and the European Court of Human Rights, two bodies that have developed very detailed, high legal standards over time.[11] In the European Union, judicial independence is anchored in Article 19(1) TEU and Article 47 of the EU Charter of Fundamental Rights. The EU employs various soft and hard mechanisms to monitor Member States' respect for this principle of judicial independence and the rule of law, such as the Annual Rule of Law Cycle and the EU Justice Scoreboard or the EU's general regime of conditionality for the protection of the EU budget. The CJEU plays a crucial role in enforcing these standards reflecting the 'essence of all the different European families of law' (chapter 7) through infringement procedures and preliminary references, contributing to a growing jurisprudence on judicial independence.[12]

Based on these legal instruments, judicial independence and its potential violation can be viewed from three key angles. The first one, independence from the political branches (external independence), highlights the need for the judiciary to operate free from undue influence by the executive and the legislature. The second angle, independence from fellow judges (internal independence), means that judges must be free from directives or pressures from colleagues, including members of superior courts and those in administrative roles within the judiciary. The third angle, impartiality, requires judges to remain unbiased and maintain equal distance from all parties involved to ensure fair adjudication and remain subordinate to the law, rather than public opinion and social pressure. The interviews in this volume offer rich reflections on all three of these various angles of judicial independence.

Freedom from the Political Branches (External Independence)

The separation of powers was never intended to lead to the complete isolation of the three branches. This is why this principle goes hand in hand with the system of checks and balances which means that both the political branches and the judiciary have constitutional means to keep each other under control. There is no one-size-fits-all model for institutionalising the relationship between them. As Smilov observes, 'most

[10] Council of Europe, Recommendation CM/Rec(2010)12 of the Committee of Ministers on the Independence, Efficiency and Responsibilities of Judges, Opinion No. 1 of the Consultative Council of European Judges (CCJE) on standards concerning the independence of the judiciary and the irremovability of judges, European Charter on the Statute of Judges.

[11] J Sillen, 'The Concept of "Internal Judicial Independence" in the Case Law of the European Court of Human Rights' (2019) 15 *European Constitutional Law Review* 114; R Spano, 'The Rule of Law as the Lodestar of the European Convention on Human Rights: The Strasbourg Court and the Independence of the Judiciary' (2021) 27 *European Law Journal* 211.

[12] L Pech and D Kochenov, *Respect for the Rule of Law in the Case Law of the European Court of Justice: A Casebook Overview of Key Judgments since the Portuguese Judges Case* (SIEPS, Stockholm, 2021).

contemporary models envisage complex systems of checks and balances or mutual interdependence'.[13]

If we look at national constitutions, we see that the political branches generally have several means to exercise control over the judicial system. These include, among others, the regulation of the organisation and functioning of the judiciary (including the basic rules on judicial accountability and self-government), the adoption of the state's budget (and thus the allocation of financial resources to the judiciary), participation in the process of selecting judges (particularly for the highest positions) and so on. In a healthy constitutional democracy, the political branches refrain from using these means to undermine the authority of the courts. However, challenges arise when the political branches exhibit a weak respect for judicial independence. In such situations, what might otherwise be considered legitimate means of democratic control can turn into tools that undermine the independence of the judiciary.

Many interviewees in this book reflect on the problematic relationship between the political branches and the judiciary. The issue they discuss most is the (potential) politicisation of the judicial appointment process and its detrimental effects on judicial independence. Grimm acknowledges that some political involvement in selecting judges is necessary for ensuring democratic legitimacy. 'Judges in general, and constitutional judges in particular, make highly consequential decisions with important political and social implications. Therefore, they need democratic legitimacy. If not from politicians who are directly elected by the people, where else should this legitimacy come from?' (chapter 6). However, he also emphasises that the involvement must be balanced to avoid partisan bias, referencing the German Constitutional Court's two-thirds majority requirement as a model. Indeed, according to the well-established case law of the European Court of Human Rights, the mere fact that either the executive or the parliament is involved in the appointment of judges does not *per se* amount to a violation of the European Convention on Human Rights (ECHR).[14] However, judicial independence requires a set of institutional and operational arrangements which must provide safeguards against undue political pressure both during the initial stages of appointing a judge and also during the execution of their duties.[15] There is a clear link between the integrity of the judicial appointment process and the requirement of judicial independence.[16] Given the prominent place that the judiciary occupies among state organs in a democratic society, and the increasing politicisation of the justice system in several member states, the ECtHR and the CJEU have been particularly attentive to the protection of the integrity of the judicial selection and removal process.[17]

[13] D Smilov, 'The Judiciary: The Least Dangerous Branch?' in Sajó and Rosenfeld (n 2) 859.

[14] *Clarke v the United Kingdom*, App no 23695/02 (ECtHR, 25 August 2005); *Zolotas v Greece*, App no 38240/02 (ECtHR, 2 June 2005); *Sacilor Lormines v France*, App no 46411/01 (ECtHR, 9 November 2006).

[15] *Guðmundur Andri Ástráðsson v Iceland*, App no 26374/18 (ECtHR, 1 December 2020), para 234.

[16] *Grzęda v Poland*, App no 43572/18 (ECtHR, 15 March 2022), paras 300–303 and 345–346, concerning the National Council of the Judiciary in Poland.

[17] From the recent case law of the ECtHR see in particular *Guðmundur Andri Ástráðsson v Iceland*, App no 26374/18 (ECtHR, 1 December 2020); *Xero Flor w Polsce sp. z o.o. v Poland*, App no 4907/18 (ECtHR, 7 May 2021); *Reczkowicz v Poland*, App no 43447/19 (ECtHR, 22 July 2021); *Dolińska – Ficek and Ozimek v Poland*, App nos 49868/19 and 57511/19 (ECtHR, 8 November 2021); *Grzęda v Poland*, App no 43572/18 (ECtHR, 15 March 2022); *Żurek v Poland*, App no 39650/18 (ECtHR, 16 June 2022); *Juszczyszyn v Poland*, App

Many of the judges in this volume also express deep concerns about the political influence of the judicial appointment process. Sterk points to the widespread trend of politicians attempting to exert control over the judiciary across Europe, citing examples from France and Spain (chapter 7). Baka (chapter 14) and Matusik (chapter 19) illustrate how ongoing pressure and strategic appointments in Hungary, most notably the election of the current Chief Justice based on tailor-made legal changes, have weakened the judiciary's integrity and public standing. Furthermore, Boljevic describes the dramatic decline in judicial independence in Serbia following the 2009 coup, which led to the arbitrary dismissal of judges, undermining the previously stable system (chapter 21).

Freedom from Superiors (Internal Independence)

Superior courts are responsible for ensuring uniformity in case law, while judicial management bodies must enforce ethical rules and maintain the effective functioning of the justice system. However, judicial independence requires that judges operate free from undue influence, not only from external sources but also from within the justice system itself. This internal independence implies that judges should not be subjected to directives or pressure from their peers or from those in administrative positions, such as the court presidents, division heads, or members of judicial councils. If adequate safeguards are not in place to protect judges' independence from their judicial superiors, this could undermine independence of the entire justice system and potentially lead to violations of the ECHR or EU law. In recent years, both the ECtHR and the CJEU have taken significant steps to protect judges who faced adverse actions such as disciplinary measures, early termination of their mandates, or the lifting of their immunity.[18] These measures were often imposed on figures who expressed concerns about legislative reforms that threatened judicial independence or who sought a review from the CJEU regarding the compatibility of national legislation with EU law.

no 35599/20 (ECtHR, 6 October 2022); *Ovcharenko and Kolos v Ukraine*, App nos 27276/15 and 33692/15 (ECtHR, 12 January 2023); *Lorenzo Bragado and Others v Spain*, App nos 53193/21 and 5 others (ECtHR, 22 June 2023); *Tuleya v Poland*, App nos. 21181/19 and 51751/20 (ECtHR, 6 July 2023); *Pająk and Others v Poland*, App nos 25226/18 and 3 others (ECtHR, 24 October 2023). From the recent jurisprudence of the CJEU see in particular Case C-824/18 *AB and Others v Krajowa Rada Sądownictwa and Others* ECLI:EU:C:2021:153, [2022] 4 WLR 36; Case C-896/19, *Repubblika v Il-Prim Ministru* ECLI:EU:C:2021:311, [2021] 3 CMLR 18; Case C-718/21, Krajowa Rada Sądownictwa ECLI:EU:C:2023:1015, [2024] 3 CMLR 14.

[18] From the case law of the ECtHR see in particular *Camelia Bogdan v Romania*, App no 36889/18 (ECtHR, 20 October 2020), *Eminağaoğlu v Turkey*, App no 76521/12 (ECtHR, 9 March 2021); *Miroslava Todorova v Bulgaria*, App no 40072/13 (ECtHR, 19 October 2021); *Kozan v Turkey*, App no 16695/19 (ECtHR, 1 March 2022); *Juszczyszyn v Poland*, App no 35599/20 (ECtHR, 6 October 2022); *Catană v the Republic of Moldova*, App no 43237/13 (ECtHR, 21 February 2023), *Tuleya v Poland*, App nos 21181/19 and 51751/20 (ECtHR, 6 July 2023); *Manole v the Republic of Moldova*, App no 26360/19 (ECtHR, 18 July 2023); *Danileţ v Romania*, App no 16915/21 (ECtHR, 20 February 2024); *Aydın Sefa Akay v Türkiye*, App no 59/17 (ECtHR, 23 April 2024). From the case law of the CJEU see in particular Joined Cases C-558/18 and C-563/18, *Miasto Łowicz* ECLI:EU:C:2020:234; Case C-824/18, *AB and Others v Krajowa Rada Sądownictwa and Others* ECLI:EU:C:2021:153, [2022] 4 WLR 36; Case C-487/19, *WŻ* ECLI:EU:C:2021:798, [2022] 2 CMLR 9; Joined Cases C-748/19 to C-754/19, *WB and Others* ECLI:EU:C:2021:931, [2022] 2 CMLR 14; Joined Cases C-357/19, C-379/19, C-547/19, C-811/19 and C-840/19, *PM and Others* ECLI:EU:C:2021:1034; Case C-564/19, *IS* ECLI:EU:C:2021:949; Joined Cases C-615/20 and C-671/20, YP and Others ECLI:EU:C:2023:562, [2024] 2 CMLR 3.

Politically influenced apex courts, such as supreme and constitutional courts, along with high-ranking officials in the justice system who lack true independence, can put undue limits on the autonomy of lower courts, as noted by several judges. Perilli raises concerns about recent Italian legislative changes that promote a hierarchical relationship with the judiciary, undermining the traditional horizontal balance of power (chapter 12). He fears that this shift may lead to bureaucratic tendencies, whereby lower-ranking judges conform to expectations rather than exercising independent judgment. Baka highlights the fact that the Hungarian judiciary faces constant indirect political pressure from the ruling party because the Chief Prosecutor, the Chief Justice, and the members of the Constitutional Court are all political appointees who can control both the input and the output of judicial proceedings (chapter 14).

In addition, judicial self-government bodies can also be exploited by governments to indoctrinate new judges, discipline dissenters, and influence judicial careers, creating a chilling atmosphere in the judiciary as illustrated by many examples recounted by judges. Aydin highlights the 2014 election for the High Council of Judges and Prosecutors as a critical moment for judicial politicisation in Turkey (chapter 20). In that case, due to various political tactics and government-supported propaganda, candidates faced a rigged system leading to the suspension of many judges post-election. Călin describes legislative changes in Romania between 2018 and 2019 that weakened judicial independence by restricting judges' freedom of expression, creating a special prosecutor's office to investigate them, and having the Chief of the Judicial Inspectorate directly appointed by the government, raising concerns about impartiality (chapter 15). The CJEU ruled that these amendments violated EU treaties, yet the Chief Inspector initiated disciplinary proceedings against those who opposed the reforms. Matusik describes the conflict between Hungary's Judicial Council (*Országos Bírói Tanács*, OBT) and the National Office for the Judiciary (*Országos Bírósági Hivatal*, OBH) after 2018, leading to personal attacks and a constitutional crisis that was eventually 'resolved' by removing Handó from the Office and positioning her at the Constitutional Court.

Freedom from Bias and Social Pressure (Impartiality)

According to the case law of the ECtHR, impartiality, in a narrow sense, means the absence of bias or prejudice in judicial decision-making.[19] This should ensure that all parties receive a fair and equitable hearing before an independent tribunal. However, this requirement goes beyond simply administering justice fairly; it also requires that justice is perceived to be fair by the public. This is captured in the principle that 'justice must not only be done, it must also be seen to be done.'[20] What is at stake is society's confidence in the fact that courts are subject to the law and nothing but the law. It is crucial for the proper functioning of democracy that judges are seen as impartial arbiters who are not influenced by political motives or personal biases. Therefore, in a democratic

[19] *Nicholas v Cyprus*, App no 63246/10 (ECtHR, 9 January 2018) para 49.
[20] See eg *Catană v the Republic of Moldova*, App no 43237/13 (ECtHR, 21 February 2023) para 77.

society based on the rule of law, attempts to influence judicial decision-making, to call into question valid judicial decisions, or to suggest that judges are morally or politically compromised based on their rulings are unacceptable.

Many interviewees in this volume emphasise the critical importance of maintaining independence from external, non-legal influences in their decision-making processes. This view is captured particularly well by Matusik who says that 'Judges must not let external factors influence their decisions. Although we are part of society and need to stay informed about what is happening, we must set aside any outside influences when making judgments' (chapter 19). In a similar vein, Grimm argues that a judge's primary duty is to interpret and apply the law correctly, regardless of its political consequences or potential misuse by others: 'one cannot expect a judge to give a wrong answer to a question deliberately just to prevent others from misusing a judgment. That would be a self-decapitation of the judiciary' (chapter 6). This commitment to judicial integrity is particularly vital in the face of the growing influence of ideology on public discourse. According to Vajda, the judiciary plays a vital role in upholding general legal principles, and it must fulfil this role even if this leads to unpopular decisions that result in the disapplication or invalidation of laws (chapter 9). Judges view their role as one of neutrality, focusing on the complexities and nuances of each case. 'A lawyer must take a side and must be partial. A judge has a distant approach, an impartial view of the law' (chapter 11). Finally, Kühn expresses his belief that judges cannot ignore cases, even those involving sensitive and divisive legal issues like transgender rights, but courts should refrain from actively participating in culture wars (chapter 18).

The exclusion of extra-legal considerations from judicial decision-making should not be confused with the mechanical application of black letter law to the facts of the case. Several interviewees emphasise the fact that judges have the freedom and duty to thoughtfully examine the meaning of the law and actively reflect on its moral implications. Titz argues that personal morals should not influence judicial decision-making, but a responsible interpretation of the law requires one to balance objective enforcement with an awareness of ethical foundations: 'I strongly believe that we cannot divorce the application of the law from its origins and moral implications' (chapter 8). Similarly, Cadelli emphasises that judges must not adhere to a rigid legalistic mindset and should not feel bound by unjust laws. She advocates for a discerning approach: 'You must go and find the right law or the least unfair law, you just must find it and interpret it' (chapter 5). Grimm argues that judges should consider the political and social context when interpreting legal norms, as these norms reflect social realities and may require judges to adapt their interpretations in response to societal changes to maintain the effectiveness of laws (chapter 6).

However, politicians and the media, especially government mouthpieces, often attack judges when they deliver unpopular judgments or make decisions contrary to the interests of political actors or the (alleged) interests of society. Many of those interviewed in this volume reflect on this concerning trend and recount specific examples. Cadelli cites the case of Cédric Herrou, a French farmer prosecuted for aiding irregular migrants, illustrating how judges are often criticised for prioritising constitutional principles over political pressures, especially in matters of human rights (chapter 5). Sterk comments on the Netherlands, where politicians frequently criticise judges, claiming they exceed their mandates or are overly lenient (chapter 7). Guglielmi addresses targeted attacks on Italian judges involved in refugee and asylum cases, particularly since 2018, where judges have been portrayed as biased when their rulings contradict government policies (chapter 10). Baka reminds us that the forced retirement of judges in Hungary after the Fidesz government came into office was accompanied by deliberate media attacks on judges, labelling them as 'Communist judges,' and leading to a significant erosion of public trust in judicial impartiality (chapter 14). Matusik highlights how both the ruling and opposition parties in Hungary undermine judicial integrity when questioning court decisions and attacking judges personally. He believes that 'These manipulative and populist messages are damaging to public perception as well as the independence of the judiciary, portraying judges as unprofessional and lacking in impartiality' (chapter 19). Călin expresses concerns about the humiliation and stress that Romanian judges face within a system influenced by corrupt political ties, leading to a lack of confidence in the judiciary among citizens (chapter 15). Kühn provides an example of how court rulings can be politicised, as seen in a 2024 decision on pension increases that was exploited by opposition politicians to frame judges as siding with the government, demonstrating the manipulation of judicial decisions for political gain. Overall, the interviews illustrate a troubling dynamic: the judiciary is under attack, compromising its independence and citizens' trust.

To regain public trust in the justice system, many judges advocate for increased engagement with citizens, while maintaining the integrity of their role. Vajda highlights the need for courts to improve their communication in order to foster understanding and respect for judicial decisions, arguing for enhanced transparency, for example by streaming hearings or providing press releases on significant cases. Frąckowiak stresses the importance of using accessible language and a more open approach within the judicial system (chapter 16). She advocates for greater interaction with the public, including participation in cultural and sporting events. Kühn emphasises that judges should share their insights in an understandable manner, avoiding technical jargon to build a supportive relationship with the public, something which is essential for judicial independence (chapter 18). Perilli argues that judges should be involved in civil society while remaining neutral in legal matters, advocating for a balance between participation and detachment from activism (chapter 12). Călin notes that judges, as members of society, should be allowed to express their opinions publicly without compromising impartiality, refuting the notion of a silent judiciary. Similarly, Frąckowiak opines that while judges should be active and open to society, they must find a balance between their judicial responsibilities and public engagement to maintain their integrity (chapter 16).

The Ultimate Guarantee of Judicial Independence: Constitutional Culture

Judicial independence can be safeguarded through various institutional guarantees. Reports and guidelines from international monitoring bodies along with organisations that assist constitution-building initiatives, illustrate a diverse array of institutional solutions that address every facet of judicial organisation and operation. Additionally, several formalised mechanisms can be employed to uphold judicial independence. These include the judiciary's participation in the legislative process, initiating constitutional reviews, utilising preliminary reference procedures before the CJEU, filing individual petitions with the ECtHR, pursuing infringement actions by the European Commission, organising public demonstrations, amongst others. However, insights from the interviews in this volume suggest that although these institutional guarantees and legal pathways are important, the effectiveness of judicial independence ultimately hinges on the attitudes of politicians, society, and judges themselves – essentially, the prevailing constitutional culture. As Sterk argues, 'of all the necessary requirements for an independent judiciary, such as good laws protecting the independence of the judiciary, a good culture surrounding the rule of law, courageous judges protecting the rights of the citizens, and the trust of the citizens, I feel it is the latter that is decisive in a moment of crisis to uphold an independent judiciary' (chapter 7). In a similar vein, Aydin notes that 'in the end, it is a matter of culture … not only for judges but for politicians and civil society, for media; they are all actors of democracy' (chapter 20).

Several judges observe that judicial independence can be sustained even in systems with limited formal guarantees, provided that politicians and society uphold the integrity of the justice system. Kühn argues that judicial independence in Czechia remains intact despite the absence of self-governance, thanks to protective legal frameworks, institutional practices, and the commitment of judges to uphold the rule of law (chapter 18). Titz notes that even though the Minister of Justice in Germany has a significant level of authority over the appointment and promotion of state judges, there is a 'social consensus' on the importance of judicial independence, and 'no Minister of Justice would be foolish enough to misuse his or her influence' (chapter 8). However, Titz expresses fears that this social consensus could weaken over time, especially if right-wing populist parties like the AfD gain power. Grimm emphasises that without the cultural preconditions for constitutionalism, politicians may not respect court rulings. He recounts how many foreign delegations sought his advice after the fall of the Berlin Wall on ensuring compliance with the Constitution, but he asserts that there's no legal solution; it relies on politicians viewing the law as a legitimate value. Based on these insights, the lesson is that the preservation of judicial independence is fundamentally tied to the prevailing constitutional culture, where the attitudes of politicians, society, and judges play a critical role in upholding the rule of law.

PART I

Insights from Western and Northern European Judges

4

We can Aim to be Part of the Solution Rather than Being Part of the Problem

LARS BAY LARSEN[1]

Benedetta Arrighini: Could you please share some key background information that you consider to be most relevant to your career or personal life?

Lars Bay Larsen: I never had a real master plan from the outset. I started by studying political science, and I completed a three-year bachelor's degree in Copenhagen many years ago, in 1976. Then I stopped and took a break, mostly because I doubted whether I wanted to complete a full degree in political science, or whether I wanted rather to combine it with law. When I started my studies, a few years after 1968, universities were not structured and working in the way that they do today across Europe and the rest of the Western world. It was a completely chaotic place, almost no matter what subject you studied. And a lot of the time went into discussions which in principle were positive, but also seemed very theoretical and endless to me, but for a while, at least, it seemed the teaching of real subjects suffered badly. In a certain way, I felt I did not become much more knowledgeable about anything by participating in these endless and fruitless discussions. So, I thought, why not study something that could be a real tool, where you could do something with it. Eventually I started studying law and I completed my law degree. I became a father twice during that period. So, I was mostly occupied with the idea that I would like to work with the law in one way or another, but I wanted to find a job which would not be completely incompatible with being a father.

And then it just happened that at the University of Copenhagen, while studying law, I had two particularly excellent external associate professors. One later became President of the Supreme Court and is still a very good friend of mine. The other one became also a judge and eventually the President of the Appellate Court in Copenhagen. At that time, they were both working in the Ministry of Justice, and I had initially a prejudice that the Ministry of Justice probably was a very stiff, conservative kind of place, because I did not know it as a workplace or in any other particular way. In the end, I felt becoming a young associate at a big law firm, where in those days they generally did not care much about family life, was perhaps not the ideal thing for me. I thought as these

[1] Interview conducted on 3 October 2024 and validated for publication on 6 February 2025.

two professors were happy to work in the Ministry of Justice, maybe I could be too. Then I sent in an application, got interviewed and got hired.

I worked in different areas, but largely on a kind of secondment to the Danish Bar Association. Technically my temporary position was based on a deal between the Ministry of Justice and the Danish Bar Association, who at that time wanted a link to the Ministry for a period of two years. But in fact they were hoping to make this kind of temporary secondment from the Ministry a more permanent arrangement. When I got back to the Ministry I was told to focus on the Danish incoming presidency in international and European police cooperation. This was before the Maastricht Treaty, so it was called the Trevi group, an intergovernmental network of representatives from Justice and Home Affairs ministries in the then Member States, created in 1976. For a year I did nothing but Trevi in the Ministry and worked with a colleague, a lawyer from the PET, the Danish internal security service, and the Danish police. That somehow got me into the world of European cooperation. My boss in the Ministry by the end of the Danish Trevi presidency wanted to appoint me as a head of the personnel section, but given my experience with police cooperation, I continued in parallel with the Trevi task. Later, I was responsible for the administration of the Danish police in the Ministry of Justice and for a while, I was also Deputy Permanent Secretary, with the same, but wider responsibilities. I was also asked to take over the law department. I remember having a brief conversation with the Permanent Secretary and I said, 'Look, I am not educated or trained for this. I have done a lot of policy work, administration, and international work. But the nitty gritty core lawyer work is not what I have really specialised in'. Eventually, I was persuaded to accept the challenge. That might have opened the door for me to go to the Danish Supreme Court which I did in 2003. If you had asked me five years earlier, it was not something that I saw as a likely opportunity to open for me.

I spent three years at the Danish Supreme Court. Then my predecessor at the Court of Justice of the European Union sent his letter of resignation, so a successor had to been found. I then got a call from the same Permanent Secretary, who had earlier asked me to take over the law department. He said something like, 'I think we had a discussion a few years ago and you made a remark that made me think that you might eventually at some point be interested in the job as a judge in Luxembourg. Would you then be interested also today, as the position will now become vacant?' And I said, 'Well, can I have some days to think about it and, and talk with my wife?' That is how I became a judge in Luxembourg almost 20 years ago.

Benedetta Arrighini: In other words, you have observed the evolution of the Trevi Group and the development of police cooperation among Member States.

Lars Bay Larsen: I was involved from the end of the United Kingdom presidency in December 1986 and for approximately the next 15 years. This presidency was followed by the Belgian presidency of Trevi for the first half of 1987. Then came the Danish presidency in the second half of 1987. I started by attending the meetings in Brussels not because it was the 'capitol of the European Community', but because it was a Belgian presidency of an intergovernmental cooperation outside the scope of the treaties. I attended all the Trevi-meetings for the next years and thus visited all of the then Member States, which were not that many in those days. As each state only has the presidency for half a year, one could cover all the Member States over a period of four to five years. I visited all the capitals and sometimes also capitals of non-Member States.

Benedetta Arrighini: In 2006 you were appointed judge to the CJEU. If you think about your 18 years of experience in the institution, how do you see your impact as a judge on EU integration?

Lars Bay Larsen: First of all, I swore an oath when I was hired, and I will not break that oath by disclosing any secrets of any deliberation. I have written some articles, some in English, some in Danish, about the way we deliberate at the Court, and some general observations, but really it is teamwork. And it is also teamwork in situations where there is perhaps at the outset and maybe also at the end, a tension between the views of individual judges. We are each a product of our personality, of our experiences, and what we have studied in more depth. Some people have been doing academic work before they came to the court. I have perhaps done less of that. I have done a lot of teaching, but not in the areas that I largely worked in later. I was teaching family law and inheritance law at Copenhagen University as an external associate professor. But I have not been teaching as regularly in police cooperation or criminal law, even though I have worked in these fields in the Ministry of Justice. It is good to not only occupy oneself with one kind of law in my view. And that is certainly what we do here at the Court; we do everything. It is the same at the Danish Supreme Court. It is a Supreme Court for all subjects, all kinds of cases, and criminal cases certainly exist there, but only in a very limited number, maybe less than 10 per cent of the cases are criminal cases. It is difficult to say much, but there are cases such as the cases Pál Aranyosi and Robert Căldăraru, which are of course some of the very important cases on the European Arrest Warrant (EAW) and on fundamental rights. I have also been the reporting judge in many cases in the Area the area of Freedom, Security and Justice.

Benedetta Arrighini: Indeed, these two cases bring us to the core of our discussion: the protection of rights in the context of growing dissensus over liberal democracy. Mr Aranyosi, a Hungarian national, was the subject of two European Arrest Warrants issued by the Hungarian courts in 2014. He was subsequently arrested in Bremen, Germany. The European Court of Human Rights found Hungary in violation of Article 3 of the European Convention on Human Rights, particularly regarding inhumane detention conditions. Similarly, the Regional Court in Bremen determined that the detention conditions in Hungary failed to meet the minimum standards required by international law. Mr Căldăraru, a Romanian national convicted and sentenced by the Court of Appeal of Braşov, Romania, was also arrested in Bremen. The ECtHR likewise found Romania in violation of Article 3 of the ECHR due to inhumane detention conditions. Against this backdrop, and in the broader context of democratic backsliding within EU Member States, the preliminary reference submitted by the German Higher Regional Court in Bremen raised fundamental questions. How has the CJEU adjusted its approach to EAW cases, and to what extent has rule of law backsliding influenced its application?

Lars Bay Larsen: Speaking very generally, you may quite often detect a certain pattern as a judge, but equally as a citizen or a lawyer from one field or another. You may have a situation, where hopefully law and national law are largely in harmony with one another. Then the Member States may decide to extend the competencies of the EU, which in time leads also to the creation by the EU legislator of new secondary EU law. Or the EU legislator decides to develop already existing secondary union law. A new directive – or framework decision as it was in older days – gives in due time rise to new cases before the Court in Luxembourg. What used to be outside the scope of European Community/EU law like Trevi and the Schengen Convention became over time part of Union law, thus eventually giving competence to the Court.

When something new calls for the introduction of a new piece of EU legislation, such provisions of EU law are altered and updated, or completely new provisions are introduced. Such developments of directives then typically call for amendments of national legislation (unless it is a regulation). Then, once it is implemented, if it needs to be implemented, then normally a few years will pass before you start seeing national cases on the application of the national law based on the new version of this directive.

What happens next? Well, then you start having cases where the national judges in Belgium, Denmark, Greece or Bulgaria – it may be any judge in any Member State – may have doubts about how to deal with these provisions. They have questions: 'How do I actually apply this? What does it mean when they have now changed this concept or developed it somehow? What should I do and how?' And to be on the safe side, because the parties might not agree how these provisions of EU law should be interpreted, then they ask a question on one aspect of *ne bis in idem*[2] or on another aspect, including aspects of fundamental rights. We, as judges at the Court of Justice of the European Union, then answer that question, and that sometimes leads to another court saying 'Yes, but that was in a situation like *this*. But what if the circumstances are slightly different, because we have a different case? Should I simply apply the same answer in my case, although there are some differences?', and if they are not sure of this, they ask new questions. Concerning *ne bis in idem*, as this principle had been codified in Article 54 of the Schengen Convention, we covered the field step-by-step and after a while we received statistically fewer and fewer referrals from national courts in that particular area because it had become a 'clarified act' as laid down in the 'Cilfit-doctrine'. The doubts that national courts may have as to the correct interpretation of EU law normally diminishes and evaporate over time as the case law of the CJEU is developing. The jurisprudence of the Court is often developing, very gradually as the Court by its jurisprudence fill in little pieces of the mosaic that hopefully fits together almost like a jig-saw puzzle and ideally becomes a complete and coherent picture in the end.

To go back to your question, there were until recently not that many cases in that particular area of democratic rights. But then maybe something factual is changing in the world. You have backsliding of fundamental rights in some Member States and that again gives rise to another type of questions that had not needed to be answered before.

[2] Editorial note: The principle *ne bis in idem* is a fundamental principle of EU law and a fundamental right of the EU. This principle prohibits a duplication of proceedings and penalties of a criminal nature for the same acts and against the same person, within the same Member State of in Several Member States.

What led to Aranyosi and Căldăraru jurisprudence is the case-law developed by the ECtHR and the CJEU, on the basis of the Dublin Convention (signed on 15 June 1990). I remember that because I was in the room at Dublin Castle when it was signed! But originally it came from the Schengen Convention, or rather the draft of the Schengen Convention. The Schengen countries – which were a forerunner group among the then EU Member States including the Benelux countries, Germany, and France at the start – were saying, 'Well, we need to do something purely intergovernmental at the outset too, because we want to see results more quickly than maybe some of the other Member States do'. And there was a long and sometimes frustrating discussion among the Member States, which was also the reason, why the European Council set up the Group of Coordinators, I think in 1988–1989, and they made the Palma document on the compensatory measures, which also covers most of what is in the Schengen Convention.

But then there was a chapter on asylum competence in an earlier draft of the Schengen Convention. At some point, there was a possibility for the Schengen Member States to take that out of their drafts and put it into the *ad hoc immigration group*, as it was called. I think this was still in the days before Maastricht and it was signed as the Dublin Convention, completely outside the treaties at first. And then the Dublin Convention was signed first by 11 Member States and only later by Denmark. That was mostly because Denmark made a technical mistake in Copenhagen. The Danish Minister was in Dublin but did not dare to sign because the Parliament had advised him not to sign it before they had had a discussion in the Danish Parliament.

Anyway, when the Aranyosi and Căldăraru cases were brought to the Court, we then had the *N.S. v United Kingdom*[3] and other good judgments of the Court in the field of asylum law, but that case-law was based on the Strasbourg *M.S.S. v Belgium and Greece*[4] case law. Belgium was judged, and Greece was judged too because of their reception conditions and their procedural responsibilities; fundamental rights were not sufficiently respected. Asylum seekers were not given enough material support, and asylum procedures were not timely processed. It was said by the Strasbourg Court (ECtHR) that Greece had violated the European Convention on Human Rights because of that. It was also said that Belgium had violated the Convention, because they had sent asylum seekers back to Greece. Belgium had argued: 'Yes, but there is a presumption that all Member States, including Greece, have signed up to the European Convention on Human Rights. How could we know that they were not respecting their international obligations?'

I think we should read the *M.S.S. v Belgium and Greece* judgments replying to this argument. 'You could have turned on your television or your radio or opened

[3] Editorial note: Case C-411/10 *N.S. v Secretary of State for the Home Department* ECLI:EU:C:2011:865, [2012] 3 WLR 1374 is a case brought to the Court of Justice of the European Union which concerned the concept of 'safe country' within the Dublin system and respect for fundamental rights of asylum seekers. For more information see the Asylum Law Database at www.asylumlawdatabase.eu/en/content/cjeu-c-411-10-and-c-493-10-joined-cases-ns-v-united-kingdom-and-me-v-ireland.

[4] *M.S.S. v Belgium and Greece* originated in an application to the European Court of Human Rights against the Kingdom of Belgium and the Hellenic Republic lodged with the Court under Article 34 of the Convention for the Protection of Human Rights and Fundamental Freedoms ('the Convention') by an Afghan national, Mr MSS ('the applicant'), on 11 June 2009. *M.S.S. v Belgium*, App no 30696/09 (ECtHR, 21 January 2011).

your newspapers or listened to Amnesty International or the United Nations High Commissioner for Refugees or whatever, and then you would have known that there were reasons at least to suspect that there could be a problem. But you did not do it. You just applied the Dublin system in spite of the special circumstances. Therefore, Belgium was responsible for the violations of fundamental rights'. This jurisprudence and this logic of the Strasbourg Court was subsequently applied by the Court of Justice in Luxembourg in the area of asylum law. First in the *N.S. v United Kingdom* judgment and later in a whole string of case law that basically applied the *M.S.S. v Belgium and Greece* ruling and made it clear that this was also the minimum protection level of the EU.

The following years I was often asked whether the same logic would also apply *mutatis mutandis* in the field of European penal law cooperation, in particular the EAW. And then for many years, I was asked about this at conferences or when I was teaching students: 'Yes, but this is asylum law. Does that also apply to the EAW? Does it also apply in the wider field of law enforcement cooperation, extradition law, etc.?' I always said, 'I would think so'. 'I cannot see why a similar reasoning should not apply in that area under Article 3 of the ECHR – or Article 4 of the Charter as it later became, when we got the Charter, and when the Charter became legally binding with the Lisbon Treaty. I cannot see why that should not also apply in the area penal law and penal law corporation. But I cannot be absolutely sure until we get the first cases on it'.

For some reason, it took several years before we actually got a case like Aranyosi and Căldăraru where the question was asked. That could be because the Member States themselves deduced that this reasoning should apply *mutadis mutandis* also in penal law and international penal cooperation. I do not know why, but it took quite some time before the first cases came, but then they kept coming and with different variations.

Benedetta Arrighini: This context is important because it is exactly at this moment that national judges also started to ask questions to the CJEU concerning the independence of judges in the context of democratic backsliding. How do you see the role of the Court of Justice in shaping the protection of fundamental rights by the Member States, but also the protection of rule of law in terms of the independence of judges?

Lars Bay Larsen: Well, I would say, generally speaking, I do not see this as the Court shaping it, because we are not like the American Supreme Court. I mean, we have great respect for them, and we have regular meetings. We just had a visit from a delegation including the President of the American Supreme Court, which was a return visit following a visit that we had in 2017 before COVID-19, and which again was a return from the visit they made in 2014. So just to not be misunderstood, they simply have a different legal system to that of the European Union. You can argue if you want that they are more integrated in some respects. You can argue that we are more integrated in a certain way, but it is simply different. And the judicial system of their Court, which is a true constitutional court, I would say, is that out of 10,000 applications every year, they pick the 60 cases that they actually deal with at the level of the Supreme Court and they have complete discretion over which cases they consider sufficiently important.

That is not how it works at the CJEU. We do maybe 800–900 cases a year, something like that. And most of them, about 70 per cent, are preliminary references. But we deal with everything that comes through our doors, in one way or another. Some are dealt with by a formation of three judges, some by a formation of five, and some in the Grand Chamber with 15 judges. Actually, we do roughly 50 cases a year in the Grand Chamber. So you could look at the 60 cases they do in the American Supreme Court and compare that to our Grand Chamber cases or plenary cases where we have maybe one or two a year or one every other year. But most cases where Union law is applied are dealt with exclusively by national courts. I do not know what percentage of EU law cases are dealt with by national judges, whether it is 97, 98, or 99 per cent. I suspect probably more like 99 than 97 per cent of the cases of applications of European Union law are dealt with by national courts, because we do not have EU courts – specifically EU courts – at a decentralised level.

Some of these applications of Union law by national judges are done by national judges who, even in the individual case, may not always reflect deeply on the fact that they are applying Union law, because their national law on extradition is quite clear, and it has seemingly correctly transposed whatever EU obligation there is. They just apply the national law; the parties may agree on this point as they have no doubts as to the concept of the law, but maybe about how you should qualify legally the facts of the case. That does not pose a problem as such.

The preliminary ruling cases that we get are obviously all selected by the national judges. We do not have a programme saying, 'OK, now it is soon to be the end of 2024, and we have now decided that in 2025 it is time to do something about the rule of law or to do something about extradition to third countries or fundamental rights'. We may have a discussion of a certain jurisprudence in general terms looking back on an academic discussion, but whether we get a case and whether that comes this year, next year, or 10 years from now or never, we do not know.

Once we get the case, we are very much like the American Supreme Court, 'one case at a time'. Then when we decide on a new case, of course, we also look at the existing jurisprudence and see if we can decide on this issue in a way that falls into place with existing case law and in some coherent way. Occasionally, we may have to change it, and occasionally, we may have to move a case to a bigger formation to be able to change or develop the case law.

Benedetta Arrighini: These are sensitive cases for the CJEU. How is the Court dealing with them?

Lars Bay Larsen: We are always trying to find the right balance in each case. And of course there may be judges who are more inclined to focus on fundamental rights themes and others who maybe have the approach like, 'Yes, but we should also look at the question or the risk of impunity – that must also be taken into the equation'. It is not a completely harmonised area because penal law is still largely a national competence, and it is sometimes very difficult to compare. You have the law, but how many years of prison can you get for importing and selling drugs just to take something that is surely unlawful – at least if it is hard drugs – in every Member State? How do you compare it? Because if you look at just the maximum penalty possible, you will be surprised.

I think it is still the case that the Netherlands is actually one of the most severe. In the Netherlands, the penalty is up to 18 years, while in other countries the same actions might not be even prosecuted. Then we look at the sentences and make the comparison. How do you compare it? It is not that easy because the systems are very much influenced by the national practice and national systems and how many prisons have you built? What is the need? Are you lacking capacity? All these things complicate the balance? Prison conditions are of course one of the things that we have had some jurisprudence on, but it came rather late.

Benedetta Arrighini: There has been much debate in a number of Member States about the decision of certain governments to limit the independence of judges. What are in your view the main threats to the independence of the judiciary?

Lars Bay Larsen: Well, I think that is the constitutional situation and context in individual Member States. We have seen that in Poland, under the previous Law and Justice government, and in Hungary. There have also been issues and doubts expressed in Romania and Bulgaria, but when you start developing a case law, you also realise that some of the rulings have consequences for some of the older Member States as well.

I am thinking of the EAW, where some German Länder and a few Member States had systems, where the Minister for justice (in practice exceptionally) might issue a direct instruction to the Director of Public Prosecution – to prosecute or not to prosecute in an individual case. The question was whether such directors of public prosecutions might still be considered as judicial authorities in the sense of the Framework Decision of EAW and thus potentially able to issue European Arrest Warrants. All Member States knew that this was the arrangement in some Member States, Denmark being one of them, as the Member States concerned had to declare this at the time of concluding the FD on the European Arrets Warrant. But the case law, which the Court had developed on the rule of law gave rise to new doubts and reflections, reasonable doubts in some of the other Member States. 'Can we give effect to a European Arrest Warrant issued by an authority who maybe once every ten or twenty years perhaps has received or will receive an order from the Minister in an individual case?' Eventually the Court took the full consequence of the recent developments of the rule of law case law. Our attention had previously not been drawn to it, but now the issue was brought to us.

In a sense, the Court invalidated all pending European Arrest Warrants issued by a prosecution authority that could receive specific instructions in individual cases. A prosecution can well be an independent judicial authority, but if they can receive instructions in individual cases, whether they do it or not, in practice they are no longer sufficiently independent and they do not qualify as an independent judicial authority under the EAW. Such authorities would then have to go back to the national (independent) court and have the court to sign the EAW-form. I have the impression that Member States were very quick to react and repair the pending EAW's in order to remedy the situation created by the Court's judgment.

More generally, you may reflect whether a serious systemic deficiency on the rule of law principles ultimately could paralyze the whole judicial system of a Member State. This would imply very dramatic consequences for the Member State concerned, but also for the rest of the EU, as it would in reality exclude the Member State concerned from any normal day to day judicial cooperation and not only from penal law cooperation.

Benedetta Arrighini: Against this backdrop of democratic decline and infringement of rights, how do you see the role of judges? The recent European election indicated a shift towards the rights. I was wondering, how do you see this current situation in the EU?

Lars Bay Larsen: I am afraid that this is not a situation that can be remedied by judges only; the judges, national and European alike, must obviously fully respect the limitations for judges. We can aim to be part of the solution rather than being part of the problem. But basically, we must do our work because that is the role of a judge: to take the right decision as best as we can together with our colleagues, like in the Court of Justice, because it is always a collegium of judges. Apart from the judicial work, we talk with judges both from EU Member States and from third countries, when they want to come here. In particular, we have had meetings with delegations from Moldova and from Ukraine. I participated in some presentations on refugee law with Ukrainian judges, and we had a delegation of Ukrainian judges at our court a while ago. But we cannot, as judges, solve the situation in Ukraine. However, I have been deeply impressed by the genuine interest demonstrated by the Ukrainian judges I have met to prepare themselves and their country also judicially for a better future, once the war is over.

Benedetta Arrighini: How do you see now the future of democracy and the future of Europe looking at these recent developments? Do you see the Court adapting to new challenges?

Lars Bay Larsen: The Court exercises the powers that the Member States have confirmed on us through the treaties. We may or we may not be frustrated by that, for instance, some aspects of foreign and security policy have deliberately been excluded from our competence by the Member States. Clearly this is one of the issues that have complicated the EU's adhesion to the European Convention on Human Rights. It is perhaps detail, although an important one, and there are historic reasons why it has developed like this.

But again, it is not up to us to decide how our competence should be. That is up to the Member States. And with the number of Member States we already have, it is not easy to change the existing treaties. I mean, I was present at the intergovernmental conferences leading to the revision of the treaties both in Amsterdam and in Nice. And Nice was just about enlargement, the biggest enlargement until now, and it was not easy to determine voting rights and the weights of votes, etc. The revision of the treaties is politically and legally difficult.

We, at the Court, have to do our legal work, that is exercise the powers conferred upon us by the Member States in the treaties. Obviously, over the years that I have been at the Court we have seen new types of cases arriving that we could have hoped never to see, about backsliding of democracy, and some Member States embracing a populist way of government nationally, which then may collide with some of the basic values that the Union is built on.

We have had to apply, inter alia, Article 2 TEU in combination with various provisions of primary law, such as Articles 19–21 TEU etc. If you look at Article 2 TEU and the common values, which are broadly described in the Treaty on European Union, if you just read the values, it looks more like the kind of statement of something very obvious, very general that you would expect to find in a preamble to the treaties or something similar. But they are in fact written into the Treaties. I for one do not regret that the Member States made that choice. It is a little bit like Article 50 TEU on leaving the European Union. Why was that put in? It was put in because there had been discussion for decades between Eurosceptics saying you should never join the European Union, because you can never get out it. And I suspect Member States were fed up with that discussion because they thought it was fake, because politically, of course, if a Member State really wants to leave, then political realities would find a legal way to accommodate that. But now they said, let us once and for all end this discussion. So the Member States made a rather general Article 50 TEU, probably assuming that it would never have to be applied. The Member States were wrong on that latter point, and then it was left to the Court in the case *Andy Wightman and Others v Secretary of State for Exiting the European Union*[5] to decide – very quickly (in two months) and in the full Court – how Article 50 TEU should be interpreted, when the UK had triggered the leave-procedure.

I am sure there will also be difficult problems that have to be resolved at the Court in some or another way in the future. We have been extremely busy in recent years, which is why we are transferring part of the competence to the General Court, especially in tax and custom cases for preliminary rulings. I am sure there will be work for my colleagues and successors in the years to come.

[5] *Andy Wightman and Others v Secretary of State for Exiting the European Union* is a case brought to the CJEU concerning the possibility of unilaterally revoking the notification of the intention of the United Kingdom of Great Britain and Northern Ireland to withdraw from the European Union. Case C-621/18 *Andy Wightman and Others v Secretary of State for Exiting the European Union* ECLI:EU:C:2018:999, [2018] 3 WLR 1965.

5

Activism is a Responsibility that Every Magistrate Bears

MANUELA CADELLI[1]

Ramona Coman: Could you briefly introduce yourself and tell me about your motivation for becoming a judge?

Manuela Cadelli: I was an assistant at the University of Namur (Belgium) until 1996 and I joined the Bar in 1992. I passed the competition to become a trainee magistrate for four years and appointed magistrate in Namur in 1999 and that is what I like – being a judge in court and spending time with people. Initially I thought I would stay on as a lawyer, but I had children, and I didn't have the pugnacity or subjectivity of a true lawyer. I love being a judge! I am going to turn 60 soon, and I cannot see myself retiring. Like the Dalida song goes: 'I want to die on stage'. At the same time, I am a research associate at CRIDS (the Centre for Research in Computer Science and Law in Namur). In court, I adjudicate economic and financial crimes at the first instance level, as well as civil law cases, and for the last four years I have also been a member of the alternative dispute resolution panel.

Ramona Coman: What do you enjoy most about your work?

Manuela Cadelli: The facts, the stories, and the questioning of power relations. Like Pierre Bourdieu, I went to boarding school at the age of five. I have a complicated relationship with authority and domination. I believe that my role as a judge is not only to dispense justice, but also to question and validate power relationships. I am motivated by the desire to deliver justice. I love people and what interests me is getting to grips with a case as closely as possible to get to the truth of the matter, knowing that we never really achieve that completely. And I like to look for the element that will appease. I like writing. Doing this job gives me meaning, especially in these times. You must do things with humanity.

[1] Interview conducted in French on 16 May 2024 at the Institut d'études européennes of the Université libre de Bruxelles. The translation was revised and validated for publication on 22 December 2024.

Ramona Coman: You have also been the President of various professional associations for judges. What led you to take on these responsibilities?

Manuela Cadelli: I was indeed the President of the Justice Association for the Rule of Law, an association set up by a Turkish judge, Yavuz Aydin (chapter 20), whom I met through the *Association Syndicale des Magistrats* (ASM, Magistrates' Trade Union Association). I am currently an administrator of the ASM, and was also its President for six years and I enjoyed the task, even though it was quite challenging. What motivates me is striving for justice, militating, fighting to resist reality as it is presented.

Ramona Coman: You are the author of several books, including *La légitimité des élus & l'honneur des juges, Radicaliser la justice. Projet pour la démocratie* (Éditions SAMSA) and *Nuremberg 1947: Le Poignard de l'assassin sous la toge du magistrat* (Éditions Anthemis, 2024). These are books with a strong message, or at least a striking vision of justice. Is activism compatible with being a judge?

Manuela Cadelli: I believe that activism is a responsibility that every magistrate bears; a burden alongside their office, a political burden in the sense of taking on the realities of life. And being an activist does not mean being a suffragette with banners. Of course you can be a suffragette with banners, and even do it better than our mothers' generation. But in reality, judges' activism is a form of existentialism; it means putting the fundamentals into practice in our rulings, in the courts, and it means respecting them. Being faithful to this commitment, that is how we uphold our honour as judges, and it consists, among other things, of speaking out in public to ensure that it is respected by politicians, and by taking civil society as a witness. In the Baka ruling in 2016, the Grand Chamber of the European Court of Human Rights said that each judge is responsible for promoting and protecting judicial independence (paragraph 138 of *Baka v Hungary*[2]). This sentence should be in the 'Pantheon' of our principles and on the pediment of every palace.

Ramona Coman: Do others in your professional environment share this view of judges' activism?

Manuela Cadelli: Compared to other countries, Belgians are very much in the minority in this regard. What is remarkable in the Netherlands, for example, is that judges don't have this culture of activism at all. Nonetheless, in 2012, 700 Dutch judges signed a petition saying that our profession was being distorted by new public management. That made a big impression on me because this culture is not in their DNA. On the Belgian side, in the French-speaking community, we are a little more indignant, but we don't say such things explicitly. The ASM does not represent a majority view at all, so it is really good to get together at ASM meetings because we're all in agreement. But unfortunately, we are in the minority.

Ramona Coman: You have written extensively about democracy and about what is happening in the justice system in both Belgium as well as in Europe. What do you see as the major trends threatening democracy and justice today?

[2] *Baka v Hungary*, App no 20261/12 (ECtHR, 23 June 2016).

Manuela Cadelli: In Belgium, there is a real problem because we have created a federalism consisting of two main parts: the Flemish and the French communities. The German community exists, and it counts, but they do not play a major role; they are not an actor or a political interlocutor. Another of Belgium's problems is also the proportional voting system. Proportional voting is very problematic in a system that can be described as a *face-to-face contest* between two antagonistic players who historically have scores to settle with each other. It means that when you (finally) have a government, the agreement that allows the coalition to form is set in stone through political guidelines from which it is impossible to deviate. Dominique Rousseau, the French constitutionalist, coined the concept of 'continuous democracy', which refers to the fact that in many countries there are transactions or arbitrations that take place between elections due to the interplay and positive action of the checks and balances. In the Belgian system, however, this is impossible. I personally am rather closely aligned with progressive parties. But when you go to them and say that some particular bill is not appropriate, they respond that it was included in the 'government agreement' when the coalition was being formed and is therefore 'locked in' as otherwise it could lead to the fall of the government. And moreover, they tell me, if the government falls, there is the danger that it will be the end of Belgium, because with each new government, the Flemish nationalist parties gain power and exert more and more pressure for further de-federalisation. In short, there is a form of blackmail. And this specifically Belgian problem exacerbates the other two difficulties: neoliberalism, which has stripped away the public good and public services and the priority given to security. Regarding the first, there is austerity imposed by the markets, and the financial markets of the world that dictate budgetary law, whatever the country. There is also benchmarking between states, between users, citizens, public services, public service workers and states. There is this competition, and benchmarking is imposed by the indicators.

Ramona Coman: How does this benchmarking approach affect the work of judges?

Manuela Cadelli: It has been accepted for some time that in Belgium we don't actually have as many magistrates, clerks and employees in the justice system as the law requires. Those in power tell us that is the way it is, it is the law of the budget like everywhere where finances dictate what happens to ordinary people. This is also true in France. For any measure today political actors first ask the finance department if they can commit a given budget. Sometimes decisions even start with the words: 'subject to approval by the finance department'. So not only are we evolving into an anti-democratic system, but above all, it is the end of the rule of law. In the same vein, most European countries that have introduced the so-called 'golden rule' of balanced budget have also made it a constitutional objective, a constitutional requirement. On the other hand, I remember governments like the one headed by François Mitterrand in France who said *l'intendance suivra*, meaning that budgets would have to be adapted to serve the collective interest. Neoliberalism imposes a blind sort of austerity. This is the first threat which I explain at length in my book *Radicalising Justice*.

The other threat, which is actually the consequence of disinvestment in the collective good, is the priority given to security and the consequent end to public freedoms and human rights. This is penal populism or the resurgence of Carl Schmitt. How are we to build a community, a collective, a cohesive whole against this background? The only way is by designating an enemy and excluding, punishing, and imprisoning 'the other' that is, each citizen or human being disqualified as an obstacle: the migrant, the delinquent, the poor, the demonstrator, etc. I was brought up with the idea that democracy is both a wager and a promise. On the one hand, you want everyone to get there and have a place, and you are going to do everything you can to make sure that it happens. In this sense, democracy is a promise. And at the same time, it is a kind of wager, because we provide the means for everyone to live safely, including the disabled, the disadvantaged, the unemployed, and migrants, in the hope that this will guarantee stability for society as a whole. But that time is gone. There is a real threat here, because in this context, justice is required to serve political objectives. The justice system is no longer required to adhere to the national and international law, and the hierarchy of norms; it is required to ensure that exclusion policies are as effective as the electoral majorities demand, in the name of the legitimacy – namely the elective principle – over which they claim to have monopoly. Justice is therefore criticised and is now seen as an obstacle. And this follows from neoliberalism. From a neoliberal perspective, judges are an obstacle to the effectiveness of security because they are described as human rights advocates, or *droits-de-l'hommistes*, as human rightist advocates.

This is what prompted me to write my second book. It was in 2016, and several things happened that inspired me. At that time, I was in Italy, in Cortona, and the *Daily Mirror* published a photo of three judges after the High Court ruled that Parliament must vote on whether the UK can start the process of leaving the Union, with the headline was: 'Enemies of the People'. At the same time, I was reading *Figaro Magazine* to keep abreast of what was being said on the right side of the ideological spectrum, and I came across an editorial by Guillaume Roquette, the editor-in-chief, published in response to a ruling of 6 July 2018 by the French Constitutional Council. The rule was based on the motto of France – *Liberté, Égalité, Fraternité* – and it sought to derive a general principle of law from the concept of *Fraternité*, thereby making it possible to invalidate the offence of solidarity in the case of Cédric Herrou, a farmer near Nice. Herrou had taken in migrants who came down from the mountains and allowed them to rest on his farm and he was prosecuted for a so-called 'offence of solidarity', that is providing assistance to irregular migrants. What we have here is an incredible misrepresentation of words. He had been convicted on this iniquitous basis – the 'offence of solidarity' – three times. The third time, he went to the Constitutional Council to find out whether it was contrary to general principles. As a reminder, the term fraternity is nowhere to be found in the Constitution, only in the motto. And the Council made it into a general principle of law. The idea of fraternity was violated by the famous offence of solidarity. A scandal! Constitutionalists were invited to appear on television programmes, and the judges were denounced for their hubris and pride, alongside criticism of the famous 'government of judges'. Guillaume Roquette wrote in this context that the ECtHR is a lair of unelected activists. So, when I saw the headline, 'Enemy of the People' in the *Daily Mirror* and the comments about a 'haven of activists', I thought I should write about it. When I say that justice is an obstacle ideologically, it is in fact now presented as an obstacle. Judges have the obligation to apply international law.

In Belgium, the Court of Cassation has made this unequivocally clear – judges are obliged to set aside national law and apply international law that is directly applicable.

But from now on, when we do that, we are treated as political, ideological, lax, human-rights advocates and so, ideologically speaking, we are already discredited, even though we are simply doing our job. So that is why we must fight in the cases, while continuing not to be influenced by the prevailing politics and ideology of security, racism, and exclusion. We have to be active on the issues, but we also have to be vocal in public. We must use the public as witness.

This is what I say in my book *La légitimité des élus & l'honneur des juges*. During the Shoah, judges bowed to the politics of electoral majorities. They did as they were told, and they were often even ideologues. The Nazi judges who were put on trial were truly Nazi, truly racist. There were not only positivist judges. Hannah Arendt says that positivism is an ideological choice; the supposed neutrality of the positivist judge does not exist. And so, to return to the subject of justice as an obstacle, in short, the justice system is now seen as a public service costing money and causing inconvenience short. The former Belgian Minister of Justice, Koen Geens, told us that we had to reduce the number of judgments that we produce are over ten pages long. Yet the Constitution requires us to respond to the arguments of the parties. We must give reasons, so that citizens can understand why they have been convicted. And this makes sense precisely because of our history. In democracies that have collapsed and which have been corrupted morally, legally and politically, judges were not required to give reasons for their judgments, but reasons are important. Especially when there is only one judge in the courtroom. The obligation to give reasons as a single judge is a kind of *disputatio* within ourselves, and which means that we can respect Kant's prescription.

Ramona Coman: So to come back to the question of democracy, judges are the target of many political decisions – you gave two examples yourself. The media often talk about limiting the independence of judges, and Poland and Hungary are the most commonly discussed examples. But tensions have always existed in other countries too. Does this mean that there is no longer a consensus on the principle of independence of judges?

Manuela Cadelli: It is even worse, because politicians are claiming that they no longer take the independence of judges into account. Take Gérald Darmanin, the French Minister of the Interior. The Constitutional Council (*Conseil d'Etat)* prohibited him from deporting a Chechen national, but Darmanin set the deportation procedure in motion anyway. The case went to the ECtHR, and the European Court also forbade him from expelling the applicant. But he deported him anyway, saying everyone has their own way of seeing things. In Belgium too, *Fedasil* (Federal Agency for the Reception of Asylum Seekers) has been condemned by the Belgian courts more than 8,800 times for failing to offer asylum seekers the reception they are entitled to under European law and Belgian law. It is ideological – it is a no-holds-barred, an uninhibited, and openly populist discourse based on the idea that the 'people' allegedly want us to deport as many people as possible. And I really believe that this is linked to this kind of drying up of the idea of collective good, a material drying up that stems from neoliberal ideology. It is the generalisation of suspicion. Everyone is supposed guilty of waste and laziness. This is the ideological legacy of Margaret Thatcher and Ronald Reagan and it has pervaded many consolidated democracies like Belgium and France.

In his book *La loi du sang: penser et agir en nazi*, Johann Chapoutot examines how the law was applied and reformed, and the way in which judges behaved during the Nazi period. He describes how there was a deep hatred of law, and law was seen as a complication, in a context of hatred of intellectuals, of dialectic, and of nuance. The hatred was framed as the promotion of efficiency, especially efficiency in terms of criminal law and migration.

So yes, I do link this phenomenon of the end of the welfare state to this shift in the 1980s. The rhetoric was the same as in the 1930s, it was the end of 'playtime', paid holidays, the Popular Front, end of all this 'disorder'. Back to order! The same ideas are also found in Michaël Fœssel's book *Récidive – 1938*. He spent a year in the bank at the *Bibliothèque nationale de France*, where he studied all the press articles from 1938. He shows an incredible similarity to what we are experiencing now, with regard to the poor and migrants, with exactly the same language. We are indeed faced with the disastrous effects of neoliberalism in terms of socio-economic equity. So how can we ensure cohesion? According to this rhetoric, by punishing, excluding, and calling for order, not by distributing wealth and taxation fairly.

Ramona Coman: What image do citizens have of the justice system in Belgium?

Manuela Cadelli: Opinion polls as a whole are quite consistent: they always suggest that about 50 per cent of citizens are happy and respectful, while 50 per cent are unhappy. And that is quite logical, because in every case there is at least one person who loses and at least one person who wins. When I go on social media platforms, I see a kind of hatred of judges and the law in reaction to certain news stories, where people say, for example, 'and of course the judges are going to set them free'. But there is also a lack of understanding of the role of the ECtHR. The law is presented as an obstacle, of course, as something for intellectuals. I left X for this reason. In real life, however, people have a lot of respect for judges. Even now, it is very rare for me to come face to face with someone who is unpleasant, rude, or disrespectful even though I adjudicate on criminal cases.

Ramona Coman: You said before that activism is important – can you tell me how?

Manuela Cadelli: I reflected on the activism[3] of judges in my book, *La légitimité des élus et l'honneur des juge*. First of all, in each case we have to take the full measure of the need for justice that is being expressed and apply and respect all the fundamentals of our oath. We must bear in mind the need for personal justice. When people enter a courthouse, they are not looking for the law, they are looking for human contact, and even if they are guilty and admit it in a criminal court, they need to be respected, and recognised as individuals. That is the first principle. Next, we must respect the idea that we are providing a public service, so we have to make our decisions in a timely fashion. You must give reasons, and the decision has to be a kind of service that you provide. We must respect these fundamental principles, which are linked to the fact that we are a constitutional authority that must be able to act as a counterweight, to oppose, to set

[3] The words used in French were *militer* and *militance*.

aside a law, and to prosecute. That is another reason why we, the judiciary, are not liked, because we constrain the power. I handed down a judgment during the COVID-19 period concerning a migrant. The judgment was 30 pages long and it was published. I know that all the lawyers who deal with migrants have used it. That is what activism is all about: it means producing a judgment that will be a useful tool, and even a weapon in every case. There are no small cases. Kafka's message in his novels *The Castle* and *The Trial* is that you can't obey the law, you must force your way in. So that is what militancy is all about, daring to be 'for' something.

Finally, the other aspect of activism is daring to speak out publicly, to exercise the duty of the whistle-blower in the media, to take the public as witness. In French-speaking Belgium, we have really set an example. I wrote an op-ed piece (*carte blanche)* in 2016 entitled 'Neoliberalism is fascism'. I thought it would create problems for me, but nothing happened. I believe I am respected because I write, but I am not very effective. Although we were able to stop a bill a year ago. We fought hard, I wrote a lot, and I appealed to the Constitutional Court challenging the amendment to the Judicial Code concerning the human resources allocated to courts and public prosecutors' offices. We will see what happens, but this work can be discouraging. And the people I work with at ASM are, like me, convinced that it is better to do something than nothing. The Baka ruling[4] is therefore fundamental in terms of judges' freedom of expression.

Ramona Coman: What forms of collective activism have you seen in your role as President of the ASM? The measures taken by the Polish and Hungarian governments to limit the independence of judges have given rise to demonstrations and expressions of solidarity by judges in other countries. Are there forms of collective mobilisation of judges in Belgium or in Europe?

Manuela Cadelli: The ASM created the MEDEL association (*Magistrats européens pour la démocratie et les libertés*). MEDEL is now a strong organisation, but it remains little known. In French-speaking Belgium, the ASM is very well known. There is also the *Union professionnelle de la magistrature*, which deals with other issues relevant to judges such as meal vouchers and pensions. There are very few Flemish members in the associations, however, and in Flanders there is really only one association left. Obviously, the challenge for magistrates is to work together.

Ramona Coman: How do you explain this low level of interest or presence in collective action?

Manuela Cadelli: It is a challenge we have to take up; I call it 'the challenge of the collective', and we are incapable of doing it even in a court house. The reason is fear – the fear of displeasing your boss. It also has to be said that this is a profession that tends to attract more conservatives rather than revolutionaries. The judiciary offers job security. Although some people also choose this profession because being a lawyer is very difficult and very demanding – that was the case with me. And then there is the

[4] *Baka v Hungary*, App no 20261/12 (ECtHR, 23 June 2016).

prevailing conservative culture exemplified by Jean de Codt, the former First President of the Court of Cassation. He wrote an article in *La Libre Belgique* entitled, 'Peut-on désobéir à une loi injuste?', in which he referred to acts such as the burning of a motorway bridge in the name of trade union freedom, or the spraying of tomato sauce on a painting by Van Gogh[5] at a time when 'civil disobedience is being invoked at every turn'. De Codt says that legalism is an important value, that 'legal positivism matters' because 'the continental judge is profoundly legalistic' and that, unlike Anglo-Saxon colleagues, 'he will tend to put forward the text that determines the solution'. A similar position was expressed by Jean de Codt in another article entitled, 'Et si l'arrêt de la Cour suprême des Etats-Unis sur l'IVG était un progrès vers plus de démocratie'[6] ('What if the US Supreme Court ruling on abortion was progress towards greater democracy?') in which he stressed that referring the right to abortion to the legislature was truly democratic. I responded to his position in an article entitled 'Renvoyer la question de l'IVG au législateur n'est pas "un progrès démocratique"', *La Libre Belgique*, 8 August 2022.[7] 'It is a fundamental freedom!', and in my article I pointed out that: 'In this role of dialectical co-normativity, the judiciary does not govern, but rather performs the virtuous function of a counter-power required by respect for the rule of law, but also by the deepening of the democratic principle, admittedly sometimes against the will and plans of elected representatives, but in the name of fundamental rights and public freedoms. And not in the service of the convictions or prejudices of its members.' An electoral majority can no longer expropriate a fundamental freedom. It is essential to say it in those terms! As far as abortion is concerned, it must now be enshrined in the Constitution.

Legalism is still firmly entrenched among my colleagues. For example, I was at a meeting where they were discussing a law that had recently been passed. I said that its unfair effects could be set aside on the basis of a ruling by the ECtHR, and a colleague turned to me and said 'But Manuela, it is the law, you don't have the legitimacy to set it aside'.

So, to come back to the question of activism, there is a lack of training in questioning the law and challenging it. The sentence in the Baka ruling about the duty of a judge should be taught. There is still a positivist culture in Belgium, and we are trained in this culture. At the Judicial Training Institute in Belgium training mainly focuses on substantive law. But we need training on the scope of the Baka ruling. This is necessary, for example, in the face of what's happening to us. When there are more than 8,000 *Fedasil* decisions that are not respected by the government, that is what we must fight against. So, we need to be taught what I call virtuous insubordination. Judges must be taught to resist.

[5] J de Codt, 'Peut-on désobéir à une loi injuste?' (7 May 2024) *La Libre Belgique*, www.lalibre.be/debats/opinions/2024/05/07/peut-on-desobeir-a-une-loi-injuste-HB574X4MSFDS5IWTC3GQMF2S2E/.

[6] J de Codt, 'Et si l'arrêt de la Cour suprême des Etats-Unis sur l'IVG était un progrès vers plus de démocratie' (14 July 2022) *La Libre Belgique*, www.lalibre.be/debats/opinions/2022/07/14/et-si-larret-de-la-cour-supreme-des-etats-unis-sur-livg-etait-un-progres-vers-plus-de-democratie-67WYJUQV3BEVNDIJGS3HSNYPDM/.

[7] M Cadelli, 'Renvoyer la question de l'IVG au législateur n'est pas 'un progrès démocratique' (8 August 2022) *La Libre Belgique*, www.lalibre.be/debats/opinions/2022/08/08/renvoyer-la-question-de-livg-au-legislateur-nest-pas-un-progres-democratique-KTDSWA3ORNDEVGAOK3KW7PONRU/.

Ramona Coman: This positivism is often presented as a characteristic of ex-communist countries. However, it seems to be more widespread than that.

Manuela Cadelli: In the Belgian case, it is a soft positivism. The law is just applied without question. There have been laws increasing the length of prison sentences. So you go to court, and a prosecutor comes along and says: 'I am obliged to ask you for the highest sentence. The law introduced a harsher sentence'. No! I must think about it first. And since there is no education, there is no education in resistance, even in questioning or drawing on the hermeneutics of suspicion, I think it is very serious. 80 years after the Shoah and the atrocities of Nazism, 80 years after totalitarianism and the moral, legal, and political bankruptcy, I think that we are not educating judges to be what the architects of the refoundation of Europe wanted them to be. In fact, we have lost our way once again. In my book *Nuremberg 47*, I say that positivism is a moral, legal and political mistake. It was Jean-Paul Sartre in *Qu'est-ce qu'un collaborateur*? (1945) who said that a collaborator, in reality, is someone who is a positivist, who bows to the direction of history. It is a form of resignation to the idea that *'C'est comme ça!'* or 'That's just how it is!' What can we do about it? Probably nothing. You must go and find the right law or the least unfair law, you just must find it and interpret it and say no. We are paid for life, and we are very well paid in Belgium. So that is all I have to do, really: question, and doubt – methodically doubt. And so, 80 years after the Shoah, I think it is much more criminal to be back in the same state as we were in 80 years ago, when you know what it leads to when judges bow down. Judges must be educated, they must be selected, and they have to be assessed on their ability to stand up. But not everyone thinks that.

Ramona Coman: Do you think that the restrictions on the independence of judges in Poland and Hungary have in some way raised awareness? Is this also a form of activism or resistance?

Manuela Cadelli: When activism is that dangerous, yes, it is resistance. Once the state is explicitly illiberal, it is resistance. The case of the Polish judge, Igor Tuleya, is very revealing. As a judge in Warsaw, he was one of those who openly criticised the Polish government and its measures and he suffered the consequences. A march was organised in Poland with the participation of judges from several European countries. This march left its mark on the public, with judges marching, not for themselves, but for a principle, and for history. The European judges joined forces to support their Polish colleagues.

Ramona Coman: Do you think that there is a growing awareness among judges of the need for a stronger link with society? Judges are coming out of their 'ivory towers' to meet the public. Is this also happening in Belgium?

Manuela Cadelli: We have close links with the human rights league, the *Ligue des droits de l'homme*. For example, we organised a citizens' café in Mons on the subject of, 'Is there class justice?' Before the 2019 elections, we set up a general movement with the *Ligue*, the trade unions, and the mutual health insurance companies. In short, we tried to copy the events of May 1968 – a form of 'convergence of struggles' against the disastrous effects of neoliberalism on public services. The ASM had to withdraw for reasons of neutrality, because the movement it had initiated was explicitly partisan in political terms. But people enjoyed the debates. When I was President of the ASM,

I often participated. But I wasn't in the same dangerous situation as Igor Tuleya. Not so long ago, I gave a talk to 200 retired people at a club in Namur. That is what I do a lot. Talk, and have discussions. The Bar takes part in activities in schools under the slogan, 'Lawyers in schools'. We should do 'Judges in schools' so that people understand what we do. Schools come to us, and we need to do this as much as possible. Judges always think they have too much work, so they prefer to stay at home and make judgments. We need to get out – the judge in the city. Even if it's obviously tricky because they have to remain a neutral third party when judging cases.

Ramona Coman: The rule of law is a common value of the EU. How do you see the role of the European Union in safeguarding this?

Manuela Cadelli: The problem with the EU is the Commission. The Commission and its ideology, and its hyper-neoliberal policy, its algorithmisation, and ardent digitisation. We have budgets for videoconferencing, to replace hearings with videoconferencing, for example. That is the problem with Europe: it is following a market approach.

Ramona Coman: The EU in general and the Commission in particular have developed a wide range of instruments and indicators for the functioning of the justice systems in the Member States. Do they make it possible to object to the dysfunctions in the justice system?

Manuela Cadelli: It depends. If you look at the European Commission for the Efficiency of Justice (Commission européenne pour l'éfficacité de la justice CEPEJ) reports, we made a lot of use of them because they showed that Belgian justice was under-funded compared to the European average – that was very interesting. What is complicated is when budgets are granted on condition that a particular objective is met. For example, I am all for digitalisation, but the hearing must remain a hearing. I am afraid that from time to time, I might have a prisoner in his cell with his mobile phone and we will do the hearing in that way. So that is the problem with institutional Europe, at the opposite end of the spectrum with the ECtHR. The Commission is all about management, rationalisation, and budgeting by indicators, and that is a shame.

What can judges do to campaign at European level? There is much to be expected and hoped for in this area. With regard to the March of a Thousand Robes in Poland, it was a decisive and historic event; it took place, and it can never be taken away from us. There are European judges who can get together when something happens, and I believe we may do it again. MEDEL also does a lot of work to support judges in danger in Turkey and elsewhere. Turkey is still a member of the Council of Europe. The dialogue between judges, the preliminary questions sent to the Court of Justice of the European Union, is also activism and in some cases, as in the Polish case, even resistance. It is daring and it takes courage. According to the New Public Management approach, if you send a case to the CJEU, you are asking for a preliminary ruling, which is not very 'pragmatic'. The Irish judge who had to send an offender back to Poland and who submitted a preliminary question to the CJEU because he had a doubt – that is militancy (n.n. translated as activism in the chapter). And the court replied that he should not be sent back. This dialogue is militant. Another positivist judge might say, 'after all, he is a delinquent, he shouldn't have been delinquent, and why bother and waste time by asking another court?' I don't like the word 'activist' as often used in English; I prefer the French 'militer'. In Belgium, the *Nieuw-Vlaamse Alliantie* (NVA, the New Flemish Alliance), the far-right party, has said it is going to fight against 'activist judges', so using the term activist, for me, becomes political […] But that too is playing with words. Because, I could say that activism is existentialism – although perhaps in English it is more neutral. What also needs to be said is that the positivist, legalist judge is also an activist because he/she bows down to authority. The very fact of bowing is not neutral – the International Tribunal set up by the Allies said so in 1947 at Nuremberg. It is an ideological choice to bow down. There is no neutrality in positivism that is a lie. And that's the point. The role of judges during dictatorships is where we need to look to support what we want, and what we reject for our present and for our democracies.

6

It is, to a Large Extent, a Matter of the Cultural Preconditions of Constitutionalism

DIETER GRIMM[1]

Viktor Kazai: Could you please share some key background information that you consider to be most relevant to your career or personal life?

Dieter Grimm: I decided to study law because of my strong interest in politics. I thought that it was the best preparation for a political career or a position in the government, a ministry, an embassy etc. In addition to law, I was enrolled in political science as well. I also had a strong interest in foreign countries and foreign law, so after having received my German law degree, I went for a year to study in Paris and another year at Harvard Law School where I earned an LL.M. degree.

After returning from the US, I got a position in the newly founded Max Planck Institute for European Legal History in Frankfurt, where I wrote my dissertation on Lèon Duguit and my *habilitation* on the relationship of constitutional and private law in the nineteenth century.

I think that my decision to seek an academic instead of a practical career developed during the work on my dissertation. Immediately after *habilitation*, I was offered a chair of public law at the University of Bielefeld. Bielefeld was a reform university, founded in 1969, and strongly oriented toward interdisciplinary scholarship, which met my own methodological approach to law. I always tried to understand and apply this approach, looking back to the conditions of its emergence on the one hand, and to the segment of social reality to which it applies, on the other hand.

In 1989, I was elected Justice of the Federal Constitutional Court of Germany and could thus add practical experience to my theoretical interests. The nomination came as a surprise. Unlike a career as a judge in the regular judiciary, you cannot plan or aim for a position in the Constitutional Court. When the opportunity arose, the decision was easy for me. I do not think any German lawyer, when asked if they would be willing to

[1] Interview conducted on 29 July 2024 in Berlin at the Institute for Advanced Study (Wissenschaftskolleg) and validated for publication on 20 January 2025.

join the Constitutional Court, would say no. At the court, I was the judge rapporteur for freedom of speech, freedom of media, freedom of assembly, freedom of association, personality rights and data protection. The time on the court was particularly interesting as it covered the unification of Germany and its consequences.

When my term ended at the end of 1999, I got a joint offer from Humboldt University Berlin and the *Wissenschaftskolleg zu Berlin*, a highly reputed institute for advanced study, whose Rector I was from 2001 to 2007. Next to my commitment in Berlin, I taught for 15 years part-time at Yale Law School and also at other US law schools and universities in foreign countries.

Viktor Kazai: Do you think being on the Constitutional Court is closely related to academia, and if so, to what extent?

Dieter Grimm: In one respect, it is closely related; in another respect, not. The way to interpret the constitution and to apply it to cases is the same for an academic and a judge. There is not one method for scholarly work with constitutional law and another for adjudicating. Therefore, I do not perceive any disparity in this regard.

The difference between scholarly work and constitutional adjudication lies elsewhere. The scholar publishes opinions and engages in academic discourse. The judge decides cases, and the decision is binding and final. However, a member of the Constitutional Court does not decide alone. This has a number of consequences. The judge cannot venture a tentative opinion and wait for the reaction of other academics. In addition, he has to pay attention to the practicability of his decision. Finally, he depends on the consent of the other members of the court. The decision is the product of deliberation. Consensus-building and reconciling different opinions is, therefore, an important part of a judge's work.

Viktor Kazai: Before we revisit your time at the Constitutional Court, I would like to ask you a few general questions about the state of democracy in Europe. After your extensive career, how do you see the current state of democracy in Germany, in Europe, and globally?

Dieter Grimm: After the seminal changes of 1989–90, it seemed as if democracy had established itself universally as a model for legitimising and regulating public power. Now, 35 years later, the acceptance of democracy is declining. Democracy is under attack from populists in many European countries and in many other parts of the world. In Germany, we are relatively better off compared to some other European countries, but we, too, face the challenge of a populist party – *Alternative für Deutschland* – gaining more support in free elections. There is also a divide between Eastern and Western Germany, with people in the East being more receptive to non-competitive and non-pluralistic democracy. So far, the AfD has not openly questioned the independence of the judiciary, since they often rely on the Constitutional Court for fair treatment compared to other parties. However, if they were to gain a majority and form a government, their stance might change, as populist parties often view an independent judiciary as a hindrance to carrying out their agenda in the name of the people.

In Europe, the situation varies greatly across the 27 Member States. The situation in Hungary, where the populist Fidesz party gained a two-thirds majority, is quite concerning, while that in Poland appears to be more optimistic since the October 2023 election. However, the current Civic Platform Polish government will face significant challenges in addressing the issues that have accumulated over the past eight years without resorting to the same problematic methods that their predecessor – the Law and Justice Party – used. There are similar challenges in other Eastern European ex-socialist countries, like Romania and Bulgaria, where the judiciary and public prosecution systems are still not functioning optimally. While problems of this magnitude are not as prevalent in most other European countries, the overall picture for Europe is quite mixed.

Globally, the number of countries that meet the standards of democracy is significantly declining. Various international institutions monitor the practice of democracy, and the number of genuine democracies has notably decreased in the last decade.

Viktor Kazai: Do you think the predictions about the proliferation of liberal democracy after the fall of the Berlin Wall were overly optimistic, and now we are heading in a negative direction?

Dieter Grimm: In hindsight, I think they were overly optimistic. I myself was optimistic, but not in an exaggerated way. This was partly due to an experience I had as a judge of the German Constitutional Court at that time. After the fall of the Berlin Wall, when so many new constitutions were drafted and constitutional courts established, we had many visitors from foreign countries – not only Eastern European countries but also South Africa – first parliamentarians who were involved in drafting or amending constitutions, and later judges of the newly established constitutional courts. Almost every delegation asked, 'How can we ensure that politicians comply with the Constitution and obey the rulings of the Constitutional Court, even if they seriously hinder their intentions?' I used to say that there is no legal answer to that question because it is, to a large extent, a matter of the cultural preconditions of constitutionalism. First, do politicians internalise that obeying the law is a value in itself and a contribution to their legitimacy? And secondly, if they don't, do the Constitution and the Constitutional Court have sufficient backing within society for it to become too costly for politicians to disobey a court ruling? Many visitors became a little bit sad when they heard this answer because they knew that these cultural preconditions did not yet exist in their country, although they hoped they might develop. This hasn't become true in all cases.

Some of these courts, for example the South African Constitutional Court, which paid a week-long visit to Karlsruhe immediately after the appointment of the judges by President Mandela, did remarkable work. I would say the same for Poland and Hungary. The Hungarian court was, however, extremely active, and some of the reactions of Prime Minister Orbán's government can be explained, although not justified, by the experience of a quite active constitutional court.

Viktor Kazai: In discussing the challenges that the judiciary faces, you mentioned that disrespect of the courts' decisions is a significant one. Besides this, what are the other visible signs of political attacks on the judiciary, particularly in Europe?

Dieter Grimm: I would emphasise above all the threat posed by populist parties. These parties, which are often but not exclusively on the right, tend to be anti-pluralist. They believe in a homogeneous society with a common interest and will and see themselves as the sole representatives of that interest. They undermine the legitimacy of opposition and of free media. They view the judiciary as an obstacle to their agenda. We see these threats manifest in various ways, such as attempting to align judges with the government, curbing the powers of the courts, or both. In Poland a series of restrictions were imposed on the Constitutional Tribunal, and that was followed by the appointment of loyal judges. Once that was achieved, the initial restrictions were eased to please the European Union, as the Constitutional Tribunal no longer posed a threat to the power of the government. This pattern can be observed in several countries, with Hungary and Poland coming to mind first, along with other countries like Israel, Turkey, and Brazil that are also exhibiting similar trends.

Viktor Kazai: Did you ever experience any political pressure during your years at the Constitutional Court?

Dieter Grimm: No, I never did. However, the Constitutional Court faced a lot of criticism due to several decisions that were unpopular with politicians, the public, or both. Around 1994–95, there were a number of contentious decisions.

Viktor Kazai: Such as the 'Soldiers are murderers'[2] and the 'Crucifix'[3] cases, I suppose.

Dieter Grimm: Yes, the 'Crucifix' decision sparked the largest protest, but the decision on 'Soldiers are murderers' also drew significant criticism, along with some other rulings. Despite the heavy criticism, I never felt any pressure or experienced any attempts by politicians to influence the court's decisions. Nor did the criticism negatively affect the functioning of the Court. As a matter of fact, the critique of individual decisions did not diminish the general approval of the Court. For a very long time, it has been the most trusted institution of the Federal Republic.

Viktor Kazai: I would like to discuss the importance of judicial independence, not just for judges and the legal system, but also for ordinary citizens. How would you explain to an ordinary citizen why judicial independence is crucial?

Dieter Grimm: This is a very important aspect. We have to try to show what is at stake. As a citizen involved in a lawsuit or considering going to court, you need to be sure that you will get an answer according to the law, based on the judges' best knowledge. Different judges may have different views on the meaning of a legal provision in a specific case, but this is not a sign of a lack of independence. If judicial independence is compromised, you can no longer be confident that you will receive an answer that is derived from the law because other factors may come into play. For the weaker parts of society, the courts are often their last resort. Imagine you live in a country where the judiciary is corrupt, and you can't afford to bribe the judges. It would be a dire situation. I would try to explain what judicial independence means for citizens in these terms.

[2] Editorial note: In the 'Soldiers are murderers' case (Judgment of 1 October 1995, German Federal Constitutional Court, BVerfG, 1 BvR 1476/91) the German Federal Constitutional Court found that using the Tucholsky quotation 'Soldiers are murderers' vis-à-vis Bundeswehr soldiers is not an insult in every case, but that freedom of expression and the protection of personal honour must be balanced against one another.

[3] Editorial note: In the Crucifix case (Judgment of 16 May 1995, German Federal Constitutional Court, BVerfG, 1 BvR 1087/91) the German Federal Constitutional Court found that the display of crucifixes in the classrooms of compulsory state schools violates freedom of religion.

Viktor Kazai: You mentioned that the German judiciary is in good shape compared to that of other countries. Have you noticed any challenges to fundamental principles like equality, presumption of innocence, or rule of law in the jurisprudence of the ordinary courts or the Constitutional Court?

Dieter Grimm: Courts have adapted to changing conditions, such as views on gender equality and sexual behaviour, or new threats to individual liberties such as data procession or atomic energy with a normal shift in their stance over time. This reflects society's evolving values or fears and can be addressed through the reinterpretation of laws and of the Constitution in line with rational legal arguments. I haven't observed a shift in Germany with regard to the basic values underpinning our Constitution. Yet, given the high number of judges and trials, I am not in a position to say that there are no outliers.

Viktor Kazai: I am asking this question partly because of the importance of the German Constitutional Court. Its decisions are cited even in those jurisdictions which are experiencing illiberalism or backsliding in the rule of law. For instance, the so-called Solange decisions of the Constitutional Court are often used by illiberal courts to justify their resistance to the European Union.

Dieter Grimm: Your observation was particularly true in the PSSP case,[4] the first case in which the German Constitutional Court declared a judgment of the CJEU ultra vires and therefore not applicable in Germany. Many commentators blamed the German Court for encouraging the anti-European tendencies in some Member States of the EU. However, unlike those states' highest courts, the German Court never declared a provision of the European treaties incompatible with the national constitution, it never denied the primacy of EU law, and it defined its reservations very narrowly. I defended the German Court against the reproach because one cannot expect a judge to give a wrong answer to a question deliberately just to prevent others from misusing a judgment. That would be a self-decapitation of the judiciary.

On the other hand, the German Court should be aware of its somewhat more visible position among the European judiciaries and explain its positions as clearly as possible to discourage misunderstandings and misinterpretations.

Viktor Kazai: Your answer brings me to a more general question about the attitude of judges. Do you think that court cases should focus solely on the legal questions at hand, or do you think that the judges can or should take into consideration the political and social context and even the potential consequences of their decisions, especially in politically salient cases?

Dieter Grimm: I would like to distinguish between questions of legal reasoning and questions of political expediency. The social context of a legal norm plays a role in the interpretation of that norm. Norms are formulated with respect to a certain state of social reality in which they are intended to have an effect, which can be either affirmative or

[4] Editorial note: In the PSPP case (Judgment of 5 May 2020, German Federal Constitutional Court, BVerfG, 2 BvR 859/15, 2 BvR 980/16, 2 BvR 2006/15, 2 BvR 1651/15), the German Federal Constitutional Court found that the European Central Bank's Public Sector Purchase Programme (PSPP) is partially unconstitutional.

reforming. However, social reality as envisaged by the legislature is in constant change. This entails the possibility that the original interpretation is no longer able to achieve the purpose of the law. In this case, a change of the law's meaning may be necessary to ensure that it again serves its legislative purpose. To this extent, it is completely legitimate to take the consequences of a judgment into account. Such an awareness of the consequences remains within the realm of the law.

Beyond these intra-legal consequences, I distinguish extra-legal consequences. Political consequences: Does the judgment please the government? Is it likely that politicians will not comply with it? Economic consequences: Does the judgment damage the German export industry? Religious consequences: Is it in line with the teaching of the Church? Unlike the consequences of a judgment for constitutional principles or norms, such consequences must not influence judgments. Considering them would be illegitimate, even in politically salient cases.

Viktor Kazai: I notice a potential inconsistency here. Earlier, you mentioned that the activism of the Hungarian Constitutional Court may have contributed to the developments in Hungary after 2010.

Dieter Grimm: Let me clarify my answer. I would argue, legally, that judges should be aware of the democratic status of the parliament as an institution directly elected by the people and accountable to the people. The parliament must enjoy a certain degree of autonomy in determining political goals and the means to reach them, and parliament and government, where most of the laws are drafted, have better access to information and expert knowledge than the judiciary. This is a functional consideration that complements the substantive consideration. It speaks to a certain deference on the side of the courts vis-à-vis the parliament.

Viktor Kazai: You mentioned earlier that there are no signs of direct political influence on the judiciary in Germany, but I believe there are some potential issues in the nomination process. For example, at the Länder level, the Minister of Justice could have significant influence over the appointment of ordinary judges. Additionally, members of the Constitutional Court are elected by political branches, just like in many other countries. How much of a problem do you think this politicisation of the nomination process is and will be in Germany?

Dieter Grimm: Judges in general, and constitutional judges in particular, make highly consequential decisions with important political and social implications. Therefore, they need democratic legitimacy. If not from politicians who are directly elected by the people, where else should this legitimacy come from? There are examples of systems in which judges are elected by the people, but such a system poses an even greater threat to the judicial function. In many states of the United States, for example, judges campaign for judgeships, invest money and make promises. This is an alternative but not a better one. If we exclude this option, then some political involvement is inevitable.

The key is to ensure that the influence is not one-sided. For the German Constitutional Court, the two-thirds majority requirement is of vital importance as it has historically prevented strongly partisan individuals from entering the Constitutional Court and ensured that professionalism plays a more significant role than party affiliation.

While party affiliation cannot be completely discounted, the two-thirds majority requirement prevents undue influence.

At levels below the Constitutional Court, such as the various federal supreme courts, the process is different. There is a committee, comprised of the Ministers of Justice of the Bund and the Länder and parliamentarians, that selects judges at the highest level with the advice of the respective courts. Lower-level appointments are handled by the Ministry of Justice on the administrative level and don't even reach the Minister. As far as I can tell, there is no significant political influence at the entry level of the judiciary. The grades in the two state exams are decisive.

Viktor Kazai: The politicisation of nomination procedures has reached an alarming extent in certain countries, such as Poland. This has led to numerous judgments from the European Court of Human Rights and the Court of Justice of the EU, which have ruled that certain judges in Poland were unlawfully appointed. Do you think this phenomenon challenges the very essence of what it means to be a judge today? If the nomination process is highly politicised, can we truly speak of lawful judges?

Dieter Grimm: The term 'lawful' refers to the existing laws. In Poland, the laws were significantly altered under the Law and Justice Party (PiS) government. While PiS lacked the majority needed to amend the Constitution, its members in the Sejm, that is the lower house of the Polish parliament, were able to change ordinary laws. Therefore, the question of what is lawful or unlawful depends first of all on the laws themselves. In Poland, the previous PiS government changed the law in its own favour, violating fundamental principles of the Constitution and the European treaties. In such cases, the intervention of European courts proved to be very beneficial. It has provided the present majority in Poland with a legal basis to denounce certain judges as unlawful. If we were solely reliant on the Polish legal system, the situation would be much more challenging.

However, neither the European Union nor the Council of Europe and their respective courts have a mandate to harmonise the judicial systems in the Member States. Each country has its own traditions and experiences. What is a problem in one country may work well in the context of another one. We should not end up with a system where a country has to seek the permission of the European institutions before it may amend its rules for the judiciary.

Viktor Kazai: Do you think that judicial independence can be restored in those countries where there are systemic rule of law problems? Do you think that rules that were deliberately put in place to undermine judicial independence need to be respected under all circumstances, or do you think that certain substantive principles of the rule of law can be more important than the formal ones?

Dieter Grimm: The rule of law requires that the laws be respected, regardless of whether the consequences are deemed useful or detrimental. Today, however, we understand the rule of law not only formally but also materially. Not any law that was passed in due form can claim binding force. It can only do so if it is also compatible with certain fundamental legal principles or values, which have found expression in the constitution or are binding for a EU Member State or the Council of Europe. Fundamental rights are such values, and judicial independence is an integral part of the rule of law.

Viktor Kazai: Aside from their usual duties, such as the interpretation of the law, what other legitimate tools do you think judges can employ to uphold democracy and defend the rule of law?

Dieter Grimm: Well, first and foremost, if judges believe political decisions or political behaviour to be illegal or unconstitutional, they must unequivocally say so, regardless of potential repercussions. I do not approve of the idea that, in order to preserve the institution of a constitutional court, judges should render incorrect decisions in the hope that things will improve over time. This is a slippery slope. What one needs in such a situation is not appeasement but clear articulation. Moreover, in situations where their independence is under threat, it is legitimate for judges to speak up publicly. Normally, it is not seen as virtuous for judges to go public outside of their rulings. But extreme threats justify exceptional means.

Viktor Kazai: We have witnessed instances in certain countries where judges have gone on strike to demand salary raises, and in other cases, Romanian and Polish judges have taken to the streets to protest the erosion of the rule of law. What are your thoughts on these forms of expression? Do you think such actions could be conceivable for German judges at some point?

Dieter Grimm: Frankly, I find it hard to imagine German judges marching down Kurfürstendamm or Unter Den Linden in protest. However, it is not beyond the realm of possibility. I recently met Brazilian judges, including members of the Supreme Court, who made public appearances to protest government plans to align the judiciary with party lines. They effectively used their platform and Court TV[5] to voice dissent against the government.

Viktor Kazai: You mentioned that several delegations from other constitutional courts regularly visited the German Constitutional Court. Do you think that international cooperation or the network of courts can be a useful tool either to resist democratic backsliding in certain countries or to support judges who are experiencing attacks on judicial independence?

Dieter Grimm: I believe that international interventions can have a certain effect. Declarations of solidarity with a judiciary under political pressure may show that such attacks do not go unnoticed abroad. Manifestations of solidarity against what is happening in a certain country might also help. It might encourage judges to resist to the extent possible, and it may also make an impression on the general public. Most countries want to appear law-abiding and if they see that the world around them is criticising what is happening, this may have a certain impact.

Viktor Kazai: Let me ask you one last question about the future. I understand that you can't predict what will happen, but what do you expect to be the most likely scenario for democracy and judicial independence in Europe? Are you feeling optimistic or pessimistic? And what are your thoughts on the European Union? Is it a solution or a part

[5] TV Justiça is a Brazilian television channel owned by the Brazilian Judicial branch and administered by the Brazilian Supreme Federal Court.

of the problem? Considering the events in Poland and Hungary, how effective do you think the European Union is?

Dieter Grimm: There is no easy answer to the first part of the question. We are in the middle of a process in which the acceptance of liberal democracy is declining, authoritarian systems are being established, and independent courts are the first targets of the transformation. And this process is not confined to Europe. We are facing a global trend. On the other hand, this tendency gives rise to reactions. Strengthening the resilience of democracy and the rule of law is the concern of the times, theoretically as well as practically. I don't expect the threat to be over soon. But I do not expect that democracy will ultimately be on the losing side. Moving on to the European Union, I believe that the recent development has shown the necessity of a means to expel Member States that consistently and seriously deviate from the Union's values. However, creating such a means would be very challenging, as it requires the consent of the countries in question. It is unlikely that this can be secured in times of crisis. But one should be mindful if a window of opportunity opens.

Additionally, I propose that the European Union enhance its own democratic foundations. I see two main avenues for this. Firstly, we should Europeanise the European elections. Currently, the European elections are a cumulation of 27 separate national elections. In contrast, Europeanisation would mean that European parties are formed and present cohesive European programs, rather than national agendas, to the electorate, in order to allow voters to influence European politics. The treaties already permit the formation of European political parties, but the national parties seem resistant to this idea, to their own detriment.

Secondly, the treaties that currently function as a constitution in the European Union are full of provisions that would be ordinary law in all Member States but are elevated to a constitutional level in the European Union. This means that they are withdrawn from the democratic process. Consequently, questions with the greatest political impact are decided by the CJEU without the involvement of the Member States in the Council and the European Parliament, which do not have a chance to change things. It is imperative to downgrade all treaty provisions that are ordinary law, leaving only provisions of a constitutional nature in the treaties. This would create space for a more robust democratic process.

Finally, the European Union should be more aware of the fact that its own legitimacy resources are rather weak and that it largely depends on the democratic resources that it receives from the Member States. A strong Member State democracy is therefore in the European Union's own interest. A constant erosion of the Member States' competencies by extensive interpretation of the transferred powers not only endangers the principle of conferral but also the democratic substance of the Member States.

7

That High Level of Trust in the Judiciary is the Best Protection You can have

KEES STERK[1]

Ramona Coman: Could you please tell us a bit about yourself, your background, your education, and the positions that you have held within the judiciary, as well as about your academic activity?

Kees Sterk: I read law at Tilburg University in the Netherlands. After that, I worked as a lecturer of commercial and civil law at that university for six years. During that time, I wrote my PhD thesis. After completing my thesis, I became a judge in the District Court of Breda, where I first worked in the Civil Division and later in the Criminal Division, including almost four years as an investigating judge. Seven years later, I was appointed to the Court of Appeal in 's-Hertogenbosch, where I again worked in the Civil and Criminal Divisions. After two years, I was promoted to Vice-President of the Court of Appeal. I was also appointed President of the Criminal Division and, as such, was a member of the Board of the Court of Appeal. Years later, the President of the Supreme Court asked me, on behalf of the Supreme Court, to join the Supreme Court in The Hague. I was on the Supreme Court for five years: three years in the Criminal Division and two years in the Tax Division. During those five years, I was a member of the Board of the Supreme Court for three years. After five years on the Supreme Court, I was selected to join the Council for the Judiciary, which is a full-time position in the Netherlands. For seven years, I was the Vice-President of the Council. My primary task was the promotion of the quality of justice, and the relations with politics, especially in the field of criminal law. For some time, I was also responsible for foreign affairs. Following my seven-year tenure at the Council for the Judiciary, I returned to the District Court of Zeeland-West-Brabant in Breda. I am also a professor at Maastricht University, where I teach topics related to the administration of European justice and its political sensitivities. I returned to the Court of first instance because that would give me more room to voice my opinions. I trained as a civil and commercial judge, but I also became a criminal and tax judge. So, I am what one could call a generalist.

[1] Interview conducted on 15 May 2024 at the District Court in Breda in the Netherlands and validated for publication on 15 January 2025.

I like to do every kind of case within the Criminal Division, where I am working now. Most people like to specialise, but I prefer to handle cases from a so-called helicopter view, based on general concepts and principles that are central to all fields of law.

Ramona Coman: What motivated you to become a judge?

Kees Sterk: After completing my PhD, I started working at the Court of Breda as an assistant to the President, writing out the judgments of the President on interim measures in civil law to approve and sign. It was love at first sight. I liked the work very much: listening to citizens, establishing facts, applying the law, all with the purpose of finding a just solution for the problems parties had within the law. The President of the Court and other senior judges asked me to become their colleague. So, I entered the selection procedure for a judge, and after one year, I was appointed. I never regretted entering the judiciary. It was and is something which suits me very well.

Ramona Coman: Could you say a few words about your activity as President of the European Network of Councils for the Judiciary?

Kees Sterk: When I was a member of the Council for the Judiciary, I was also in charge of foreign affairs, and I joined the ENCJ in 2014 as a member of the project on Independence and Accountability. A few years later, I became the President of that project, and in 2018, I was elected President of the ENCJ. And of course, this was the time when, in Poland, the takeover of the judiciary by the Law and Justice government was happening – not secretly, but openly. So, I rallied support for our Polish colleagues by making statements, which we are still doing. If the Polish Council for the Judiciary (*Krajowa Rada Sądownictwa,* KRS) was no longer independent, then we had to suspend it from the ENCJ. It was not very easy to get the members of the ENCJ to accept this. There was fear among representatives of the national councils. Who would be next? There was also fear about how the national executives would react towards them: would it create tensions? This was, for instance, the fear of the Spanish and Slovak Councils. Some councils felt that we might become too political. And, of course, suspending a member was totally new to the ENCJ. But according to the statutes of the ENCJ, members must be independent from the executive branch. And if it is obvious to everyone that the Polish Council for the Judiciary does not meet that criterion, we must take a position and say that we don't accept them as a full member anymore, otherwise we would not be taking our own statutes seriously. So I was very happy that in September 2018 the ENCJ voted for suspension, with only the Polish Council itself voting against it. This was rather remarkable: all the councils were able to overcome their fears. Since the ENCJ decided on suspension and not on expulsion, the Board of the ENCJ initiated a monitoring mechanism of the Polish Council. Every three or four months, a delegation under my leadership went to Warsaw. The delegation always consisted of three members of the Board, which always included a representative from Central Europe (ie Lithuania, Hungary, or Croatia), myself, and someone from Southern Europe, to represent the different families of law and different experiences as to the independence of the judiciary. This was done on purpose so that the Polish government could not accuse the delegation of being biased and of not understanding their history.

The delegation usually started with a visit to the Dutch Embassy to learn about the political situation in the country. As I said, it is difficult to assess developments in a country if you don't understand the language, you are not able to read the newspapers and you don't know which people and which news sources can be trusted. In that case, you need reliable sources of information. It was helpful to begin by obtaining a good understanding of the context of the developments in Poland from the embassies of EU Member States. Usually, we started with the Supreme Court, talking to the First President and other members of the Supreme Court, then to representatives of the judges' organisations Iustitia and Themis and to representatives of the Free Courts organisation. We also visited the Office of the Polish Ombudsman, Adam Bodnar (who was appointed Minster of Justice in Poland in December 2023), and talked extensively with him and his staff. We went to the Polish Council of the Judiciary. Our schedule always included an appointment with the Minister of Justice or a Deputy Minister of Justice of Poland. Only once, however, was this a real conversation, because all the other appointments were cancelled just one hour before they were meant to take place. It was obvious that the government was not interested in talking. But the Polish KRS always did. The dialogue with the KRS was always very difficult. The President of the KRS at the time, Leszek Mazur, was open to discussion, but others were not, including some members of the Judicial Council who have all since been appointed to the Constitutional Tribunal. During the visit, they reproduced what I would say is Law and Justice propaganda, without any intention for dialogue. But I thought it was good to have the meeting anyway. In the end, this process led to the conclusion that the KRS did not want to go in the direction of independence. That led to a proposal to expel the KRS on the basis of the reports that the delegation made on all of our visits. After two years of visits, the conclusion was that they knew what they were doing: deliberately destroying the independence of the judiciary. The KRS does not want to mend its ways, and so there is no reason for it to be in our organisation. We had to expel it. We reached that conclusion in 2020, during the COVID-19 pandemic. I did not think it was a good idea to have such a potentially difficult discussion online, because expulsion was a new phenomenon that had never been seen before in the ENCJ. I knew about the sensitivities in different councils. Therefore, we postponed the meeting to a later date, and that is why the decision to expel the KRS was taken in 2021 and not in 2020. In 2021, although I was no longer the President of the ENCJ, I was still very much involved in the expulsion. I even wrote the expulsion paper, which was adopted by the Board of the ENCJ.

I am still involved in many developments at the ENCJ. In July 2024, I was invited to the annual meeting of the ENCJ in Rome. In June 2024, I was invited to Warsaw to speak at a conference about the restoration of the independence of the judiciary in Poland in the Senate building of the Polish Parliament. I am also involved in a lawsuit against the Council of the European Union. Four European judges' associations – Association of European Administrative Judges (AEAJ), European Association of Judges (EAJ), MEDEL and *Rechters voor Rechters* (Judges for Judges) – launched this lawsuit with the CJEU, and I am one of the initiators, along with colleagues from Madrid, Dublin,

Groningen, etc. The lawsuit[2] is about the Council's decision to disburse EU funds as part of the Recovery and Resilience Facility despite ongoing rule of law concerns in the country. The case was referred to the Grand Chamber of the General Court in Luxembourg, which ordered an expedited procedure. Since it gave that order, however, everything went very slowly. In the end, the General Court rejected the standing and legal interests of the four organisations, on – in my view – rather unconvincing reasons. The four organisations appealed to the Court of Justice of the EU in August 2024. They argued that the measures adopted by the Polish authorities insufficiently insure the effective protection of the independence of judges and the judiciary. The case is still pending.

In July 2024, I went to Munich at the invitation of the Bavarian Judges Association to speak about the safeguards that the Dutch system of self-government provides to the judiciary. It is very important to have good laws to protect and guarantee the independence of the judiciary, but we learned from the situation in Poland that you do not have to change the text of the law to undermine the independence of the judiciary. The Polish Constitution has not been changed, not one sentence or one word. And yet the PiS government still managed to undermine judicial independence. Why was the PiS government able to do this? I have gone to Poland every year since 2015. And at a certain point I said to the leadership of the judges' associations, that they must prepare for the time after PiS. Because no party and no party leader lives forever. So there will come a time after PiS, when it will no longer be in power. I encouraged them to analyse why these attacks on the judiciary occurred and why there was not much support from citizens for the independence of judges in Poland. Eventually they concluded that they had made mistakes. They thought that simply doing their job and being protected by the law was enough to protect their independence. The main Polish lesson for judiciaries is that the protection of the law is not enough. Of course you must do your job. You must do it well. But you must also reach out to the public, and you must try to gain and maintain the trust of the public. Because at the end of the day, it is the trust of the public that will be decisive in whether you lose your independence or not, when attacked by (populist) governments.

In the Netherlands, we recently had a survey of trust in the judiciary. It monitored the trust of citizens in the police, the judiciary, the parliament, the government, and many politicians in general. For many years now, the trust of the population in the Dutch judiciary has been between 70 per cent and 75 per cent. And it is rather stable. Usually, there is a kind of competition with the police. The police usually score a little bit below the judiciary, but they also do very well. And trust in politicians, the parliament and the government is at 25 per cent. So there is a huge gap between the judiciary and police on the one side and politics on the other. That high level of trust is the best protection you can have. Of course, trust can be undermined by fake news, by attacks, by politicians, etc. Yet of all the necessary requirements for an independent judiciary, such as good laws protecting the independence of the judiciary, a good culture surrounding the rule of law, courageous judges protecting the rights of the citizens, and the trust of the citizens.

[2] Joined Cases T-530/22 and T-533/22 *MEDEL v Council* ECLI:EU:T:2024:363.

I feel it is the latter that is decisive in a moment of crisis to uphold an independent judiciary. If you look at the situation in the Netherlands, our main problem is not the laws or the trust of the population but the rule of law culture, which might undermine the trust of citizens in the long run. For the last ten years, I would say, politics have been very much involved in the maximisation of efficiency, and getting political problems 'fixed' by bypassing the law. To some extent, I feel, this was probably necessary, but what I see is that the efficiency of the system and the fixing of political problems by bypassing the law seem to have become the dominant point. We fail to ask ourselves why are we doing certain things? What (legal) values we must uphold?

The internal rules of the bureaucratic system have become too dominant. In my opinion, that is not how criminal law should operate. A judge must decide on the case of an individual citizen and his or her personal circumstances. And, in my view, this focus on efficiency and fixing problems by bypassing the law has moved the centre of attention away from the values on which our criminal law was founded: the values of democracy and the values of the rule of law. This is true not only for criminal law, but also more broadly. And that, I feel, threatens to undermine the trust of citizens in the judiciary in the Netherlands in the long run. The child support scandal in my country is the obvious example. In essence, this scandal revolves around the way misuse of child support, as perceived by some political parties, was organised. The legislator introduced a strict regime of which the core was that every fault/mistake in an application (even spelling your name wrongly by one sybil) resulted in an irrefutable duty to pay back all the child support ever received, even as it was established that it was received in accordance to the law. It pushed tens of thousands of innocent citizens into misery and poverty.

But the problem goes deeper than the child support system. We now have a new government, and it has agreed – on paper – to respect the law and the international treaties. That is good, but it is not enough. What we need in the Netherlands is a defence and a restoration of the pathos and the values of our society in legal practice, a restoration of the balance between justice and efficiency. Increasingly, this restoration means more justice and less efficiency, but it must be done anyway.

Ramona Coman: Are there tensions in the Netherlands between politics and justice or threats to judicial independence in some way, perhaps indirectly?

Kees Sterk: There are attacks and criticism, usually from the right end of the political spectrum. That includes three of the four parties in the present government. Usually, the criticism is about climate cases, criminal law and immigration law. There was a famous climate case between Urgenda and the Dutch government. The criticism was that the judges were overstepping their mandate. So, yes, there are some tensions between judges and some politicians in that area of law. But there are also some tensions in the field of criminal law. In that area, when there is a major crime, certain newspapers usually ask the judges to give the suspects as severe a sentence as possible. Some politicians echo this cry that there must be severe sentences. So there are tensions in the areas of criminal law and immigration law. Of course, some politicians and newspapers accuse judges of being too soft.

In my view, however, for some years now, most politicians are unable to solve certain problems in the fields of immigration, climate, crime, and in my country housing, and they feel powerless to do anything because of the (international) complexity and the magnitude of the problems of society. Other populist politicians do not seem to be interested in solving problems of society, although they say they do, because they offer only simple, usually symbolic solutions, and do not care whether the law allows these solutions or not. Both kind of politicians do not want to look powerless in the eyes of voters, so when the problems of the voters are still not solved, they blame judges instead of looking at themselves.

The politicians who try to solve the problems of society have been making vague laws for years, or laws that are based on different, conflicting principles without making it clear which principles should be upheld first and which second. In cases where the content of a law is unclear, I, as a judge, cannot refuse to make a judgment on the basis that the law is unclear. By law, I am bound to give a judgment based on the law. If some politicians are not happy with the outcome, then they should make clearer laws. Politicians are not always successful in doing this in a country like the Netherlands, where there is always a multi-party government. The present government consists of four parties, and the last government was also a coalition of four parties. To govern, they need to make compromises, so they make vague laws. That is one point. Another point is that sometimes the laws are not vague, but they are very harsh. Take the example of child support and allowances. The law states that if a citizen provides incorrect information on an application for child support in a certain year, he or she will not only have to pay back everything he or she received in that year but will also have to return the benefits of previous years. The consequences of breaking the law by the applicant were clearly out of proportion to the mistake or fault: even spelling your name incorrectly could have led to these harsh consequences. It is no wonder that this law resulted in a huge scandal. A lot of citizens were pushed into misery and poverty because of it. I feel that one of the issues involved here, apart from the law itself, is that the Council of State, which is the highest administrative judge in this field, was too close to politics to be able to judge that these consequences were not proportionate. It upheld the harsh consequences of the law, while, in my view, it obviously should not have done so, because the consequences were not in proportion to the fault/mistake. It is delicate for me to say this, because I was a member of the Dutch Supreme Court, but I really feel that if these cases had gone to the Supreme Court and not to the Council of State, this scandal would probably never have happened.

Ramona Coman: We have discussed the Netherlands and Poland. What is your view of the state of democracy in other Member States in the EU and outside of the European Union?

Kees Sterk: I usually focus on the judiciary, of course, because I am a judge. When you talk about democracy, you are usually also talking about politics. As a judge, I must restrain myself from any comments on politics, with one exception. I am allowed by the ECtHR in Strasbourg to talk about the judiciary and its independence in cases where the independence of the judiciary is in danger. The Court has held that in those circumstances, I have a duty to speak out on that subject. Otherwise, I must refrain from comment.

Ramona Coman: Let's then talk about the independence of the judiciary, which is a very important component of liberal democracy.

Kees Sterk: What worries me very much is that there are quite a lot of attempts by politicians to get control over the judiciary. Appointments of judges are, of course, a very useful instrument for that. And that is what you see everywhere, not only in Central European countries but also in other countries in Europe and elsewhere. In 2013, I was at the *Cour de Cassation* in Paris. There was a meeting about the relationship between the French Council for the Judiciary (*Conseil Supérieur de la Magistrature)* and politics. The President of the French Republic was also the President of the Council, but the French judges at the time did not want to be under the political supervision of the President of the Republic. They wanted to free themselves from that supervision, because most French judges feel that the most important appointments in the judiciary have a political element. I remember talking about the Dutch system, which, in my view, is one of the few systems in Europe where there is, until now, no political influence whatsoever on the appointment of district and appeals court judges, or president of these courts. That is one of our main safeguards in the Netherlands. At the Paris meeting, there was a huge outcry by a former prime minister and other politicians, who were very much against the independence of the French Council. They did not want to give up power, but they framed this as part of their duty to protect the judiciary.

I had another experience in Spain, where a good friend of mine was a member of the Spanish Council for the Judiciary. She has been a member for a longer period than the law provides for, because the Spanish Parliament has not been able or willing to elect a new Council. And why is that? I think that this is still due to the aftermath of the Spanish Civil War, and that the left-wing majority in Parliament now feels that the judiciary has too many right-wing people in its ranks.

Ramona Coman: Some observers are comparing the situations in Poland and in Spain. Are these situations similar in terms of judicial independence and political influence on the judiciary?

Kees Sterk: Poland and Spain have different histories, of course. In both systems, however, the Council for the Judiciary is appointed by the parliament. This is against European standards, which hold that the selection of judges for a council for the judiciary should be done by peers, meaning judges. So, in both countries, the selection of judges for the Council for the Judiciary by the parliament should be changed. As I said, both countries have different histories. Poland comes from a communist system, in which there is no separation of powers but just one central power. In that system, the judges had to do what the Communist Party said they should do. What is interesting is that the PiS government, which was very anti-communist, very much used the instruments of the communist past in trying to bring the Polish judiciary under its control. That was very strange to witness. In Spain there is a different history: the Civil War, which Franco's forces won. When Franco died, Spain turned to democracy and the country had a more outward look towards the world and to Europe. But it seems – at least, according to some politicians – that the Spanish judiciary still recruits too much from among people and families who were on Franco's side of the Civil War, and not from both sides. I think that is where the problem began, and I don't know whether it is true or not. The Spanish Socialist Party feels that the judiciary is more or less the instrument of the right-wing party. It looks as if the civil war over the judiciary has not yet ended.

Ramona Coman: Poland and Hungary are different, not in terms of the measures that their governments, the Fidesz and PiS governments, have taken, but different in terms of the reactions to these measures within the judiciary and within society. How do you see this difference between Poland and Hungary?

Kees Sterk: Orbán gained power in 2010, and right from the beginning, he started to seek control over the judiciary. I feel that one of the major mistakes of the European Commission at the time was that they did not see this happening, or chose not to see it happening, or they thought it would go away of its own accord, without interference from Brussels. I feel that the European Commission made a huge mistake at the time. It was perhaps also relevant that Hungary is a rather small country, with a difficult language, so the focus was not on what was happening there. Orbán was not raising his voice against the EU, which might be another explanation. He used the first years of his government to get control of the judiciary. The Commission realised this only after four or five years. Then Orbán started playing the Commission. He proposed different laws, but each with the same goal as the previous one: getting control over the judiciary. And the Commission did not have the inside information or the political courage and will to deal with this. These were Viktor Orbán's tactics to get control over the judiciary. They were totally different tactics from Jarosław Kaczynski's in Poland. Kaczynski always acted openly; Orbán mostly acted secretly, with more or less hidden tactics.

Comparing Polish and Hungarian judges, the Polish have a kind of tradition of fighting for things that are important to them. Otherwise, they would have lost their country in the past. Poland was divided between Russia, Prussia and Austria for more than 100 years. They had to fight in World War II. It is in the mentality of the Polish people that if you do not fight for what you believe in, then you will lose your independence. Independence as a country, but also independence as a judge. In Hungary, in the first five years of his government, Orbán already gained quite a grip on the judiciary. The Hungarian judges were not supported by Europe because Europe did not see or did not want to see what was happening. There was no such resistance as there was in Poland. Yes, of course, there were some examples of very brave Hungarian judges. As President of the ENCJ, I supported and visited the Council for the Judiciary in Hungary, which was not under Orbán's influence at the time. Orbán did not care about that, however, because the Council did not have any decisive powers and was neglected by the executive branch and by Parliament.

Ramona Coman: Perhaps one of the differences is that there are more disciplinary proceedings against judges in Poland than there are in Hungary.

Kees Sterk: Yes, there are. For example, there is the case of the Polish Judge Waldemar Zureck, who still has the most disciplinary procedures against him. Right from the start, he refused to recognise the disciplinary chambers dealing with these cases. And he is not the only one; others include Dariusz Mazur, who is now a Deputy Minister of Justice in Poland, and Judge Igor Tuleya. But there are not just two. There are at least 20, 25, 30 Polish judges facing many disciplinary proceedings. These proceedings put these people under huge psychological pressure and create a chilling effect. Because of that, these judges have the support of European judges. When I went to Poland every year,

I did not have to say much; my presence was support enough. I was not the only one: there were also the Portuguese Judge Jose Igreja Matos of the European Judges Association (chapter 11), who is now the President of the Court of Appeal in Porto, and Tamara Trotman, who is the President of *Rechters voor Rechters*.

The ad hoc support evolved towards more sustainable, structured support for judges. For the first time, I must say that we, the judiciaries in Europe, are really working together. And that is a very important development. In 2013, when I entered the ENCJ as part of the project on Independence and Accountability, we said that we must establish standards about independence in Europe. This was not an easy task, given the divergences between the different families of law in Europe. The project met three times a year with the goal of a deeper understanding of the essence of judicial independence. Conversations during the meetings were not easy, because every participant simply advocated for his or her own system. It took us a year to realise that we had to look further than our own national systems. In the end, the project was able to create standards for the whole of Europe that everyone agreed to. All these standards were accepted unanimously. These standards are still in progress, and European judicial organisations are working together to push them forward. It is an important development from national judges operating within their national systems and meeting judges from other countries to inspire each other. There is a sense of urgency among European judges because of the threats from politicians against their independence. There is a practical solidarity and a willingness to act, although, as I explained earlier, this is always difficult for judges due to the restraint required. Not every European judge is involved, but there are a few people who do this in Europe and who are comfortable doing it. As for myself, I would say that I am a traditional judge. I don't like to get involved in politics. But when it comes to the independence of the judiciary, I have learned to be vocal in the press and in parliaments, including the European Parliament. It is not enough to have laws protecting you; judges must reach out to the public and politicians, work together and support each other. This is quite different from the traditional way in which I, and many judges in Europe, were trained.

Ramona Coman: This raises a question about the role of judges. When we witness the dismantling of judicial independence and see attacks on fundamental pillars of democracy and core values, it inevitably leads to a broader question: what is the ethos of judges, and what is their role within society?

Kees Sterk: As the intensity of the attacks on the judiciary is relatively new, the first reaction of judges is traditionally to avoid getting involved. But I feel that things have changed, and among many European judges, there is now a common feeling that we judges should act. And what is very helpful in this respect is the judgment from Strasbourg holding that when judicial independence is threatened, a judge has a duty to act, at least to raise his or her voice. Interestingly, this duty was already part of the standards of the ENCJ, of the CCJE and of the EAJ. These standards are of course not law; perhaps one could call it soft law. The courts in Luxembourg and Strasbourg use these standards as a kind of inspiration for their judgments. And then suddenly some of these standards become hard law, since they reflect a common idea of what independence in Europe should be. There are always critics and sceptics who ask why you would develop standards that have no official legal status. My answer is that they reflect the essence of all the different European families of law about what judicial independence should be in Europe. Therefore, these standards get more traction when we work together, and we facilitate the courts in Luxembourg and Strasbourg, the Commission and the European Parliament. The standards have proven to be influential.

Ramona Coman: Could you elaborate on the mobilisation of judges that you mentioned earlier, specifically on the movement in Poland and the support that Polish judges received? It was significant for them to see that what was happening in their courts mattered not only to their colleagues in Poland but also to judges from other countries, like the Netherlands. If I recall correctly, judges from 22 European countries, including non-EU states like Turkey, showed support.

Kees Sterk: Yes, this is a form of transnational solidarity among judges that is developing. I think it was not a one-time occurrence, as we can see from the continued response. For instance, every three months the presidents of the European judges' organisations meet online to discuss the state of affairs with respect to judicial independence, and what action should be taken and by whom. There is even a WhatsApp group of judges from all over Europe. I am a member of this group, and we share information with each other.

In October 2023, PiS was voted out of the Polish government, and some people now argue that the problems of judges in Poland are solved, and our Polish colleagues no longer need solidarity from their peers in Europe. My clear answer to this position is: no, I don't think so. Before, the goal of the international solidarity was to support the Polish judges and to stop the undermining of their independence. Now, it is to support the Polish judges in building the best judicial system possible, which is connected to citizens, and which is there for the citizens. That is why, in 2024, I visited the Polish Senate to talk about experiences in the Netherlands with the Dutch system of judicial self-governance. I did not argue that Poland should simply copy the Dutch system, as was argued about standards of judicial independence in 2013, at the beginning of the ENCJ project on Independence and Accountability. No, I simply wanted to give an example of how self-governance could be organised and to give the Polish judges and politicians some inspiration, always keeping in mind that they can do with that what is best for them. This is what is happening now, and I think it helps very much. The Polish judges of Iustitia has a working group on the restoration of judicial independence. Sometimes they ask me to come to Poland and to express my views on proposals – not, as I have said, to impose any decisions, but just to help by sharing my experience. Sometimes they follow my advice; sometimes they do not – it is their choice and their responsibility. But this kind of international cooperation among judges is rather unusual. Before the movement of European solidarity among judges began, such cooperation usually happened between governments, if at all. The Polish government could ask the Dutch government through the Polish Ambassador how its system of judicial self-governance worked. Now, this flow of information is not the only one on the subject: there is also a direct flow of information from judges to judges.

Ramona Coman: How do you see the role of the European Union?

Kees Sterk: I don't think that the first Commission under Von der Leyen is a champion of the rule of law, to put it mildly. She's not, and to some extent I understand that because of the threats coming from Russia. This geopolitical situation in Europe made it very, very difficult to prioritise the rule of law. But what I find very strange is that we say in Europe that we are democracies under the rule of law, and we want to protect our way of living, and that is why we don't want to be under the power of Moscow. But, in order to be able to fight Moscow, we allow EU Member States to undermine the rule of law. This is very strange and seems to be a kind of vicious circle. How do you stop this kind of vicious circle? We must find ways to do that. That is one of the reasons I'm involved in the lawsuit I've mentioned, the aim of which is to establish in law that if the Commission is not willing to uphold the independence of the judiciary, then the judges' organisations at the European level should be able to take over the defence of independent judiciaries in the EU before the CJEU.

Legal standing and legal interest for these organisations are not included in the wording of the treaties, nor in the jurisprudence of the Luxembourg Court. So, if the CJEU does not want it to happen, it would be very easy for Luxembourg to say no. However, the Commission, which is responsible for upholding the treaties, is not protecting the independence of national judiciaries in the Member States for political reasons. Considering this fact, and considering the purpose of the treaties, European judicial organisations must, in my view, be allowed to fill the gap. It is essential that the gap be filled to uphold the uniform application of EU law. Without the uniform application of EU law, there can be no European Union.

Ramona Coman: The President of the Commission announced that the Article 7 TEU procedure against Poland, which is not as powerful as it was supposed to be, may be closed. We know that, given the situation on the ground, it is too early – things have not changed. It is difficult for the new government to undo the past.

Kees Sterk: I trust Adam Bodnar, the new Minister of Justice, perfectly well; I think he has very good intentions. But that still leaves the Polish President, Duda, who doesn't want an independent judiciary and is using his veto power to prevent it. The neo-KRS is still working and still selecting judges, whom Duda is still appointing – the situation has not changed.

Ramona Coman: So would closing Article 7 TEU be premature?

Kees Sterk: It is too early, based on the facts. It is clearly a political decision. And this is true of the Commission decisions on the Hungarian judiciary as well. Orbán used his veto power to block decisions that the other Member States consider essential just to get a little bit more funding, which had been withheld because of the conditionality mechanism. And the Commission usually gives in in the end. So, there must be another mechanism in Europe to uphold the independence of the judiciary. One of the solutions could be that the Court of Justice of the EU gives legal standing and legal interest to judges' associations in Europe in defence of judicial independence.

Ramona Coman: What can the judges' associations do?

Kees Sterk: They can bring lawsuits against decisions of the Commission or the Council, for example if the rule of law conditionality mechanism is not properly applied. This would have huge political implications. You must have very brave judges to do that. But if it is not done, the rule of law and the independence of the judiciary will remain caught up in the political game of I scratch your back, you scratch my back. And that is not where it is supposed to be. The rule of law is the framework of society. Within that framework, there is political wheeling and dealing, and I accept that perfectly well. But the judicial system itself should not be a part of the wheeling and dealing of daily politics.

Ramona Coman: Do you think that there are many judges in EU Member States are able and ready to defend their independence?

Kees Sterk: You do not need everyone to be brave and courageous, only a few people. I am hopeful. Why am I hopeful? In 2018, the CJEU held that all national judges are also European judges. And because they are European judges, the standards for independence on the European level apply to national judges as well. This was not predicted at all in the academic literature. Everyone was surprised. The decision was made in a case which the Portuguese Judges Association[3] lost, actually, so it took some time to realise what the court had said. The President of the Court of Justice of the EU in Luxembourg, Koen Lenaerts, said that this judgment is one of the three most important judgments the court has made since it was established. It took a little time to understand what was going on. This President is still in office. There are many more judges. But it is possible. It would be very helpful: it would enormously limit the power of the EU Council and the Commission to give in to pressure from countries where the independence of the judiciary is being undermined. On the other hand, it will also help those institutions, because the President of the Commission can tell Orbán, when he uses his veto power to pressure have funding unblocked, that the Commission cannot do so because the Court has ruled that the Commission is not allowed to deblock the funding. Ursula von der Leyen can say to Orbán: We can talk about it, but it is not possible, because it is outside the realm of political wheeling and dealing.

Ramona Coman: There must also be some political will on the other side, because there are already cases on judicial independence, and there is a judgment from the CJEU concerning the disciplinary courts in Poland.

Kees Sterk: That is true. But, you know, Europe has the power of the purse, and that usually works – not always as I want to, but it works somehow. It did not move the PiS party in Poland to change its policies, but I am not sure one could say it did not work in the Polish general elections. The voters were well aware that enormous amounts of money had been blocked by the EU, money that was necessary to address problems of society, of climate, of immigration. Many felt that they were facing threats from China and Russia. Polish voters believed that they needed the EU – and its money – to deal with these problems.

Ramona Coman: I think that this is an important point, as in many countries, judges have received support from civil society organisations. But in the end, the question is whether we really receive justice in return for our support of independence for judges'

[3] Case C-64/16 *Associação Sindical dos Juízes Portugueses v Tribunal de Contas* ECLI:EU:C:2018:117, [2018] 3 CMLR 16.

independence? But to do what? How is this connected to us as citizens? This independence has a purpose.

Kees Sterk: I think that is a very important connection. Citizens do not understand why judges must be independent if judges do not protect citizens rights. Therefore, there must be a connection to the general ideas of justice in society. This is one of the things that I am teaching young people who are in training to become judges. The law is developed by individual judges and lower courts, and not by the Supreme Court. The Court gets different opinions from the judges, all well-argued, and the Supreme Courts chooses one of them. The Supreme Court does not develop an opinion; it chooses from among different options. This view on the role of the Supreme Court gives judges some liberty to do justice. They know the judgments of the Supreme Court, but they can still make distinctions for this or that reason for the sake of justice. This is how I see the role of judges in society and in the judiciary.

Ramona Coman: In some countries there is still a lack of democratic culture or a culture of the rule of law. Is this something that you have experienced in your work?

Kees Sterk: It is very interesting that you mention this. I went to Bosnia and Herzegovina at the invitation of the Bosnian and Herzegovinian Council for the Judiciary, who asked me to conduct a review along with judges from Belgium, Finland and Norway. For two weeks, we conducted interviews with all the members of the Council and many senior staff members. We made a report, in which we essentially said to stop discussing the system and start making the system work. Bosnia and Herzegovina more or less copied the Norwegian system of judicial self-governance. That system is in accordance with European standards, and so is the Bosnian system of judicial self-governance. But such a system only functions well when there is a strong rule of law culture in the judiciary. I will give you an example. There was a scandal involving a former President of the Bosnian and Herzegovinian Council for the Judiciary. He had allegedly accepted bribes to interfere in a civil case. The case came before the Disciplinary Chamber of the Council. It ruled that there had been no disciplinary offence because the president was not acting as a judge but as a member of the Council, and – formalism again – the law had a loophole for disciplinary offences of members of the Council. There was an enormous outcry in the newspapers that the members of the Council were protecting themselves against corruption allegations. The review committee told the Council to interpret the law in such a way that the system works. To achieve that, a good rule of law culture is absolutely necessary. Another example: the Bosnian and Herzegovinian Council for the Judiciary is responsible for appointing judges, disciplining judges and managing the courts. The review committee noticed that the Council spent almost all its time talking about appointments. It didn't manage the courts. Not at all. We talked to a lot of presidents of courts, and we asked the Council members, as well, what they were doing to manage the courts. They were not very interested in good management of the courts, probably because they are judges, while this task is essential for citizens.

In many countries, judges are not really interested in good management of the courts. This is also true in the Netherlands. In my opinion, judges need expert help managing the courts. Experts on financial management, human resources and ICT, for example, can help judges to develop the competences required to manage the courts. In Bosnia and Herzegovina, however, there is still a lot of political interference with the judiciary, which makes it difficult to develop these competences. But even in places without political interference in the judiciary, like the Netherlands, developing these competences is difficult enough. In my experience, most judges do not recognise enough that a lack of sufficient management skills could become the Achilles' heel of judicial self-government. Apart from that, a model of self-governance can only function well when the values underlying the model are lived in practice. A culture that upholds and supports these values must be developed. That's necessary in the Netherlands and everywhere in Europe. Good rules on judicial independence are important, but focusing only on rules is clearly not enough to uphold judicial independence. There must be a culture in politics, society and the judiciary that upholds the values of democracy under the rule of law. In my opinion, the absence of this sustaining culture in the Netherlands is the biggest threat to the independence of the judiciary. In the last decade, Dutch politics have been more focused on efficiency and fixing problems by bypassing the law in all areas of society. Efficiency and this kind of problem solving has become so dominant that it displaces values in society, which undermines the trust of citizens. Again, think of the child support scandal. In my view, that dominance is a threat to the judiciary in the Netherlands. Protecting judicial independence is about good rules, about a good culture sustaining the rules, and about courageous judges. It is about doing justice to citizens.

8

We cannot Divorce the Application of the Law from its Origins and Moral Implications

ANDREA TITZ[1]

Viktor Kazai: Could you share with us why you became a judge and what were the most important experiences of your judicial career?

Andrea Titz: I decided to become a judge while I was at university, thanks to an internship I did that included placements in courts. I discovered my love for this work early on and dreamed of becoming a judge. In Germany, aspiring judges must pass two state exams and undertake a training process called *Referendariat* between the exams, which involves spending a lot of time in courts and public prosecutors' offices.

I was certain that being a judge was the right path for me. It wasn't easy, as becoming a judge depends on your academic achievements, and only the top performers have a shot. I was grateful for the opportunity and have never looked back. The job is incredibly interesting, since it covers various aspects and fields of law. I also enjoy working with people, rather than just doing research alone in an office. As a judge, I can engage with people, which is a priority for me. I also value the ability to switch between different fields of law and roles throughout my career. This flexibility has allowed me to pursue diverse areas of law and to adapt to different positions. And now, here I am.

Viktor Kazai: Even within the judiciary, you were not just an ordinary judge; you were also a spokesperson, president, and Vice-President of a judges' association and a prosecutor, for shorter terms. What prompted you to pursue these different roles?

Andrea Titz: When I began my career, I became a regular member of the German Association of Judges. Shortly afterward, I was invited to join the newly elected board at the regional level. I tend to have a 'Why not?' attitude and rarely turn down tasks, so I accepted the opportunity. As I became increasingly involved, I began attending meetings of the Bavarian Association, where the former president saw potential in me. When

[1] Interview conducted in English on 16 May 2024 at the German Judges' Association in Berlin and validated for publication on 2 December 2024.

he asked if I could imagine joining the Bavarian Presidency board, I once again replied with a confident 'Yes, why not?' I believe it is crucial to participate actively in such work, advocating for the rights of our colleagues at various levels. It is not always a battle; however, standing up for the rights of judges and public prosecutors is crucial. It is vital for us to have a voice, and our professional association provides us with a platform for that. I think that is what motivates me to engage in this kind of work.

And why did I change my position while working in Bavaria? In Germany, the justice system is organised on a state level, with each state, or 'Land' having its own unique system. In Bavaria, it is common to switch between being a judge and a public prosecutor. So it was quite natural for me to start as a public prosecutor, transition to being a judge, and then move to a higher level at a public prosecutor's office again. This kind of career development is typical in Bavaria. Of course, some people choose to settle in a judge's position for their entire career, but that's not my style. I prefer changing roles every now and then.

I became a spokesperson because the former president of the Higher Regional Court in Munich knew me. When the NSU proceedings began – a lengthy, high-profile case against a group of three people responsible for ten racially motivated murders across Germany – the court faced negative press due to some initial communication problems. The former president asked if I could join as a spokesperson, working alongside the former spokesperson. I agreed, and when the former spokesperson became ill and had to step down, I took over. That was the beginning of this chapter of my life. My career has been influenced by many random coincidences, but in the end, everything turned out fine.

Viktor Kazai: And the result is a very rich career. I was wondering whether, based on your many years of experience in various fields, you have any general thoughts about the state of democracy. Let's start with Germany, and then perhaps you could share your thoughts on Europe and the international scene.

Andrea Titz: I believe that Germany is still operating as a functioning democracy. However, as in other countries, democracy is under threat. It is particularly threatened by increasingly influential extremist movements, especially those on the right-wing populist end of the spectrum – such as the political party AfD – which are gaining popularity in the country.

It seems that people are feeling increasingly insecure about their future, the state of the nation, their health, security, wealth, and welfare. These insecurities seem to stem from the various crises we have faced in recent years, starting with the pandemic, followed by the Russian war in Ukraine, and now continuing with the conflict between Israel and Hamas in Gaza. It is becoming apparent that the long-standing assumptions of peace, prosperity, and stability for all no longer hold true.

In Europe, we are facing the challenge of an influx of refugees, which has created numerous issues within our society. These issues range from housing shortages to the integration of refugees into schools and workplaces. This situation has led to many concerns and insecurities among the local population. For instance, if a small village of perhaps 1,000 or 2,000 residents suddenly gains 200 refugees, it necessitates a considerable adjustment. It is not about the refugees being bad or unwelcome, as helping them is our humane responsibility. However, in a small village where residents may never have encountered a different language or culture, it becomes incredibly challenging. The refugees struggle to integrate due to the language barrier and often face limitations in finding employment. This leads to a situation where they are forced to live in substandard housing, further exacerbating the feeling of insecurity among the local population.

I believe that the crises mentioned above, including the refugee situation, contribute to instability and insecurity in Germany. This prompts people to seek solutions. Although right-wing populist parties lack real solutions, they pretend otherwise. In Germany, like in other countries where the same influences can be seen, they often claim to have the answers, typically by opposing everything. This is a significant problem in Germany and poses a threat to our democracy.

Viktor Kazai: And do you see any impact of this growing political extremism on judicial independence?

Andrea Titz: Currently, the independence of the judiciary remains unaffected by political controversies. It is paramount for us to uphold and protect this independence, not just as a theoretical idea but also in our everyday professional conduct. This responsibility is crucial for maintaining a stable and impartial judicial system, even in cases that are potentially divisive and politically significant. This principle should be universally acknowledged and put into practice to reflect its significance in every aspect of our work.

We have witnessed significant attacks on the independence of the judiciary in both European and non-European nations. Consider Poland, Hungary, and even Israel. A year and a half ago, I travelled to Israel for the International Judges Association, and we were impressed by the stability of the Israeli justice system. However, just a few months later, there were disturbing assaults on the independence of the judiciary.

On the other hand, these instances illustrate how acutely people recognise and resist unjust efforts to erode judicial independence. Consider the massive mobilisation in Poland, where not only members of the judiciary but also hundreds of thousands of ordinary citizens took to the streets in a show of solidarity. Their actions underscore the widespread understanding of the crucial role that an independent judiciary plays. This gives hope that the majority of people value the concept of liberty and recognise the pivotal role of judicial independence in upholding it. While some prioritise security over liberty, the crucial point is that a considerable number of people still appreciate the significance of upholding liberty through an independent judiciary.

Viktor Kazai: I agree that social support is crucial for judicial independence. However, are there any invisible problems in the system that could become serious issues if circumstances change, such as a loss of social support or the rise of political extremism in Germany?

Andrea Titz: The problem in Germany is that we lack independent judicial self-administration, unlike many other European countries. In our case, the judiciary is organised at the 'Länder' (state) level, but in each 'Land', the Minister of Justice holds the ultimate authority over all members of the judiciary. Although there are some opportunities for cooperation and consultation through various boards, in many 'Länder', the Minister of Justice is responsible for appointing and promoting judges and public prosecutors. In a stable democracy where the independence of the judiciary is universally recognised, this would not be an issue. However, when problems arise, it is crucial for the Minister of Justice to consider all relevant factors when appointing and promoting judges and public prosecutors.

There is a concern that one day in one of the 'Länder', right-wing populist parties like the AfD could gain significant influence, even if they do not hold a majority. This could lead to the necessity of forming coalitions with them. For instance, it is conceivable that the Minister of Justice might be a member of the AfD, which would allow them to appoint their allies as judges. This could gradually erode the independence of the judiciary, and our concern in this situation is the lack of proper self-administration.

The situation in Germany has raised some concerns within the European Union. This has been the system for the last 75 years, and we haven't been able to change it. Currently, the influence on politics and the judiciary isn't a problem because there is a social consensus. In the near future, however, this consensus might fade. Every Minister of Justice is already theoretically able to appoint whomever he or she likes as a judge, as long as the person meets the requirements of being a German citizen and passing the two state exams. This influence may become an issue if the social consensus weakens, but for now, due to the understanding of judicial independence, no Minister of Justice would be foolish enough to misuse his or her influence.

Viktor Kazai: Have you been aware of any cases in which the political elite tried to influence judges?

Andrea Titz: I haven't personally heard of any cases in which that happened. I don't believe that this is a real issue, because, as I mentioned earlier, there is a widespread consensus that judicial independence is crucial. Therefore, if a Minister of Justice or any other politician were foolish enough to attempt to exert influence on the judiciary, he or she would face severe consequences.

Viktor Kazai: Are you aware of any disagreement within the judiciary over fundamental values? Are there cases in which some members of the judiciary deviate from the mainstream and challenge fundamental values of the constitutional system?

Andrea Titz: My colleagues, particularly those from the eastern states of Germany, have mentioned to me that the influence of the right-wing party is quite significant. They have also noted that there are supporters of the AfD within the judiciary. Keep in mind that in Germany, unlike in some other countries, judges are allowed to be involved in political movements or work and even to be members of a political party. Although there are no openly declared members of the AfD within the judiciary, there are certainly supporters of the party.

Some of my colleagues have observed that certain judges, particularly in Eastern Germany, include sentences in their judgments that are at least aligned with the policies of the AfD. These sentences are not overtly racist, but there seem to be potentially racist tendencies. For instance, they may issue sentences that seem to make things harder for migrants or people with non-German passports during legal proceedings. It is not a widespread issue, and it is subtle enough that you couldn't outright declare it problematic. However, there are subtle nuances in these judges' wording and in the reasoning within their judgments. This is what my colleagues have told me. Personally, I haven't noticed anything like this, but they believe they can see and sense it. There are colleagues with whom you wouldn't want to be associated because they seem to be supporters, at least to some extent, of the AfD. So, while it may not be a widespread problem, there seems to be a problematic tendency.

Viktor Kazai: As for the European Union, have you noticed any anti-EU sentiments or anti-EU trends in the judiciary?

Andrea Titz: I don't believe so. Naturally, hardcore supporters of the AfD tend to oppose the EU, as that position aligns with the party's core beliefs. They advocate for a future outside the European Union. However, I haven't observed any influence of this position within the judicial system.

Viktor Kazai: You mentioned that politicians claim not to influence the judiciary, but I wonder whether the AfD criticises the judiciary in specific cases, such as migration cases.

Andrea Titz: The leadership of the party does not openly criticise the judiciary, but this does happen through social media and via criticism from influential party members. It is uncertain whether those who criticise the judiciary and express disdain for judges are affiliated with the AfD. Based on the wording of some of the criticisms, one might assume so, but there is no general consensus about that. The AfD wouldn't openly criticise the judiciary, since the party claims to support a strong state, including the judiciary. However, it is unclear what their vision of a robust judiciary entails. While they claim to support the judiciary conceptually, we don't want their endorsement.

Viktor Kazai: I was wondering whether judges and courts have a responsibility to consider societal and political opinions on sensitive issues, or whether there should be a strict separation between law and politics. Do you think there should be a relationship between politics and law in the court system?

Andrea Titz: I strongly believe that we cannot divorce the application of the law from its origins and moral implications. Merely enforcing the law without considering its formulation and its moral underpinnings would mirror the approach taken by judges and the judiciary between 1933 and 1945. Back then, they focused solely on enforcing the law and disregarded its moral basis. I consider such an approach wrong.

As a judge, one cannot impose one's personal morals. While personal beliefs should not dictate the law, it is equally important not to disregard how laws are created and their implications. It is not about being apolitical; it is about enforcing the law without the interference of one's personal views.

The Judges Association bears the primary responsibility for shaping the law. It is crucial for us to participate actively in the law-making process and to express our concerns about significant societal changes from a judicial standpoint. While an individual judge cannot impose personal morals in his or her rulings, he or she must conscientiously apply the law ethically. However, it is also the duty of the Judges Association to voice concerns and to contribute to the formation of laws, which we are committed to doing diligently. We have the right to be heard when new laws are being formulated, and we strive to use our influence in this regard.

Viktor Kazai: What other legitimate ways are there for judges to voice their opinions? In Poland and Romania, for example, we have seen demonstrations.

Andrea Titz: As judges, we have the right to express our political opinions, but it is important not to overdo it. While it is legitimate to participate in demonstrations, we shouldn't make a habit of doing so for every minor issue. However, in cases like those in Poland or Israel, it may be necessary for the judiciary to voice collective opposition to certain measures. It is within our rights to demonstrate and raise our voices, but it is often best for our association to represent us in public matters. Going on strike, however, is prohibited by the Constitution.

Viktor Kazai: Does the German Judges Association have a relationship with associations from other countries? And has this relationship ever been more than a protocol or a diplomatic relationship? Like, have other organisations relied on the support of your organisation to, I don't know, resist political events or attacks?

Andrea Titz: Yes, we have strong connections with various associations within and beyond Europe. Within Europe, we are members of the EAJ and the International Association of Judges (IAJ). We also maintain close ties with other member states. Furthermore, we actively participated in events such as the March of a Thousand Robes,[2] and we showed our support for our Turkish colleagues and raised our concerns publicly. Even though our voices may not be taken seriously by foreign ministers or presidents, it is crucial to show solidarity with our colleagues in other nations.

Our support goes beyond mere protocol; we also provide practical assistance as a form of transnational solidarity, such as providing financial aid to our Turkish colleagues facing professional setbacks. Additionally, for the past 30 years, the German Judges Association has actively supported the families of our colleagues in Columbia who had been killed or were imprisoned. We are committed to doing our best to offer support and help wherever we can.

Viktor Kazai: Have the roles and duties of judges changed over time, especially in light of the challenges in Europe? Is being a judge today the same as it was 10, 20, or 30 years ago?

Andrea Titz: I believe that the values of judicial work remain constant. While some values may hold more significance in today's context, the core values remain unchanged. Traits such as impartiality and courage have always been important, but in today's world, they may require greater emphasis. Upholding these values and giving your best efforts in your daily work is crucial, both now and 30 years ago.

It seems that these days, being a judge requires even more courage. The rise of social media has increased the potential for political influence, making the job more challenging. The way people talk to and about judges has become harsher. For example, a

[2] This event saw thousands of people, including judges and lawyers from many EU Member States, march through Warsaw on 11 January 2020 to protest against the government's attempts to curb the powers of the judiciary in Poland.

colleague of mine recently had to take time off after facing a lot of public scrutiny due to a high-profile murder case. Even after 30 years of experience, she had never encountered such a situation before. It's clear that being a judge today requires even greater strength and resilience than in the past.

Viktor Kazai: The European Court of Human Rights and the Court of Justice of the European Union have raised concerns about certain judges and courts in Poland not being lawfully appointed, which could undermine societal confidence in the judiciary. This raises questions about the politicisation of the judiciary and the legitimacy of certain judges and courts.

Andrea Titz: The issue at hand is undeniably significant. A lack of confidence in the judiciary, particularly in Eastern European nations, stems from a longstanding tradition of judges being appointed in ways that aren't perceived as lawful. When people believe that judges are chosen arbitrarily by the president or because they are politically convenient candidates, trust naturally diminishes. Without trust, the effectiveness of the judiciary is compromised. The appointment and removal of judges without transparency and for unclear reasons are evident problems. We've seen the consequences of these issues in countries like Hungary, Poland, and Israel. The potential for a government to overrule the rulings of the Constitutional Court also poses a serious concern. Fortunately, this isn't currently an issue in Germany.

Viktor Kazai: To conclude, what are your predictions for the future of democracy and judicial independence in the European Union? Do you anticipate improvement or deterioration? And what is your opinion on the role of EU institutions in addressing these issues?

Andrea Titz: I truly believe that there are numerous stable and well-established democracies in Europe, and it is crucial to embrace and uphold democratic values. In Eastern Germany, we can see that people who haven't been exposed to democracy from an early age tend to struggle more with societal issues and are less firm in their democratic principles. However, I am hopeful that the majority of European countries are on a path of stable democratic progress. Despite the recent rise of right-wing and nationalist movements in several countries, I remain optimistic that the pendulum will eventually swing back. The resilience of people in upholding democratic values, as demonstrated by protests in Poland and Israel, gives me hope for the future.

The European institutions have the potential to play a constructive role in addressing certain issues. For instance, they can decide to withhold the substantial funds they typically provide from countries that no longer maintain stable democracies or uphold the rule of law, as in the case of Hungary. This approach could be effective in certain cases. However, it is essential to recognise that dealing with European institutions is not straightforward. Their decision-making process is often slow due to their dependency on Member States and the requirement for either a majority or a unanimous vote to enact measures. Despite these challenges, I believe that the European Union and its institutions can be part of the solution.

I am not entirely pessimistic, although I believe we will face tough years ahead as we must stand strong against these movements spreading across most European countries. Consider Italy and perhaps France, where the Minister of Justice is openly confronting judges and public prosecutors with whom he had disagreements when he was a lawyer. This behaviour reflects undemocratic practices and a disregard for the rule of law, yet nobody is quick to label France or Italy as non-democratic. Even in traditionally strong democracies like Finland and other Northern European countries, similar movements are emerging. The hope remains that we will be able to confront and overcome these challenges.

9

How can Courts and Legislators Co-exist?

CHRISTOPHER VAJDA[1]

Ramona Coman: Could you please describe your personal, academic and professional background?

Christopher Vajda: I read law at the University of Cambridge, and I wanted to study abroad, because I had an international perspective. That is how I ended up studying at the *Institut d'études européennes* of the *Université libre de Bruxelles*, thanks to the very generous support of the Wiener Anspach Foundation. This is important to mention because I could not have financed my studies myself. Before applying to the Foundation, I went to see a retired professor of comparative law at Cambridge whom I knew very well, and he highly recommended that I study abroad. I received a scholarship from the Wiener Anspach Foundation in 1977–78, and I came to Brussels for a year to study in the postgraduate programme. I enjoyed EU law very much, and I wanted to practice it. I was lucky enough to practice EU law as a barrister. I spent the first five years of my career in Brussels and then moved back to London.

Ramona Coman: What motivated you to pursue a career as a judge?

Christopher Vajda: When I began my career, I was not sure whether I had any ambition to be a judge. In England, the system is quite different from that of many continental countries, because we don't have a judiciary that you can enter after university. In the UK, you can only be appointed a judge after you have been in practice for several years. For example, for a senior post, meaning a High Court judge, you need to have practiced for 15 years. As a result, a 'young' judge in England would be somebody in their forties. I became a part-time judge handling criminal cases when I was in my forties. I was hesitant as to whether I should become a full-time judge or not. Then my predecessor at the CJEU retired, and a number of people suggested I should apply. I did, and I was appointed.

Ramona Coman: You were a judge at the CJEU from 2012 to 2020, a period during which the European Union faced many crises, from the Eurozone to the response to migration, not to mention Brexit and the dismantling of the rule of law in some Member

[1] Interview conducted on 29 April 2024 and validated for publication on 9 January 2025.

States. This leads me to the topic of our book, which is about dissensus over liberal democracy. What can you tell us about the impact of these challenges on the Court of Justice? And, more generally, what is your perspective on the state of democracy, in the European Union but also in the individual Member States?

Christopher Vajda: The Court is not, and should not be, a democratic institution. The members of the Court – judges and advocates general – are not elected. The role of the Court is to ensure that the rule of law is applied and safeguarded. What do I mean by that? The Court is there to decide legal disputes according to the law, namely EU legislation and the Charter of Fundamental Rights. Making the laws is the task of the democratic legislator. How can courts and legislators co-exist? Occasionally, the Court is asked to rule on whether a law has been properly adopted, that is to say, on whether the democratic process has been observed. More often, its task is to decide what those laws mean, when there is a dispute, and to ensure that those laws are enforced. It is not the role of the Court to determine whether a law is good or bad; that is for the democratic legislature to do. However, the Court does have the power to declare national laws contrary to EU law and indeed to invalidate EU legislation that is incompatible with the Charter of Fundamental Rights. Some of these cases are high-profile and have a large political dimension. But the Court does not enter the political arena. It is independent of politics. Its sole role is to rule on the interpretation and legality of the law. In doing so, it must, of course, give a reasoned and understandable judgment.

Ramona Coman: How do you explain the assault on the courts that has taken place in some EU Member States, where governments have limited the power of judges? Key tenets of liberal democracy are under strain: the rule of law and the independence of judges.

Christopher Vajda: We are living in an era where the social and political landscape has changed a lot. It is an era of social networks and an enormous use of the Internet but also of the diffusion and rapid propagation of fake news. We are also living in a less deferential society than before, which is something I personally welcome, provided it is within limits. This context has led to the rise of political parties that claim to have a solution to the problems we are facing, such as the immigration of non-Europeans coming to live and work in Europe. Measures to combat climate change are another sensitive issue. Since the global financial crisis of 2007–08, many people's living standards have been reduced, not just in Europe but also in the United States. And now living standards have been reduced further, at least in Europe, as a result of the Russian war in Ukraine, which has increased energy costs. We are no longer in the same situation as in the 1950s and 1960s, when there was rapid economic growth and living standards were rising. The 1970s were difficult, but Europe's economies recovered in the 1980s. Since then, the Berlin Wall has fallen, and the EU has expanded to the east. Now, the social and economic context in Europe is not benign. Governments are under pressure to deliver on their own promises and to respond to citizens' concerns. In this context, the role of judges is often portrayed in a simplistic way: that out-of-touch judges and out-of-touch courts are thwarting the will of the people. However, the role of judges is to apply the law as it was made by the democratic legislator. To command respect, judges must be independent and free from political interference.

One must also remember that both within the EU and indeed with Europe there are certain fundamental principles that even a legislator must respect. After the Second World War, there was a consensus in Europe about the need to codify and enshrine such fundamental principles, which culminated in the European Convention on Human Rights. These principles are intended to ensure that we do not slide back into what happened in Nazi Germany and that there can be no tyranny by the majority governing party or, as one former UK politician said, 'an elective dictatorship'. This is part of the system of checks and balances in a liberal democracy. It means that courts will occasionally deliver judgments that may be unpopular because they hold a piece of legislation to be in breach of fundamental rights. In the less deferential world that we live in now, such judgments are sometimes criticised in the most vitriolic terms. Hence the temptation in some states to limit the power of judges (and this phenomenon is not just limited to Europe).

Ramona Coman: And this leads me to the next question. What are the implications of the democratic erosion of judicial independence for judges and for citizens?

Christopher Vajda: It is all the more important that the independence of judges be protected. The principle of independence is not just some theoretical principle but a central bastion for everyone in our society to ensure that the law is impartially applied and obeyed. Fortunately, both the EU and the United Kingdom have wholly non-political criteria for the appointment of judges. When the Treaty of Lisbon was adopted in 2009, an important innovation, which is actually credited to the United Kingdom, was the establishment of a committee now known as the Article 255 Committee. The Committee is required to produce an opinion on every judicial candidate put forward by Member States for the General Court or the Court of Justice. That has been extremely important. I don't think anybody quite realised what a valuable tool it was. It has become a safeguard against appointing people who do not meet the standards required to be a judge at one of the EU courts. Although the Committee's opinions are, legally, only advisory and not binding, no candidate who has received a negative opinion has been appointed, as far as I am aware. In fact, the previous Polish judge at the CJEU remained much longer than he wished to because the previous Polish government did not put forward a candidate who would satisfy the Article 255 Committee. So, it is very important now to have procedures to ensure the appointment of properly qualified judges. One can probably say that the judges in the EU courts are better qualified than they were 20 years ago. They are also clearly independent. This is important because, with the expansion of EU law into areas such as criminal justice, asylum, and immigration, as well as the adoption of the Charter of Fundamental Rights, there are many more politically sensitive cases than there were 20 years ago.

I think that, in this regard, the EU system is good, but it could be improved. At the General Court or the Court of Justice, a judge has a mandate of only six years, and Member States may be tempted to substitute somebody else after six years if, for some reason, they are dissatisfied by the current judge or they wish to appoint someone who they know shares their political outlook.

My own view is that a judge should be appointed to an EU court for one term of twelve years with no renewal. That would give them total independence. The European Court of Human Rights adopts a similar approach, albeit with a term of nine years and not 12. Nine years would be too short a time, in my view, for a career as a judge at an EU court. The UK has also a judicial appointment system which is out of the hands of the politicians. I think it is fair to say that one reason that English law is such a popular choice of jurisdiction internationally is the reputation of the English judiciary, which is seen as well qualified, fair and independent. A former Lord Chief Justice in England once asked rhetorically who would want to live in a country where the government wins every case. The very fact that judges are not elected is a very important safeguard.

Now, you asked about citizens. One point I think is very important is that courts need to communicate more with citizens than they have done in the past. The problem is that judges can be attacked in the media, and, indeed, now they are sometimes attacked by politicians. No one should be immune to criticism, and that includes judges. But in the past, that criticism was largely confined to the legal academic community, and, whether one agreed with a judgment or not, the judgment was respected, particularly by the government. It is obviously inappropriate for any judge to answer these criticisms, because then the judge would be stepping out of the judicial role and into the political arena. The judgment must speak for itself. However, it is important for courts to be more transparent so that citizens can be aware of what is happening. In practice, this means streaming more hearings and issuing more press releases in important cases to make cases more accessible to journalists and the general public. This would ensure that debate on a judgment is better informed.

Ramona Coman: Today, many issues are very polarised and divisive. Values are contested and courts have a role to play in cases dealing with issues related to abortion, rights, freedoms, etc. From your perspective, which values are more contested today than in the past?

Christopher Vajda: Let's look at the big picture. Everybody in Europe today is in agreement on fundamental rights. And within the EU you have the Charter of Fundamental Rights and the European Convention on Human Rights. When the Convention was established in 1950, after the Second World War, one of its explicit aims was to protect minorities. The Convention was not intended in any way to be anti-democratic. On the contrary, the Convention was intended to entrench certain rights that were considered essential to democracy, such as freedom of speech and freedom of assembly. It is true that some of the judgments of the Strasbourg ECtHR and the Luxembourg CJEU have been controversial where the notion of fundamental rights has been developed and expanded. This has led to tensions between governments and the courts, because the governments say that the courts are engaging in judicial overreach.

I had a case when I was at the CJEU, called the Coman case, about same-sex marriage. It could be said to be quite a technical question. Coman, a Romanian national, married his partner, who was not an EU citizen, in Brussels, and then he wanted to come back to Romania with his spouse and enjoy rights under EU free movement law. This was refused on the basis that Romania did not recognise same-sex marriages. The hearing was quite interesting because a number of governments intervened and the governments that intervened on the side of Mr Coman were from Western Europe. The governments that intervened on the side of the Romanian government were essentially governments from Central and Eastern Europe. The argument that Romania and its supporting governments made was, in effect, to say that they did not join the EU to be told whether they had to accept same-sex marriage in their country. 'We don't believe in this. You should keep out of it', some said. I am slightly exaggerating. But as a matter of law, the issue was not that difficult, because the question was whether or not Mr Coman's partner was a family member in terms of the EU legislation, which did not refer to marriages between persons of a different sex. We held that he was a family member, but we were careful to emphasise that EU law does not require Romania to recognise same-sex marriages. That is a matter for Romania. I have no idea what happened and how that case was received in Romania.

But I think there are two things that the Court needs to do. First of all – and this was not possible when I was a judge, but it is possible now – is the streaming of Court hearings, which I have already mentioned. The streaming of hearings in Luxembourg only began as one of the very few benefits of the COVID-19 pandemic. Now it is used in all Grand Chamber cases. There is a stream with a short delay. As an example, the UK Supreme Court has been streaming for quite a long time. It heard the two Miller cases. The first case was on the question of whether the UK Parliament had to approve the proposal for the UK to withdraw from the EU. Then there was a second case in which the then Prime Minister, Boris Johnson, used his prerogative power to stop Parliament sitting, which meant that Parliament would not be able to extend the period for which the UK was a member of the EU, and hence the UK might leave the EU against the will of Parliament. Both those cases were livestreamed on YouTube, and they attracted millions of viewers. It showed that there was a great interest in these high-profile cases that could easily be followed by everyone via a computer screen. Going back to the Coman case, it is unrealistic for people in Romania to come to Luxembourg just to listen to the case. But, obviously, if you are sitting in a university faculty or at home, the fact that you can actually watch proceedings on your computer is really important, because you can see how the process works and how judges do their job in court.

Secondly, courts can issue a press release that summarises what the judgment is about. The European courts do this, the UK Supreme Court does this, and I think the German courts and possibly other courts in the EU do as well. Unfortunately, if you are not a lawyer, you may not feel inclined to read, or be able to understand, a long judgment. So it is very important to have a press release that sets out clearly what is at stake and that summarises the judgment. This means that citizens can be much better informed as to what the Court has said, rather than just getting that information from some clip on the Internet, which may be inaccurate.

Ramona Coman: My next question is about the role of the courts. How do you perceive the role of courts in addressing highly polarising or politicised issues? What roles should courts play in a context of increasing tensions between law and politics but also in a context of democratic decline? Should courts be more active?

Christopher Vajda: The problem with the term 'judicial activism' is that it is a slightly pejorative term. It gives the impression the judges are really doing more than they should do. One of the criticisms of the Luxembourg CJEU is that it is activist. But the CJEU does not have a political agenda. Or, I would say, any agenda. It decides each case on its merits. However, it is also a fiction to pretend that courts do not develop the law. This is particularly true in the case of the EU, as everyone knows that the CJEU has played what is probably the major part within the EU in developing EU law. Think of the principle of direct effect, the importance of fundamental rights, and state liability for breaches of EU law. Think also of the general principles developed by the EU courts. One of them is the principle of the rule of law, which is now enshrined in the Treaty on European Union. This principle, like many principles, has developed incrementally over time. Thus, the principle of having one's case heard by an independent tribunal was in fact first articulated in a case I was involved in in 2008 about a lawyer's right of appeal against a decision of the Luxembourg Bar refusing his request to be established in Luxembourg. The principle was then developed in a case about cutting the salaries of Portuguese judges. Then came the cases about the independence of Polish judges and about the lawfulness of imposing a regime of conditionality relating to the rule of law in an EU budget Regulation 2020/2092.

While principles can be developed by courts, courts must also, in my view, act with self-restraint. A good example is the right to abortion. One of the most controversial decisions of the US Supreme Court was *Roe v Wade*, in which the Court used the right of privacy to create a right to abortion. In my own view, it would have been preferable if the right had been granted by the legislature, as has happened in Europe. That would give the right a democratic imprimatur that a court decision lacks. Another example is the right to die and to have an assisted death. This is a highly controversial issue. If possible, I think it is better that those rights be determined by the legislator and not by the courts. This is effectively what the UK Supreme Court said some years ago in a right-to-die case.

Ramona Coman: These are controversial issues within society. How do judges deal with them? How, if at all, are different opinions or views expressed within courts?

Judge Vajda: When I became a judge, I had to take an oath not to reveal the secret of the deliberation inside the court. But I think what I could say is this: the CJEU is, I think, very unusual among supreme courts now in not permitting dissenting opinions. The Strasbourg Court permits dissenting opinions, as does the German Constitutional Court, but not, I think, the Italian Constitutional Court. I would be in favour of permitting dissenting opinions in the CJEU, at least in the big cases – and by a big case I mean a case that would be in the Grand Chamber of the CJEU, where 15 judges sit.

There is no provision that says dissenting opinions are not permitted. The Court could change its policy tomorrow if it wanted to. But I think there are two reasons that there has been no change. First of all, there's a language issue, because, obviously, if dissenting opinions were permitted, they would have to be published in all the official languages of the EU, of which there are 24. That would be quite an additional burden. Secondly, and this is probably the most important reason historically, there was a feeling that dissenting opinions would somehow undermine the authority of the judgment if it were known which judges did not agree with the majority. But in those days, the EU (originally the European Coal and Steel Community) was a fragile plant. Dissenting opinions could have undermined the authority of judgments. I think we have long passed that stage. The EU has flourished, grown stronger, and expanded to 27 Member States. The CJEU needs, in my view, no such protection today. I don't think anybody can seriously say that the Strasbourg Court's judgments command less respect because there are dissenting opinions.

Ramona Coman: Are there any debates on this issue of expressing dissenting opinions?

Christopher Vajda: It has been, and remains, the subject of informal debate. For example, I was at a conference recently with judges and former judges from the supreme courts of Germany, Slovenia and Italy. There was a debate on this issue. I am sure there have been academics who have written about it as well. My own view is that it is unlikely that the CJEU will move in this direction unless there is a groundswell from outside the Court. The Court has been an undoubted success during its 70 years of existence. It would be a radical change to permit dissenting opinions. So, if it is going to happen, there will need to be a public debate on the issue.

Ramona Coman: In the context of the rule of law dismantlement in Poland and Hungary, judges from different Member States joined forces to support their colleagues. See, for example, the March of a Thousand Robes in Poland, when judges from 22 Member States marched in the streets of Warsaw in support of the rule of law and judicial independence in Poland. How do you see this movement of professional solidarity? What is the role of judges when their independence is undermined?

Christopher Vajda: I always had mixed feelings about that, because I strongly believe that the role of judges is to stay inside the court (other than explaining their role or judgments in a lecture). A judge should not be seen taking sides in a political debate. Going on a protest march, in my view, goes beyond explaining judgments or what a judge does.

Ramona Coman: My last question is about the role of the EU in this context of crisis of democracy. Is the EU a solution or an additional problem in the context of the challenges that we have addressed in this conversation?

Christopher Vajda: My view is that the EU is very much a solution. Although the EU has faced huge challenges in recent years, it has sought to address those challenges in a democratic way via the EU legislature. The EU courts, for their part, have had to rule on what EU law means, including developing important principles such as that of the rule of law. In my view, the EU has strengthened democracy and respect for the rule of law where it has been under threat. In that sense, the EU has been a bulwark for democracy. The fact that states still wish to join the EU, but can do so only if they are democratic, is a testament to its success.

Ramona Coman: To conclude, what does it mean to be a judge today? What are the challenges and what are the lessons learned from this long period of crisis?

Christopher Vajda: Judges must be both independent and also representative of society. In other words, we must represent the diversity in our countries. It is a great privilege to be a judge. Judges have to decide issues that are important not just for the parties to the litigation but also for society as a whole. The challenge is to show that judges remain independent and fair. In a world of soundbites, a particular challenge is to write judgments that are clear and well-reasoned. If any lesson has been learned from this long period of crisis, it is that judges need these qualities of independence and fairness more than ever. They are in the public eye more often than before and, as I have said, often subject to quite severe criticism. As it has always been, it is not the role of judges to solve today's problems but, rather, in accordance with the judicial oath taken by judges in England, to do justice according to the law.

PART II

Insights from Southern European Judges

10

The Independence of the Judiciary is not the Privilege of a Group of Professionals

MARIAROSARIA GUGLIELMI[1]

Leonardo Puleo: I would like to start with a general question about your background, in particular what led you to pursue a career within the judiciary?

Mariarosaria Guglielmi: Besides my years at the Superior Council, my professional track within the magistracy has always been focused on prosecution. In Italy, judges and prosecutors are part the same body of civil servants and share the same institutional framework. Once I entered the magistracy, my original ambition was actually to serve as a judge, but I eventually decided to take a position as public prosecutor. I have never regretted my early decision. Prosecutors are a key juncture of the justice system, and key actors in upholding the rule of law. This is becoming strikingly clear now that the current government is planning extensive constitutional reforms, which perhaps we can discuss later.

In our system, public prosecutors play an active role in criminal proceedings since they can directly carry out investigations and – according to the Constitution – directly coordinate of judicial police officers. Mandatory prosecution is a fundamental principle in Italy and despite some reforms introducing a certain degree of bureaucratisation and reinforcing internal hierarchical powers, the role of the public prosecutor – thanks to the constitutional framework and to the independence currently enjoyed by individual prosecutors when exercising their functions – is still that of a primary guarantor of fundamental rights and freedoms.

Regarding my motivation to pursue the judicial career more broadly, I must admit that the study of law was quite a late passion. In high school, my main interest was indeed for classical languages, and my ambition was to continue studying literature at university. I switched to law due to the better employment perspectives, and immediately after graduating, I decided to take part in different public competitions for positions in the civil service. After being admitted to the ranks of the *Avvocatura dello stato* (ie the authority in charge of representing public bodies in court), I decided to also try the competition to be admitted to the magistracy. It is a very difficult merit-based

[1] Interview conducted on 17 May 2025 and validated for publication on 24 January 2025.

competition, involving a set of complex written and oral tests. I did not feel that my chances of being admitted were high, but I got some extra confidence from the example of my sister and of other friends who had been admitted shortly before.

It is worth mentioning that my generation was particularly motivated to pursue a career in the magistracy in light of the historical and political context at that time. In Italy, starting from the 1970s, several magistrates were killed by terrorist and mafia criminal organisations. Among them was the Vice-President of the Superior Council of the Judiciary, Professor Vittorio Bachelet, who was killed by the terrorist organisation *Brigate Rosse* in 1980. Then Rosario Livatino, brutally killed by mafia in Sicily in 1990, when he was only 37 years old. In May 1992, it was the turn of Giovanni Falcone and his wife, judge Francesca Morvillo, followed in July 1992 by Paolo Borsellino, all murdered together with their security details. All these traumatic events marked our history. Falcone and Borsellino were killed with bomb blasts, in a manner that represented symbolic 'declarations of war' against the state and our democracy. Additionally, we had the example of the group of prosecutors who launched the so-called *Mani Pulite* ('clean hands') investigation, which successfully brought to trial the key political actors involved in this a high-level system of bribery.

All this made many of us feel that it was possible to contribute to solving the crisis of a country severely affected by organised crime and corruption and help protect our democracy under attack.

I wish to stress that, like many Italian judges and prosecutors, I have always perceived my involvement in judicial associations as an integral part of my professional role. From 2016 to 2021 I served as the General Secretary of *Magistratura Democratica* (one of several judicial associations of different cultural orientations currently active in Italy under the umbrella of the *Associazione Nazionale Magistrati* (ANM, *National Association of Magistrates*). Since 2008, I have also been active in MEDEL, of which *Magistratura Democratica* is a founding member. My experiences within judicial associations over the years, together with my institutional experience at the Superior Council, have enriched my reflection on the role of public prosecution, and the importance of its independence but also of its accountability. MEDEL has always been committed to these issues and even recent developments, such as the collapse of the rule of law in Poland, have confirmed that the guarantees of an independent and accountable public prosecutor are essential for the independence of the whole judiciary and the fair and impartial administration of justice.

Leonardo Puleo: What is your general assessment of the evolution of the state of democracy in Italy and in Europe, in particular with regard to the rule of law and judicial independence?

Mariarosaria Guglielmi: I share the perspective of MEDEL, focused on judicial independence as a key component of the rule of law. MEDEL acts as a unique observatory, which combines a view of the situation across Europe, and even beyond its borders, with the experience and knowledge of what is happening in national contexts. This has allowed us to constantly monitor the process of democratic erosion and rule of law backsliding in Europe that has taken place in recent years.

The European landscape is composed of democracies that are still structurally fragile, and serious deficiencies in the rule of law persist or new ones constantly emerge, even in EU Member States. Rule of law backsliding is not limited exclusively to Poland and Hungary, although these are the clearest examples of the seriousness of the democratic regression in Europe. The situation in Romania and Bulgaria, for instance, is also quite problematic. Although the European Commission formally closed the Cooperation and Verification Mechanism, the Bulgarian judiciary faces a critical situation with judges under significant pressure. The lack of any effective accountability of the Prosecutor General had been longstanding issues in Bulgaria, as had the lack of any mechanism for judicial review of prosecutors' decisions not to open investigations, and both of these are serious obstacles in the fight against high-level corruption in public administration. Two months ago, MEDEL, along with three European associations – the Association of European Administrative Judges, the European Association of Judges, and *Rechters voor Rechters* – sent a letter to European institutions expressing concerns about the situation of the rule of law in Bulgaria and the pressures and intimidating conduct against individual judges.

Our association recently reported about the Belgian government's[2] blatant refusal to comply with domestic court injunctions concerning asylum seekers: a situation that triggered a systemic crisis of the rule of law, directly affecting the guarantee of effective protection of fundamental rights. In February, the European Parliament passed a resolution expressing serious concerns about rule of law and democracy in Greece, highlighting severe corruption, attacks on journalists' freedom, issues regarding migrants' fundamental rights, and frequent attacks against civil society organisations.

As for Italy, I consider my country to be a sort of laboratory where experiments that are very dangerous for democracy have been taking place for a long time. Since the March 2018 elections, we have witnessed a radical change in the Italian political scene. We had a government that openly labelled itself as populist, with a Prime Minister who boasted that they were 'the lawyer of the people', and a Minister of Interior (and Deputy Prime Minister) who radically changed migration policy, launching the so-called 'closed ports' manifesto, and raised the level of the attacks on the judiciary, portraying judges and prosecutors as 'enemies' of the people and suggesting that their decisions concerning migrants were politically motivated.

Italy still has a constitutional framework that, in its tenets and main features, has not changed since the moment in 1948 when the democratic and republican Constitution came into force after the fall of the fascist regime, providing solid guarantees for the rule of law and judicial independence. Within this framework, public prosecutors are – as I already mentioned – firmly isolated from the influence of the executive power and the Minister of Justice; as part of a single entity, both judges and prosecutors are governed by the Superior Council of the Judiciary, with a majority of members being elected by their peers, while the Council is chaired by the President of the Republic acting as a guarantor of constitutional values.

The overall constitutional framework is now the subject of radical reform proposal aimed at giving more power to the Prime Minister while weakening the roles of the President of the Republic and the Parliament. Other constitutional reform proposals radically reshape the magistracy, including the status of prosecutors and the structure

[2] For more information see www.questionegiustizia.it/data/doc/3900/i-belaid-eng-ok.pdf.

and competences of the Superior Council of the Judiciary. In particular, the envisaged separation of careers alongside the establishment of two distinct Councils are the two main features of moves to disrupt the constitutional framework that has guaranteed and protected the independence of the whole magistracy in our system.

The proposed reforms will also impact the current constitutional status of prosecution that guarantees the full independence of prosecutors vis-à-vis the Minister of Justice and the executive power, thus ensuring the effectiveness, impartiality, and fairness of investigation and prosecution.

We can see further clear signs of autocratisation and democratic regression in the attacks on media freedom and individual journalists, as well as on civil society organisations. This is part of a broader process composed of multiple policies with regressive effects on the protection of individual rights and freedoms, affecting different fields and restricting the scope of action of civil society. The most blatant example here is the rules adopted by the current government to impose limits on the activity of the NGOs rescuing migrants at sea.

Leonardo Puleo Have these trends that you described from 2018 onwards been also associated with pressures on individual judges?

Mariarosaria Guglielmi: We are witnessing an increase in public attacks from political actors and media against judges' associations, such as our umbrella association, the *Associazione Nazionale Magistrati*. These attacks occur simply because our associations speak openly about constitutional reform proposals and express concerns about them. At the same time, there have been increasing instances of politically motivated attacks on individual judges and prosecutors, especially people dealing with high-level corruption trials and investigations.

This tendency has old roots in Italy, but it has never before posed this level of danger to the rule of law. The attacks aim at a judiciary that is going through a crisis of distrust since it is not in the position to ensure that justice is delivered in an efficient and timely manner. Also, the facts disclosed a few years ago during an investigation, concerning ethical failures by some members of the Superior Council, seriously impacted the public perception of the judiciary. In such a context, the charges of 'politicisation' are frequently triggered by decisions that are 'unpopular' (as those concerning the protection of migrants) or, however, perceived as distant or fully detached from collective expectations in terms of 'security' fuelled by crime control policies based on the highest possible deterrence and harshness of punishments. Today, it is like as if judges are asked to 'take one side', and to declare which this is, while it is no longer accepted that they must stay – always and solely – 'on the side' of rights and guarantees. If those who challenge the role of the judge as an impartial actor have a government position, and exploit it to amplify their voices in the media, one easily obtains a dangerous delegitimisation of the judiciary and its constitutional role. It is again necessary to stress the relevance of this within the overall picture of the attacks against judges dealing with refugee and asylum cases. Such attacks come following decisions that do not align with the new government policy, notwithstanding the fact that these are based on reference to constitutional, European, and international norms. Yet, attacks always follow the same script: 'You are in favour of migrants. You are against our government's policy. Therefore, you are not impartial'. Government members recently led a media campaign that accused judges of boycotting national migration policies on ideological grounds and claiming they are playing a political role. This continues a trend that started in 2018 when the then Minister of the Interior clearly stated that he wanted to blacklist any judges who participated in conferences and public events on migration, engaged in cultural activities, or wrote articles on these topics.

Leonardo Puleo: In Italy and also in Europe, we are witnessing increasing polarisation around fundamental values such as migration, human rights protection, and constitutional checks and balances. Do you think the debate on these issues influences citizens' perception of the judiciary?

Mariarosaria Guglielmi: The question of citizens' perception is an important aspect of the complex situation we are dealing with. The deterioration of judicial independence and the intense attacks on judges who get portrayed as political opponents or as otherwise politically motivated in their decisions, lead to a delegitimisation of judicial functions which undermines citizens' trust in the judiciary. This is a dangerous general trend in Europe. The Polish 'muzzle law' is a good example of this trend, but cases elsewhere are also multiplying. Last year in France, some members of the Parliament proposed introducing legislation stating that judges must remain 'impartial' even when speaking as members of a judicial association and on issues concerning democracy, fundamental rights, and the rule of law. The inaccurate reference to the value of impartiality here is clearly nothing else than a tool to limit the expression of judges' opinions and negatively reinforce the image of a judiciary governed by ideological and political biases.

The distorted use of the concept of impartiality in the public debate can be easily observed in Italy as well. As I mentioned earlier, decisions issued by judges on international protection cases (but also many concerning criminal cases), are often presented by the media and politicians as political decisions 'against the government', with a clear impact on the perception of judges' impartiality.

The Italian situation is definitely a difficult one. As I said, we are facing a serious crisis of public confidence in the judiciary. Judges are 'paying the price' for the inefficiencies of our judicial system, which has to deal with a huge workload and lengthy proceedings. The problems affecting the efficiency of our justice system are of a structural nature that cannot be reduced to the idea of 'negligent judges' – although of course there can be individual cases of negligence – but rather are rooted inter alia in constant underfunding and inadequate procedural framework. Yet the inefficiency of justice is widely perceived by citizens as a problem related to judges, and the portrayal in the public debate of magistrates as members of a 'privileged elite' certainly furthers this perception.

This decreased level of public confidence in the justice system can facilitate the advancement of reforms that endanger judicial independence. The current situation is therefore quite different from what occurred in the past in contexts where judges and prosecutors also came under attack. Notably, during *Mani Pulite* and Berlusconi's season of '*ad personam*' laws,[3] it was clear that judges and prosecutors were the targets of instrumental political and public attacks, yet the judiciary enjoyed the trust of citizens. Today, because of the lack of public confidence, it is very difficult to make people understand that the independence of the judiciary is not the privilege of a professional group, but a key component of the rule of law and a guarantee of citizens' rights and freedoms.

Leonardo Puleo: Do you see a trend towards polarisation surrounding fundamental values also growing within the judiciary?

Mariarosaria Guglielmi: Regarding the current Italian context where individual judges or prosecutors are under pressure or are accused of being partial or acting against the government, one can observe different cultural approaches among the various judicial associations that are part of the *Associazione Nazionale Magistrati*. Some associations, like my own, *Magistratura Democratica*, have always been in favour of the judiciary playing an active role in the public debate concerning democracy, rule of law, and fundamental rights. The differing visions and views of interpreting the role of magistrates, the limits and the forms of their participation in the public debate, can lead to divisions within our umbrella association and make it harder to adopt unified public stances.

But the most recent Italian experience also proves that, when it comes to the core values of the defence of the rule of law and judicial independence, judges and prosecutors, and the different judicial associations, stand united around these values.

I feel that, at the European level, the experience of Turkey and Poland in recent years has led to a new model of judicial associationism, with the capacity to understand the values at stake and to establish a common front around them.

With several joint initiatives, for instance concerning the dialogue with European institutions, but also through symbolic events such as the March of a Thousand Robes in Warsaw in January 2020 the European associations proved how strong the bonds are – made of shared values – that unite judges and prosecutors today from different countries within a broader community of jurists committed to defending the rule of law.

This cohesion, built on the impact of the experiences of first Turkey and then Poland, made all European judges and prosecutors acutely aware of the fragility of the rule of law and judicial independence.

Leonardo Puleo: In your opinion, has the meaning of being a judge or a prosecutor changed in this context? Do you think that there are new challenges for the profession and its internal ethos today?

Mariarosaria Guglielmi: I feel that the essence of the role of judges and prosecutors has not changed. They must impartially guarantee rights, freedoms, and legality. However, this role has become much more difficult. First of all, the demand for justice is increasingly complex, involving new rights and increasing inequalities. Judges have to

[3] Editorial note: During Berlusconi's time in office, several laws were proposed by his governments and approved by parliament, which protected his interests and delayed his trials. (see C Dallara, 'Powerful Resistance Against a Long-Running Personal Crusade: the Impact of Silvio Berlusconi on the Italian Judicial System' (2015) 20 *Modern Italy* 59.

play their role and provide effective justice even when there is no clear legal framework, and this is a frequent occurrence. The trends of democratic erosion and populism that we discussed add a further layer of complexity, since it is the very idea of the impartial guarantee of fundamental rights and freedoms that is, per se, under attack.

The projects and attempts to reform the judicial system in order to bring it under the control of the executive cannot be considered an unprecedented challenge to the rule of law, but they now take a new, broader meaning. They are now indeed part of the effort to advance a new overall idea of society that is no longer based on equality but rather on identity. The role of judges as impartial guarantors of fundamental rights is under attack because of its nature as a corollary of the principle of the universality of rights and freedoms. When judges apply our constitutional charters, the European Convention on Human Rights, and EU law to guarantee fundamental rights for migrants they are simply upholding this principle of universality. This role of impartial guarantor is exactly what is under threat.

Leonardo Puleo: During the Polish rule of law crisis, we witnessed an unprecedented level of mobilisation and transnational solidarity among judges' associations. Do you think the Polish experience is showing us a path for the future in terms of creating alliances within society, or was it an isolated event?

Mariarosaria Guglielmi: The Polish experience is crucial in this respect as well. It shows that independent judges and prosecutors can support the resilience of independent justice by acting as European judges and engaging in dialogue with European courts. Polish judges used the mechanism of preliminary reference to the Court of Justice of the EU to reaffirm the core values of the rule of law and they acted at both the institutional and judicial levels. They strengthened relationships with other judicial associations, including European judicial associations. At the national level, they were able to open a dialogue with civil society, effectively explaining the values at stake and demonstrating why an independent judicial system is so crucial, as well as helping build a bulwark for the defence of the rule of law, together with lawyers, scholars, the free press, and NGOs. They had a specific communication strategy to convey the right messages, often simplifying complex issues to reduce the distance between judges and civil society.

This is an important example for everyone and is certainly true for the Italian judiciary in the current context where they face difficulties in explaining why changes to the structure and competences of the Superior Council of the Judiciary and to the status of prosecution imply serious risks for the rule of law.

More generally, the difficulty of having an effective dialogue with public and proactive communication with citizens is also due to the fact that democratic erosion is often a silent and subtle process. Governments tend to present radical changes as being low-profile reforms in line with their electoral mandate and based on the popular will. We have clearly observed this trend in Europe: the process of rule of law has been backsliding, even in the absence of dramatic events such as the Turkish coup attempt in July 2016, and proceeded 'silently', often receiving support at the ballot box.

It is therefore important to identify the early signs of democratic erosion and understand that radical changes can be implemented without the public immediately understanding their impact. All this reminds us of the importance of having a strategy to communicate effectively with the public, so we can explain why an independent judicial system is essential and how certain reforms can alter the balance between democratic institutions.

Leonardo Puleo: What do you think are the prospects for the future regarding challenges to judicial independence and the rule of law in Italy and Europe?

Mariarosaria Guglielmi: The current scenario is not very well defined. We are facing an international context of devastating wars. We are on the eve of elections for the European Parliament which could increase support for radical political projects. These projects may not question the EU directly, but rather undermine it by emphasising national identity and national sovereignty as primary values.

I believe that Europe will continue to face a serious process of democratic erosion within its borders, and democracy will have to prove even more resilient. The Polish experience shows that we have many instruments to address rule of law backsliding. Although these instruments were used in Poland in a more assertive way than in Hungary, we have to remember that they did not show a capacity to stop and reverse the process of rule of law backsliding. Democratic erosion is therefore still 'alive and kicking' within the EU and clear signs of this can be observed in several EU Member States, including Greece and Italy.

I do however believe that Europe still harbours 'antibodies' to combat the rule of law crisis. It is crucial to stick to the idea that the European community is united by fundamental values, and that there must be no backtracking from our achievements in terms of freedoms, rights, and democracy. I also believe that we will see a stronger civil society acting in defence of the rule of law, values, and democracy: this is my feeling and my hope.

11

We must Decide with Our Conscience, with the Sole Comfort of the Law

JOSÉ IGREJA MATOS[1]

Ramona Coman: Could you please describe your personal, academic, and professional background?

Igreja Matos: I have been a judge for 34 years now, since 1990. In the Portuguese judicial system, we start at a young age! I started my career when I was around 25 years old and I followed what could be considered a normal career path as a judge: I started at the school of judges in Lisbon, I was a trainee judge for two years, and after that I worked first in smaller courts. I am now the President of the Court of Appeal of Porto, a second instance court. In our system, the president is elected by their peers. I was elected on 21 October 2021 and I have now two years left of my mandate. I have worked extensively in different regions of the world. I was involved in activities in several Portuguese-speaking countries, particularly in Africa but also in Latin America, especially in Brazil. I have served as the Vice-President of the International Association of Judges since 2012, and I was also involved in several projects with the United Nations. I worked in Latin America, mostly on human rights and on the fight against corruption. I managed one project against corruption in Latin America addressing the judiciary. But my main work has been in Europe. I was President of the European Association of Judges from 2016 to 2021, and then President of the International Association from 2021 to 2023. My mandate as President of the EAJ coincided with the rule of law crisis particularly in Poland and Hungary. I worked with many colleagues and different institutions from these countries, mostly in Poland. Also, I joined efforts with international institutions, mostly the OECD and the Council of Europe (CoE). Recently, at the end of 2023, after being a member of the working group, I was elected Vice President of the Consultative Council of European Judges (CCEJ), which is a body within the CoE that issues opinions on the independence, impartiality, and competence of judges. I also try to support the work in the United Nations regarding the judiciary. I am a member of the advisory board of the Global Judicial Integrity Network of the United Nations

[1] Interview conducted on 24 May 2024 and validated for publication on 22 December 2024.

Office on Drugs and Crime (UNODC), which means that I have worked also in other continents, for example in countries in Asia.

Ramona Coman: You have an impressive record of international activity in many countries around the world. What motivated you to become a judge?

Igreja Matos: That is a very good question. Thinking about it, one could say that I always liked to approach complexity from different angles of the same narrative. And that is the role of a judge – our role is to listen to the different sides of the same story, to be aware of subtility and nuances. The truth is not black and white, and this idea of the complexity of the facts and of the law was one of the main triggers for me to decide to become a judge. A lawyer must take a side and must be partial. A judge has a distant approach, an impartial view of the law. I also like working with real people, and with real cases. I could have decided to stay in academia, but for me it was more interesting when I was young to work in the court and to work with concrete cases. What motivated me most was this idea of impartiality, of taking some distance, of having the possibility to approach the same issue in different ways without being committed to only one side of the story, like lawyers or prosecutors rightly must do.

Ramona Coman: In many countries, being a judge is very prestigious. Is this still the case in Portugal?

Igreja Matos: I will emphasise the word 'still'. When I began working, the profession was more prestigious than it is today. There is an issue of trust in judicial systems, and this is not specific to Portugal, it is present everywhere. The lack of trust in the people of the judiciary and in judges has an obvious impact on the prestige of judges.

Ramona Coman: You have vast experience in many countries. How do you regard the state of democracy in these different regions, in Europe or in Portugal?

Igreja Matos: My assessment is negative in comparison with previous years, especially in Europe, but not only here. We can observe a decay of the rule of law and limitations on judicial independence in the context of the rise of populist parties. There is a 'democracy fatigue' within younger generations and this is an additional problem. The World Justice Project has clearly shown that in recent years the rule of law has been declining in most countries, especially in the context of the COVID-19 pandemic. Portugal is a bit different because we don't have a real problem with judicial independence. The major problem that we have is a problem of trust, of people's confidence in their judiciary. In this respect we have reached perhaps the lowest level ever. There is also a problem of efficiency regarding some big corruption cases that we had. The lack of efficiency largely explains the lack of trust.

Ramona Coman: Many EU Member States face problems with the independence of their judiciaries. Why is the situation in Portugal different?

Igreja Matos: In a more formal way there is internal independence. We don't have any problems with our Judicial Council interfering with the decisions of the judges. The presidents of the court are totally detached from the decisions of their colleagues. They can decide whatever they want, and there is no interference in their decisions. There is also external independence. Until now we have not had political parties or populists challenging this independence. However, now we have a right-wing party (Chega) which is winning votes in elections.

Ramona Coman: Is this party challenging the independence of judges or the organisation of the judiciary?

Igreja Matos: To be honest, no, I do not see that. I may be wrong or too optimistic, but I don't think this party is a real threat, at least for now and in my assessment. It is just a party which is taking advantage of the negative view of politicians by a large part of the electorate, at least for the time being. Historically, Portuguese fascism, our totalitarian regime, was a 'light' one. It was not like the Nazis or Mussolini or Franco. And even our populist, radical party now is not very eager to change things regarding the rule of law, especially if you compare it with Germany, France, or, perhaps the worst example, with Hungary.

Ramona Coman: Since you mentioned the state of democracy, is this a topic of debate within the judiciary or between judges, either in Portugal or at the European/international levels based on your experience in different associations?

Igreja Matos: Absolutely, yes. We are constantly debating the state of our democracies and how judicial independence could be put at risk. I was in Poland recently to receive an award. By the way, it was the best I ever had – a very informal one, basically just a frame with a set of photos of dozens of Polish judges, each of them in their offices holding a sign with the word 'Thank you' on it. It was a very emotional moment. But the more important aspect was the possibility for us, independent judges, to gather in the Polish Senate and to speak freely about judicial independence.

Anyway, returning to your question, the state of democracy is always a topic for us, especially now we are seeing problems in so many countries – Slovakia, for instance, with the new government in place. Judicial independence is never a given. It is always a fight; it is always something that could collapse. And my early experience in Latin America maybe helped me to better understand the present European challenges. What happened in Latin America a few decades ago is very similar to what has been happening in recent years in Europe. Autocrats use the same approach to attack the judges, the media, the opposition … Controlling the judges and the media makes it inevitable that such leaders will also be able to control societies to perpetuate their power. I saw that repeatedly in Latin America. It was curious because autocracies could be from the left or the right – radicalised ones, obviously – depending on specific contexts. For the moment, maybe the most worrisome example regarding the EU would be Hungary since Orbán's regime has an agenda based on his concept of 'illiberal democracy'. For instance, in Venezuela, we have an autocratic regime labelled as 'leftist' where judicial independence is just a mirage.

Ramona Coman: The state of democracy is indeed a matter of concern for judges too. What are the main threats that you observe, or which have been discussed not only in relation to Poland and Hungary but also in other countries?

Igerja Matos: In Europe, I would say that in general the ex-Soviet countries or ex-communist countries are more at risk now. Outside the EU, you can see it in Serbia, in Montenegro – everywhere actually, there is a temptation, a constant compulsion, to control the judiciary. It is, in a way, the resurgence of the old Soviet way of appointing judges at the supreme court or constitutional court, or presidents of the courts and judicial councils to have the power over the top judicial bodies, and then to have the possibility to determine some judicial rulings. They don't need to do much, they don't need to give a public speech about controlling the courts. They control the key points within the structural system of the judiciary, and the rest will go smoothly. We can see this temptation in many countries, and it is subtle. It does not make the media headlines nor is it in the newspapers. It is not spoken out loud. But if you talk with judges, we can detect that these concerns are always pending.

Ramona Coman: How do you see the role of judges in this context? What role should they play? Should they take a stance and be active, or embrace self-restraint? Are these more normative questions about the ethos or the code of conduct of judges also debated within the profession?

Igreja Matos: This is a very interesting question because our genetic code or the way we are trained is mostly to be silent; thanks to our professional role we are prepared more to listen than to speak. To be a judge is a professional career. We are not politicians. For us, being a judge is lifelong work, it's for life. So, our normal way to react when politicians want to take control is to be more or less silent, to not intervene but to leave things as they are, and hoping that the future will be better since the political background is fluid and in constant change.

Our professional approach is based more on being passive than active. We are educated to know the laws and apply them, but not so much to consider the political organisation in a broader sense. And in fact, I must say, most of the cases that we deal with are 'anonymous' since they affect normal citizens not visible in the public arena. Those in power don't care much about such cases. The problem is when we have powerful people – or those who are around those in power – getting involved in judicial cases. When I was the President of the EAJ, it was difficult to mobilise the judges for this issue, in particular if they didn't feel this pressure in their own country, in their daily work, on their own skin, or in their own soul. For them, it was something that happens in other countries, they do not feel very concerned. It comes and goes. 'We are not politicians': This is a phrase that we always hear, and it is absolutely true. When I speak about these topics I always try to explain why, for instance, in Hungary, judges were mostly passive. Because it is not our culture to speak out. Our culture is different, it is a culture of acceptance of the rules that are fixed by others. That is why we have recently tried to have a more proactive approach in this regard. If you read, for instance, the Opinion 25 of the CCEJ[2] about the freedom of expression of judges – an opinion in which I was involved since I was a member of the working group – we underlined the fact that judges have a duty (not only the right) to speak when rule of law and judicial independence are at stake. We are trying to slowly change the perspective a little bit to say that judges, if they want to be judges, must also have a commitment to judicial independence. It is a kind of ethical commitment. It is as important to be impartial as it is to be

[2] Consultative Council of European Judges, Opinion No. 25 (2022) on freedom of expression of judges, rm.coe.int/opinion-no-25-2022-final/1680a973ef%0A%0A.

outspoken when defending the independence of courts, a value that protects not the judges, but the citizens.

Ramona Coman: In our conversation about the relationship between law and politics, you mentioned that 95 per cent of cases that judges deal with are not of interest for political actors while the rest are more sensitive. Do you think that it is still the case today that only a small proportion of cases are sensitive for political reasons?

Matos: You are right – maybe it is not 95 per cent anymore. There are indeed new concerns, see for example the cases – some on a small scale – related to the protection of the environment. I think environmental protection will be a major issue for judiciary over the next ten years. I worked closely with the Global Judicial Institute on the Environment, an organisation composed only of judges, within the United Nations, in which we had these discussions about environmental law. So the concrete enforcement of environmental law and its measures of protection of the planet will be a major topic for the judiciary in the next ten years.

We are at a crossroads, we have the laws and we have public concern, especially amongst younger generations. But we don't have the enforcement, and we don't have the proper tools. It seems clear to me that there will be one or two possibilities to continue to have these 'light' discussions about defensive environments or to give real tools to the judiciary to punish damaging behaviours. Enforcement is always about the judiciary. Regarding the environment, we can see in Brazil, for instance, that the destruction of nature is very worrisome. What I am discussing with my colleagues from Brazil is that they have very good laws, but in the end, they are not applied because there are still issues about implementing the laws concretely in the courts. In my opinion, this will be a major topic for the future.

Another topic is migration, and this is a double challenge. I was recently talking with some colleagues from the UK, and they complain about the stress and burnout they feel when dealing with those cases, also because of the huge backlogs. Indeed, that's a third one, judicial well-being, that will be at the top of the agenda for us in the future, or even now already. Stress and burnout are increasing in particular for judges who work with migrants and on the issue of refugees or asylum seekers. Another major source of stress is family courts. Talking with other colleagues from Portugal, I was amazed by the levels of stress that they are now facing with all the existing pressures from different quarters.

Ramona Coman: Do you encounter other conflictual topics besides climate and migration on which judges have to make decisions?

Igreja Matos: We could mention here all the cases that deal with challenges for modern societies such as abortion, discrimination against minorities, and the use of technology in the workplace, for instance. You see the latter in Asia, for instance, in China, where there is an attempt to control the private and the professional life of citizens now and we also have the technological tools to effectively do so. This is another factor of concern for the future. To this I would add the 'usual' topic which is the fight against corruption. It is not politically correct to say this, but I think most intentions to control the judiciary have to do with corruption in Europe, Latin America, and the United States. The goal is to have a lenient system, for governments to have the possibility of doing their own business without anybody interfering. Corruption, at large – including abuse of power, nepotism, influence peddling, and lobbying – will be always a conflictual area for judiciaries.

Ramona Coman: Some of the issues that you mentioned are often seen as divisive – are they also divisive within the judiciary?

Igreja Matos: Absolutely. How to tackle these issues is not straightforward for us. Let me give you an example: In Turkey when the political power wanted to control the judiciary and to put their people in key positions, there was a huge, huge replacement of judges. More than 4000 were newly appointed after Erdogan came to power. In Poland too, several hundred judges were appointed during the PiS government. It is clear that judges have different approaches depending on the circumstances of their appointment. The younger generations are not children of the Second World War, or they don't have memories of the fascist times, because it was decades ago, nor do they have memories of the years after the construction of freedom and of a liberal state. Therefore, their background and memories of history are different, posing new challenges. Because they were born, fortunately, in this new environment, they are not so preoccupied with trying new models for society. Judges who are in their forties, fifties or sixties are very keen and they know what dangers always persist in the shadows. I always try to alert younger generations and advise them to go to these museums of memories in Europe, or to read and to think how fragile democracy is. For most of them democracy is a given. Some of them will say, 'Oh, this is fine but maybe we should try something else'.

Ramona Coman: What does it mean to be a judge today? And what does it mean to interpret the law or to apply the law?

Igreja Matos: The work of judges is controlled every day for reasons of productivity. You open your computer, and you have the cases on which you must make a ruling. The next day you have more, and so it continues. When I began, everything was done on paper but now it is totally different. You can control your work to the second if you are running late on your decisions, and this leads to an additional factor of stress. We have a burnout problem. Why? Because thanks to technology, statistics are everywhere; we are controlled to the day, to the minute.

The second issue is a lack of means. It is not popular for the state to give resources to the justice system, and it doesn't get anyone votes. It is better to open a hospital or to build a road than to have modern courts, and to have proper resources for the justice system. The lack of resources is a key problem, and indeed a transversal problem.

Another problem is solitude, something which is inevitable because our job is a very, very lonely one. We must decide with our conscience, with the sole comfort of the law. We are always talking and debating to ourselves when deciding. As a judge, when I finish a trial, I have my first impressions, but then I go home, I think about it again and another option appears for the decision. It is always a struggle to escape from the routine, to be open to all the possible solutions and always be aware of the peculiarities of each and every case out of the thousands we adjudicate over the years.

Ramona Coman: What tools are available for judges to stand up and defend the independence of the judiciary?

Igreja Matos: One tool is judicial cooperation. Being in the EU is an asset for us. You can see that if you look at countries that don't belong to the EU, like the former Soviet countries. What is also positive is that we have many opportunities to interact with other judges and many informal networks of communication to cooperate with judges from different countries. Not to mention that we can all now communicate in English. It is easier than in the past when we were facing a language barrier. In Poland, judges have been courageous, and colleagues from many countries have expressed solidarity with those brave Polish judges. Many initiatives have been taken by national associations of judges, as well as by European associations. In Portugal we have one professional association which represents 90 per cent or more of the judges.

Ramona Coman: What is the outcome of this transnational solidarity between judges? Can you give two or three examples of this?

Igreja Matos: The main issues are education about justice to help build closer ties with civil society as well as communication challenges. That is quite evident for me. There are networks of transnational associations who support those who are in danger so that they feel not alone. I can give you many examples. In Turkey, for instance, EAJ created a solidarity fund and we raised more than €300,000, giving €900 to each family of Turkish judges and prosecutors who were in prison or exile. There were more than 2,400 judges in prison after 2016.

A big network of assistance was created, and they didn't feel so alone. Hundreds of letters were received at the headquarters of the IAJ in Rome addressed to Turkish judges and their families, and they were very moving. They convey this idea that somewhere in Europe, someone is watching what happens, they are concerned and want to supported the judges to help their families. And this kind of solidarity is essential for a human being. This is an extreme example, obviously, but there are many other examples in smaller circuits with different kinds of problems, for example, in cases of disciplinary procedures against judges for being outspoken on judicial independence, where people will come together to support them to have lawyers to defend them.

Lawyers are decisive in this struggle for rule of law. I always try to cooperate very closely with lawyers and their organisations. They are on the front line protecting human rights. It is not only about judges and transnational communication among judges. Defending democracy and the rule of law is also about lawyers, jurists, and about academia. It is also about civil society. If you have a civil society committed to the rule of law, it is much more difficult for those in power to dominate the judiciary. If you don't have civil society on your side, it is a much bigger problem.

When I was in Poland at the March of a Thousand Robes, what impressed me most was all these thousands of people. Some of them were crying. The mobilisation of civil society was impressive. During the march, an elderly woman approached me with tears in her eyes. She expressed her gratitude, engaging in a heartfelt dialogue. 'Dziękuję, Dziękuję' – 'Thank you, thank you' – she said to this foreign, anonymous judge. In the end, we embraced and continued, feeling comforted, amidst the crowd. The work and mission of defending the key values of judicial independence and the rule of law will forever be shaped by the clear and tearful eyes of that elderly woman.

12

Judges can be a Big Obstacle for Authoritarian Regimes

LUCA PERILLI[1]

Ramona Coman: Could you briefly introduce yourself and tell me about your motivation for becoming a judge?

Luca Perilli: After passing the bar exam in Italy, I worked as a lawyer for a year and a half in a law firm in Vicenza until I received the results of my application for the judicial position, having taken the written exam two years before. Since there were over 15,000 candidates who took the competitive examination to become judges, the examining Committee took almost two years to assess and compare thousands of written papers, and fewer than 300 candidates were finally admitted to the oral exam. Having passed all the procedural steps to become a judge, I quit the profession of lawyer and started the initial judicial training at the Court of Venice. Since then – that was in 1995 – I have worked as a judge for more than 29 years, in the courts of Milan, Rovereto, Trento and Catania. In my judicial position, I have reached the highest 'degree', the seventh, in the sense that I have passed all seven professional appraisals. Throughout my career, I have adjudicated cases in basically all areas of justice, at different levels, in first and appeal instances, and in both civil and criminal law. I've also dealt with bankruptcy, commercial, labour, and even agricultural law cases.

Since 2020, I have been dealing with international protection and migration law. This has only become a relevant issue for the ordinary jurisdiction in Italy in recent years. After the 'great refugee crisis' of 2014–2017, more than 600,000 migrants reached the Italian coast, and most of them filed asylum claims. It is in this context that, in 2017, the specialised sections for international protection were created and since then a new branch of jurisdictional activity has started to become increasingly important. These cases amount to almost one third of the cases of the regional courts, a huge number of cases.

Apart from that, I was frequently involved in international activities. For a long time, I worked as an independent expert for the CoE and the EU. As an EU independent expert, for almost ten years I carried out periodical peer review missions to assess the

[1] Interview conducted on 16 May 2024 and validated for publication on 11 January 2025.

progress made by candidate and potential candidate countries to the EU in the context of the judiciary and fundamental rights, in countries including Croatia, Turkey, North Macedonia, Montenegro, Serbia, and Albania. During country visits I had the opportunity to interview representatives of the institutions, especially judicial institutions, representatives of the associations of judges, lawyers, members of the civil society, and NGOs.

Ramona Coman: You have had some very impressive international activity! How were you able to accommodate this experience alongside your duties as a judge?

Luca Perilli: It was a big challenge, because I carried out the international activity in parallel with my work as a judge, without being exempted from my cases in court. Sometimes I was on leave, sometimes not, but I was always authorised by the Judicial Council with the consent of the President of my Court. In addition, having accumulated such international experience, since 2006 I have also been involved in many conferences organised by the CoE, the EU, and other international organisations in the areas of the rule of law and protection of fundamental rights. I stopped my activity as an EU independent expert after the collapse of the rule of law in Turkey. My last mission was executed in June 2015 in Southeast Turkey in the context of the visa liberalisation process, to assess the security legislation that was affecting especially the rights of millions of Turks of Kurdish nationality living in Southeast Turkey. In 2016, after the attempted *coup d'état*, almost 3,000 judges and prosecutors were arrested in Turkey. Many of those arrested had served in the Turkish Ministry of Justice and were working on the portfolio of the negotiations for the accession of Turkey to the EU. I was personally very close to some of them because of the professional relations we developed over the years. Some of these judges are now refugees in Europe, some are even in Belgium.

More recently, I have been involved annually as a speaker at the Fundamental Rights Agency of the EU in Vienna, in seminars for judges about the applicability and the effects of the Charter of Fundamental Rights for European judges. Since 2016 I have also been the national contact point for the Agency of European Union for Asylum, Courts and Tribunal sector. This represents a total of 20 years as an international expert and 10 years as an EU-independent expert in the EU enlargement. In the same period, I regularly discharged my judicial activities.

Ramona Coman: What was your motivation for pursuing a career as a judge?

Luca Perilli: I would not say that I really wanted to become a judge. I was interested in law and economics and what I really wanted was to work at the international level. When I finished *lyceum* (secondary school in Italy), I was attracted by economics and passed the competition to enter Bocconi University in Milan, but in the end, I decided to study law. I think it is mainly because of family tradition. In my father's family, there were nine siblings and all five brothers graduated in law. My father was very proud at the idea of seeing me as a judge. Having this option, when I had to decide between being a lawyer and a judge, I went for the latter partly because there was a family desire for me to pursue this path. But also, the profession attracted me, and the context was important too. I completed my legal studies in the beginning of the 1990s. In 1992 I took the written exam to become a judge, and in 1993

I passed the bar exam and started to work as a lawyer. I then entered the judiciary in April 1995. It was the period when the public prosecutors in Milan started to unveil the *Tangentopoli* system. The investigation was known as *Mani Pulite* (Clean Hands) and became a scandal that involved high-ranking politicians. That investigation revealed a system of political power rooted in corruption. In the same years, on 23 May 1992, Judge Giovani Falcone was killed by the Mafia, and then a few months later, on 19 July 1992, Judge Paolo Borsellino was also killed. I took the exam in 1993. There were more than 15,000 applications for 300 judicial positions available. This huge number of applications shows that, at that time, being a judge was a very attractive profession for Italian lawyers. This is how I started.

Ramona Coman: We will come back to the prestige of the profession later. You became a judge in a tumultuous political context in Italy in the 1990s which completely changed the nature of the political regime and to some extent strengthened the independence of Italian judges. We are currently living in a context in which democracy is also under strain, in particular the independence of judges. How do you see the situation in Italy and in Europe?

Luca Perilli: First, I would like to share with you my experience on this point as an international expert. I have witnessed the deterioration of the state of democracy and the disruption of the rule of law most dramatically in Turkey. In the years between 2007 and 2012, there was hope for a brighter future and development of democracy in Turkey and the reinforcement of the protection of fundamental rights of individuals. And I could see the positive evolution from close up. The Constitution of Turkey has always been seen as an example of democracy in a country in transition and in those years important constitutional reforms were implemented to reinforce it. A new Judicial Council was set up, the majority of whose members were elected by judges and prosecutors, in accordance with the model recommended by the CoE, a model that is not followed even by most European countries. A very advanced constitutional framework was established, through amendments to the original text, to strengthen the independence of the judiciary and to ensure the protection of the fundamental rights of people. An individual application was introduced for a remedy to the Turkish Constitutional Court for the protection of individual fundamental rights. There was a lot of progress.

However, in 2013 the situation changed radically due to political reasons. I tend to believe that the political majority ruling the country never took ownership of these reforms which were strongly advocated and supported by the EU. A clear sign of this was the reaction of the political branches to growing independence of the magistracy that manifested, for instance, in the initiation of corruption-related criminal investigations against members of the Turkish government. December 2013 was the turning point when the Judicial Council was shaken up and then put under the control of the executive power. New legislation was adopted to undermine the independence of the judiciary and, after a few years, in 2017, the Constitution was again amended to ensure political control over the Judicial Council. But what is shocking and unpredictable was the arrest and detention of judges. In July 2016, two days after the attempted *coup d'état* a list of almost judges was made public by the Judicial Council. It was a list of judges who were identified as terrorists by an already politically controlled Judicial Council.

Immediately after this, almost 3,000 judges and prosecutors were arrested and detained and more than 3,000 were fired. It was a shock to see how the state of democracy can be disrupted overnight.

In subsequent years, the situation has changed in Europe as well and we have witnessed attacks on the judiciary in European countries, including EU Member States. Judicial independence is the key value for the protection of the rights of individuals, especially in times of change and constitutional transitions, and judges are those who can and must protect those rights. However, this requires that their independence from political power is guaranteed. Judges can be a big obstacle for authoritarian regimes. This is why the independence of the judiciary is the first target of autocrats. The experience in Turkey as well as Poland and Hungary shows that the first immediate target of an executive that is willing to control the judicial power is the constitutional court, particularly in countries in which the constitutional court exercises control of constitutionality over the legislation and where, as in Turkey, it is also the guardian of respect for individual fundamental rights. The first two arrests in Turkey in 2016 targeted precisely two judges from the Constitutional Court; one of the two, Alparslan Altan, was the Deputy President of the Court and a member of the Venice Commission of the Council of Europe. Three years later, in 2019, he received a decision of the European Court of Human Rights in Strasbourg which held that his right to liberty had been violated by the Turkish State under Article 5 of the European Convention on Human Rights.

Ramona Coman: In the early 2010s, important changes happened in EU Member States as the rule of law was dismantled by elected politicians in Hungary and in Poland alongside other Member States that have been less discussed in the media. In those states, judges were not imprisoned like in Turkey, but they were dismissed or replaced, and courts were packed with new judges. There are also concerns in Romania, Bulgaria, Slovakia, Malta, and Spain. Judicial independence is no longer an 'Eastern European' phenomenon; is it also a source of concern in Western Europe?

Luca Perilli: Indeed. In Hungary, the judicial reform of 2011, which entered into force on 1 January 2012, impacted the self-governing independent National Judicial Council – that had been set up in 1997 – depriving it of many of its competencies which were transferred to a newly established body, the National Office of the Judiciary, along with its President. Over the years, the political control over the National Office of the Judiciary and its President has allowed heavy political interference in the independent exercise of judicial power. In Poland, the Parliament (Sejm) adopted ordinary legislation to gain control over the Polish National Judicial Council and the Constitutional Court and, finally, over the judiciary. A 2017 law that forced many members of the Polish Supreme Court to retire was the subject of an infringement procedure launched by the European Commission. In June 2019, the CJEU held that Poland had violated judicial independence. Also, the 2019 establishment of a special body, a disciplinary chamber in the Polish Supreme Court, was declared to be contrary to the principle of judicial independence by the CJEU in 2023.

However, as you said, judicial independence is not only a problem in Central and Eastern Europe; let's talk about the situation in Italy. In June 2024, the Council of

Ministers adopted a draft constitutional amendment to change the governance of the judiciary and the composition and functioning of the Superior Council of the Judiciary. The text was adopted very rapidly, on the eve of the June 2024 European elections. The plan was to separate the careers paths of judges and prosecutors by having two different recruitment processes in place and two Judicial Councils. Further, the draft constitutional reform envisages the creation of a High Disciplinary Court. These provisions have no clear justification, apart from the aim of creating mechanisms of political control over the prosecution service and putting pressure on judges. The separation of the careers of judges and prosecutors is already a reality in the Italian judicial system: since a 2007 law was passed, judges and prosecutors have been forced to change 'judicial district' if they apply for a change of functions, while another law of 2023 – the so-called Cartabia reform adopted by the Draghi government – allows judges and prosecutors to change functions only once in their professional career. Basically, 'changes of career' only happen when a judge applies to the General Prosecution Office of the Court of Cassation, an Office that does not perform any investigation but only issues opinion 'in the interest of the Law' (similar to the role of the General Attorney of the CJEU). On 26 April 2024, the EAJ deemed this draft reform 'a serious attack on the independence of the Judiciary, an undermining of the existing balance of powers in Italy, and a clear infringement of the European standards'.[2]

Ramona Coman: In some EU Member States we have seen an increase in disciplinary sanctions against judges – is this also the case of Italy?

Luca Perilli: The Italian disciplinary system for judges complies with the European best standard. A judicial independent body – an independent department of the Judicial Council – adjudicates over the indictments. Principles of legality of infringements and legality of sanctions are in place. There are a wide range of authorities that can start a disciplinary proceeding, including the Minister of Justice, which ensures a large control over the ethical behaviour of judges and prosecutors. The disciplinary decisions adopted by the Judicial Council are ultimately subject to the scrutiny of the Unified Civil Sections of the Court of Cassation upon appeal. There are then two levels of jurisdiction. First, the Council and second, the Court of Cassation. The system works in such a way that many disciplinary cases are launched every year against judges and prosecutors. Italy is one of the Council of Europe countries with the highest number of disciplinary proceedings against judges and prosecutors. It is therefore very clear that the government's aim is to change a system that complies with the best EU standard with a view to creating a new disciplinary body separated from the judicial system – a sort of special court.

Perhaps this new body will be sensitive to the political winds? This High Court would be composed of 15 members, nine judges, and six lay members. One problem is that those nine judges will be selected from the offices that are on the top of the system – the General Prosecution Office and the Supreme Court – whilst, currently, only two out of 20 judicial members of the Judicial Council are elected by the Supreme Court members,

[2] European Association of Judges, 'Resolution on the Endangered Independence of the Judiciary in Italy', uhs.hr/wp-content/uploads/2024/05/EAJ-Resolution-Italy.pdf.

the remaining being elected by lower jurisdictions. Is this a surreptitious way to create hierarchies in a judiciary that is instead constitutionally characterised by the horizontal share of power? What is most worrying is that the appeal against the decisions of this High Court will be heard by the same High Court, in a sort of self-referential circuit.

Ramona Coman: How is this development perceived today by judges in Italy?

Luca Perilli: In 2016, a study titled 'Magistrati e cittadini' was published by the School for the Judiciary (SSM) in cooperation with the Italian National Association of Judges (*Associazione Nazionale Magistrati,* ANM). The research shows that there is a big gap between how judges perceive themselves and how citizens perceive them, and it showed that judges' self-perceptions of judicial independence and impartiality are far stronger than citizens' perceptions. This gap in perception is very problematic because judges feel independent, but this independence is not strongly rooted in society and makes the judiciary weak vis-à-vis the political power.

The vast majority of judges and prosecutors and also the ANM, which represents more than 90 per cent of Italian magistrates, are strongly critical of the last draft reform of the judicial system; however, this position might be presented by the ruling politicians and the pro-Government media as a form of corporatism. The promoted by the government is that the new legislation will increase judges' independence and impartiality; it might be possible that a big section of Italian society that does not perceive judges as independent or impartial will be ready to support the reform.

Ramona Coman: How do you explain this gap in how judges are perceived more generally within society and how they perceive themselves?

Luca Perilli: I think that there are two main reasons for it. It might be explained on one hand by the way judges approach citizens in courts and hearings, in other words, how the judges communicate with citizens, not about the content of their decisions. On the other hand – and this is more important – it might be due to how the media, and especially politically-oriented media, depict judges. Silvio Berlusconi, who was Prime Minister for a long time, did not refrain from using strong words to attack the judiciary and even individual judges in public speeches and the press or on television – parts of which were controlled directly by him and his family. He referred to judges as being 'mentally disturbed'. Trust in judges was very high in the 1990s, in the context of *Mani Pulite* and at the time of Giovanni Falcone and Paolo Borsellino's investigations against the mafia, but it has declined since then. This superficial attitude of attacking judges and the judiciary in the media has not stopped even now Berlusconi left the public scene. Nowadays the main target is judges who deal with migration.

Furthermore, the Italian judiciary has always been perceived as very inefficient because court proceedings are exceedingly long, and citizens are not able to understand that this is mainly due to a lack of resources that should be provided by the Minister of Justice. Several reports issued by the CEPEJ of the CoE show that the Italian court system lacks sufficient human resources to deal with the high caseload. In this situation, judges are perceived as a privileged category of public employees, being well-paid, but lazy and slow. And there is a widespread perception that they do not do enough to protect the rights of the citizens. The endemic situation of there being insufficient human resources for the judiciary was finally addressed thanks to the funds and support from the EU: 12,000 judge-assistants have been hired in the last two years as part of the Next Generation EU programme, with the specific aim of helping judges and courts reduce the backlog of cases and bringing the length of trials in line with the principle of reasonable duration.

Finally, there is a problem of judges not perceiving the importance of 'procedural justice'. Italian judges are mainly focused on legal issues. However, courts are not only accessed by the parties to trial. There are also a huge number of people who go to court to get a service: for example, for the appointment of a guardian for a vulnerable person, which is a very common situation in Italy. If a court is not able to provide a proper and timely service for these citizens, then the citizens will have the perception that judges do not do enough to protect their rights. Changing behaviour, attitude, and organisation is a key. To do so, judges need to change their way of thinking about their role as a service, and not only as a power.

Ramona Coman: Is the degree of confidence that citizens have in the justice system a topic of debate within the judiciary?

Luca Perilli: Reflections on this question started 20 years ago when the so-called observatories for civil justice were created. These observatories are associations that include judges, lawyers, and academics, as well as representatives of NGOs who are interested in the functioning of the justice system. Members of the observatories meet periodically at the local and national levels and discuss how to improve the service to better serve citizens' interests. There has been a very positive approach that brought to the elaboration of so-called 'protocols for civil justice' between courts and bar associations to agree on informal procedures to make the judicial service easier, more open, and nonconflictual. In my court we have also implemented two of these protocols.

However, I would say that these efforts have involved only a minority of judges. There is still a big portion of the judiciary that thinks that the role of the judge is listening and then deciding, and that this is a matter of impartiality, rather than being actively involved in civil society associations. I instead consider it a misinterpretation of the idea of impartiality. Impartiality means being distant from the interest the parties have in the case but not that they are distant from the service that the judge must provide to the parties.

Another way to improve the service is judicial training. When I was one of the directors of the judiciary school, we organised consistent training about the quality of justice, which also included reflection with psychologists and experts of communication on how to treat the parties. This was also based on studies performed in Northern European countries, according to which, if the parties are treated properly by the judges, they will be much more ready to accept the final decision. This is part of the appearance of the impartiality of the judge. Another example: we also organised training on the psychology of judges on how to recognise and prevent bias. This is important, especially in the field of migration, where bias and prejudice can severely affect the process and the decision for many reasons including cultural distance, lack of knowledge of the social and political context the migrant comes from, or the behaviour of the asylum seeker who might be scared, traumatised, or wary.

Ramona Coman: You mentioned migration which is a very politicised topic in many EU Member States. What is the situation in Italy and to what extent does this create tensions between justice and politics?

Luca Perilli: There are three main fields of judicial activity where tensions can arise between judges and political actors. One is related to criminal investigations and criminal cases regarding politicians, such as cases of corruption at a high political level or cases where there is major economic interest. To refer to a recent example, this year there has been an investigation of corruption regarding the Governor of Liguria, an Italian region, which has triggered harsh political reactions. As an answer to the investigations, some high-rank politicians called for the reform of the judicial system and the change of the Constitution. The Italian Constitution of 1946 provided the judicial power with strong independence from external influences, especially from the executive. This independence also extends to the prosecution service and it has made criminal investigations possible in every context of social and political life. When Silvio Berlusconi was in power, there were attempts to change the Constitution and curtail judicial independence. These attempts failed because changes to the constitution require a very large political consensus.

Another field of tension is the area of family law and bioethics. In Italy, a Catholic country – and the same can be seen in other Catholic European countries – judicial cases can become a field of political battle, fostered by those political parties that claim the protection of Catholic religious values. This happens, for example, in cases of the rights of children of same-sex couples or in cases of judicial decisions regarding the end of life. Some of these situations are not fully regulated by the law, because it is difficult to find a political compromise in this context. Normally, the judges have wide discretion in applying constitutional and sometimes supranational principles and rules, and this creates a clear field of tension. At the political level, in Italy, a debate has even recently restarted about abolishing the right to abortion, like in Poland.

The third issue is migration. Migration is the most important emerging field of tensions not only in Italy but in the whole of Europe, because increasingly often at the political level the protection of the national identity is invoked as a key value. This automatically becomes an obstacle to the protection of third-country nationals. It creates a division between those who are part of a national community and the others who are not. The message supported by some political parties is that migrants put the Italian identity at risk; the message is accompanied by misinformation about the reasons why asylum seekers migrate, as well as about their conditions and their culture.

This situation can also have consequences at a legislative level, especially when the legislation conflicts with constitutional or international values concerning the protection of the individual fundamental rights of the asylum seekers. Let us consider, for example, the EU Pact on Asylum and Migration, a set of rules aimed at managing migration at the European level. The consensus about this new Pact was reached by the EU in last May after many years of discussion and negotiations that started in 2016. Robust amendments to the Common European Asylum System have been voted on by the European Parliament and were upheld by the European Council of Ministers just before the June elections for the European Parliament. We could argue that this agreement has been reached at the expense of any guarantee for migrants that they will receive fair treatment when reaching the EU's external borders. There is a potential clash between the new rules and the fundamental individual rights of asylum seekers, protected by the Treaty on European Union and the Charter of Fundamental Rights of the EU, especially in the context of the new screening and border procedures. In the first comments released by experts, scholars, and even by the Office of the United Nations High Commissioner for Human Rights (UNHCR), some provisions of the Pact have been identified as containing a potential violation of the rights to liberty, access to justice, and the principle of the best interest of the child.

We are speaking about values that constitute the foundations of the European Union's democratic architecture. These conflicts will be certainly brought to the attention of the European judges dealing with international protection cases. In deciding the case, judges will have to refer to those fundamental values enshrined in the Charter, the national constitution, and the UN Geneva Convention, because asylum seekers are holders of fundamental rights, exactly like national or European citizens. There is no difference. These rights must be protected according to the democratic system that we have. And judges are the people who must protect their rights. Judges are the last resort, and the independence of judges is the pre-condition for the protection of the individual rights of these people.

In Italy, we had a very clear example of this potential clash between judges, protecting the rights of migrants, and the political level invoking the application of national legislation. In the night between 25 and 26 February 2023, in Calabria, a few kilometres away from the coast, a boat of migrants sunk; of the 159 migrants on the boat, only 54 survived. In the headlines, there were many controversies about the delay in the rescue operations and a criminal investigation was even started to identify those who were potentially responsible. The Government delivered an unexpected and inconsistent response; it issued an urgent legislative decree – which unfortunately is known as '*Decreto Cutro*', named after the beach close to which more than one hundred people died – that severely restricts the rights of the migrants, especially those fleeing from countries that Italy designates as 'safe third countries of origin'. The new provisions allow for the detention for such asylum seekers. At the same time, the list of safe third countries of origin was greatly enlarged by a government decision, to include countries like Nigeria, Cameroon, Cote d'Ivoire, Colombia or Bangladesh, ie countries that judges have often found unsafe for the asylum seekers in past judgments. Large parts of Nigeria are considered unsafe even by the European Union Agency for Asylum policy documents. According to a European Directive (Procedure Directive recast), a country can be considered 'safe' if there is no systematic persecution of individuals and effective remedies are in place against persecution or inhuman and degrading treatments.

A few months after the adoption of the new legislation in Italy, some asylum seekers were detained according to the new provisions and brought in front of the judges in the Court of Catania for the validation of the detention. The judges in Catania adopted parallel and subsequent decisions in different cases and decided not to validate the detention, deciding that the new legislation goes against the European Directive and the general fundamental values enshrined in the constitution and the Charter of Fundamental Rights of the EU about deprivation of liberty. Some members of political parties of the ruling political majority presented it as a situation in which legislation adopted by the parliament was blocked by the judges. This was followed by harsh attacks on the person of the first judge who adopted a negative decision. The judge was attacked in the media for what her son did at the university, for a Facebook post of her husband, and for how she rode a motorbike. But this was not even the most worrying part. A video was circulated of this judge five years before, in 2018, at a time when she was not dealing with migration law. The video shows the judge taking part in a meeting of citizens at the Catania harbour, which was organised in the summer of 2018, by Catholic organisations among others, to protest against the holding of migrants for many days on a boat named *Diciotti*, moored in the harbour of Catania. A decision adopted by the Ministry of Interior prevented the migrants from disembarking although they were exhausted and had been kept on the boat for 14 consecutive days, after having crossed the Mediterranean in awful conditions. Afterward, the holding of migrants gave rise to a criminal investigation against the Minister of Interior.

What is unclear is why the judge, who attended the meeting together with thousands and thousands of citizens five years before, was recorded on video, who was the author of the video, why this video was kept for such a long time, and how it was found and disseminated. After this video was circulated, politicians and politically-oriented media started to question the impartiality of the judge in rejecting the validation of the detention in the 2023 case. A unanimous statement was adopted by the *Associazione Nazionale Magistrati* to protect the independence of this judge. However, this created a debate within the judiciary about the judge's behaviour. In this way, political tension finds its way into the courts, into the judiciary, and into the associations of judges, but not in the way it should. Criticism of the content of the decision would be legitimate; the personal attack on the judge is instead an attack on judicial independence. As for the decision, the government made an appeal to the Court of Cassation and the procedure was suspended, and the Court sent a preliminary reference to the CJEU. After the preliminary reference was sent, the government even withdrew its appeal to the Court of Cassation.

Ramona Coman: This example and the internal discussions within the judiciary pertain to some extent to the ethos of the profession, and to the question of what judges should or should not do.

Luca Perilli: Among the new generations of judges, there is less discussion than before about the role of the judge and professional ethics. In the last 15 years, I have seen a tendency, supported by changes in the legislation, to promote a sort of hierarchy in the judiciary, something that we never had before. In our system, we have always experienced a horizontal share of judicial power within the judiciary; supreme court judges, appellate court judges, chief justices, and first instance judges do not have a position in a hierarchy, but they simply play different and equally valuable judicial roles; they also earn the same salary, depending on how long they have been in service. In the new legislation on the judiciary, I now see an attempt to introduce a hierarchy between judges. The risk here is the bureaucratisation of the judiciary, that lower-rank judges will do more what is expected from them. This also leads to ever less participation of young judges in the activities of the judicial associations, and this is problematic for the future of the judiciary.

Ramona Coman: Would this mean that there is a danger here of creating a system in which there is more passivity?

Luca Perilli: Yes, those are the right words: risk of passivity. We see this passivity, especially in the young generations. This might be also because we have not managed our independence very well. In 2020, a big scandal occurred when some members of the Judicial Council gathered in a hotel in Rome together with a politician who was under investigation by the Rome prosecution office. They gathered to discuss and negotiate, outside the formal institutional context, the appointment of the next chief prosecutor of the Rome prosecution office, which is one of the most important positions in the Italian judiciary. The conversation was intercepted, and a criminal investigation started. The members of the Council resigned from their positions and, several years later, received heavy disciplinary sanctions. One of them, Luca Palamara, was dismissed from the judiciary. This case brought a lot of shame on the judiciary vis-à-vis general citizens. But it also generated distrust in the young generations of judges vis-à-vis the Judicial Council which they considered to be under the control of invisible powers existing within the same judiciary (*le correnti*). This was a hard blow to the internal independence of the judiciary. On the other hand, on a positive note we have to consider the fact that the same Italian judiciary was able to counteract the situation in question. Prosecutors started the investigations against their colleagues and the participants in the meeting were sanctioned by the same Judicial Council, which is composed mostly of judges and prosecutors. This might be a sign of the vitality of judicial independence.

Ramona Coman: It seems to me that many other issues are under debate within the judiciary. Do you discuss the dramatic deterioration of the rule of law in EU and non-EU Member States, for example? There have been some manifestations of solidarity on this issue – what was the position of Italian judges?

Luca Perilli: After the arrest of almost three thousand judges in Turkey in July 2016, the Italian National Association of Judges organised protests in Milan and Rome, sent letters of solidarity, and collected funds to support the families of judges who had been detained. There was also an important reaction by the International Associations of Judges. The associations of judges at the European and international levels can be a shelter for national judges who are under attack, and Turkey is a clear example of this. In 2016, the European Association of Judges, *Magistrats Européens pour la Démocratie et les Libertés*, the Association of European Administrative Judges, and the association *Rechters voor Rechters* created the 'platform of an Independent Judiciary in Turkey' with the aim of protecting judges hit by the crackdown. This platform has been very active in issuing statements, sending letters to European institutions, preparing reports, and collecting funds. This intervention has been very important for keeping the attention of the European institutions and international organisations on the collapse of the rule of law in Turkey, but it is also very important for the judges who are under attack, are in detention, or are refugees to know that their international colleagues support them.

In January 2020, judges from 20 European countries, including representatives of national and European associations of judges, gathered in Warsaw on a silent march to protest repressive measures imposed on Polish judges. The Polish Association of Judges,

Iustitia, which unites almost 20 per cent of Polish judges from courts of different levels, resisted attacks against the independence of the Polish judiciary. This was also thanks to the support of international associations of judges. The situation is different in Hungary, where judges' associations are very weak and the protection of the rule of law is left to brave individual judges, as illustrated by the case of András Baka (chapter 14), previous President of the Supreme Court, who was dismissed three years before the end of his mandate for criticising the government. Afterward, the ECtHR in Strasbourg held that Hungary had violated the freedom of expression of Baka to speak publicly about judicial reforms.

Ramona Coman: What does it mean to be a judge today?

Luca Perilli: Being a judge today is a very difficult and challenging task. It requires high professional and ethical skills. It is not sufficient to simply have knowledge of the national law, even if this is a precondition to becoming a judge and is the main focus of national competition to access the judiciary in Italy. The judge must also have consistent knowledge of the European Union law that governs cases that falls into its scope of application, and the scope of application of EU Law is becoming broader and broader. Further, the application of EU Law often triggers the Charter of Fundamental Rights of the European Union. Moreover, the judge must be aware of the case law of the CJEU and the European Court of Human Rights, when the protection of people's human rights is at stake. The Charter and the Convention might interact with the provisions of a national Constitution. Therefore, judges nowadays, especially in the fields I mentioned – family law, bioethics, international protection – must not only investigate the facts of the case but also identify the rule applicable to those facts, which might emerge from the interaction of national and supranational sources of law. This operation often implies the interpretation of national law consistently with the national constitution or supranational sources of law. Sometimes it even implies the disapplication of the national law in cases where non-compliance with EU law has a direct effect.

The disapplication of the national law or its interpretation in line with supranational principles might not meet the expectations of the political majority and it might lead to political pressure or even attacks on the judiciary, as in the cases at the Court of Catania mentioned above. To perform her/his work the judge needs therefore broad legal knowledge and clear awareness of her/his role, but also a strong independence from political power. For example, in Hungary, to prevent judges from applying EU law or sending preliminary references to the CJEU, the concept of national constitutional identity has emerged in the decisions of the Constitutional Court. Sending a preliminary reference to the CJEU could potentially lead to the initiation of a disciplinary procedure in Hungary. In Italy too, members of the government have made statements in public contexts saying that judges should first pay respect to the Italian Constitution and only apply EU law as a secondary approach.

Furthermore, the task of the judge is very difficult because to be fully professional, judges must also develop soft skills, the capacity to communicate with the parties, the ability to identify and prevent bias, and to manage time. Improving these skills takes training and time. However, judges struggle with scarcity of resources and lack of time, and with the internal and external pressure to reach high targets of quantitative performance (in terms of the number of cases processed). This situation might induce judges to take a bureaucratic approach to the work, with the main aim of 'producing' decisions instead of devoting enough time to each situation.

This is why the associations of judges are so important for protecting judges' independence, especially in times of crisis. When a judge faces a disciplinary proceeding because she/he raises a preliminary reference to the CJEU, the external support from the association of judges can capture the attention of public opinion and of the European institutions. The associations of judges can also play an important role in warning the public that pressure for performance and scarcity of resources are at the detriment of the judicial service and the protection of citizens' rights. However, we must recognise that also in my country, there is a significant decrease in participation in the activities of the judicial associations amongst younger generations. This might be a sign of disinterest or distrust which is not very promising for the important role the judicial associations must play.

Ramona Coman: Given this very fast-changing context in which rights and values are contested from the top and from below, how do you see the role of the EU, for example in restoring the rule of law in countries where it has been dismantled?

Luca Perilli: The EU's role is essential. There is good primary legislation in place in the EU, not only the TEU but also the Charter of Fundamental Rights, and secondary legislation. This legislation generally reflects the fundamental EU values of democracy and the protection of human rights. A legal framework at the European level that cannot be changed unilaterally or by a minority of Member States is a shield for the rights of individuals, also in times of change or deterioration of the rule of law.

However, at the same time, the EU does not always seem fully committed to those values. I could mention here again the example of Turkey and the 2016 EU-Turkey deal to stop immigration from reaching Europe through Turkey. From an international legal point of view, it is not even clear whether the EU is formally party to the deal, or only Member States are. However, politically, it is clear that the EU reached an agreement on a very sensitive issue, the fundamental rights of asylum seekers, with a country in which, at that time, the rule of law was clearly in ruins and the existence of an effective remedy for the protection of the migrants' rights was very questionable. A few months later, the negotiations for the accession of Turkey to the EU were suspended but the deal on immigration was not. Another example of a possible clash between EU law and the EU Charter of Fundamental Rights and a national constitution is the EU Pact on Asylum and Migration mentioned above.

Internally, in the European Union, since January 2021 there is potential reinforcement of the protection of the rule of law in Member States through the general regime of conditionality for the protection of the EU budget, which might lead to effective financial measures against the countries that do not abide by the rule of law. However, critical situations will be inevitably brought before national judges, especially in these times when respect for the rule of law is not self-evident in many EU countries. In 2018, the CJEU, in a preliminary reference procedure initiated by the *Associação Sindical dos Juízes Portugueses* (Association of Portuguese Judges), stated for the first time that national judges are responsible for the protection of the rule of law at the EU level. This principle has been reaffirmed by the Court in cases regarding the deterioration of the rule of law in Poland. The burden of safeguarding the rule of law at the EU level is therefore placed on the shoulders of the national judge, possibly in cooperation with the CJEU or the national constitutional court. This challenging task requires that judges are able to rely on solid external and internal independence and that they have a clear awareness of their irreplaceable role.

13

We can Best Uphold Democracy and Defend the Rule of Law by Listening to Citizens

JAVIER HERNÁNDEZ GARCÍA[1]

Giulia La Torre: Could you briefly introduce yourself and tell me about your motivation for becoming a judge?

Javier Hernández García: Since the time I started law school, I have always liked the law as a system. During my university years, I also discovered the decisive role that judges play in making the legal system work. The judicial function is enormously demanding, intellectually nourishing, and very socially engaged. It was very stimulating. I liked legal theory, and I realised that through the judicial process there is a way to build the legal system and recreate the legal norm that benefits society. It is also true that, 37 years ago, a law graduate from a middle-class family did not have many professional opportunities beyond a relatively limited range of choices. I think there are far more possibilities today. At that time there were not many career options available, but the judicial function seemed to me to offer something like an existential choice. So by the time I received my law degree, I had no doubts.

Giulia La Torre: In 1986, Spain became a full member of the European Economic Community (EEC). You began your judicial career in 1989, another historic year. The period from the late 1980s up to the mid-1990s was an age of optimism, characterised by people's faith in the advancement of liberal democracy and the consolidation of rule-of-law standards. How did you experience the period as a new judge?

Javier Hernández García: You are right in saying it was an optimistic time. The fall of the Berlin Wall was an important event. In that same year, in 1989, the industrial crisis that had plagued Spain since the 1970s began to ease and all the social conflict that had emerged in the early 1980s was somehow overcome. Nobody was looking back, the Franco regime was far behind us. By 1989, the Spanish Constitution had been in force

[1] Interview conducted in Spanish on 21 January 2025 and validated for publication on 10 February 2025.

for more than 10 years and we truly had a demiurgic Constitutional Court, a deeply respected Constitutional Court that allowed Spanish judges to approach legal reasoning in a different way. There was a change in the modes of argumentation through which Spanish judges reached their decisions. Those who joined the judicial ranks during those years – in 1987, 1988, 1989, or 1990 – approached the justification of judicial decisions differently to those judges who had been appointed under Franco. There was a certain enthusiasm for the role of reasoning in judicial decision-making, and I remember that the shift towards new forms of argumentation brought very important new ideas.

Giulia La Torre: How did you first come into contact with EU law and what was your first understanding of how EU law is practiced?

Javier Hernández García: During my first years as a judge, I did not perceive the European Economic Community as a normative actor. It is true that, during those years, Spain passed some laws in which the relevance of the EEC was evident. I was a civil judge at that time, and I remember working with the Spanish General Consumer Protection Law on some cases. The General Consumer Protection Law brought about profound change in how the contract and burden of proof regarding certain risk activities were conceived in Spain. And this law draws clear inspiration from Community Law. Indeed, around exactly the same time as I entered the judicial profession, Spanish judges began to have a certain familiarity with legal concepts that until then had been completely alien, such as decision or even directive. However, I was unaware of the true scope of the normative role of the EEC. I had a purely descriptive knowledge of what the EEC was and, perhaps, a superficial knowledge of European legal sources. I gradually became aware that the EEC was an important normative actor which could directly influence my work. But it was a process. And I began experiencing this process of expanding awareness while I was a judge, not in law school.

Giulia La Torre: Based on your own experience, do you think that EU law, together with the case law of the CJEU, has a real and appreciable impact on how the judicial function is exerted in Spain?

Javier Hernández García: I think so. The day-to-day reality of my colleagues in the Social and Civil divisions of the Supreme Court is very much marked by the decisions of the CJEU. For instance, the entire Spanish structure of real estate law has been greatly affected by the CJEU's case law. For a while, the field of criminal law and procedure remained sheltered from EU intervention. But that changed with the Tampere and Stockholm programmes. Right now, a good chunk of the Spanish criminal process is Europeanised. And so, whenever I face a new problem, I always check to see whether or not there has been a response from the CJEU, whether or not there is a connection with EU law, or whether or not EU directives tell us how Spanish law should be implemented. I often find myself quoting CJEU case law in the decisions that I take. One time I was engaged in deliberation with the 15 members of the Criminal Division of the Supreme Court and the CJEU suddenly delivered a ruling on the issue of the scope of the right to be informed of the accusation. Well, on that occasion, I remember saying: 'I believe we cannot continue deliberating until we all study the ruling of the CJEU, for it may well modify the course of deliberation'. That is the extent to which some judgments of the CJEU can be decisive. Moreover, the CJEU is gradually becoming more important than the European Court of Human Rights. We are beginning to see a battle of titans there, and I believe that the decisions of the CJEU are gaining ever more weight – this notwithstanding the fact that the minimum standard of protection is set by the ECtHR. CJEU case law is also easier to apply than that of the ECtHR.

Giulia La Torre: And how do Spanish judges generally approach the EU legal system? Do they engage with the sources of EU law directly, or do they rather see EU law through the looking glass of national law?

Javier Hernández García: I believe that a majority of Spanish judges stay informed about developments in both EU law and CJEU case law, though I recognise that there are different levels of involvement. For me, at least, EU law is a constant companion. When I'm faced with a transposition law, for instance, I always try to refer to the recitals of the EU directive. Why? Well, I do so in order to interpret the normative concepts that have been employed in the national law – in other words, to provide these concepts with a genuine meaning. Nevertheless, I have to say that EU law is weighed down by its size. There is rather a hyper-production of law in the EU; that is, an enormously productive regulatory activity at EU level. The speed and breadth of normative output sometimes undermines the principle of *iura novit curia*. All the more so in today's fragmented legal landscape, where there is such a massive plurality of legal sources. In my field of practice, criminal law, this is less the case. But my colleagues in the Administrative and Social Divisions of the Supreme Court have to deal with many different bodies of law: parliamentary law, treaty law, EU law, CJEU case law etc. Identifying which law is applicable to a specific case is far from easy.

Giulia La Torre: I suppose that the abundance of laws and the plurality of legal sources not only make it more difficult to determine which law is applicable, but they also increase the likelihood of norm conflict. How do Spanish judges generally deal with conflict between national law and EU law?

Javier Hernández García: In situations like that, what usually happens is that we judges will use the preliminary ruling procedure to ask the CJEU for clarification on what to do. Of course, sometimes the CJEU will already have ruled on a similar issue, and so, in accordance with the *acte claire* doctrine, there is no need for clarification in the first place. In that case, if the conflict of norms persists, we are, indeed, obliged to disapply the rule of national law. As far as I know, there have been no instances of disapplication within my jurisdiction. But it may yet happen. Let me give an example. The Spanish Code of Criminal Procedure sets time limits for the completion of criminal investigations. And so, anything obtained outside these time limits cannot be considered as evidence admissible before the Spanish courts. The CJEU has ruled that these time limits do not apply to investigations of criminal offences affecting the financial interests of the European Union. Why? Because the CJEU considers that the rules governing the temporal limitation of criminal investigations are not rooted in axiological premises. Thus, if we were faced with an issue of admissibility of evidence due to the expiry of the investigation period, provided that the crime being investigated affects the financial interests of the European Union, I believe that we judges would have an obligation to disapply the relevant national rules on procedural time limits.

Before doing so, we would most probably ask for a preliminary ruling from the CJEU – just to be absolutely sure. We, continental judges, feel a deep connection to the law. To set aside a valid rule of law is something that we are all terribly afraid of. We are not prepared to disregard the existing law. And so, in some sense, the primacy doctrine does pose a challenge for national judges.

Giulia La Torre: Some jurists believe that the doctrine of primacy alters the hierarchical structure of the legal systems of the various Member States and, ultimately, calls into question the supremacy of national constitutions. In your view, can the supremacy of the constitution be made compatible with the primacy of EU law?

Javier Hernández García: I believe that the CJEU should exercise some measure of self-restraint when applying the doctrine of primacy. The primacy of EU law cannot be enforced at the cost of respect for the Member States' national constitutional identity. It is a difficult balance to strike. But I think that the primacy of EU law can only be secured through the supremacy of the national Constitutions. In this connection, the *Taricco* case proves interesting. In the *Taricco I* case,[2] the CJEU paid no mind to the national constitutional identity clause in Article 4(2) of the Treaty on the EU. However, the preliminary ruling of the Italian Constitutional Court in the *Taricco II* case[3] made it clear to the CJEU that respect for the Italian constitutional identity was what was at stake. On this occasion the Italian Constitutional Court said: 'You should tread carefully when answering questions about issues that strike at the heart of the way in which we conceive our rights-based political system'. Beyond this tension, we should also think hard about the question: 'Primacy in relation to what areas of competence?' The Spanish Constitution allows for exclusive competences to be conferred upon the EU. If we do not guarantee the primacy of EU law in those areas in which the EU enjoys exclusive competence, then we are indeed going against what the Constitution plainly permits. However, the matter is less clear-cut in areas of shared competence between the EU and the Member States. And, with regard to these areas of competence, the CJEU has to reflect more on the subsidiarity and proportionality of EU action. It is here, in the areas of shared competence, that I believe the real problem lies, and where the friction is greatest.

Giulia La Torre: The *Taricco* case, which you mentioned, speaks to a reluctance on the part of the Italian Constitutional Court to recognise the absolute primacy of EU law over the Italian Constitution. In this regard, it is interesting to note that many high courts across the EU have, at some point or another, shown a similar disinclination to give blanket acceptance to the doctrine of primacy. Indeed, some Member States' Constitutional Courts, such as the German *Bundesverfassungsgericht*, have gone so far as to develop a list of exceptions to the primacy of EU law. How do you explain the persistent disagreement about the primacy of EU law between the CJEU, on the one hand, and the national Constitutional Courts, on the other?

Javier Hernández García: The authority and integrity of national constitutional systems is increasingly under strain, and so it must be protected. There is a delicate balance

[2] Case C-105/14 *Taricco and Others* ECLI:EU:C:2015:555, [2016] 1 CMLR 21.
[3] Case C-42/17 *M.A.S. and M.B.* ECLI:EU:C:2017:936, [2018] 2 CMLR 15.

between the need to protect national constitutional systems and the duty to respect the primacy of EU law, and inevitably there will be conflicts. There is a primacy-denying defence of the supremacy of the national constitution, and, at times, there is also a supremacy-denying defence of the primacy of EU law. But one does not come at the expense of the other. Constitutional supremacy is an essential feature of the EU legal system itself. The preservation of national constitutional systems is the best guarantee of the continued development of the EU legal system.

Giulia La Torre: Some years ago, the Polish Constitutional Tribunal issued its famous judgment in the case *K3/21*.[4] This judgment is read as a broad rejection of the doctrine of primacy and deplored as an assault on the basic foundations of the EU legal system. Some believe that the judgment should be situated within the larger context of the rising tensions that I mentioned between the CJEU and national constitutional courts. Others argue that the content of the judgment goes well beyond the usual reservations expressed by national constitutional courts and is thus related to the particular circumstances of the so-called 'rule-of-law crisis' in Poland. What is your opinion on this matter?

Javier Hernández García: I am not familiar with the details of the Polish judgment, but it seems to me that it is part of what we might call a 'reactive' constitutional jurisprudence. And so I think it is necessary to take into account the national political climate in which the judgment is made. The Polish Constitutional Tribunal is a reflection of an increasingly polarised society, and, clearly, there are some in that society who perceive their national identity to be under attack. But national identity is understood here in the negative sense of the term, in the sense of preserving certain formulas that I believe did objectively compromise the principle of the rule of law.

Giulia La Torre: Moving on to consider the situation in Spain, although the Spanish Constitutional Court has not been inclined to question the case law of the CJEU, it has also expressed some qualms about the doctrine of primacy. A good illustration is the *Melloni* case,[5] the first time when the Spanish Constitutional Court requested a preliminary ruling from the CJEU. Following the response of the CJEU in this case, the Spanish Constitutional Court issued a judgment in which it warned against unconditional acceptance of the doctrine of primacy. In its judgment, the Spanish Constitutional Court referred to 'the material limits of the competences conferred on the European Union' and 'the preservation of the sovereignty of the Spanish people'. What is your assessment of the judicial dialogue between the CJEU and the Spanish Constitutional Court in the context of the *Melloni* case?

Javier Hernández García: In the *Melloni* case, the CJEU dismantles the non-regression clause in Article 53 of the Charter of Fundamental Rights of the European Union. The CJEU essentially told the Spanish Constitutional Court: 'if you consider that your national level of protection of fundamental rights is more important and, therefore, refuse to apply the Framework Decision on the European Arrest Warrant, you will compromise the effectiveness of EU law'. Thus, when having to choose between

[4] Judgment of 7 October 2021, Polish Constitutional Tribunal, No K 3/21.
[5] Case C-399/11 *Stefano Melloni v Ministerio Fiscal* ECLI:EU:C:2013:107, [2013] 3 WLR 717.

protecting the right of the accused to be present at their own trial and securing the effectiveness of EU law, the latter must prevail. In the face of this pronouncement, the Spanish Constitutional Court said: 'although we maintain that the right to be present at trial is an absolute right at the domestic level, at the level of the European Union we defer to the CJEU's interpretation of the Framework Decision on the European Arrest Warrant'. This formulation does not seem particularly convincing to me. But it is plain that the CJEU does not regard the issue in the *Melloni* case as an axiological problem. As the CJEU sees it, the laws of the Member States of the European Union are sufficiently homogenous with respect to the grounds of trial *in absentia*, and it is precisely this homogenisation that allows the European Arrest Warrant mechanism to operate properly. Nevertheless, the non-regression clause is a normative clause that appears in the Charter of Fundamental Rights of the European Union, and this clause makes it clear that fundamental rights must not be interpreted in a way that lowers the level of protection provided by the legal systems of the Member States. So, I found the preliminary ruling in the *Melloni* case quite shocking. The CJEU is really making a purely functional bet. Their argument is: 'I do not care about your reasons, do not block the mechanism and do not alter the rules of the game'.

Giulia La Torre: The argument of effectiveness does indeed play an important role in the legal reasoning of the CJEU. It emerges in the case law as a general principle of EU law, ie the principle of the effectiveness of EU law. This principle is arguably rooted in the EU values of equality and justice. Nonetheless, some jurists believe that these values are yet to be sufficiently articulated by the CJEU. Thus, the axiological dimension of the principle of effectiveness of EU law is still not well understood. This point relates to a common critique of the judgments of the CJEU, which is that they do not always contain detailed, value-based arguments. Do you agree? What is your view of the decision-making practice of the CJEU?

Javier Hernández García: I think there are two questions here. The first question is 'On what basis does the CJEU carry out the practice of argumentation?' In the preliminary ruling procedure, the CJEU relies on the law and facts provided by the national judge. What has sometimes been criticised about the CJEU's judgments is that they confer something akin to a presumption of infallibility onto the national judge's representation of the law and the facts. My colleagues in the Civil Division of the Supreme Court often complain that ordinary judges do not provide an adequate description of their respective national legal framework when referring questions for a preliminary ruling. That is to say, referring judges do not always give a faithful account of the national legal norms, case law, or administrative practices applicable to the case in the main proceedings. And so, what the CJEU does is collect information from the national judge and, on this scanty basis, build a judgment.

The second question is 'How does the CJEU argue?'. The discourse of the CJEU is, for the most part, sober in tone. The CJEU usually delivers short judgments with very synthetic formulas reminiscent of the decision-making style of the French *Conseil constitutionnel*. But why? This is because the CJEU judges are not allowed to issue dissenting opinions. In other words, the expression of judicial dissent is prohibited. This prohibition makes judgments more operative, because, more often than not, the final elements of the decision will have a clear-cut rationale. However, it is true that sometimes you are left wanting for more. The reasons for the decision may be clear, but other, perhaps more significant reasons are missing. This boils down to a circumspect attitude, and this attitude is explained by the absence of dissenting opinions. At the CJEU, dissent must be dealt with internally. Many CJEU judgments are, therefore, lowest common denominator agreements, and, in this sense, they can be unsatisfactory.

Giulia La Torre: The preliminary ruling procedure is doubtless a cornerstone of the EU legal system. Given what you know about the interaction between national judges and the CJEU, what do you think are the consequences of the preliminary ruling procedure at the domestic level?

Javier Hernández García: In Spain, every judge can ask the CJEU for a preliminary ruling. Thus, we have what might be called a polycentric model. In my view, this model encourages a trivial and somewhat manipulative use of the preliminary ruling procedure. The CJEU has also not helped matters. For many years, it has taken a deferential approach to accounts by national judges. Moreover, it has a history both of reconstructing poorly formulated questions and admitting references that have little connection with EU law. All of this has led to reforms of how the justice system is organised in Spain, with the consequence that enormously important decisions are no longer taken by a court endowed with an exceptional *auctoritas*. It is interesting to note in this regard that many preliminary rulings are issued by chambers of three or five judges, and very often without the participation of the Advocate General. Regardless, it is clear that the preliminary ruling procedure is cracking under the weight of its own success. The number of preliminary references has been steadily growing for years. And at some point, this trend will force a change of model in Spain, the introduction of a filtering mechanism at the CJEU, and a rethinking of the preliminary ruling procedure more generally.

Giulia La Torre: In light of all that you have said, is there, do you think, a problem when it comes to guaranteeing legal certainty within the European Union?

Javier Hernández García: On paper, the normative model of the EU is well-articulated, rigorous, and appealing. The EU legislature creates law on the basis of principles and by means of regulations, decisions, and directives, while the Member States have the task of implementing EU law and, when necessary, of transforming EU legislation into clear, accessible, and foreseeable norms. If a national judge has doubts about the interpretation of a regulation or the transposition of a directive, they can refer questions to the CJEU for a preliminary ruling. In theory, this is an ideal model that safeguards the principle of legal certainty. In practice, the virtues of this model sometimes get lost under an avalanche of laws. There is an undeniable tendency towards the administrativisation of EU legislative activity, and an astonishing number of micro-regulations. Indeed, you can find EU regulations on the most unusual aspects of any activity whatsoever. Thus, national judges are confronted with numerous legal rules, many of which may be difficult to interpret or may be subject to uncertain conditions of applicability. Add to this the challenge of multilingualism, and it is clear that national judges find it difficult to know and apply the law in the EU. So, there is a problem of legal certainty because there is a problem of knowing which law is applicable.

Giulia La Torre: The EU institutions have expressed concerns about the rule of law in Spain. More specifically, the European Commission has denounced the politicisation of the system for appointing members of the Spanish Council for the Judiciary, which is the judicial self-governance body in Spain. Do you agree? If so, why do you believe the process for selecting the members of the Spanish Council for the Judiciary has become politicised?

Javier Hernández García: The Spanish Council for the Judiciary is inspired by the Italian *Consiglio Superiore della Magistratura*. When the Spanish Constitution was being framed, its creators faced the challenge of reorganising the judicial branch in Spain, and so they wanted a model of judicial governance that would help shield the judicial selection process from undue political influence. Naturally, they looked to the Italian *Consiglio Superiore della Magistratura*, which embodies the ideal of guaranteeing the autonomy of the judiciary from the executive branch. According to the Spanish Constitution, the Council for the Judiciary should consist of the President of the Spanish Supreme Court and 20 individuals, 12 of whom are to be selected from among judges. Furthermore, in a Law of 1980, the Spanish legislator stipulated that these 12 members of the Council for the Judiciary were to be elected by judges themselves. Strictly speaking, this is what the Constitution intended. However, we have to place ourselves in the political context of the time. The Spanish Constitution was adopted by referendum on 6 December 1978 and came into force on 29 December of the same year. Franco had died on 20 November 1975. What was the Spanish judiciary like in the late 1970s and early 1980s? Politically, it was deeply conservative, for the vast majority of judges had been appointed under the Franco regime. There was no post-transition purge of Spanish judges. So at that time entrusting judges with the power to appoint members to the body of judicial governance meant strengthening the conservative character of the judiciary. In the face of this, Spanish legislators ask themselves: 'What can we do to make the judiciary more pluralistic?' Thus, in 1985 the Spanish legislator decided to initiate a reform by which the Spanish Parliament would be vested with the competence to elect all 20 members of the Council for the Judiciary. In 1986, this reform was ruled constitutional by the Spanish Constitutional Court. Nevertheless, the Spanish Constitutional Court warned that transferring this competence to the Spanish Parliament involved the risk of politicising the system of judicial self-management. In the view of the Constitutional Court, this risk could only be offset if, first, the election of all the members of the Council for the Judiciary is made subject to a qualified majority vote in Parliament and, secondly, political parties use the power to elect the members responsibly and judiciously. So the Constitutional Court established some guidelines for an acceptable, indeed optimal, model of judicial governance. However, as we have seen over the last few years, what ends up happening is that Spanish political parties use the majority rule to block the renewal of the Council for the Judiciary. And so, the system for appointing members of the Council for the Judiciary is sometimes perceived as a tool in political bargaining.

Giulia La Torre: Indeed, Spain's main political parties were unable to reach an agreement on the renewal of the Spanish Council for the Judiciary for over five years. It was only a few months ago, in June 2024, when Spanish politicians decided to set their differences aside and strike a deal for the renewal of the Spanish Council for the Judiciary. This was largely possible thanks to Didier Reynders, the then European Commissioner for Justice, who played an important mediating role in the process. Do you believe that this five-year blockade, described by some as a full-blown 'institutional crisis', is a symptom of a deeper set of problems of political interference in the Spanish judicial system?

Javier Hernández García: The Parliament elects the members of the Council for the Judiciary, which, in turn, makes appointments for top judicial positions. However, I do not believe that political parties have a direct influence on who is or is not appointed by the Council for the Judiciary. The Council for the Judiciary is not political in its functioning. Doubtless it should be more transparent when making appointment decisions. But we should bear in mind that these decisions are subject to the scrutiny of the Spanish Supreme Court. In fact, the Spanish Supreme Court has annulled a significant number of appointment decisions over the last few years, and it has done so for two main reasons: first, because the Council for the Judiciary did not provide sufficient justification, and secondly because the non-appointees' professional achievements greatly exceeded those of appointees. Thus, there are institutional checks and balances designed to prevent a situation developing like the one in Poland. Of course it is true that political parties decide on the composition of the Council for the Judiciary. This is undeniable. And, naturally, there might be an ideological component to the decisions of the Council for the Judiciary. But what model of judicial governance does away with all ideological elements? All in all, I would say that the Council for the Judiciary fails to adequately perform its most sensitive function, which is precisely the appointment of top posts in the judiciary. We will probably have to rethink our model of judicial governance, and we will most definitely have to put the power to elect members to the Council for the Judiciary back in the hands of Spanish judges. This will make the influence of political parties far less evident.

Giulia La Torre: So, would you say that judicial independence in Spain is adequately protected?

Javier Hernández García: I sincerely believe that judges in Spain enjoy high levels of external independence, comparable to those of any advanced democracy. When performing my tasks as a judge, I have never felt constrained by a power external to the judicial branch. And I believe that the levels of internal independence are also quite high. The Council for the Judiciary does not have a jurisdictional function, meaning it cannot review what ordinary courts decide. It is true that the Council for the Judiciary has disciplinary powers. However, these powers do not extend to the content of judicial decisions. Of course, there may be some judges who, in attempting to secure a position at one of the higher courts, give up their internal independence to please the members of the Council for the Judiciary. But this has more to do with the constitutional commitment of each and every judge. My belief is that the constitutionally guaranteed levels of both internal and external independence are optimal, although there may be judges who choose not to optimise them. In Spain, there is no political element to the judicial selection process although there is a degree of politicisation of the system by which members of the Council for the Judiciary are appointed.

Giulia La Torre: If, as you say, there is no a priori reason to suspect that Spanish judges are partisan, what do you think of the recent proliferation of criminal cases against politicians in Spain? Does this show the judicialisation of politics or is it more a sign of the politicisation of justice?

Javier Hernández García: What is clear is that there is today a crisis of representative democracy. When parliaments become polarised, when there is no consensus and, therefore, no real possibility of enacting reform, the underlying source of conflict remains and, more often than not, ends up coming before a judge. And when this happens, there is need for an answer that goes beyond black letter law. Judges are therefore sometimes forced to come up with creative solutions. But back to your question about the judicialisation of politics: I would say no. If there are politicians who have allegedly committed crimes, then both the principle of equality and the fight against corruption and abuses of power make it absolutely legitimate for politicians to be subjected to criminal proceedings. As for the politicisation of justice? I rather think so, yes. When politicians are caught in a compromising position, a certain number of protection mechanisms are activated. And what is the most effective mechanism which politicians can deploy to protect themselves or get immunity from liability? It's the politicisation of justice. They try to delegitimise the courts. They try to portray judicial decisions as politically motivated and judges as actors at the service of political interests. The judicialisation of politics and the politicisation of justice are, therefore, two sides of the same coin. First, it is constitutionally unquestionable that a politician suspected of a crime should be investigated and punished if appropriate. Secondly, politicians, insofar as they use political messaging to delegitimise the judicial system, promote the politicisation of justice as a way to stave off scrutiny. In such scenarios, there may well be instances of judicial misconduct. However, that is a different matter. If a judge misbehaves, there is a path to correction. There is the possibility of appealing to higher courts. In Spain, I believe, the criminal prosecution of politicians responds to adequate objectives. If there is a plausible *notitia criminis*, then a criminal investigation must be carried out. Doing otherwise would signal a disregard for the rule of law and the equal administration of justice.

Giulia La Torre: Let us stay on the topic of the rule of law. Over the past decade, there have been instances in Poland or Romania where judges have openly criticised and even protested the erosion of rule-of-law standards. What are your thoughts on these forms of expression?

Javier Hernández García: This question captures a basic constitutional dilemma: how can judges reconcile their responsibility to administer the law impartially with their right to express themselves in the public arena? How do we balance the judicial duty of impartiality with the freedom of expression of judges? The European Court of Human Rights has developed a substantial body of case law on this issue. In a nutshell, the ECtHR considers that judges have the right to express their opinions on matters relating to the proper administration of justice, including the rule of law, separation of powers, and judicial independence. Indeed, I myself would say that it is not so much a right as an institutional duty, that is, a duty of institutional cooperation. Judges contribute to the health of the Constitutional State. Their opinions matter, and so their freedom of expression must be protected.

The judgment of the ECtHR in the *Baka v. Hungary* case[6] is, to my mind, illustrative of what I have just told you. Baka was a judge whose mandate as President of the Hungarian Supreme Court was prematurely terminated in 2012. Following the termination, Judge Baka lodged an application with the ECtHR. He alleged that his dismissal was not the consequence of an organisational restructuring of the judiciary, as the Hungarian government contended. Rather, Judge Baka claimed, his mandate had been terminated as a result of views that he had expressed publicly, in his capacity as President of the Supreme Court, concerning the Hungarian government's policies of judicial reform. The ECtHR upheld Judge Baka's claim on the grounds that his right to freedom of expression had been violated. That is to say, the ECtHR found that, though the right to freedom of expression is not absolute and may be subject to limitations, Judge Baka was within his rights to express his opinion on legislative reforms affecting the judiciary. The rationale behind this is the following: Judge Baka's statements called for a high degree of protection for his freedom of expression insofar as they concerned questions that are enormously important for the preservation of a democratic State governed by the rule of law.

Giulia La Torre: How do you regard other forms of mobilisation such as strikes and demonstrations, then? Is it right to say that judges can and should take part in such actions when they oppose judicial reforms? And do you think it is conceivable for Spanish judges to go on strike or organise a demonstration in defence of their independence?

Javier Hernández García: Although the Spanish Constitution recognises the workers' right to strike, the Spanish legislator is yet to regulate the conditions for the exercise of this particular right. Strictly speaking, therefore, Spanish judges face no restrictions on using their constitutional right to strike. Nevertheless, I object to this reading of the Spanish Constitution. A prime minister, a member of parliament, a judge cannot go on strike. Why? Because they all have been entrusted with the exercise of constitutional powers. And just as the Constitution cannot be suspended, so too the exercise of judicial power cannot be suspended. So I have serious doubts that judges can exercise the right to strike in the same manner as any other worker. Regardless, judges in Spain have indeed gone on strike in the past – but never against judicial reforms or public policies. Rather, they have launched strikes to demand wage increases and better employment conditions. So, Spanish judges have not, thus far, threatened strike action for reasons of democratic accountability and the rule of law.

As for the right to hold political demonstrations – well, it is a tricky issue. As you already noted, judges in Poland and Romania have staged demonstrations against government plans for judicial reform, and rightly so. As I see it, judges have an obligation to actively protest legislation that threatens or could threaten judicial independence. Nevertheless, I do not believe that judges have a *carte blanche* to take a proactive stance

[6] *Baka v Hungary*, App no 20261/12 (ECtHR, 23 June 2016).

on any and all political initiatives. Personally, I found it unfortunate that Spanish judges organised demonstrations against the Spanish government's proposed amnesty bill (ie a bill that would grant immunity to all those prosecuted for their involvement in the Catalan secessionist movement). Of course, those who protested argue that with this draft law, the Spanish government was making a mockery of the separation of powers. But I am not convinced by that argument. I think that judges must only consider demonstrating as a last resort. There are, doubtless, some reasons that can justify active forms of protest. I have in mind cases where there is a reform agenda to eliminate existing mechanisms of transparency in the system of judicial appointments, or, indeed, to lower the retirement age of judges, without providing for any kind of transitional regime. However, the demonstration against the draft amnesty bill is taking place against a different backdrop. This is not a good example of how judges can fulfil their duty to preserve democracy and the rule of law. Rather, it is an example of reckless conduct that is likely to compromise the appearance of judicial impartiality.

Giulia La Torre: You mentioned the demonstration against the draft amnesty bill. If Spanish judges had attended this demonstration as private citizens, without wearing their judicial robes or gathering in front of courthouses, do you believe that they would have also compromised – or risked compromising – the appearance of judicial impartiality?

Javier Hernández García: In my view, a judge who joins a demonstration in their capacity as a private individual, without flaunting their status as a member of the judiciary, is merely making use of a right accorded to every other citizen, namely the right to freedom of assembly. Nonetheless, judges must exercise particular caution when engaging in public acts of protest. As a judge, you must not only be impartial; you must also avoid giving the impression that you are not impartial. In this regard, it is important to point out that the ECtHR has distinguished between subjective impartiality and objective impartiality. Per the requirements of subjective impartiality, I cannot sit in judgement on cases involving my partner, my family members, or persons with whom I have either a friendship or an enmity. Why? Because each and every one of these relationships gives rise to the assumption that I am prejudiced for or against one of the parties to the case. But the ECtHR has created another standard of impartiality, one that is not contingent on there being a prior relationship between the judge and the litigants who appear before him. This standard is known as 'objective impartiality'. Under this standard, a third party should not be able to reasonably entertain a doubt that the judge hearing the case is not impartial. Even if the judge has no personal bias against any of the parties to the proceedings, they must avoid behaving in a way that would allow someone standing outside of the proceedings to reasonably believe otherwise. Objective impartiality is not measured in terms of self-perception. Rather, the measure is based on an external observer's perception. Thus, the appearance of impartiality, understood as people's perception of impartiality, is of crucial importance.

Giulia La Torre: So in your view, what are the tools that judges can employ to uphold democracy and defend the rule of law?

Javier Hernández García: The most important thing that we, as judges, can do is to faithfully discharge our duties under the Constitution. I believe that we can best uphold democracy and defend the rule of law by listening to citizens, justifying our rulings well, and enforcing fundamental rights. We help maintain the democratic constitutional order, and therefore we shoulder responsibility for preserving a robust constitutional democracy. We should not forget that the quality of our decisions has a bearing on the overall quality of justice and democracy in our countries. In Spain, moreover, ordinary judges can count on the Spanish Constitutional Court to protect citizens against arbitrary governmental action. Spain has a centralised model of constitutional review of legislation. This means that if a Spanish judge believes that a rule relevant to the case is not in compliance with the Spanish Constitution, they must raise a so-called 'question of unconstitutionality' before the Spanish Constitutional Court. And, of course, another powerful mechanism for the protection of constitutional values is the preliminary ruling procedure.

Giulia La Torre: The instruments ordinarily available to judges, those commonly understood as being part of the judicial function, might, however, turn out to be ineffective for resisting authoritarian efforts to undermine liberal democracy and the rule of law. Do you agree and, if so, can you think of any alternative legitimate instrument?

Javier Hernández García: As judges, we must take care not to be dragged into an authoritarian system. I have always said that if I had to apply the death penalty, I would resign from my position as judge. For me, the death penalty is absolutely immoral. My objection to it is unsurmountable. I would not be able to perform judicial duties in a State that allowed for capital punishment. And so back to the question at hand: what role can judges play in the face of liberal democratic regression? We can apply the law in the light of the Constitution. We can also alert the Constitutional Court to an unconstitutional statute. But what if neither of these options is available because the law is increasingly unjust and the Constitutional Court is tightly controlled by an illiberal government? We will have to leave the judicial bench and take the plunge into politics. I can see no other alternative. We simply cannot go beyond the realm of what is permitted by our role as judges.

PART III

Insights from Central and Eastern European Judges

14

The Judiciary [...] has Power over the Meaning of the Law

ANDRÁS BAKA[1]

Viktor Kazai and Ramona Coman: Could you provide some information about your career and why you decided to enter the judiciary?

András Baka: After graduating from university, I had plenty of job opportunities. Despite being one of the top students in my class, I did not pursue a career in the judiciary or as a lawyer, which was quite popular at the time. Instead, I chose to work at the Legal Institute of the Hungarian Academy of Sciences. Even though it offered the lowest salary in the legal profession, intellectually it was a great job. I was first part of the Comparative Law Department and later the Constitutional and Administrative Law Department of the Institute, focusing on human rights and minority rights. As a member of the Institute, I was involved in drafting various laws, including the initial, 1989 version of the National Minorities Act, which unfortunately was not enacted. Later, I became the Director General of the National School of Public Administration and a professor of constitutional law. After that, I was the head of the school's International Law Department.

In 1991, I was honoured to be appointed to the European Court of Human Rights, which felt like a natural continuation of my career. At the age of 39, I was among the youngest judges on the Court at that time. I was re-elected in 1998, when the Court became permanent, and re-elected again in 2001. After the conclusion of my international career in 2008, I was elected as the President of the Supreme Court of Hungary. My presidency was relatively short-lived due to the political circumstances. When my mandate was prematurely and illegally terminated, I turned to the ECtHR as an applicant,[2] a position I had never imagined myself in. My main goal was to draw international attention to the situation of the judiciary in Hungary at that time.

Before retiring, I was elected to the Administrative Tribunal of the Council of Europe, where I also served as deputy president. I left the Administrative Tribunal after my second term ended in April 2024. So, this summarises my journey thus far.

[1] Interview conducted on 7 May 2024 and validated for publication on 15 December 2024.
[2] *Baka v Hungary*, App No 20261/12 (ECtHR, 23 June 2016).

I rarely grant interviews. Although various agencies, organisations, and media outlets approach me, I have chosen to limit my public appearances. However, this does not mean that I am not actively considering the future. I am deeply engaged in discussions and planning related to the future of the judiciary in Hungary with some colleagues and friends.

Viktor Kazai and Ramona Coman: We have a follow-up question regarding your appointment as a judge at the ECtHR. You mentioned that it was a natural continuation of your career. We are curious how you viewed your role as a judge at the ECtHR compared to your role as a scholar? And when you transitioned to a position in the ordinary judiciary in Hungary after leaving the Strasbourg court, how different did you find that new role?

András Baka: I considered it a natural continuation because of my background in human rights. I was honoured to serve as a visiting scholar at the University of California, Berkeley, Columbia University, and the University of Virginia School of Law, and as a professor at Santa Clara University in California for a semester, where I taught international human rights. I also led the International Law Department focusing on human rights at the School of Public Administration when it became a university-level institution. This gave me the chance to apply my theoretical knowledge in a practical setting.

The ECtHR was highly esteemed and had a traditional structure. Initially, from April 1991 until 1 November 1998, the Court was not permanent, so the judges would split their time between their home countries and Strasbourg. We spent seven to ten days per month in Strasbourg, where we received extensive case files. I prepared my cases in Budapest and then returned to Strasbourg for deliberations and decisions. I was the director general of the School of Public Administration in Budapest at the same time.

When I compare my experience at the ordinary court with my time at the ECtHR in Strasbourg, I find that everything felt quite different. The case-law system, procedures, behaviours, and detailed knowledge of national laws were completely different. It was challenging for me to catch up and acquire the skills and specialised knowledge that my colleagues already had. Later, as the President of the Supreme Court of Hungary, I could make good use of what I learned in Strasbourg. I was surprised and even shocked by the disparity in digitisation between the two courts. In Strasbourg, we used various computer programs, whereas in Budapest, even the Word processor seemed outdated. As well as the level of digitisation, the working methods were significantly different, which made it a difficult transition for me. Being a national judge at any level is a completely different job compared to being on the ECtHR, and it was a challenging time for me.

Viktor Kazai and Ramona Coman: We will move on now to the focus of this interview, which is the state of democracy and its impact on judicial independence. We would like to begin with a general question: What is your view of the current state of democracy, particularly in Hungary and Europe but also from a broader global perspective?

András Baka: I hold strong opinions about the state of democracy in Hungary, which is no secret. In my view, Hungary has shifted away from being a democracy. It appears to have become an authoritarian state where the separation of powers is non-existent. Without this separation, there can be no rule of law, and without the rule of law, it is difficult to call the system democratic. It seems more like a one-party system.

As for the current state of the judiciary in Hungary, I believe it resembles the judiciary of the 1970s. Although the courts generally operate freely, every aspect of their work is under the heavy influence of the ruling party. The ruling party, and by extension the government, exercises decisive control over Parliament. True democracy seems to be lacking. Nevertheless, I acknowledge that the judiciary is fairly independent and seems to be functioning reasonably well, but it is under permanent political pressure.

We must consider that the judiciary's input and output are tightly regulated. What does this mean? In criminal cases, the prosecutors control the input. The prosecutor's offices are overseen by the Chief Prosecutor, and essentially, no one supervises the prosecutors. So, for ordinary criminal offences, like shoplifting, or even serious ones like murder, the cases proceed through the system without interference. However, if a crime involves a high-ranking political figure, it never reaches the court. With no charge, there's no case. This is what I mean by 'controlled input'.

Furthermore, the output of the judiciary is overseen by the Constitutional Court, which has the authority to determine the constitutionality of final judgments. There is obvious political influence when a single party cherry-picks the judges, nominates and elects all the judges of the Constitutional Court, as it happened in Hungary. In ordinary cases the Constitutional Court bases its decisions on legal arguments. However, in politically sensitive cases the Court consistently take the side of the government either by deciding in its favour or by delaying the effect of unfavourable decisions. While I do not want to delve too deeply into this area, I believe that both the input and the output of the judiciary are strictly regulated.

The current President of the Supreme Court, a former prosecutor with strong ties to the ruling party, had never been a judge prior to his election. He became eligible for the position due to tailor-made legislation, and his appointment as President of the Supreme Court means that the government wants decisive influence over the court system. The President of the Supreme Court openly questions the principle of the separation of powers and the rule of law. As president, he has full administrative jurisdiction over the judges of the Supreme Court, and, as the head of the chamber mandated to guarantee the uniformity of case law, he wields significant power to influence legal practices at lower-level Hungarian courts. This approach indicates that the judiciary is intended to be used for the purpose of implementing the will of the ruling party.

In a broader sense, I believe Hungary is a country where the ruling Fidesz party holds all the power. The government controls about 90 per cent of the press and the media, and with a two-thirds majority in Parliament, they can manipulate the electoral system. They have changed electoral law and the Constitution multiple times, showing a disregard for democratic values. This is the current situation in Hungary, and while I do not mean to paint everything with the same brush, this is what is happening.

As for Europe, I think it is in a better position overall, but there are still challenges on another level. During my time at the ECtHR, I did not fully realise the extent of these challenges. However, the situation has worsened since the beginning of the war in Ukraine and the European Union's internal rule of law crisis. The European institutions seem relatively weak and often have to compromise. That is a good thing in some ways, but it also hinders their ability to act quickly and efficiently, especially when it comes to influencing the actions of certain countries. This is true for the Court of Justice of the European Union as well: it takes a considerable amount of time to make decisions on major issues. Therefore, I believe that EU reform is almost inevitable, and I hold the European institutions responsible for allowing the situation in Hungary to deteriorate to its present level.

On a global scale, we are concerned about the possible consequences of the United States elections in November 2024. What impact might they have on the rule of law and democracy? We must acknowledge that countries that uphold the rule of law and democratic principles represent a relatively small minority worldwide. Therefore, we must prioritise the protection and preservation of our democracies. Democracy must always be safeguarded.

Viktor Kazai and Ramona Coman: Could you please elaborate on the threat to your independence as a judge? How did you feel when you were personally attacked by the government for your opinion?

András Baka: During my time as an international judge, I can honestly say that I never encountered any form of interference in my duties. No one ever approached me, whether directly or indirectly, to influence my decisions, not even my colleagues. Throughout my 17 years at the ECtHR, I did not experience any political interference, even when the Court handled cases with serious political implications.

In Hungary, I was elected as President of the Supreme Court in 2009, the year before Fidesz, the current ruling party, came to power. During that year, we developed a comprehensive reform programme for the judiciary. When it was finalised and the new government took office, we presented it to them. However, they completely ignored it. Instead, from late 2010 to early 2011, they launched an attack on the judiciary. There was a widespread media campaign against the judiciary, with rhetoric about 'blood judges' from the 1950s and doubt cast on the legitimacy of Hungarian judges, despite the fact that 74 per cent of them were appointed after the regime change in 1990. For around two months, the government undermined the authority of the judiciary in the press and media. After that, they introduced a new law mandating early retirement for judges. In Hungary, the retirement age for judges had traditionally been 70 since 1869. Forcing judges to retire at 62 was not only inhumane – especially considering that it was introduced within days – but also an egregious attack on the judiciary, particularly given that the new age limit was the lowest retirement age for judges in Europe at the time.

I vividly recall a quotation from the President of the Supreme Court of the Netherlands, Geert Corstens, who drew a parallel between the situation in Hungary and the Nazi occupation of the Netherlands. In his book,[3] he emphasised how the lowering of the retirement age for Hungarian judges, who were promptly replaced with loyal appointees after they retired, mirrored a similar scenario during the Nazi occupation. This was a severe blow to the independence and stability of the judiciary. The forced early retirement of a significant portion of the Hungarian judiciary, including Supreme Court judges and senior officials from lower courts, resulted in widespread human tragedy. The rapid replacement of these experienced judges with new appointees represented a direct and unprecedented political assault on the judiciary. I strongly opposed that, and that is why I was removed from office through a tailor-made constitutional change.

Viktor Kazai and Ramona Coman: The impact of changes in the Hungarian judiciary is crucial, not just for judges and institutions, but also for individuals. Can you explain further how these changes affect citizens?

András Baka: There was a deliberate and widespread attack on the judiciary by the government-friendly media. This included constant reports on 'communist judges' presiding over cases. This seriously undermined the public's trust in the impartiality of the judiciary. Ordinary citizens were led to question whether their cases were being handled impartially due to the presence of these so-called 'communist judges.' This relentless assault on the judiciary by the government erodes its credibility, which in turn weakens the foundation of our entire legal system.

The judiciary is an integral part of the state apparatus, and its strength is crucial for maintaining a healthy and functioning state. In Hungary, however, the government's actions have severely undermined the judiciary's authority. This has a direct impact on the principle of equality before the law, as a politically influenced judiciary goes against the fundamental tenets of the rule of law.

The initial attack was just the beginning. The judiciary has faced ongoing pressure through evolving methods ever since. For example, high-ranking judicial officials have been appointed in order to influence the judiciary. This personal form of control has significantly affected civil society, the public, and the standing of the judiciary, leaving it less robust, honourable, and respected than it should be.

Viktor Kazai and Ramona Coman: Is the diminishing independence of the judiciary reflected in the way courts make decisions? Do you see any courts or areas of law where political influence can be detected?

András Baka: I find it challenging to pin down specific areas of law, but there are individual cases that stand out. One particular case involved a judge who referred a case to the CJEU for a preliminary ruling.[4] The Hungarian judge asked the CJEU whether the

[3] G Corstens, *Understanding the Rule of Law* (Oxford, Hart Publishing, 2017) 5.

[4] In 2019, a judge at the Central District Court of Pest, seised of criminal proceedings brought against a Swedish national, referred some preliminary questions to the CJEU regarding, inter alia, judicial independence in Hungary. The CJEU declared that on the basis of the primacy of EU law, a national court must disregard any national judicial practice which is prejudicial to its right to make a reference to the Court of Justice. Case C-564/19 *IS* ECLI:EU:C:2021:949.

judicial system was sufficiently independent. The Chief Prosecutor opposed the decision to refer the case to the CJEU and initiated a case against it. Ultimately, the Supreme Court ruled in favour of the Chief Prosecutor, prohibiting judges from making such referrals. I consider this a political and unlawful decision: judges should have the basic right to refer cases concerning EU law for preliminary rulings. This ruling denies them this right regardless of the circumstances surrounding the case.

Viktor Kazai and Ramona Coman: How do you see the judiciary's role in protecting its independence and defending democracy? What are the appropriate methods that courts can legitimately use to achieve these goals? How can they effectively accomplish them?

András Baka: Your question is essentially about the specific role and responsibilities of courts. Court plays a crucial role in safeguarding democracies. Generally, judges make independent decisions as a natural part of their role, which inherently helps protect democracy. Among the different branches of power, the parliament is responsible for establishing the framework of the state and, of course, the judiciary, while the government's role is to execute laws and decisions. By contrast, the judiciary has the authority to interpret legal measures, which is an effective tool: it has power over the meaning of the law.

I believe that the interpretation of legal rules is the primary tool with which the judiciary can uphold democracy. This is particularly pertinent in Hungary, where there are ongoing attempts to restrict judicial interpretation, as has been made clear in several speeches by the Minister of Justice. Limits to judicial interpretation – such as the restrictions in Article 28 of the Fundamental Law of Hungary, which dictate how legal rules should be interpreted – pose a serious threat. Restricting the judiciary's power, and especially its right to interpretation, undermines its fundamental purpose. I believe that maintaining an unrestricted right to interpretation is imperative to preserve the independence of the judiciary.

As for engaging with the public, the judiciary has many opportunities to connect with civil society. I believe civil society plays a crucial role in upholding the independence of the judiciary. Citizens can be advocates for the judiciary, conducting research and raising public awareness. The judiciary can also establish connections with international judicial organisations, but there are limits to this cooperation, as participation in these international bodies tends to be limited to court leaders and is not possible for ordinary judges. This method may also be less effective in Hungary due to the political appointment of court leaders. On the other hand, international judicial organisations play a valuable role in setting standards for judiciaries and judges.

Viktor Kazai and Ramona Coman: What does it mean to be a judge in a context where the independence of the judiciary has not just been eroded but has been dismantled completely? How does this radical transformation affect judges and their profession? In some countries, judges have taken to the streets in solidarity to defend the independence of the judiciary, while in others, the response has been more hesitant. What does it mean, then, to be a judge in a context where independence is completely dismantled, and what are the implications of this solidarity movement between judges from different countries? For instance, we have seen Polish judges supporting their counterparts in Romania and Hungary, as well as judges from the Netherlands joining a march in Poland in January 2020, with the participation of judges from 22 EU Member States. How do you see the significance of these transnational movements of judges to support their peers in different Member States?

András Baka: You have essentially asked two questions. To start with the first one, what does it mean to be a judge today under changing circumstances? Today, the role of a judge remains unchanged despite the evolving circumstances. It is crucial for a judge to work independently, deliberating and making decisions on cases while free from external influence. In Hungary, the ordinary court system operates without interference, allowing judges to render verdicts based on their expertise and legal principles. However, if a judgment proves politically sensitive or raises constitutional concerns, the Constitutional Court may review it, potentially altering the outcome. This aspect of the process is politically driven, but the fundamental function of a judge has remained consistent, both during previous regimes and in the present day.

As for the second question, let me tell you this story. I was invited to Poland in 2016 to attend the inaugural Congress of Polish Judges. I was not entirely sure what the event would be like. I prepared a lecture for 50 judges. Upon my arrival, I learned that there would be around 1,000 participants, with the potential for another 200 to join online. In response to the unexpected scale of the event, I rewrote the entire lecture overnight. It turned out to be a critical gathering for the Polish judiciary to protect its independence, and I am convinced that such meetings are incredibly valuable and efficient.

Poland and Hungary represent two different situations. In 2011 and 2012, there were no demonstrations in Hungary for the protection of the judiciary. In Poland, however, the brutal attack on the judiciary led to mass demonstrations, including by judges, for its protection. The attack in Poland was against the entire judiciary, whereas in Hungary, the judiciary was intentionally divided by politicians. By removing top-level judges, the Hungarian government created tempting vacancies for many judges. The government's deliberate division of different professional groups – be it doctors, teachers, or another group – was intended to weaken potential protests and create enemies. This is an ongoing phenomenon in Hungary, where social solidarity and civil society have traditionally been weaker than in Poland.

Viktor Kazai and Ramona Coman: As we conclude, we are curious about your thoughts on the future of democracy in Europe, especially within the EU. Do you see Europe, specifically the EU, as part of the solution or the problem when it comes to the challenges we are currently facing? You mentioned earlier that European institutions are not strong, and that Hungary is not the only cause for concern; other Member States are also raising issues. While the situations in different states vary greatly, we wonder whether Europe is contributing to or alleviating the problems we are seeing in different Member States.

András Baka: I believe that the EU, or Europe, as you referred to it, can be a solution rather than a problem. The key issue is making European institutions more effective and efficient in safeguarding the interests of Europe. Broadly speaking, there are two approaches: the federalist approach and the approach of national sovereignty. Personally, I am inclined towards a stronger and more efficient integration of the European states.

I believe that most of the basic problems Europe faces cannot be effectively addressed by individual states based on national sovereignty alone.

Given the current issues – such as the Ukrainian crisis, relations with Russia, environmental protection, migration, the challenges of establishing a European Common Defence Force, and maintaining common legal standards – I do not believe that these and other issues can be resolved independently. They require robust harmonisation and viable solutions for the EU Member States. Challenges such as COVID-19 or safeguarding Europe from threats posed by Russia require a high level of unified cooperation among the European states. To achieve this level of cooperation, significant changes within the EU are necessary.

15

The European Commission Abandoned the Honest Judges

DRAGOŞ CĂLIN[1]

Leonardo Puleo: I would like to start by asking you to provide some general information about your background and what motivated you to pursue a career as a judge.

Dragoş Călin: I graduated from the Faculty of Law at the University of Bucharest and the National Institute of Magistracy in Bucharest and later earned my PhD in law from the University of Bucharest, Faculty of Law. In terms of my career, I have held a variety of positions. I have been a judge at the Bucharest Court of Appeals since April 2009, and since 2010 have also been a founding member and Co-President of the *Asociaţia Forumul Judecătorilor din România* (AFJR, Romanian Judges Forum Association). In the early 2000s, Romanian society was eager for political change and there was a consensus about joining the EU and NATO. Politicians promised to break with the communist past. Becoming a judge was perhaps the only option for me at that time because meritocratic exams had been introduced since 1998, so it was practically the only chance for a law graduate to continue working in the profession and not end up working as a taxi driver.

Leonardo Puleo: Could you please elaborate a bit on what specifically motivated you to become a judge in Romania? Were there other judges and lawyers in your family?

Dragoş Călin: No, we don't have a family tradition of going into the magistracy. It was very complicated to be a lawyer in the 1990s and 2000s because you needed an experienced lawyer to guide you. Paradoxically, becoming a judge was simpler because there was a truly meritocratic exam. Furthermore, in 1997, the government created the National Institute of Magistracy to improve the procedure, modelled on the French system. The contest involved around 3,000 to 4,000 candidates competing for 100 judicial traineeship positions. A framework was established to help young people

[1] Interview conducted on 15 April 2024 together with Viktor Kazai and Ramona Coman and validated for publication on 16 July 2024.

deepen their understanding of the aspects necessary for serious preparation for the subsequent profession of magistrate. In contrast, becoming a lawyer or notary required the endorsement of an experienced lawyer or notary in office. These professions were closed castes. As a result, the judiciary became the only option for young law school graduates without personal connections to influential elites.

Leonardo Puleo: I would like to hear your opinion about the current state of democracy in your country and, then more generally within the European Union.

Dragoş Călin: In Romania and many other countries in Eastern Europe, we are seeing a weakening of the judicial system and there are daily attacks against the judiciary in the media, often perpetrated by judges seeking political positions. There was also a case in Romania where a judge – president of the *Uniunea Naţională a Judecătorilor din România* (UNJR, Romanian National Union of Judges) was put forward to be Minister of Justice. The UNJR supported counter-reforms in the judiciary between 2017 and 2019. It supported the creation of a special section for investigating judges, the fragmentation of the powers of the National Anti-Corruption Directorate, the replacement of meritocratic promotion exams with formal interviews, among other measures. Recent years have been characterised by severe polarisation and a global wave of democratic decay. This decay happens when there is a significant decline in key aspects of a country's formal democratic system. Autocratisation occurs when political leaders in government reduce the capacity of other branches of the state to check their powers, often accompanied by crackdowns on civil society. In recent years, there has been a visible decline in the rule of law in several EU Member States. The Court of Justice of the European Union has increasingly focused on rule of law issues, particularly on measures meant to weaken checks and balances on government actions. Hungary, Poland, and Romania have emerged as the countries with the largest number of unimplemented rulings from the Court of Justice of the European Union and the European Court of Human Rights.

Leonardo Puleo: How do you see the evolution of Romanian democracy, not only as a judge but also as a citizen? How does the situation now compare to the period before EU accession in 2007?

Dragoş Călin: It was better in 2007 because we saw a different face of both judiciary and politics. But then there was a huge crisis in 2018, when the Parliament changed the laws on judiciary. The government started to attack the judiciary, but in Romania, unlike Poland, the attacks were indirect, using a part of the judiciary.[2] Now we are experiencing a significant decline in democracy. As a judge, I cannot indulge in political opinions. However, we now have a coalition that controls 75 per cent of parliament and all the most important state authorities. So it is hard to characterise Romania – or the Romanian political system – as a true democracy. In Eastern Europe, there are alarming tendencies such as the refusal to comply with CJEU judgments, partial compliance, and only partially addressing systemic problems without tackling underlying issues.

[2] As the CJEU established in the Judicial Inspectorate case. See Case C-817/21 *Inspecţia Judiciară* ECLI:EU:C:2023:391, [2024] 1 CMLR 31.

Hundreds of parliamentarians, a former prime minister, thousands of ministers, judges, prosecutors, and mayors were convicted of corruption related offences in Romania from 2010 to 2018. At the same time, a vigorous campaign against anti-corruption legislation is being waged by TV stations that are owned by people convicted by the National Anticorruption Directorate and the High Court of Cassation.

Leonardo Puleo: What challenges are faced by courts and judges in Romania in terms of judicial independence? Have you faced any threats personally?

Dragoş Călin: Between 2018 and 2019, several harmful legislative amendments were adopted in the field of justice. These included limiting the freedom of expression of judges and prosecutors, establishing a new separate prosecutor's office for investigating offences committed by judges and prosecutors, and introducing unacceptable provisions regarding the personal and financial liability of judges and prosecutors. The Chief of the Judicial Inspectorate was nominated directly by the government using an emergency ordinance. In May 2021, the CJEU ruled that these legislative amendments were contrary to the TEU. However, after that, the chief inspector opened disciplinary proceedings against key judicial figures who opposed these amendments.

The importance of the independence of the Judicial Inspectorate stems from its extensive jurisdictional powers, which significantly impact the careers of judges and prosecutors. These powers include conducting disciplinary investigations, which are a mandatory preliminary stage for initiating disciplinary action against judges or prosecutors. The Judicial Inspectorate also assesses whether the conditions for the exercise of judicial functions were met in bad faith or with gross negligence in the event of a miscarriage of justice. Moreover, it investigates the integrity of candidates in the competition for promotion to the position of judge at the High Court of Cassation and Justice, and conducts checks at courts and prosecutor's offices to ensure compliance with laws and regulations. In this framework, the Chief Inspector holds key powers, which were strengthened by the 2018 legislative amendments (Law No. 234/2018). These powers include appointing judicial inspectors, designating inspectors with executive functions, and managing the work of the Judicial Inspectorate and disciplinary proceedings. The Chief Inspector organises the allocation of cases and determines the specific areas of activity for control. The Chief Inspector is also responsible for issuing instructions/orders and has the authority to initiate disciplinary proceedings or endorse/confirm an inspector's decision to close a complaint during preliminary checks. As a result of these changes, the Judicial Inspectorate has effectively become a pyramidal public authority, unique in the judicial system, controlled by a single individual with significant discretionary powers. This includes authority over the adoption of the organisational regulatory framework and the confirmation or reversal of decisions made by judicial inspectors. Within this structure, judicial inspectors, appointed by the Chief Inspector, are fully subordinated to him, which poses a risk to their functional independence.

I was one of those who were harassed for almost two years, but the accusations against me were then dismissed by the Superior Council of Magistracy and the High Court of Cassation in May 2023. The attacks on myself and others were a chilling attempt to intimidate the magistracy in Romania. In November 2021, the Judicial

Inspectorate launched a serious and unprecedented accusation against judges using vindicative and shocking language. The Judicial Inspectorate initiated disciplinary proceedings against me, Laurenţiu Grecu (Mehedinti County Court, member of the AFJR), Anca Codreanu (judge at Braşov County Court, former co-president of the AFJR), Alina Gioroceanu (Olt County Court, member of the AFJR), and Cristi Danileţ (Cluj Regional Court, former member of the Superior Council of Magistracy from 2011 to 2016). We were accused of violating Article 99(a) of Law No. 303/2004 in connection with messages allegedly posted on a Facebook group. The content of these messages reportedly focused on the establishment of a special prosecutor's section for investigating offences in the judiciary, as well as criticism or praise for the conduct of specific members of the Superior Council of Magistracy (including the Minister of justice) and criticism directed at the Judicial Inspectorate or Constitutional Court (showing that these authorities ignored the CJEU rulings regarding the rule of law).

However, no evidence was presented to authenticate these messages. Despite this, the Judicial Inspectorate, represented by its Chief Inspector Lucian Netejoru, decided to bring us before the Superior Council of Magistracy – Section for Judges. The Judicial Inspectorate accused us that we were trying to put pressure for obtaining a position within the new Superior Council of Magistracy. It was delusional, because we did not state any wish, either publicly or privately, to become members of the Superior Council of Magistracy. And none of us were candidates for the new Superior Council of Magistracy. They accused us of using funds from the professional associations in order to escape disciplinary liability; it was absolutely shocking. After nearly 18 months of trial, the Section for Judges rejected the disciplinary action in September 2022, citing the lack of evidence for the authenticity of the messages. The appeal on a point of law, filed by the Judicial Inspectorate, was definitively dismissed by the High Court of Cassation and Justice in May 2023, more than two years after the disciplinary action was initiated.

Leonardo Puleo: Some of the judicial reforms in 2017 were introduced by emergency decrees by the government – can you tell me more about that?

Dragoş Călin: Yes, this was criticised by the Venice Commission. In response, during 2019, the Romanian President organised a referendum, where citizens voted against these emergency ordinances. However, the government continues to use this mechanism, and the Constitutional Court has not issued any rulings on the use of emergency ordinances since the 2019 referendum. The challenge here is the fact that emergency ordinances can only be challenged in the Constitutional Court through a judiciary action, and that takes several years. The Ombudsman of Romania could also challenge them, but appointees to that office are nominated by political parties. So, it's almost impossible to quickly contest these emergency ordinances in the judiciary, and this poses a significant challenge to the rule of law in Romania.

Leonardo Puleo: Romania, Poland, and Hungary are often regarded as being similar when it comes to governmental measures limiting the independence of judges. But in Romania, it seems the struggles are more internal to the judiciary – do you agree?

Dragoş Călin: Not exactly. The chief inspector was nominated directly by the government. On 11 May 2023, the CJEU found that the Judicial Inspectorate was using its powers to conduct political scrutiny of judicial activity in Romania. This included my case and those of some prominent judicial figures like Laura Codruța Kövesi (former chief prosecutor of Romania's National Anticorruption Directorate and current European Chief Prosecutor) and Cristi Danileț.

Leonardo Puleo: Is there growing tension and polarisation within the judiciary, then?

Dragoş Călin: Instruments like the Judicial Inspectorate can be used to intimidate the judges who still resist. Nowadays in Romania, the Judicial Inspectorate continues to harass judges and prosecutors, introducing appeals against disciplinary decisions by the section of the Superior Council of Magistracy. Some judges who have been excluded from the magistracy by the Superior Council of Magistracy later win their cases at the High Court of Cassation. Yet no one is held responsible for the stress and terror inflicted by these rulings and investigations.

All the inspectors who have harassed magistrates, judges, and prosecutors have been allowed to stay in office and have even been promoted, while the Superior Council of Magistracy remains unresponsive, even when the CJEU has confirmed these issues. The CJEU ruled that political control of judicial activity in Romania was being carried out through the Judicial Inspectorate, directly targeting judges and prosecutors.

We had a problem with the European Commission because it abandoned the honest judges and prosecutors in Romania who stand up for the independence of the judicial system. We are constantly humiliated, harassed, and blocked in terms of promotion and career advancement within the judicial system because half of the judges who supported the judicial reforms in 2018 and 2019 were promoted by the Superior Council of Magistracy or appointed to various positions by the Minister of Justice. This is why we are tired and stressed. It is not a normal society. There is probably a link between parts of the judicial system and politicians as, for example, the Constitutional Court also counts former politicians among its members. The result is that citizens lack confidence in justice because, in corrupt societies, corrupt politicians are protected by weak judges.

Leonardo Puleo: You mentioned an important point about the image of judges within society. What do you believe are the implications of the deterioration of judicial independence for citizens?

Dragoş Călin: Trust in the judiciary is linked to the eradication of corruption, and this is the main problem in Romania. Corrupt politicians are protected by weak judges (or prosecutors) using instruments like the Judicial Inspectorate, as the CJEU mentioned in the case C-817/21.[3] According to the Eurobarometer, only 50 per cent of Romanians trust the judicial system. Independent surveys such as the Romanian Civic Barometer

[3] Editorial note: This case concerns the reference for a preliminary ruling regarding the interpretation of Article 2 and the second subparagraph of Article 19(1) TEU and Commission Decision 2006/928/EC of 13 December 2006 establishing a mechanism for cooperation and verification of progress in Romania to address specific benchmarks in the areas of judicial reform and the fight against corruption. Case C-817/21 *Inspecția Judiciară* ECLI:EU:C:2023:391, [2024] 1 CMLR 31.

have shown that 74 per cent of respondents believe that judges and prosecutors are no longer fulfilling their duties. Only 8 per cent of respondents have total confidence in the judiciary, according to this independent survey.

So, we have many problems regarding people's trust in the judiciary in Romania. But on the other hand, let us not forget that in December 2017, more than 200,000 people protested in Bucharest for the independence of the judiciary. Many citizens supported our public demonstration for judicial independence in Romania.

Leonardo Puleo: Have there been cases of judgments that were criticised for being favourable to corrupt politicians?

Dragoş Călin: There are numerous cases in Romania where judges have been criticised. On 9 June 2018, government parties organised a large-scale rally against judges and prosecutors in Bucharest, with over 100,000 participants. The message of the rally explicitly targeted judges. There was a harsh political discourse, with accusations that judges were corrupt and Stalinist, using the unacceptable term 'rats'.

Leonardo Puleo: What should judges do when their independence is challenged? Which strategies can a judge implement in order to protect their position and resist these trends against judicial independence?

Dragoş Călin: It is complicated because we are employing all the strategies available. The most crucial strategy has been engaging with the CJEU. The CJEU has traditionally been a steadfast ally of Romanian judges, indeed perhaps the only reliable one, as the European Commission has often inexplicably neglected its role outlined in the founding treaties. This lack of serious involvement from the Commission in countering the negative effects of recent changes to Romania's judiciary laws is evident. Although the Commission published several Cooperation and Verification Mechanism reports, these have had little real impact, despite the Commission's responsibility and capability to ensure treaty compliance in Romania. The Commission repealed this mechanism in 2023, despite the Venice Commission's opinions being disregarded by the Romanian state. Regrettably, Romanian judges were compelled to pursue actions to safeguarding their independence which were not supported by the European Commission. No infringement procedure has been completed, no action by the European Commission for the application of the Cooperation and Verification Mechanism (CVM) has ever been before the CJEU. The CVM had a scope of application that was wider than EU law generally, as it also applied to purely national corruption cases (without EU funds being involved). This passivity on the part of the European Commission sets a dangerous precedent, gradually eroding judicial independence, and it may serve as a troubling example for other EU Member States. Currently, Slovakia faces a similar situation, and it's conceivable that other countries in Eastern Europe may follow this path in the future.

Through the efforts of a few individual judges supported by our professional association, preliminary rulings from the CJEU became possible. These judges were harassed by the Judicial Inspectorate, highlighting that their resistance was indeed the most serious form of fighting to preserve the rule of law in Romania.

Leonardo Puleo: And how do you explain this attitude of the European Commission?

Dragoş Călin: I remember a meeting in June 2022 with Věra Jourová (Former Vice-President of the European Commission for Values and Transparency), where she proposed to halt the CVM mechanism. I believe this was linked to the situation in Ukraine, as Romania's cooperation with the EU in military matters theremight have encouraged this tolerance regarding governmental attacks on the judiciary.

Leonardo Puleo: How have judges and the judges' associations responded to this new political context and the changed framework of the relationship with the EU Commission?

Dragoş Călin: We collaborate on a daily basis with the European Commission's rule of law unit in Brussels, but there are rumours reports are sometimes modified by the Commission's President or Vice-President. The reaction from judges and our professional associations is legitimate and necessary, especially when the functioning of the judicial system is threatened. Public protests and dialogue with international bodies were essential in Romania. We also collaborated closely with colleagues from Poland, Germany, and university professors, which was very motivating. For instance, Dariusz Mazur (currently deputy Justice Minister), a judge from Poland, joined us at protests alongside Romanian judges.

However, the main issue lies with the European Commission. Romanian judges and prosecutors were compelled to take actions when the Commission itself hesitated to act. While it was crucial to have referrals to the CJEU, the Commission refrained from initiating infringement cases against Romania. It remains unclear why the Commission responded so weakly.

Leonardo Puleo: Do you believe that a strategy of international solidarity can help overcome this impasse?

Dragoş Călin: This strategy is essential, and I believe it is our only solution. Transnational exchanges are absolutely crucial in times like these. As judges, we have witnessed similar reactions in Poland and Romania, for instance, but not in Hungary or Bulgaria, where they also face significant rule of law issues. Judges' associations in those countries do not bring these problems into the public debate. In Romania, the judiciary laws were changed in 2022 due to forceful reactions from judges at that time. However, we still face many problems. For example, one major issue is the subordination of judges to court presidents, leading to processes for promoting judges to higher functions that lack meritocracy. The High Court of Cassation only promotes certain judges who are comfortable with members of the Superior Council of Magistracy.

Leonardo Puleo: You mentioned that the attitudes of Polish and Romanian judges are very different from those of their Hungarian or Bulgarian colleagues. Has the Romanian judiciary traditionally been more assertive than its Bulgarian and Hungarian counterparts?

Dragoş Călin: In Romania, the National Institute of Magistracy, established in 1997, helped change the mentality of judges. We now have a younger generation of judges with a new mindset, trained by this institute. They are knowledgeable about the case law of the CJEU and the European Court of Human Rights, and this has fostered their sense of independence. The reactions of our association are crucial, and it's also important for countries like Bulgaria, Romania, Hungary, and Poland to have strong and independent associations of judges.

A judge is a member of civil society and cannot be expected to live in isolation from reality. In some post-communist societies, civic attitudes may not yet be fully developed, and the public may not immediately react to abuses of power. Judges and prosecutors should be allowed to express their opinions publicly as long as their impartiality is not compromised. The judiciary should not be envisioned as a silent entity where only heads of courts or prosecutor offices can speak out, leaving others condemned to perpetual silence.

In Romania, over 4,000 judges and prosecutors signed a memorandum in October 2017 in support of the independence of the judiciary. This figure represents more than half of the approximately 7,000 judges and prosecutors working in courts and prosecutors' offices in Romania at the time. This shows that the majority of judges are fighting for judicial independence.

Leonardo Puleo: Low salaries are another common threat to judicial independence – what is the situation in Romania regarding the renumeration of judges?

Dragoş Călin: In Romania we have some of the best salaries globally for judges compared to other professionals in the country. The improvement in salaries began with Minister Monica Macovei in 2006 and was then followed by decisions from the High Court of Cassation and rulings from the Constitutional Court which further increased judicial salaries. So salary is not a problem in Romania, and we also have robust retirement provisions. For instance, judges can retire from the magistracy after 25 years of service, meaning we have cases where judges as young as 47 or 48 retire.

Leonardo Puleo: How do you see the future of democracy and judicial independence in Romania and within the EU?

Dragoş Călin: For Romania, I believe the European Union represents the only viable solution. We must fight for the European Union. As I mentioned earlier, the CJEU has been a steadfast ally for judges in Romania and other states, for example Poland, that are facing political crises and autocratic tendencies. It is crucial that the appointment of judges to the CJEU is controlled not by governments but by independent commissions consisting of academics and former judges of the court. Judges in European courts must act independently and free from influence by the state that appointed them. They must have the courage and freedom to make decisions without external pressure, particularly in cases involving the independence of the judiciary. The CJEU stands as the last bastion of independence, and it is imperative that we do not lose this independence. Politicians will always attempt to control the judiciary, not only in Eastern Europe but also in Southern Europe, as seen in Italy and Spain, where they have been refusing to nominate members to the Superior Council of Magistracy since 2015, indicating serious issues with judicial independence.

Leonardo Puleo: Do you think that further threats to the independence of the judiciary will emerge after the upcoming elections in Romania?

Dragoş Călin: Who knows? It is possible, yes. We need to wait and see because, as the polls show, a significant portion of the population in Romania tends to vote for anti-establishment parties. In many European countries, such parties garner around 30 per cent or more of the vote, making it challenging to form a new parliamentary majority. However, we will have to wait and see how this situation unfolds and to what extent it will affect the independence of judges.

16

Judges cannot Speak Only Through their Judgments

MONIKA FRĄCKOWIAK[1]

Ramona Coman: Could you please tell us a bit about your personal, academic, and professional background?

Monika Frąckowiak: I graduated from university with a law degree in 2000. Following that, I was in training for a period of two years, and then I worked for one year as an assistant of a judge in the regional court of Poznan, Poland. In 2004, I was appointed as a 'judge in training', which means that I worked as a regular judge for a preparatory period that lasted three years. Following that, I was approved to become a full judge, and in 2007, I was appointed as a judge by the President of Republic. Currently, I am still working in the civil division of the District Court in Poznan.

Ramona Coman: What motivated you to pursue a career in law?

Monika Frąckowiak: It was a coincidence that I chose law, as I did not know what to do with my life. After a period of two or three years, I began to feel that it was not my path or my preferred direction. But then, by coincidence, during the second half of the 1990s I participated in some workshops dedicated to fundamental rights, along with some judges, including ones from Europe. At these meetings, there were also international judges who worked in former Yugoslavia after the war, and they inspired me. After those meetings, I was then 100 per cent sure that I wanted to graduate with a law degree and become a judge. So that is when and how I decided to pursue a career in law.

Ramona Coman: What was the reputation of the profession at that time?

Monika Frąckowiak: Well, at that time, I thought it was quite a conservative profession. But the judges I met from elsewhere in Europe gave me another picture of who and what a judge can be. On the other hand, I considered judges in Poland to be a very closed community.

[1] Interview conducted on 3 May 2024 at the Institut d'études européennes of the Université libre de Bruxelles and validated for publication on 20 January 2022.

Ramona Coman: The state of democracy in Poland has often made the headlines. How do you see the situation today compared to the situation under the previous government? What has changed since the last elections?

Monika Frąckowiak: Well, we are in a very difficult moment in Poland now. Obviously, we were so happy in October 2023 after the opposition's victory over populists. It was an incredible result. However, it is not easy to restore the rule of law after eight years of demolition. First, it is difficult to avoid using the same instruments the previous government was using. And we are still limited by the law which was created under the previous government, plus President Andrzej Duda is still in position at the end of the legislative process. His signature is needed on every legal act. He already declared that he is going to veto every legal act that tries to change the legal system constructed by the PiS, and he is going to be President for another year. Regarding the judiciary, for example, we still have disciplinary officers appointed by the former Minister of Justice. These people have no integrity, they have breached all possible rules, however according to the law, it is very difficult to replace them now. So we are in a really difficult transitional period. And at the same time, there are so many people who are aware of the difficulty, and feel very disappointed seeing 'bad judges' still in their positions. I must admit, it is also difficult for me.

Nevertheless, I think that Adam Bodnar, the new Minister of Justice, chose the right path by seeking to make changes through small, but consequent steps. I like that he is trying to bring back good practice. So, for example, according to the binding law, the Minister of Justice has absolute discretionary power to appoint presidents of courts. But Bodnar encourages judges to elect presidents among themselves. Before he makes appointments, he takes the judges' opinion into consideration. It is still not perfect, but much better than just applying the law that is still binding.

Ramona Coman: In your opinion, what are the other pillars of democracy that the previous government managed to weaken or even destroy?

Monika Frąckowiak: I think that the people lost trust in institutions, and it will be very difficult to rebuild it. Despite the result of the elections, it is very difficult to convince the majority of people that the legal order, institutions and the constitution exist to guarantee the protection of their rights. It will take years to regain people's trust. And I am very afraid that sooner or later populist parties are going to win in Poland again, undoing the changes and repair made by the democratic government. So from this point of view, it is better to act with a lot of caution.

However, in some areas prompt action was necessary, as in the case of the public TV when the new government replaced the top management of public television. I had mixed feelings in December 2023 when the new government took control of public television on the basis of controversial decisions. You need to know that under the PiS government, public TV was worse than what I remember from the 1980s. It was full of hateful propaganda. When the new government decided to get rid of the PiS propagandists, they occupied the TV building. It was quite shocking and dangerous, because they could have inspired some riots by using the media in this way. I do understand the urgency, nevertheless, from a legal point of view, it was controversial. Sooner or later, the issue will have to be decided in the court. But that was a political decision.

Ramona Coman: Regarding the media, how often is the state of the judiciary discussed now versus before? Do you see many journalists with an interest in this topic?

Monika Frąckowiak: There is more interest in the judiciary than there used to be before 2015, before the PiS government. Of course, it is not a major topic, but still, Adam Bodnar is one of the members of the government who is quite often seen in public media. So, there is still an ongoing discussion on the rule of law because we still have the problem to resolve related to the Constitutional Court, the Judicial Council or the 'neo-judges'.

Ramona Coman: What about in other Member States – do you see similar or different trends?

Monika Frąckowiak: Yes. We can observe similar trends in Romania, Bulgaria. And to tell you the truth, in the case of Bulgaria, the problem is even worse than it used to be in Poland. For reasons which I don't fully understand, this situation is not so well regarded in Brussels. I consider the situation much more complex in Romania too. But even in old democracies like Italy or France, there are more and more influential populists saying that judges are enemies of the people. Unfortunately, the populists make 'perfect' use of social media. So, there is a growing tendency to have ever more control over the judiciary.

Ramona Coman: You mentioned France, but not Spain. What are the challenges there?

Monika Frąckowiak: It took me a lot of time to try to understand the situation in Spain because everything that is happening there is somehow linked to the country's history. I have never heard of any situation in Spain in which a judge would be under pressure to deliver judgment in one way or another. Never. But the fact, that Spain hasn't had a proper Judicial Council for a few years is really alarming. The internal problems in Spanish politics obviously influence the tensions in the judiciary. However, I wouldn't compare Spain and Poland in terms of judiciary.

Another example is Portugal, which has always seemed to have a well-functioning system. What I have always admired was the high level of independence of prosecutors. In 2023, Portuguese prosecutors did their job and launched an investigation concerning their Prime minister and this led to new elections. After the last elections, it seems that the judiciary has become a problem for many politicians. We will see what direction it will go from there.

Ramona Coman: What are the main challenges in your day-to-day activity? How do you see your work and what are the challenges of the implications for your daily work of the political context in Poland ?

Monika Frąckowiak: I have realised for myself that we cannot go back to the situation we had in 2015. We need to learn from what happened in Poland. That means that judges cannot only speak through their judgments. It is something that we know to be 100 per cent true. Magistrates need to be active and open to society. But, at the same time, it is difficult to find the right balance between being simply a judge and being an activist, because a judge should always be limited by the position they hold. There are some limits and boundaries they cannot cross. We must keep our integrity, remembering that we are judges, not pop stars.

Ramona Coman: Should judges be active in society?

Monika Frąckowiak: Yes, for sure. Most judges in Poland have understood that we must change our language to be much more comprehensive and more easily understood. We need to drop the tendency to use our patronising tone. And, within the court, we must open the institution to activities other than just delivering justice. Courts should be open to students, pupils, and society in general. We should be present at public events such as sport, cultural or even rock festivals.

Ramona Coman: What role do associations play here in relation to different types of activities? And more generally, what is the role of the judges' association?

Monika Frąckowiak: The role of associations is crucial for obvious reasons. It is a network with various structures making it much easier to organise events anywhere in the country. This is true for the Polish Association of judges Iustitia as well as other associations. The associations make it much easier to cooperate with other NGOs, and also help us be heard by media. And in difficult times, working together gives you strength, there are people around you offering support.

Ramona Coman: There are two points here. First, can you give us an example of collaborations with civil society and organisations in Poland? And second, have you received support from professional associations elsewhere in Europe?

Monika Frąckowiak: We have cooperated with many Polish NGOs, for example *Akcja Demokracja* (Action Democracy), *Helsińska Fundacja Praw Człowieka* (Helsinki Foundation for Human Rights), *Komitet Obrony Demokracji* (KOD, Committee for the Defence of Democracy), Amnesty International, *Wolne Sądy*, Tour de Konstytucja. And outside of Poland there is MEDEL, *Rechters voor Rechters* from the Netherlands, the European Association of Judges, the European Association of Administrative Judges, and other organisations.

MEDEL advocated for Polish judges in the context of the struggles over the rule of law in front of some European institutions as well. They were also writing open letters to European Commissioners and to the Council of Europe, and there were some actions to support particular judges like Igor Tuleya. The culmination of our cooperation with European organisations was the March of a Thousand Robes, the march of judges organised in Warsaw in 2020. It was an amazing event, and one of the most touching moments in my professional career. It had importance not only for Poland and for Polish judges, but for the whole judicial community in Europe. And that was the defining moment for many of us. It became obvious that we belong to the same judicial community. We still are in close contact with some of those who came to the march, and we created a European network to connect magistrates from various countries.

Ramona Coman: Has this become a formal, institutionalised network now?

Monika Frąckowiak: No, it is informal, but it operates whenever there is a need to act in defence of judicial independence. Currently, we are supporting Judge Vladislava Tzarigradska from Bulgaria.

Ramona Coman: How united or divided are the judges on such issues? Are there disagreements, for example about how to act, how to express dissatisfaction and so on? Is it true that having more judges makes for more opinions?

Monika Frąckowiak: Yes, more opinions, exactly! That is why it is an incredible success that we have all achieved so much together. We were able to publish and release so many statements, organise events, conferences. Although there are some different opinions on particular issues, what unites us is the dedication to fundamental rights.

Ramona Coman: How many associations per country are represented by MEDEL?

Monika Frąckowiak: There are no strict rules. From Poland we have not only Iustitia, but also Themis and Lex Super Omnia, which is the prosecutors' association. From Spain there are two, from Belgium as well, but there is only one French association. So it depends on the country.

Ramona Coman: Is the EU generally a help or a hindrance for the independence of the judiciary, or for democracy? How do you view the role of the EU, considering that you have also been in contact with European institutions, I suppose?

Monika Frąckowiak: We already have some European standards for the judiciary which were mainly established by the European Court of Justice, and European Court of Human Rights. Many important rulings were issued in the Polish case. It is a kind of roadmap for all European countries and EU institutions. So, in the case of Poland, the role of EU institutions was crucial, but without active civil society and Polish judges, they might have been more reluctant to do anything about the rule of law in Poland. As for the role of the EU – apart from what the European Commission is already doing, the key issue is education, promoting awareness in the field of rule of law. Knowledge and education are the only weapons against populism.

17

The Very Status of a Judge Requires Deep Reflection

MAŁGORZATA MARIA GERSDORF[1]

Ramona Coman: I would be grateful if you could share some information about your career and why you decided to enter the judiciary.

Małgorzata Gersdorf: I come from a family of lawyers: my father was a law professor, my mother was a judge, and my son, Dr Maciej Giaro, is a lawyer. My husband is also a lawyer and the former President of the Constitutional Tribunal. I always wanted to be a judge. For many years, I worked in academia, but I also practiced as a legal advisor. I graduated with honours from the Faculty of Law and Administration at the University of Warsaw in 1975. I then began my judicial training, which I completed in 1979, passing the judges' exam with a very good result. In 1986, I passed the exam for the position of legal adviser, again with a very good result. From 1991 to 2004, I was a member of the Supreme Court's Office for Studies and Analysis (formerly the Judiciary Office). Then, until 2005, I was the Supreme Court's general counsel.

On 15 July 2008, I was appointed by the President of the Republic of Poland to serve as a judge on the Supreme Court. This was the fulfilment of my dreams and my family destiny. My father deserved to attain this position, but the political circumstances at the time did not allow it. He did not want to join the communist ruling party, even though it is a great honour for any lawyer to become a Supreme Court judge. After six years as a judge on the Supreme Court, I was appointed First President of the Supreme Court on 30 April 2014. I held this office until 30 April 2020. This was a great honour, but it was also a great responsibility, especially during the years of holding this position under the PiS government. I have therefore achieved everything that can be achieved in the legal profession.

Ramona Coman: In addition to your work as a judge, you are also a teacher and are active in the academic world.

Małgorzata Gersdorf: In parallel with my judicial career, I have pursued an academic career. I earned my doctorate and *habilitation* and held a professorship and various

[1] Interview conducted on16 October 20204 and validated for publication on 15 December 2025.

university functions, up to the position of Vice-Rector of the University of Warsaw. I am also in legal practice as a legal advisor. I have written more than 230 academic publications on individual and collective labour law and social security, including seven monographs and several leading commentaries. I am also the author of several dozen popular science books and legal essays. I still work at the Faculty of Law of the University of Warsaw as the chair of Labour Law and Social Security. Because my tenure [as president of the Supreme Court] was marked by attacks by the ruling PiS coalition on the independence of the courts and of judges, I constantly had to oppose these attacks, including by giving lectures on the issue at home and in several other European Union countries. I also organised an international conference on the future of Europe based on the rule of law in Warsaw in April 2019. The conference was attended by the presidents of the supreme courts of most European countries.

Ramona Coman: You have experienced several waves of transformation in your country and have been affected by measures the PiS government has introduced. What is your view of these transformations in Poland and in Europe more broadly?

Małgorzata Gersdorf: Let me start with a rather disturbing reflection. We are living in an era of decline of the world as we know it. There have been many such times in history, and these periods of turmoil have almost always meant the same thing: a struggle, not necessarily an armed one. However, I have no hope that the EU and its Member States will continue to function as before. The period of prosperity and of the post-war model of democracy, based on traditional party alignment and the so-called liberal consensus, is irrevocably coming to an end. It will only get more difficult from now on. The crisis of the Western world mainly lies in the fact that with the emergence of new electronic media and the prospect of a new division of the political pie, the traditional democracy-rule of law pair loses its appeal. Unfortunately, this happens first in the nations that joined the peloton most recently and are its 'weakest links': the newest EU Member States and the countries that are, in various ways, under the political and economic influence of the EU. There is ample evidence. For example, this has been the case in Poland, Hungary or Turkey. Each case is a little different in its details, but all are very telling. Fortunately, the elections in Poland in 2023 put an end to the devastation of democracy and of the rule of law. The effects of this devastation will be noticeable for a long time to come.

Historically, in each of these countries, the leader of the ruling formation – the de facto dictator of a new type of autocracy – finds an effective way to instrumentalise the law in the extreme, under the banner of restoring its 'proper' meaning, of course. In Poland, this was done by subterfuge; in Hungary, by bribery and by winning a constitutional majority; and in Turkey, largely by violence. Despite their differences, the new regimes in all these countries have some common features. One of these is the façade of democracy: elections are held even in outright dictatorships such as Belarus. The electoral competition is no longer equal, and a large part of the population is politically represented by parties that pursue their own goals rather than acting for the common good, especially parties that are in power in authoritarian countries. In the face of the skilful manipulation of public sentiment and various forms of bribery among an increasingly degenerate elite, the supreme power of the people becomes a fiction. People are being groomed through microtargeting and trolling on social media and online, which is exacerbated by a reduction in the diversity of traditional media. In the twenty-first century, comments on X are becoming the equivalent of tanks and guns on the streets of twentieth-century cities. It is not surprising that the judgments of constitutional courts that are staffed by carefully selected cadres are associated with political struggle and not only with the common good. Theoretically, in Poland, this should be largely behind us, but the Constitutional Tribunal formed in the previous period [before the 2023 elections] is still a pale imitation of what it should be. The same applies to the National Council of the Judiciary and many court presidents who were appointed by PiS.

Ramona Coman: It has been often argued that these transformations are specific to 'new' democracies. What is your view of the situation in the EU or Europe as a whole?

Małgorzata Gersdorf: I think that the Western Member States of the European Union should not pretend that it is not involved and that all this is happening only in the 'wild East'. What is happening on the other side of the Oder and the Nysa is only holding up a distorting mirror to the decay of democracy in those countries that have, generally, happily enjoyed it since at least 1945. Post-industrial civilisation has produced tools against which the traditional regulator of human behaviour – the law – is becoming ineffective. Instead of speaking and listening, citizens stare at smartphone screens in search of sensationalism. It used to be possible, at least in theory, to argue about truth and justice. And today: *Quid est veritas?* This is a problem that both the new and old Member States of the EU share. Using electronic tools, the new autocrats are, step by step, undermining true democracy and the rule of law in a party power struggle.

I believe that EU reform cannot only involve the EU itself but must also involve the Member States themselves. The guarantees of the tripartite division of power are too weak in the face of a genuinely unchecked executive power, which is becoming increasingly widespread. The overwhelming preponderance of political power often leaves judges sitting completely alone in the courtroom. In countries that have moved away from democracy, judges are sometimes pitted against all other organs of the state, along with the entire state propaganda apparatus and power of repression. Let the actions of Zbigniew Ziobro, the former Polish Minister of Justice, be a warning. With the permission of PiS leader Jarosław Kaczyński, he aimed to create a disastrous image of judges who were independent and not subordinate to him. Government-controlled television incited the public against the 'judicial caste'. Using similar methods to those used by the police to fight judges, the Ministry established a special department within the highest prosecutorial unit in which one man – the Minister of Justice and the prosecutor general in one person – had the power to control every element of criminal proceedings, from the presentation of charges to the final conviction. In turn, the National Council of the Judiciary became extremely politicised, because it was filled with the Minister's people and acted in a completely non-transparent way. The Kelsenian model of the Constitutional Court also became a pure fiction: new judges on the Constitutional Court were recruited from among unknown rank-and-file lawyers who held the 'right' views, because no one with an appropriate reputation wanted to accept such a dubious 'honour'. The Minister of Justice was also given a fifth role, becoming not only the supervisor of the judiciary but also 'judge of judges'.

Ramona Coman: The PiS has declared war on judges in various ways. And the Polish judges' response has been an unprecedented mobilisation. What is the role of judges when not only independence but also rights are at risk?

Małgorzata Gersdorf: The doctrine propounded by PiS was a huge threat to the independence of judges in Poland. In one of his public speeches, the leader of PiS openly made it clear that he considered the judiciary just another corporation within the party- state that pushes its interests at the expense of the general public. Therefore, in the interest of the latter, they should be controlled by the party's Minister and subjected to a system of rewards and punishments under his authority. He was wrong, and not only because no one in Europe would accept such a vision of the tripartite division of power. First and foremost, the Polish judges themselves did not accept this view, in the service of the values that constitute the essence of judicial power. They did not believe that judges had a duty to remain silent in the face of such actions by political authorities. They did not keep silent, and for this, they were repressed. That is why many of them suffered the consequences of opposing autocratic 'legalism' under the PiS government. They were suspended from their duties and faced disciplinary proceedings. The Polish judges were steadfast. They had the courage, for example, to rule on the illegality of the constitution of the National Council of the Judiciary in our country. The true spirit of Solidarity lives on in such people! The judges did not abandon their repressed colleagues. They have, indeed, already won. They defended their independence. The bar association and some of the prosecutors stood behind the judges. They also had the support of groups associated with civil society, such as Free Courts (*Wolne Sądy*) and the Citizens of the Republic of Poland (*Obywatele RP*). They therefore had the support of the nation, which was aware of the importance of the tripartite division of power. European judicial associations also showed great merit in their defence of Polish judges. During this time, Kees Sterk (chapter 7), the President of the management board of the European Network of Councils for the Judiciary, visited Warsaw several times, supporting me in my efforts to promote the rule of law in Poland. Sterk also sent a letter to the President of the European Commission, Ursula von der Leyen, which was also signed by Jean-Claude Wiwinius, President of the European Network of Presidents of Supreme Courts and himself the President of the Supreme Court of the Grand Duchy of Luxembourg, and by José Igreja Matos (chapter 11), the President of the European Association of Judges. Frans Timmermans, Vice-President of the European Commission, has been the face of the struggle for the rule of law in Poland and Hungary for years. He was a regular guest in Warsaw, where he repeatedly drew the attention of the governments of 'good change' to the departure from the principles of the civilised state of law. On behalf of the Polish judges and the Polish judges' associations, all of these parties deserve warm thanks, and perhaps even busts and monuments. Without international support and the support of Polish citizens, little would be achieved in the fight against the autocratic rule of law and the opportunists and careerists who support it.

To answer your question, judges' importance in defending democracy is enormous. Judges must be independent and sovereign. Hence, the selection of judges should be recognised as a huge responsibility. In Poland, the newly politicised National Council of the Judiciary is still in place today. This body presents new judges to the President for nomination. We call them 'neo-judges'. The problem of their place in the judiciary is still unresolved in Poland. The President opposes this. Citizens and judges want these appointments to be verified by a National Council of the Judiciary that was elected in accordance with the Constitution. The same applies to the Constitutional Tribunal, which in its current composition is only a façade of what the Constitutional Tribunal is supposed to be. The independence of the judiciary applies in equal measure to judges of the ordinary courts and judges of the supreme courts. The only difference is substantive: we demand more expertise from judges of the higher courts.

Ramona Coman: As First President of the Supreme Court, were you subjected to pressure from the executive branch and from Parliament?

Małgorzata Gersdorf: I was not a favourite of the authorities. On the contrary, I was not spared grievances and humiliations. I have always expressed my views in line with my conscience, referring to the principles and values of European legal culture. There were even attempts to remove me from office before the end of my term. A special provision was passed lowering the mandatory retirement age for judges. The 'lex Gersdorf' provision was unconstitutional, so I did not submit to it and served my full term as First President of the Supreme Court.

The provision failed thanks to resistance within the country and from international institutions. Disciplinary proceedings have been brought against me, and they continue to this day. These proceedings are conducted by the disciplinary ombudsman, Schab, who was appointed by President Duda. I have been subjected to a lot of hate. The criminal cases of people who spread hatred about me online and even threatened to kill me recently came to an end. These people had clearly been manipulated and hated me for no apparent reason.

There was a fatal motorcycle accident, which I had nothing to do with (I had driven on the same road, but earlier), and yet it was attributed to me. The ONET news outlet and the journalist Stankiewicz claimed that I killed a man and fled the scene. It was very tragic. My husband and I were summoned to the prosecutor's office in Suwałki, 300 kilometres from Warsaw, and our car was taken away. The car was held for weeks, and the results of the accident investigation were not reported, because I was only granted the status of a witness, which meant that I could not call on an expert and demonstrate the absurdity of the accusation. The case is still ongoing.

Ramona Coman: Given the current context of a global crisis of democracy, are the guarantees of judicial independence strong enough to protect citizens' rights?

Małgorzata Gersdorf: I believe that the very status of a judge requires deep reflection. Of course, I know that in countries such as Germany, for example, the judge's status as a *sui generis* official does not damage his or her independence in any way. Today, no one from the government would even dare to comment too openly on the judgments of the highest courts, dismiss 'disobedient' court presidents or manipulate judicial appointments. But are the guarantees provided by a certain political culture sure to be sufficient? Modern populism is like a tsunami wave: it destroys all conventions and principles.

And citizens' faith in the independence of the courts from politicians is not as strong everywhere in the West as it is in Germany today – take Spain, for example. After the European Court of Human Rights' judgment in Case C-26374/18, *Guðmundur Andri Ástráðsson v Iceland*,[2] and the Court of Justice of the European Union judgments in the Cases C-585/18, *AK and Others v Sąd Najwyższy*[3] and C-896/19, *Repubblika v Il-Prim Ministru*,[4] it is difficult to pretend any longer that Member States are free to establish procedures for the appointment of judges as they see fit. This claim is now hypocritical. I believe that ensuring the autonomy of judges and courts will require rethinking some minimum requirements for them at the EU level and, arguably, may require constitutional changes in many Member States.

Secondly, judges cannot be obliged to remain silent on matters that are deemed to be 'political'. The world is changing dynamically, and even the British no longer support Lord Kilmuir's once famous 1955 rules, which banned all statements to the media outside the courtroom. This does not mean that those entrusted with the power of adjudication should undertake normal political engagement, because, after all, the separation of powers and the impartiality of the judiciary should be taken seriously. However, there are issues of principle about which one must not be silent, and the statements formulated in legal judgments do not have sufficient resonance in society. It is the duty of every judge to defend the values and principles enshrined in the Constitution and to demand the same loudly from every authority, under all circumstances. Let us therefore allow judges to be whistle-blowers of the constitutional system. A judge should not be afraid to interact with the new media and to provide reliable information about what the law says. After all, to assume that someone else will reliably inform the public if there is a disturbing anomaly in the legal system is tantamount to naïveté towards party politicians. The ECtHR jurisprudence regarding Article 10 of the European Convention on Human Rights, in *Kudeshkin v Russia*, *Baka v Hungary* or *Kövesi v Romania*, for example, sets a clear standard as regards the freedom of expression of judges. This standard should become a reality in all EU Member States.

Ramona Coman: What role should the EU, and not only the EU, play in safeguarding democracy in its member states? Should judges be more active in this regard?

[2] Editorial note: the case *Guðmundur Andri Ástráðsson v Iceland* originated in an application against the Republic of Iceland by an Icelandic national, MrGuðmundur Andri Ástráðsson ('the applicant'), on 31 May 2018. The applicant complained that his criminal conviction had been upheld by a 'tribunal' which was not 'established by law' and which was not independent and impartial, in violation of Article 6 § 1 of the Convention. *Guðmundur Andri Ástráðsson v Iceland*, App No 26374/18 (ECtHR, 1 December 2020).

[3] Editorial note: Case C-585/18 *AK and Others v Sąd Najwyższy* brought to the CJEU is a request for a preliminary ruling made by CP and DO, Judges of the Sąd Najwyższy (Supreme Court, Poland) concerning their early retirement due to the entry into force of new national legislation. Case C-585/18 *AK and Others v Sąd Najwyższy* ECLI:EU:C:2019:982, [2020] 2 CMLR 10.

[4] Editorial note: the case C-896/19 *Repubblika v Il-Prim Ministru* brought to the CJEU is a request for a preliminary ruling of Repubblika, an association registered as a legal person in Malta, the object of which is to promote the protection of justice and the rule of law in that Member State, and Il-Prim Ministru (Prime Minister, Malta) concerning a popular action seeking, inter alia, the conformity with Union law of the provisions of the Constitution of Malta ('the Constitution') governing the procedure for the appointment of judges. Case C-896/19 *Repubblika v Il-Prim Ministru* ECLI:EU:C:2021:311, [2021] 3 CMLR 18.

Małgorzata Gersdorf: I am not a politician, and I cannot draw scenarios for the development of democracy in the EU. I do know one thing. The future belongs to the young generation, and they should be educated now. Young people must know that democracy must be fought for. It is not a given, once and for all. The Polish association Iustitia's activities aimed at young people (such as distributing booklets about the importance of judicial independence) and even at first graders (for example, visits to courts, including the Supreme Court), as well as activities aimed at all citizens (like meetings about the Constitution conducted by prominent judges and professors throughout Poland) are examples of how to achieve this.

18

Constitutional Courts are not the Sole Guardians of Liberal Democracy

ZDENĚK KÜHN[1]

Ramona Coman: Could you please describe your personal, academic, and professional background?

Zdeněk Kühn: I graduated from law school in Prague in 1997, and I started working in a legal practice and in an attorney's office. At the same time, I also started being a professional academic. I started at the Charles University Law School at the Department of Jurisprudence in 1997, and in 2001, I got my PhD in Prague. In the same year, 2001, I went to the United States to study at the University of Michigan, Ann Arbor, where I received an LLM degree in 2002 and a S.J.D. degree in 2006. I spent two years in Michigan, and then I came back in 2003, and became an associate professor in 2006. In 2008, I joined the Supreme Administrative Court. So, as an academic and as an associate professor of jurisprudence, I joined the Supreme Administrative Court, which was only established in 2003, so at that time it was a relatively young court. Yes, during communism, there were no administrative courts! And in the 1990s in Czechia, even though the Constitution provided for the Supreme Administrative Court, the politicians did not establish any such institution, it was only established in 2003. It was a very unique court because it started from scratch. That's why, unlike the regular Supreme Court, which was equipped with career judges, the Supreme Administrative Court was about 50 per cent career judges, and the remaining 50 per cent were academics, attorneys, and various kinds of legal professionals. That was how I became a judge in 2008. Ten years later, in 2018, I became a full professor in Prague, again at the Department of Jurisprudence, and then in December 2023, the President of the Republic appointed me to the Constitutional Court. For the next ten years, I am a Constitutional Court judge in Brno. I am still a judge of the Supreme Administrative Court, but now it is suspended because now I am a judge of the Constitutional Court. By the way, Brno is the judicial capital of the country. The three high courts – the Supreme Court, Supreme Administrative Court and Constitutional Court – are all located in Brno.

[1] Interview conducted on 1 July 2024 and validated for publication on 20 January 2025.

Ramona Coman: Can you tell me what motivated you to take up a judicial position?

Zdeněk Kühn: It was because I was always interested in judicial matters as an academic. I was writing about judicial reasoning. As an academic, I have written several books about legal argumentation by judges, and I have been very critical of the post-communist legal culture. That is why I got the offer from the Chief Justice of the Supreme Administrative Court, who was interested in my writings on the judiciary. In the Czech Republic, it is usually the chief judge, the president of the court, who selects judges for the court. As a matter of law, it is the government and the President, but it is based on the motion of the president of the court, the Chief Justice. So, the Chief Justice approached and told me: 'Ok, you are writing a lot about the judiciary, and you are very critical. I think we need someone like you at the Supreme Administrative Court', and that that was the reason. I have been always interested in judicial reasoning. I was motivated both academically and professionally.

Ramona Coman: Let's move on to address the topic of the book, which is the state of democracy, the dissensus over liberal democracy, and the independence of judges. How do you see the state of democracy in your country first, and then maybe also in Europe more generally?

Zdeněk Kühn: In my country, so far, so good. Because we were quite fortunate in many respects. The situation in Czechia is quite stable, especially if you compare it with the situation in the overall region, with Slovakia, Poland and Hungary. But this is also due to pure political coincidence. Today we have a quite stable Parliament here and the government, which is a pro-European. We do not have any major political party which would be an open threat to democracy and the rule of law. But that can change.

With respect to the judiciary, we have not experienced any major crisis like our neighbouring countries. I would say that one reason for this is that even problematic presidents we had in the past did not pay much attention, for instance, to the nominations of judges to the Constitutional Court or judges to the general judiciary. This includes our last president, Mr. Miloš Zeman, whose mandate ended in 2023. Like American presidents, our President has a unique power to nominate judges to the Constitutional Court. But Mr Zeman was not interested in this power, especially at the beginning of his term. That is why he made appointments based on the advice of his friend, who was a Chief Justice of the Constitutional Court, and the Chief Justice put forward quite decent people, renowned scholars and great judges. Those were perfect nominations. It was only at the end of his term, that Zeman realised that perhaps he was missing out on a chance to use his power and so he started to make more problematic appointments. But it was at a moment when there were not many vacancies, and it did not impact the court at all, as the Senate also resisted some of his problematic nominations. So, generally, I would say the situation here is quite stable. Even the Czech populists, mainstream populists like Mr. Andrej Babiš, a previous Prime Minister, follow the 'rules of the game'. I cannot say that during the Babiš term in office there were any problematic tendencies with respect to the judiciary. To answer your question, I would say no, he did not try to undermine the independence of the judiciary. He did not attack the prosecutor's office, and he did not attack the public media. So, even though he is a friend of Viktor Orbán at the EU level, he did not practice Orbán-style politics at the domestic level. Indeed, so far, we have been quite fortunate, but there is no guarantee that it will stay like this in the coming years.

Ramona Coman: How do you see the situation in other EU Member States? Are you saying that the independence of judges is not (or no longer) a problem specific to Central and Eastern Europe? Is this a European problem? How do you understand this new trend in Europe where we are seeing an assault on courts and judicial independence not only in recent democracies, but also in well-established democracies?

Zdeněk Kühn: Yes, it is clear that there is a crisis of democracy and the rule of law in Europe, in many countries. Why is it so? I believe that we are facing deeper social problems. I am afraid that the unrestrained economic neoliberalism of the 1990s has contributed to those problems – plus unfortunate culture wars which also radicalise many citizens. There is no question that this is a global crisis of liberal democracy.

Ramona Coman: And how do you see the role of judges in this context of rights being contested?

Zdeněk Kühn: First of all, I believe that it is dangerous if we concentrate too much of our attention on constitutional court judges. This is one of the specificities of our region – everyone in Europe talks about constitutional courts and the fact that they are the sole guardian of liberal democracy and so on. I think it is a mistake, because in order to protect democracy and the democratic constitution, and constitutionalism, we need to have a strong and robust ordinary judiciary.

At the same time, we, the constitutional justices, should be self-restrained, I believe. We should not actively pursue some political agenda, and if possible, we shouldn't intensify culture wars, which have the tendency to further split citizens into opposed groups. So, the court shall protect and guard the ultimate values and principles of the constitutional order. But without an independent judiciary, there is no workable democracy in the long run. If you compare it, say, with the Hungarian situation, the judiciary there is more and more under the control of the executive branch, which is not the case in Czechia. That is surprising as, like many European countries, we don't have a supreme judicial council that would be in charge of judicial self-governance. Again, it might be a pure coincidence because our legal settings are also dangerous. It is just that until now we haven't had politicians who will abuse that. What I mean by 'legal settings' is the fact that the Czech judiciary is under the oversight of the Ministry of Justice. So, all those technical issues, allocation of money within the judiciary, promotion of judges, appointment of judges, and judicial training – it is all managed by the ministry. This is unlike most countries in Europe, where these are the responsibility of the supreme judicial council.

Ramona Coman: So how do you explain this? Do you think that there is a judicial culture in Czechia, for example, which is weaker or even doesn't exist in other countries in the region?

Zdeněk Kühn: According to the law, for now, all important powers relating to the judiciary are in the hands of the Ministry of Justice. But, as a matter of fact, those powers are much more decentralised. They are shared between the Ministry of Justice and the regional court chief judges. The Ministry of Justice has the power to promote judges to the appellate courts, for example, but at the same time, such promotion depends on the approval of the chief judge of the appellate court. So, it is not that the Ministry of Justice has the sole power to run the judicial system, which is actually decentralised and in fact, there are more important players than just the Ministry of Justice. There is the President of the Republic, there are the 14 chief judges of the appellate courts, and chief judges of the supreme court and supreme administrative court. You cannot nominate judges to their respective courts without their approval at the same time. So, on paper, the Ministry has the executive power, but it is dependent on the cooperation with the judiciary.

Secondly, the Czech Constitutional Court has also made some important decisions which have strengthened the independence of the judiciary. Some things that are happening in Poland would be impossible here. One example is that the Czech executive branch cannot dismiss a chief judge at will. In 2006, the Czech President, Václav Klaus, tried to dismiss the Chief Justice of the Supreme Court, which technically according to the letter of law was possible. The Chief Justice of the Supreme Court defended herself by filing a constitutional complaint. The Constitutional Court concluded that the executive branch cannot dismiss a chief judge of any court, including the Supreme Court, and this is now a constitutional principle in our country. So, just like what was happening in Poland during the government of the PiS since 2015, one sees that the current Polish government is employing the same practice again to get rid of appointees, and basically, they dismissed most court presidents there. But that would be impossible here, as it would be proclaimed unconstitutional. So, it is another important principle, ruled by the Constitutional Court, which contributes to the stability of the judiciary.

The question is: why don't we have a supreme judicial council? I think that one reason for that is not that the Czech judiciary would be so weak, but that Czech politicians are very sceptical about this institution, especially after taking careful notice of what was happening in Slovakia when they established supreme judicial council at the beginning of this century. It ended in disaster. For Czech politicians, and I must admit also for Czech judges, the Slovak example is a warning that it might end very badly. So, when we saw what was happening in Slovakia, many Czech judges who were originally in favour of a supreme judicial council changed their minds. I think the Slovak example and the abuse of the supreme judicial council by judges themselves, served us as a lesson. Perhaps our legal regulation, even though it's old fashioned – it dates back to the end of the nineteenth century – is actually not too bad. And the situation in Czechia is similar to that in Austria and Germany, by the way. It doesn't function too badly, it works quite well in a way.

Ramona Coman: I understand that the situation in Czechia is different to that in other countries. What challenges is the judiciary there is facing? What are the main issues that you would identify as problematic for the judiciary?

Zdeněk Kühn: One issue, in my opinion, is the fact that the judiciary has a natural tendency to isolate itself in an ivory tower. This is seen in the recent political debates to get rid of lay judges. We follow the German example of having a mixed bench in many cases, especially in criminal and labour law cases. A mixed bench means that there is at the first instance level one professional judge and two lay judges. Now there is a legislative proposal in parliament which is about to abolish mixed benches. And I am afraid that if we delegate and assign all those powers only to professional judges, I think it will not contribute to a better functioning judiciary, but that it will contribute to the isolation of judiciary from real, practical daily challenges, and indeed from the people. I am a supporter of the participation of lay people in the exercise of adjudication – that is why I am critical of that proposed law.

A second example might be, for instance, the way people are appointed as judges. This is something where Czech law is searching for a proper balance. About 20 years ago, we changed the law. We set a minimum age limit of 30 to become a judge, which is not bad. Now the question is how to select new judges. Every regional court selected its judges in a different way. By the way, officially it is the President who appoints them and the ministry who makes those decisions. But in reality, in the Czech scenario, the Ministry of Justice only has a power of veto. This is a good example of how things function in reality. The situation was quite disorganised until recently because every regional court was doing things in a different way; some regional courts were selecting the candidates through non-transparent procedures such that no one knew why they were selecting the nominees. Then, about two years ago, the Ministry of Justice decided to standardise procedures. But the system became so bureaucratic and formal and time consuming that a lot of talented people decided to join private legal practice instead of waiting for the very uncertain result of these tedious proceedings. I am afraid this might lead to the judiciary losing out on some of the most talented candidates, and it might endanger the status of the judiciary. However, it was a decision of the Ministry which was acting on the advice of some prominent members of the judiciary who were critical of the previous system, when it was basically decentralised. But it has resulted in the opposite extreme, with very bureaucratic, and time-consuming proceedings. I think this is also dangerous. But the judiciary still acts in a nonpolitical way, and nominees to the judiciary are not selected in a political manner, which is good.

There might be other problems, such as the fact that, if you are a relative of an important, influential judge in that region, you might have an advantage. I do hope that this isn't too common, however, and I still believe and hope that those are the exceptions and not the rule.

Ramona Coman: How do you perceive the role of courts in addressing highly polarising or politicised issues? You mentioned culture wars as well as also other issues; what is the situation in Czechia, and how do you see the role of judges at the more general level?

Zdeněk Kühn: Let me give an example. Two months ago, the Constitutional Court decided on a case about transgender rights. It was the case about castration. According to Czech law, in order to change gender, you have to undergo genital surgery. So, we had the case of a person who was assigned female at birth who wanted to change their legal gender. If they decided to do this, they would have to undergo full gender reassignment surgery including genital surgery. The person in question was challenging this law And I told you that I preach self-restraint, and I don't want courts to engage in those culture wars, but at the same time, courts cannot ignore such a case. We had a human being who exercised their basic rights and we protected them and annulled the law which required mandatory 'castration' in that way. Of course, we did completely the opposite of what I said a few minutes ago about self-restraint. But here there was no way to exercise self-restraint. We cannot say that this is constitutional, especially in light of the case law of the ECtHR. So, this is an example of when we actively engaged in culture wars. I was not happy with that, but this was our judicial duty to engage. We did not say that there should be no regulation for that. In fact, there must be a regulation made by the legislature. So, we annulled the law, but we delayed the effects of annulment of the law for more than one year. The legislature would have time to make a new law, which could provide for the conditions for someone to change gender.

Ramona Coman: Should I understand that when there is no political consensus to decide something, and when the legislature doesn't have a clear view on the matter, the question is brought to the court?

Zdeněk Kühn: That is correct. This is how we acted. There were some tendencies that we shall resolve once and for all. And we might annul it, and say, 'There shall be no conditions for gender reassignment', but in my opinion, that would be too much. Yes, of course, the legislature has every legitimate right to have a say, especially with respect to impulsive decisions. For the decision to change someone's gender, there must be some regulation. Of course, the legislature might say there is no regulation, everyone can decide on their gender as they want to decide. But if the legislature wants to have a regulation, it is necessary to provide them with the time to make such a regulation. So, at the end of the day, the complainant on the one hand succeeded in bringing about the annulment of the law. But because we delayed the effects of annulment of the law, the complainant did not succeed because we dismissed their complaint and said, 'You must wait till a new regulation is enacted'. Of course, there will be a very interesting case if the legislature does not act and enact a new regulation by summer 2025, when our judgment will take effect. Then there will be chaos. But the chaos will come because of the legislature, not because of us, because we provided the chance for the legislature to create a new regulation. If they don't create a new regulation, ok, it will be unregulated. And anyone can say, 'Today I am female' and, they will have a right to say so. So, I hope that the legislature will make a new regulation.

Ramona Coman: How was the decision of the court received by civil society and other actors?

Zdeněk Kühn: Of course it was received in a divided way. Liberals celebrated the decision, and conservatives were criticising the court for activism. But what we have as an advantage is that so far, judicial decisions are generally respected by all principal players and all political factions. No politicians, even from the extreme right, claimed that we should be ignored. We have the advantage that so far, our judgments are being followed. There is, of course, no guarantee that what is happening today will happen tomorrow.

Another example of that was the decision at the beginning of this year [2024] when we decided on a very technical legal issue – the increase of pensions – an important decision for millions of pensioners because the current government decided to lower the speed rate of the increase of pensions in the country. And the question was a very technical, legal issue: was the adopted legislation retroactive, or not? According to our decision, it was not, but politicians started to use the court as a card in their political games. The opposition filed a constitutional complaint against the law, enacted by the parliament, and they started to say that 'Those judges in Brno, they sided with the government that has the majority in the Parliament, the post of President of the Republic, and now they have the Constitutional Court'. So, the opposition started to become more popular and stated that people have to vote for them in the next elections (2025), since the governing party is 'controlling everything'. So here, the Constitutional Court was abused in a political game, even though it was a very technical decision about retroactivity.

Ramona Coman: Are there different voices within the judiciary and within the Constitutional Court? Are there ever contrasting or divergent views, or dissenting opinions?

Zdeněk Kühn: It has happened. So, in both cases I referred to just now, there were dissenting opinions. And it is natural these dissenting opinions have been quoted: they have often been quoted by those who disagreed with the judgment. But that's normal. And they were not many different views: in the transgender case, I think there were two, while in this pension case there were three dissenting opinions.

Ramona Coman: What does it mean for you to be a judge today in this specific context where there are so many challenges? How do you see your work today in this specific context?

Zdeněk Kühn: First of all, it is a responsibility, because I am one of those actors who might be blamed by our successors for accelerating a crisis of the rule of law and democracy. If you are working at this type of court, of course you have the responsibility you bear. It's a burden. I must be aware that I could be the person who might accelerate the problems of the political system. Or, on the other hand, I'm the person who has the capacity to prolong the stability of our political system. If you ask me generally about the position of being a judge, I believe that judges must be aware that they live in very dangerous times. That's why not only Constitutional Court judges, but all judges in Europe today must be aware of their responsibility to democracy and the rule of law, and to the system they were appointed to as well as the system they are supposed to defend.

Ramona Coman: So, what the role do you think they should play? We have seen judges in Poland taking to the streets, protesting, and having different forms of associations with other judges from other Member States, civil society. And there are also actions and cases brought to the Court of Justice of the European Union and so on. How do you think, for example, judges could protect their independence and other values?

Zdeněk Kühn: With regards to what was happening in Poland, I was reading and watching that with a lot of attention. I believe this is precisely what judges in times of crisis are able to do and must do. So, it's not only talking about their job, but also their judgements in extreme situations. Taking to the streets, protesting and protecting democracy. What I liked about Polish judges, was their main slogan – Constitution. They had t-shirts with the text 'Constitution' written on them, and some of those judges were then subjected to disciplinary proceedings. I believe – and this is something which is also approved by the case law of the European Court of Human Rights – that judges have the power to act in this way, to be engaged in discourse about the protection of democracy. I also believe that judges are supposed to be visible. So, this is what I try to do. For instance, I have no problem giving interviews to journalists about my judgments, explaining my judgments in more detail for normal, ordinary people who do not like to read overly technical legal language. I think it is also the responsibility of judges not to use too many legal technicalities in their judgments, because we are writing these for normal, ordinary people. We should write judgments in a way which will be accessible and understood by the people. Because at the end of the day, members of the public should be the allies of the judiciary, and they should also contribute to the protection of the independence of the judiciary.

Ramona Coman: You said that you followed the actions of the judges in Poland. Have you been involved in any of the petitions or the activities they organised?

Zdeněk Kühn: Yes, I have, of course. I am in touch with some of my Polish colleagues, so I like providing them some assistance, explaining for instance when the previous Polish government tried to defend themselves by making comparisons with the Czech law. I tried to provide them with my legal opinion, how it actually works. For, as I told you, even though Czech law looks pretty authoritarian, and it gives a lot of power to the ministry, in reality it doesn't function like that. I even quoted a former Minister of Justice under the Mr. Babiš government; after he stepped down from the office, the former minister wrote that he realised that the power within the judiciary is not only in the Ministry of Justice, and that the power within the judiciary is dispersed everywhere. He also said that as a minister, it is extremely difficult to change anything because you do not have the real power. I tried to provide those perspectives to my Polish colleagues. I also met with them, attended presentations and public speeches. I tried to provide my friends in Poland with my support. Moreover, the previous Czech chief justices of the Constitutional Court, Supreme Court, Supreme Administrative Court, the previous Ombudsman and previous Prosecutor-General issued a common memorandum supporting the Polish judiciary and Polish prosecutor's office in times of crisis. So, they harshly criticised what was happening in Poland. And I know that my Polish colleagues were really happy about it – they were happy that they were getting support from the neighbouring country.

Ramona Coman: And the Hungarian case is exactly the opposite. There we saw silence, and the judges were more passive. How do we explain the fact that, despite the measures which have been adopted by the government, the Hungarian judges remained silent from the beginning of the process?

Zdeněk Kühn: There is a big difference between Hungary and Poland, because in Poland there were many manifest violations of the law and the Constitution. For a judge, it is much easier to protest, and to talk about it, if there is an open and gross violation of the law. In Hungary, the government controls everything and they have a constitutional supermajority. The government was able to follow the Constitution because they were making the constitution, and they amended the constitution many times. So, the Constitution will of course fit their agenda. For a judge, as a lawyer, it's much more difficult to criticise or fight assaults on the judiciary, because it seems that everything is in compliance with the principle of legality. And then, unlike Polish colleagues, of course, Hungarian colleagues had much more difficulty working out what to criticise because everything fit the law. Plus, the strategy of the Hungarian government was much more sophisticated. So, whereas the Polish government resisted the decisions of the European Court of Human Rights, and resisted decisions of the Court of Justice of the EU, the Hungarian government did, for instance, comply with decisions of the Court of Justice. The government did not disobey the judgments of the European Courts openly, and therefore I understand my Hungarian colleagues and their reluctance to be more visible.

The Fidesz party's control over the country is also much stronger than the control of the previous government in Poland. In Poland, they had natural allies and a strong opposition. In Hungary, the opposition is very weak and fragmented. There were actually only a few isolated judges who talked about what was happening in Hungary, or spoke against it. A few years ago, when I was visiting Hungary as a judge of the Supreme Administrative Court via an exchange programme funded by the European Union, I saw a completely different atmosphere than in Poland. The judges were always looking at me, or they were talking very softly. They looked around to check that no one was listening to the conversations. And only then did they start to talk to me in a more open way. So, it is evident that the atmosphere in Hungary is completely different: it has become a soft, authoritarian regime.

Ramona Coman: I have a question about professional associations: Do you have them, and how active are they when things happen, for example, in relation to events in other countries like Poland or Hungary? How active are associations in defending judicial independence and other values within Czechia, but also outside?

Zdeněk Kühn: We have a Czech Judicial Union and approximately one third of judges are members – 1,000 out of 3,000 judges in total. These are the most active judges, and I must say that the Czech Union of Judges (*Soudcovská unie České republiky*) actively took part in what was happening in Poland. The representatives of the Czech Judicial Union were marching and protesting together with our Polish colleagues in the streets of Warsaw. The Czech Union of Judges is a renowned association, which dates to the early 1990s. It was established by some of the most famous and most renowned Czech judges of the 1990s, and it focuses on the independence of judiciary and things like that.

Ramona Coman: How is the role of judges perceived in your country? Some judges in this book have argued that judicial independence cannot be protected without support from civil society.

Zdeněk Kühn: Yes, I am afraid that if we get into a situation like a Poland, we will not get much public support. I can think of one example from 2006. The former Czech President, Václav Klaus, dismissed the Chief Justice of the Supreme Court. As an associate professor of law, I claimed that this was unconstitutional and the Constitutional Court ultimately proclaimed that the dismissal went against the separation of powers, and the President angrily accepted the decision. At the time, I was surrounded by members of our law faculty, many of them from the old era, who were claiming that the president can dismiss a judge at any time because the president exercises state power. And, to my shock, that is what most academics said at the time, twenty years ago.

Further, at the conference about this issue in 2006 there was a presiding judge of the High Court in Prague who stepped up and said if he were dismissed by the President, he would not hesitate even for a minute to vacate his office. He continued by saying that the president has the right to dismiss judges at any time. Not surprisingly if the legal professionals had this opinion in 2006, the ordinary people did not care, did not pay attention. The fact that legal professionals held this view, this came as a huge shock for me. Only a few academics and professionals said in 2006 there was something wrong or unconstitutional with the dismissal. Many legal professionals actually pursued a very stupid idea, claiming that the Chief Justice was not a good manager after all and so the President should have the power to remove her. Perhaps, she was not the best Chief Justice in our history, but that does not matter. It was unconstitutional. We were fortunate that we had judges at the Constitutional Court at the time who said the action was unconstitutional.

On this issue, I saw a communist or authoritarian thinking at work. This was a complete denial of the idea of the separation of powers. I simply could not understand why anyone could have the view that President of the Republic can do whatever he wants with regards to the judiciary.

But to get back to your question, do I believe that we will gather the support from ordinary people? I don't think that we will get the support unless we are able to link this to some future dramatic situation, such as an assault on the independence of the judiciary, with something more concrete, something more visible to the people. I don't believe that people will take to the streets just to protect the independence of judiciary, because for them it's too abstract.

A few years ago, we had about 300,000 people on the streets of Prague when a demonstration was called in favour of the independence of judiciary. It happened during the previous government, under Prime Minister Babiš, who is now the leader of the Czech opposition. He is an oligarch and populist, and he had replaced the Minister of Justice. There was a fear that the new minister would put the independence of judiciary at risk. So a demonstration was called for the independence of the judiciary. However, it was much more a political demonstration against the government. I don't think that most people gathered in order to support independence of judiciary. People gathered because they disliked the government of Mr Babiš. Plus, I didn't believe that the replacement of the Minister would put our judiciary at risk at all. I did not believe for a single second, because I knew the new minister, and I knew that this was a decent person who would never, ever, push or abuse her powers within the judiciary, which she did not. So even though the protests were called demonstrations for 'the independence of judiciary', they were much more political demonstrations against the government.

Ramona Coman: Thank you. As we come to the end of the interview, the last point for me is about the role of the European Union. How do you see the role of the EU, and the Commission in particular, as well as other institutions, in rule of law problems in the Member States? For example, in Poland and Hungary, but also Romania or Slovakia. How do you perceive the role of the European Union? Is it a solution or a problem?

Zdeněk Kühn: I would say that the EU is neither a solution nor a problem. It can contribute to solving the problem, but it can also contribute to extending the problem.

Generally, I have a positive view of the case law of the European Court of Justice, which protects independence of judiciary starting with the Portuguese judges' case. I think it can help. But it's not like some kind of magic which will solve all our problems, because at the end of the day, those problems must be solved by the elections of local people. We must vote for politicians who will not attack the judiciary and the rule of law. And even if we vote for populists, hopefully, we must vote for the populists who will not put the independence of judiciary at stake. I was talking with some Italian professionals, discussing what the Italian government is doing with Italian judges. They told me that so far, so good. In their opinion, the Italian government is not trying to exercise its undue influence over the judiciary. That might change – because I do not trust those neo-fascist parties – but at least the Italians I have talked to in recent years told me that the government is not doing anything improper.

But to give a short answer, I support the case law of the Court of Justice. I think it can help. And I believe, for instance, that with respect to Hungary, the influence of the EU is keeping Viktor Orbán's government within some limits. If Hungary were not in the EU, I think Viktor Orbán's government would react very differently. They would run and exercise their power in a far wilder and much more authoritarian way. On the other hand, of course, someone might criticise the EU for helping to create this monster. It's also true that the authoritarian Hungarian regime is being built by European money. But, I repeat, I believe without the EU the situation would have been far worse.

19

When your Independence and Integrity are Called into Question, you must be Prepared to Respond

TAMÁS MATUSIK[1]

Viktor Kazai: We would be grateful if you could tell us about whatever aspects of your personal or your professional background that you find relevant.

Tamás Matusik: I come from a family that lived on the outskirts of Budapest, specifically in Buda. Both of my parents were engineers, so it wasn't a given that I would choose to study law. In fact, there were not any lawyers in my family, except for my grandma's older brother in the first half of the twentieth century. It was not until high school that I realised I was interested in the humanities, which led me to pursue a law degree.

At university, it was a big surprise for me to see the amount of reading material we received in the first year, and that made me question if I was on the right path. During my time at university, I interned at a law firm focusing on civil and economic matters, but I discovered my passion for criminal law. I found the logical and accountable nature of criminal law to be more appealing, and better aligned with my mindset than other areas of law.

I enjoyed my time as an intern at the law firm because I had a lot of freedom. I could come and go as I pleased, and the office environment was very accommodating. However, I soon realised that the graduated trainee lawyers were essentially overworked, putting in long hours in the hopes of achieving success in the future. They were working until 7 pm every day, starting my career with such long hours did not appeal to me at all.

During my time at university, I also had the opportunity to speak with fellow students who were doing internships at courts. They shared their positive experiences, which made me interested in pursuing a similar path. One of them recommended a judge at the Central District Court of Buda, in the Buda Hills, and I decided to reach out to her. She welcomed me, and I ended up interning there for a short period, around

[1] Interview conducted in English on 3 April 2024 at the Central District Court of Buda and validated for publication on 13 January 2025.

three to six weeks. Despite the brief duration, the experience left a lasting impression on me. I found the atmosphere and the sense of duty of being a judge very appealing. I found myself specifically drawn to criminal law, and that became my primary focus during my university years.

Upon completing university with a summa cum laude degree, I felt a sense of success, despite the fact that it took me six years instead of the expected five. I admit I was somewhat lazy in the beginning, but in the end, I successfully finished. With such a prestigious degree and good results in the language exam, I naively believed I would easily find my place at the courts. However, I soon realised that breaking into the judiciary was far from easy at the time. There was no official entrance system back then, people just relied on family connections and friendships. I learned the hard way when I submitted an application to a court, only to receive a polite rejection stating that there were no vacancies.

The head of the criminal division contacted me via email expressing that they were in need of clerks. This was not a judicial position, but rather an opportunity to work in that capacity for a period of six months to a year, and the plan was to transition into a trainee position afterwards. I was living with my parents at the time without financial obligations, so I saw this as a good opportunity and I accepted it. However, towards the end of the summer, there was a change in plans as that position had also been given to a family member or relative of a court executive. However, the head of the division intervened and convinced the president that I had been promised a position in the court, leading to my immediate appointment as a trainee judge. During that year, there were 15 new trainee judges at the Budapest courts, and I recall being one of the very few who were not related to judges.

My path was unconventional because I never worked as a trainee at a district court, only at the Metropolitan Court. As a result, I did not have a regular assignment at district court level back in 2006. At that time, there were major controversies involving the wrongful detention by investigative judges of numerous protesters who were demonstrating against the government. This led to internal professional inquiries into how these incidents occurred. Witnessing these events made me realise that there were deficiencies in the investigative judiciary and that improvements could be made at a higher professional level. The idea of being an investigative judge increasingly appealed to me. I understood that this role required greater autonomy than usual with strong human rights approach, quick thinking, and the ability to make decisions in an extremely short timeframe. The cases were intriguing, but I believed they could be handled with greater professionalism rather than the practice of blindly accepting every motion filed by the prosecutor.

So, that was my plan. When I shared it with my superiors, they were surprised. No one had wanted to be an investigative judge before, as that role was seen as a punishment for those not performing well in trial work. They questioned why I, with good skills and results, would want to do it. But I was determined. I did not have experience with normal cases at a district court, but I could picture myself in this role. Initially, I started as an assistant judge in this department and finally managed to convince the president to support me when a position opened up. At that time, there was no ranking system, so selection was subjective and not based on objective criteria.

Viktor Kazai: Have you ever thought about changing fields?

Tamás Matusik: About 10 years ago, in 2014, I spent a year working in the Judicial Office as the head of the International Relations Department. It was a significant change for me because, as a seconded judge, I was not allowed to handle cases. Instead, it was primarily office work, and I held a middle management position. After that year, I never had the desire to switch to another field in the judiciary. Since 2015, I have been leading the Investigative Judge Department after applying for the position through an open application process. I am in my second term now, considering that court leaders serve six-year terms. Our department is quite large, with 18 judges, and we are responsible for the entire investigative judiciary in Budapest. Our jurisdiction extends over the entire city, and the work is genuinely fascinating. We are on duty every day, including weekends, and judges contact me if there are any administrative issues. Me and my deputy are essentially on call all the time. I can't say that I'll stay here forever, but for now, I have no plans to change career.

Viktor Kazai: For a considerable amount of time, you also held another position as a member and later as the president of the National Judicial Council[2] – how did that come about?

Tamás Matusik: In 2018, the mandate of the former members of the Judicial Council (*Országos Bírói Tanács*) came to an end. I believed they were not effective in fulfilling their main task, which was supervising the President of the National Office for the Judiciary,[3] Tünde Handó. I was not seeking confrontation, but I was prepared to stand up for my belief if necessary, and I applied for the role with that understanding.

The judges elected a Council with a majority of members who shared a similar attitude to my own. When we began our work, we were promptly met with resistance from the President of the OBH due to our professional criticism and inquiries. She not only refused to acknowledge our concerns but also launched personal attacks against me and other council members in court and in the media. This led to a challenging period of one and a half years during which she completely shut down cooperation with the council, causing a constitutional crisis. It became clear that there was a lack of collaboration between the two most crucial judicial bodies, namely the OBH and the OBT, and the issue remained unresolved within the judiciary. Despite using all available legal means to address the situation, including presenting a case to Parliament for the dismissal of the OBH President, no action was taken on the merits of our motion. Consequently, the systemic checks failed to resolve the issue, and only a political solution emerged: the President was appointed to be a Constitutional Court justice and thus removed from the judicial system. Ultimately, we emerged victorious from this conflict. The most intriguing aspect was that it wasn't resolved solely through institutional means but required an external political decision by Parliament.

[2] Editorial note: Since 2012, the National Judicial Council (OBT) has been the supervisory organ of the central administration of courts in Hungary. The President of the Supreme Court (Kúria) is delegated by law, while the other 14 judge members are elected by their colleagues.

[3] Editorial note: The National Office for the Judiciary (OBH) is responsible for the central administration of the courts. Its work is supervised by the National Judicial Council (OBT).

I am immensely proud of the six years of hard work despite the challenges we faced, especially in those one and a half years. It was an extremely demanding period, and I must admit that it had its downsides as well. It took a toll on our personal and private lives, and we continue to grapple with the consequences. Nevertheless, I believe that we played a crucial role in safeguarding judicial independence in Hungary and combating detrimental trends. Our efforts contributed to slowing down or even obstructing negative developments, ultimately leading to a significant judicial reform in 2023. This reform substantially strengthened judicial self-governance and independence in Hungary, a change that was not only demanded by the European Union but also made possible through our relentless advocacy and activism. Without our perseverance and dedication, this positive transformation would not have materialised.

Viktor Kazai: You and your colleagues at the OBT did not run for re-election, even though you could have been theoretically re-elected. What was the reason?

Tamás Matusik: The reason was that the possibility of re-election stemmed from tailor-made legislation. We were the only ones who had the opportunity to rerun for the position, not the former or future members of the council. This made it a one-time opportunity, a transitional rule in the law. We criticised the President of the Supreme Court, András Zs. Varga, for having accepted his nomination that was enabled by tailor-made legislative amendment, so we felt it was only right to decline our opportunity to run again. In my opinion, it's also unhealthy to get re-elected as member of a supervising body. Running for a new campaign can affect your objectivity. With almost 3,000 judges in the country, it is not ideal to have a council with returning members. There should be a wide selection of judges.

Viktor Kazai: The next important topic for our conversation is the relationship between the state of democracy and judicial independence. There is extensive academic research and numerous international indices and findings from EU and CoE bodies that point to democratic erosion in many European countries, particularly in CEE and including Hungary. What do you think about the impact of democratic erosion on judicial independence in general, and specifically in the case of Hungary?

Tamás Matusik: It is essential to acknowledge that erosion, should it occur, does not happen abruptly. In most cases, this process involves small and gradual steps. For many people, and for numerous judges, it is not immediately evident what direction these changes are taking nor how individuals in the judiciary consciously perceive the evolving nature of their judicial careers and their roles. Unfortunately, in Hungary, many judges lack self-awareness on numerous counts. Not all judges consider it important to participate in the process of safeguarding the separation of powers, which is, of course, very significant. Despite the long-standing tradition of judicial irremovability, in 2012, a considerable number of judges were compelled to retire abruptly due to an unconstitutional law. This action was framed by the CJEU as a matter of discrimination,[4] even though it was clearly a matter of judicial independence. Countless judicial leaders were

[4] Case C-286/12 *European Commission v Hungary* ECLI:EU:C:2012:687, [2013] 1 CMLR 44.

immediately ousted from their positions, with no chance of reinstatement. This was the first instance in which fundamental principles were challenged in practice.

Viktor Kazai: There is a very long list of measures that have threatened or still threaten judicial independence in Hungary. What are the most important challenges – including those that are less visible – when it comes to the independence of the judiciary?

Tamás Matusik: The most aggressive move to threaten judicial independence was the forced retirement of judges, which had a significant impact. In addition, there were improper appointments of court presidents and senior judges. This irregular practice, as stated in council decisions from 2018 and 2022,[5] affected the judicial leaders and, later, in particular the senior judges in the Supreme Court.

Additionally, there were limitations on freedom of expression, and the execution phase of the well-known *Baka v Hungary* case[6] is still ongoing. Disciplinary actions against council members were initiated, but many cases were left unfinished, with chilling effect. There were visible smear campaigns against judges including myself and one of my colleagues. These campaigns, which saw publication of over 400 articles in a single month in the government-friendly press, are unique within Europe. What is surprising is that these articles not only criticise our decisions as council members but also attack our ethics and question our independence as judges.

There have been instances of discrimination in the workplace over the one and a half years, which I addressed in the context of our challenges of the former President of the Judicial Office.

There is another issue that still persists, which remains the most pressing concern: judicial salaries in our country are the lowest across the entire EU. This is a significant problem. I understand that it may not be very popular to discuss this matter because it is often seen as merely a financial concern, but it is crucial to acknowledge that fair wages are an integral part of judicial independence; they reflect our dignity and the respect of our profession. As judges, we receive very low salaries, and our judicial staff are also not remunerated adequately to secure their livelihoods. Consequently, many of them are leaving the judiciary, resulting in a substantial turnover that significantly impacts the functioning of the courts. It is becoming increasingly difficult to operate without our colleagues. This issue has gained significant prominence recently and needs urgent attention.

Viktor Kazai: Have you personally ever experienced anyone wanting to interfere in a specific case?

Tamás Matusik: Never in the sense of being instructed how I, as a judge, should decide. However, there are other types of pressure. Two weeks ago, I faced an attack in the press again regarding a judicial decision associated with me. Initially, it was reported that I made a decision in a sensitive case, which was untrue as I was not even the judge involved in that case. Criticising judicial decisions is normal and acceptable, but the problem was that they were questioning my character, connecting this order with my

[5] Resolutions no. 59/2018, 60/2018 and 50/2022 of the National Judicial Council.
[6] *Baka v Hungary*, App No 20261/12 (ECtHR, 23 June 2016).

previous actions, like meeting the US ambassador on behalf of the National Judicial Council. After realising their mistake, the journalists changed their angle, blaming a subordinate in my department but still making out that my character had something to do with the decision. This version was published in the printed press nationwide. The main issue is not the criticism of the decision but the personal attack against me, claiming that I am not independent as a judge.

Viktor Kazai: Independence of the judiciary is crucial for the entire justice system and for judges themselves. However, it is also important for ordinary citizens. What are the negative implications and consequences of a decline in judicial independence from a citizen's perspective, and how is it perceived?

Tamás Matusik: It is concerning to see the public's declining trust in the judiciary, and surveys also reflect this sentiment. I am no expert on the matter, but it seems that public trust is constantly diminishing. Cases remain unresolved, with parties either reluctantly accepting the outcomes or challenging them. There is a prevailing belief that judicial decisions are influenced by personal or biased motives, which is exacerbated by media coverage and public assertions.

Moreover, politicians from both the ruling and opposition parties question judicial decisions, not just on legal grounds but also by attacking the integrity of the judges involved. This creates a significant issue, and things are unlikely to improve unless both sides refrain from making populist statements following court decisions. For example, the Prime Minister criticised the decision to desegregate Roma communities, citing it as just one example of a troubling trend. Then there is the former opposition leader, who also serves as a mayor, publicly targeted judges who ruled against him, even going so far as to label them as biased and to plan to publish a list of their names online. Additionally, a Hungarian member of the European Parliament accused judges of being traitors and communists, prompting a response from judicial leaders who condemned such statements as unacceptable. Furthermore, there were cases where lawyers demanded compensation for prisoners subject to inadequate prison conditions; for this the lawyers were accused of involvement in 'prison business' and this label was endorsed by a former Minister of Justice, who also said that the legal practice is on the side of the criminals, undermining the legal system's integrity. These manipulative and populist messages are damaging to public perception as well as the independence of the judiciary, portraying judges as unprofessional and lacking in impartiality.

Viktor Kazai: When dealing with politically or morally sensitive cases, the judiciary can only rely on its own authority because general acceptance from the public is needed for judgments to be executed. When you are deciding on sensitive cases, do you take into consideration either public opinion or the potential consequences of your decisions?

Tamás Matusik: Judges must not let external factors influence their decisions. Although we are part of society and need to stay informed about what is happening, we must set aside any outside influences when making judgments. It is crucial for courts to operate with transparency and to have professional communication, and for judgments not to be influenced by political or ideological biases. In Hungary, there is a concerning trend of ideologies seeping into various aspects of public discourse, including court cases. When public debates on the judiciary start emphasising labels such as left-wing, liberal, or Christian conservative, it can create unnecessary pressure on judges. Although judges should not let this influence their decisions, the danger still exists if public debates continue in this direction.

Viktor Kazai: In your experience, have the fundamental principles of constitutional democracy in general, or more specifically in criminal law, been questioned by individuals outside of the judiciary or even by the judges themselves? For example, in relation to principles such as presumption of innocence, due process, or equality.

Tamás Matusik: In Hungary, the meaning of the term 'rule of law' has become distorted in public debates. It is sometimes portrayed as a message from Brussels that runs contrary to our domestic values, and this is simply not true. The rule of law is a fundamental aspect of Hungary's constitutional system and its Fundamental Law. Unfortunately, it has been politicised and is often misrepresented, leading to misconceptions among the public. For example, the notion of proportionality in legal matters has raised the public expectation of harsher judgments and punishments, especially in high-profile cases. This trend is reflected in changes to the criminal code, where the potential prison sentences are continually being extended. Furthermore, the media's approach to reporting legal cases often lacks objectivity and fairness, leading to unjust harm to individuals' reputations and undermining the principle of presumption of innocence. As a result, those wrongfully portrayed as criminals in the press face a prolonged and arduous process when seeking justice and reparation.

Viktor Kazai: Based on your professional experience of over 20 years, what do you think it means to be a judge, and has this changed since you began your career?

Tamás Matusik: When I first started as a trainee, the situation was much better since there was a greater sense of dignity among the judges compared to now. I believe this is a challenge not only in Hungary, but all over the world. This is not just happening in new democracies or in Central and Eastern Europe; there are new challenges for judges everywhere. A judicial career does not have the same appeal as it used to. For instance, the ENCJ has launched a new project group focused on making judicial careers more attractive. Many countries face the perception that few lawyers want to work in the courts, and this issue needs to be addressed.

It is not just about salaries but also working conditions and public trust. In fact, this fundamental issue is often related to populism. At a recent conference, I heard a Croatian colleague mention that all political parties are targeting judges because they are an easy target. Judges cannot respond to these attacks like politicians can with press releases or press conferences. It is easy for politicians to blame judges for the country's problems. For this reason, even older democracies are not immune to such populist approaches.

Being a judge in these times is challenging if you value your independence and are vigilant about protecting it. We cannot all be expected to have an X [formerly Twitter] account and communicate on these issues daily. By the way, I have an X profile, and I actively use it to express my views on issues relating to judicial independence. Although traditional judicial associations have a role in addressing these challenges, they are often preoccupied with fighting for better salaries, which is a major issue in Hungary. Despite the challenges, they are doing important work in this area.

Viktor Kazai: In the jurisprudence of the European Court of Human Rights and the European Court of Justice, there is evidence that the politicisation of the judiciary has reached such an extreme level in certain Member States that judicial appointment processes have become unlawful or irregular. In particular, in the case of Poland, there are many judges who were appointed unlawfully, making their positions technically not lawful. Have you observed similar unlawful appointments of judges in Hungary?

Tamás Matusik: As a former member of the OBT, I would like to say something about the decision we made in 2022 regarding the appointment practices of the President of the Supreme Court. We criticised the president for deviating from the rules of the selection process – something he still denies. In his statements he called our criticism unfounded. However, we maintain that the process was unlawful. Our concern was not about specific judges, but rather the overall practice. In this sense, some of the judicial appointments in Hungary can be questioned, although the issue is not as widespread here as it is in Poland. We also found irregularities in the process of appointing judicial leaders during the presidency of the former President of the Judicial Office. These concerns led us to make inquiries as a council, and we concluded that there were indeed irregularities in the appointment process.

Viktor Kazai: That law required consultation with the Judicial Council regarding the election of the current Chief Justice. What was the Judicial Council's opinion on his election?

Tamás Matusik: We did not support his candidacy. This was for two main reasons.[7] First, he lacked courtroom experience because he had never been a judge before. Although he served as a Deputy Chief Prosecutor of Hungary and was a member of the Constitutional Court, the Constitutional Court is not part of Hungary's judicial system and has a different appointment process; its members are political appointees and not integrated into the regular court system. Second, his path to candidacy was facilitated by two legal changes in the legislation, which we viewed as being tailored specifically for him, and this raised questions about his impartiality for the role. Despite our lack of support, the legislature overlooked our objections, and he was appointed President of the Supreme Court by the Parliament. We had to work with him together as he also became an ex officio member of the Judicial Council after his appointment.

Viktor Kazai: For a couple of years it was possible for members of the Constitutional Court to be appointed as ordinary judges in Hungary, even if they did not meet the general eligibility criteria. What do you think about this? Do you see any place in the judicial system for judges with backgrounds outside the judiciary, for example in public administration? Or do you think that the judiciary is only for career judges who start from the very beginning as clerks or interns and then move up the ladder?

Tamás Matusik: The possibility of becoming an ordinary judge for Constitutional Court justices and applying to a judicial position from the outside are two different phenomena. In the former case the appointment is automatic and candidates are not checked

[7] Resolution no. 120/2020 of the National Judicial Council.

for any eligibility criteria. Moreover, former members of the Constitutional Court are immediately promoted to high positions in the ordinary judicial system.

Nevertheless, I believe the judicial system should not function like an exclusive club. Instead, it should be accessible from all corners. I generally believe that the previous shifts in this direction were necessary. Not only because it is unrealistic for someone to accurately decide on a lifelong career in their 20s, but also because an overly closed institution is not conducive to justice. The current application and ranking system is a significant improvement over the previous subjective approach. Although it will never be flawless, it is a step in the right direction. This system allows for objective criteria and a more open selection process, which is crucial given the declining quality of training due to low salaries and reduced opportunities. We need to consider candidates from different backgrounds to ensure a diverse and competent judiciary. While institutional knowledge is important, it is not essential for every judge to have followed the same career path.

Viktor Kazai: Different jurisdictions vary significantly regarding judges' freedom of expression. In some countries, judges can freely express their views in public, including participating in radio or television interviews. However, in other countries, there are more constraints on their expression. What is the extent of judges' freedom of expression in Hungary, both in relation to the legal framework and the attitudes of the judges?

Tamás Matusik: There has been a debate about freedom of expression for judges, prompted by a specific case. As a member of the OBT, I have been involved in the adoption of a new Code of Ethics.[8] The code emphasises that judges should not be prohibited from commenting on political issues, and that defending their independence is part of their duty and they should not be criticised if they do so. However, the code has been challenged by the Supreme Court President before the Constitutional Court for various reasons, and the outcome of the challenge is still pending. I disagree with the reasons presented by the Supreme Court President, particularly the argument that the Judicial Council cannot adopt a new Code of Ethics.

Viktor Kazai: Do you think that the judiciary, or judges in general, are still trying to expand the limits of judicial self-expression, or have they accepted the situation?

Tamás Matusik: The judges seem to be downplaying or ignoring the reality of the situation. Many judges refuse to comment further, which, in my opinion, is not a good way to behave. When your independence and integrity are called into question, you must be prepared to respond. In the past, the failure of judges to react was a significant issue, particularly when it came to forced retirements – the most serious violation of our careers, positions, and profession. No one, not even the Judicial Association, took action.

Viktor Kazai: In some countries like Romania and Poland, judges have shown their self-expression through actual protests on the streets. What are your thoughts on seeing

[8] Resolution no. 16/2022 of the National Judicial Council.

these examples in other countries? And do you think something similar would be imaginable or acceptable in Hungary?

Tamás Matusik: There are excellent examples in other countries that we can learn from. It is not just about the *Magyar Bírói Egyesület* (MABIE, Hungarian Association of Judges) adopting their approaches, methods, or tools, but also about the mindset of the Hungarian judges and people. The public mindset in Hungary is different, and it may lead us to accept certain deals within the community. In Poland, for instance, only one Hungarian judge participated in the March of a Thousand Robes that took place in Warsaw in January 2020 and that person faced criticism in the press. Such demonstrations by judges are unimaginable in Hungary due to the differing mindsets.

Although judicial self-governance was strengthened during our six-year mandate at the Judicial Council, the local councils' competences remain weak. However, new legislation and reforms provide some promise for the future. Yet, these changes alone are not sufficient. Continuous monitoring is crucial to understand how these new tools of the Judicial Council are being implemented and used in practice.

The point that I always emphasise in interviews and conferences is the importance of judicial solidarity. This is not my original idea; it was also a topic of the ENCJ. Solidarity among judges can prevent the decline of independent judiciary. When we share knowledge, challenges, and solutions, and show solidarity with each other – and examples here include both the EAJ and the IAJ, we can convey information to the European Commission more effectively. As a Judicial Council, we have shared information and recognised common challenges we have faced, such as judicial salaries and political populism. By joining forces and sharing our thoughts and results, we can find higher-level solutions to these common challenges. Our judicial reform efforts even reached the table of the European Commission, thanks to the collaboration of the international judicial community.

Despite being called traitors of our homeland, we proudly continued to inform and collaborate with the international community and have achieved significant success. This was symbolised by the Judicial Independence Award we received from the IAJ in recognition of our efforts for judicial independence in Hungary. The award was evidence that Hungary is a country where judicial independence must be protected and fought for.

Viktor Kazai: It seems that in recent years, in many countries, including Hungary, there has been a growing closeness between the judiciary, judicial associations, and civil society actors, including human rights NGOs. What is your view of the cooperation – or possible cooperation – between judicial associations and civil society actors? Do you see any areas where they can collaborate on a permanent basis?

Tamás Matusik: I believe that NGOs, alongside other organisations, conduct important reports, surveys and research. Judicial associations can also play a significant role in this. Currently, it seems that official joint training activities are restricted. However, I have personally participated in professional conferences organised by NGOs focusing on investigative judiciary. Unfortunately, my involvement led to criticism in the press. The current political atmosphere often portrays NGOs as adversaries of the state, which makes it challenging to cooperate with them. Nevertheless, it's crucial to defend judicial integrity. While we should not be unduly influenced by NGOs, participating in professional communication or conferences should not be criticised on the basis of ideology, as often happens in the press.

It is also difficult to engage judges in research due to concerns about the potential negative effect on their careers. The fear of being associated with NGOs in the context of research creates hesitancy. Additionally, as a judge, when I give interviews, it is essential to understand that I am representing myself as an independent judge, not as the head of any department. Although I take pride in my past role as the president of the National Judicial Council, I am no longer in that position, so I only represent my own views now.

Viktor Kazai: As we wrap up the interview, I would like to ask you about the future. The EU and the Council of Europe have made significant efforts to protect judicial independence in Hungary. Do you think these European mechanisms have been effective in safeguarding and strengthening judicial independence in Hungary? If not, where do you see room for improvement? How could they be enhanced to better support judicial independence?

Tamás Matusik: I believe that the particular legislation adopted by the Hungarian parliament to unfreeze the EU funds[9] was more effective than any other because it led to an increase in judicial independence and self-governance in Hungary, which was a unique occurrence in the last decade. However, its practical impact and effectiveness need to be continuously monitored. It is not my role to make judgements prematurely. The true effectiveness of this legislation in the daily operations of the judiciary and society cannot be determined instantly, it takes time to evaluate these. It is the responsibility of European stakeholders to oversee this, not as a punishment or consequence, but in order to maintain our alignment with the values of the EU and to make necessary improvements when needed.

Viktor Kazai: Are you optimistic about the implementation of judicial reforms?

Tamás Matusik: I was satisfied with the text of the legislation. It met about 99 per cent of the requirements set by the EU, which is great. Although some civil society and NGOs have raised objections, I believe it fulfilled most of what was needed. What happens next depends on the people involved. It would be unfair to be pessimistic, but also unrealistic to be overly optimistic.

Editor's note: After the interview, the National Judicial Council (OBT) signed an agreement with the Ministry of Justice, which makes any salary increase for judges and court administrators contingent upon the implementation of additional judicial reforms. Judicial associations and individual judges, including Judge Matusik, have expressed concerns about this agreement, suspecting that the planned reforms by the Ministry of Justice will further erode judicial independence in Hungary.

[9] Editorial note: In 2023, Hungary passed legislation to improve judicial independence, addressing concerns raised by the EU. As a result, the Commission decided to partially unfreeze EU funds to Hungary.

PART IV

Insights from Neighbouring European Countries

20

I Went to Bed a Judge and Woke Up a Terrorist

YAVUZ AYDIN[1]

Leonardo Puleo: Could you tell me a bit about your background, and especially what motivated you to enter the judiciary.

Yavuz Aydin: I graduated from Ankara University law faculty. After completing my master's, I was appointed as a judge in 2002 at the age of 27, which felt too early for me. I worked for several years as a sitting judge in a town on the border between Greece and Turkey.

After the start of the negotiation process for Turkey's accession to the EU, I was invited to be a part of the negotiation team and to align Turkey's legislation with the EU *acquis* and best practices. Preserving my title as a judge, I worked in the Justice Ministry for some years. After obtaining a master's degree from Exeter in the UK, I was sent to Brussels to work as the Justice Counsellor at the Permanent Representation of Turkey to the EU. There, my role was to follow developments in the EU and facilitate the flow of information between Brussels and Ankara regarding the areas of judiciary and fundamental rights during the accession negotiations. But those were the good old days.

Starting from 2011, we witnessed a shift towards authoritarianism in Turkey. A significant conflict emerged within the judiciary beginning with the Gezi protests in 2013. Actually, starting from 2012, my position was very explicit and clear: I was openly criticising the government's policies, and as a result of this, I was called back from Brussels to Turkey, and sent to a remote, heavily overworked court, where I worked for two years until July 2016, the infamous coup attempt took place. I can explain more about that, but maybe it could be defined as a 'false flag operation' rather than a botched coup attempt.

Leonardo Puleo: Could you clarify why the coup could be described as a false flag operation?

[1] Interview conducted on 24 May 2025 and validated for publication on 3 February 2025.

Yavuz Aydin: The coup attempt took place on 15 July 2016. On 16 July, the following day, a Saturday, I woke up as a 'terrorist'. It was like falling into a Kafkaesque universe. I summarise this process as 'I went to bed a judge and woke up a terrorist', like thousands of other colleagues. Between 9 and 11 o' clock that morning, before the coup attempt was fully suppressed, the judges' council had convened and suspended 2,800 judges and prosecutors within two hours only. Simply calculated, giving one minute to discuss on each of these 2,800 judges would normally take about 46 hours without any break, but they managed to suspend 2,800 judges in just two hours. When I woke up, I found several missed calls from my colleagues, and I learned that I was on that list of purged judges.

At that moment a different phase started in my life. First of all, I must say that I was not ashamed to be on the list – it was even an honour to me. Not being on that list would have been something to be ashamed of because the list was apparently prepared two years in advance, in 2014. Some colleagues who had passed away in 2014 were still on that list, and the workplaces of many people indicated on the list were the same as they had been in 2014, though they were transferred to different cities in the meantime. We have evidence that it was prepared in advance, as far back as 2014, long before the coup. Being on that list was like a confirmation of my stance against authoritarianism and dictatorship, and my support of the rule of law and democracy.

After that day, most of these 2,800 suspended colleagues were arrested and detained. I waited at home for the police to come to pick me up. We learned that there was an arrest warrant for each and every one of these suspended judges. That was like suspending the Constitution. I realised how brutal and lawless the situation was, and as I was lucky and was not being visited by the police until the evening of Saturday, I had the opportunity to leave home. I was at large for almost two months. Then, with the help of human smugglers, we paid $40,000 to buy our freedom as refugees and together with my family and after an unimaginably dangerous journey of 32 days, we ended up in Romania. That's the story.

To understand the real scale of the purge, we need to look at the figures. On 15 July 2016, the day of the attempted coup, there were around 14,500 judges/prosecutors in Turkey. After the suspension of the first 2,800, the number of suspended judges climbed to 4,560 in the following weeks. Currently there are around 21,000 judges and prosecutors in Turkey. This means that, having 'cleared the way' by sacking and imprisoning thousands of judges while sowing fear among those remaining, the Erdoğan government hired 11,000 'accredited' new judges over a period of in four years and consolidated power through the judiciary from 2020 onwards. Having secured his 'new order', Erdoğan changed the structure of the judicial council and placed it under the full control of the executive. This fact was recently underlined once again in the report of the Venice Commission of the European Council in December 2024.

To a certain degree, the same developments occurred in many governmental departments including the police, military, education, etc. In the end there were a total of 152,000 civil servants who were purged without trial and without any chance to defend themselves, even before a disciplinary chamber. After this 'cleansing' as Erdoğan calls it, everything became 'lawful' as there was no longer any legal framework. The newly accredited judiciary opened around two million investigation files on more than 600,000 individuals, including judges, prosecutors, academics, teachers, and even housewives. In total, 263,000 people were detained.

Following the declaration of the state of emergency on 20 July 2016, four days after the coup attempt, the judiciary was captured, while the army and police forces were re-structured, and the system of checks and balances was paralysed. So, whatever might happen in state institutions after a successful coup, also occurred under the state of emergency. The words of Numan Kurtulmus, the then speaker of the ruling Justice and Development Party (*Adalet ve Kalkınma Partisi,* AKP) captured the situation perfectly. During a live TV programme, Kurtulmus openly stated that under normal circumstances it would take at least five years to remove a single judge, whereas this time the government could dismiss thousands overnight thanks to the state of emergency. It was really frustrating for me and many colleagues when we heard the same sentence expressed by a prominent opposition member of parliament with a prosecutor background.

These are only a few of the reasons that make me think that the coup attempt may be defined as a false flag operation. This also explains why Erdoğan called the coup attempt 'a gift from God' on the night of 15 July, long before full control was re-established. The memoirs of Michael Pompeo and John Bolton, both of whom had access to top-secret U.S. government information during those years, reveal that Erdoğan took every opportunity to consolidate authoritarianism in Turkey. Pompeo, in his book *Never Give an Inch*, wrote: 'Ever since a purported "coup" in 2016, President Erdoğan had gone full Islamist-authoritarian'.[2] It is unlikely that Pompeo used the word 'purported' lightly to describe the coup attempt. Indeed, this choice of wording alone casts doubt on the accuracy of the Erdoğan government's narrative.

Leonardo Puleo: So, do you believe there was there a sort of grand design already planned for capturing the entire judiciary?

Yavuz Aydin: Yes, the plan was already in place, and the government actually did not hide its intentions. The year 2014 is important for understanding this process regarding the judiciary because the election for the High Council of Judges and Prosecutors of that time took place in October 2014. A few months before that election, the government formed a platform called the 'Judicial Unity'. This platform comprised judges and prosecutors from different political, ethnic, and religious backgrounds, which may sound fine on paper. However, when we are talking about the judiciary, impartiality, independence, and the ability to act freely regardless of your background are critical. So, preparing such a list of candidates was like a Trojan horse from the government to take over the judiciary. The propaganda activities of these candidates were fully financed and supported by the government through open declarations from the prime minister and justice minister of the time.

It was like all the cards were reshuffled because the government claimed they had members from left-wing and right-wing backgrounds, alongside certain religious groups, plus the Alawite group, and so on. But the platform was formed and financed by

[2] M Pompeo, *Never Give an Inch: Fighting for the America I Love* (New York, Harper Collins, 2023).

the government – it was a sheer act of politicisation of the High Council and judiciary as a whole. It became clear that judges had been profiled during the discussions prior to the election for the High Council. The list of the first 3,000 judges to be suspended and arrested was fabricated just after the controversial victory of the High Council through the platform of 'Judicial Unity', which was later further strengthened in the form of an association. In 2014, thousands of judges like myself stood up against this alongside the YARSAV Association, the only legitimate and legal association of judges in Turkey at that time. Murat Arslan, chair of YARSAV and a laureate of the Václav Havel Human Rights Prize, should be mentioned at this point. He is one of hundreds of colleagues who have been imprisoned for over eight years. We should also remember those who lost their lives in Turkish prisons, in refugee camps in Germany, and in the cold waters of the Mediterranean Sea while trying to escape persecution in their homeland. It should also be noted that both of the Europe-wide umbrella organisations for judges, namely MEDEL and the EAJ opposed the Turkish government's stance, and they still recognise YARSAV as their only member association from Turkey. The IAJ also adopted the same firm and principled stance on this matter. The government executed its plan step by step. First, any judge or prosecutor who posed a potential 'danger' was transferred to different corners of the country. All their investigations and cases were taken away from them, and they were intimidated through continuous judicial inspections. There were rumours that thousands of people would be purged from the judiciary by the government, which masked its actions behind rhetoric of dismantling an alleged 'parallel state structure'.

Following this victory, the government attacked all the judges and prosecutors who did not agree with its policies. They accused all the judges of being associated with Fethullah Gülen and his group with whom the government had close relations for many years. Then, after 2013, when the conflict between the government and the Gülenists started, the government used this fight as the perfect pretext to call all the thousands of judges and prosecutors who posed a risk to them as Gülenists, labelling us as parallel state structure elements, Gülenists, and then terrorists after 2016. In this way, they justified the purge and justified jailing all of us. That is the story in a nutshell.

It is clear that everything was prepared in advance not only in judicial matters but in all other areas. We can see this now years later. We can complete the puzzle after years, after seeing the minutes from the courts or the evidence that comes up or after the fights between government officials, where they expose some secrets afterwards. So, everything was planned. At least, the evidence shows that there is a high probability that everything was planned in advance. We were sacrificed to the gods of dictatorship.

In fact, the attacks and threats started even earlier. Since then, they have escalated step by step. The government attempted to redesign the judiciary through some minor adjustments over time. However, they couldn't do everything at once due to resistance from within the judiciary. Thousands of judges didn't agree with the government's policies and dared to stand up against them. The government couldn't destroy all the bridges with the CoE, the EU, and the rest of the world, so they needed a pretext to proceed: this pretext was precisely the failed coup. It seems that they planned all these actions in advance, or at the very least, they used the coup attempt as a perfect pretext to implement their plans. After July 2016, any judges and prosecutors who were seen as a potential threat to the autocracy were declared to be terrorists and were then purged.

There is a famous sentence that anyone of our generation in Turkey knows by heart: 'The perpetrator of an act is usually the one who benefits most from it'. This was apparently the point of view of Mr Kemal Kılıçdaroğlu, the former chair of the opposition party, when calling the events of 2016 'the controlled coup'.

Leonardo Puleo: Hearing this story, it's astonishing how the Turkish situation shares similarities with other cases such as Hungary. In your opinion, is there a sort of playbook that aspiring autocrats and their governments are using to capture the judiciary in Europe and beyond?

Yavuz Aydin: First of all, I need to make one thing clear. In the first phase of the Erdoğan leadership, between 2003 to 2011, he was so cautious, focused, and oriented towards the result, namely the support of the EU. We can see his plan clearly now. But at that time the consequences of his actions were still not clear to us. Judges are not politicians; we are not involved in politics. While involved in the accession negotiations with the EU, we were trying to advance the rule of law and judicial independence within the context of negotiations with the EU. And indeed, those years were the times when, in all the EU Commission reports, CoE reports, UN reports, the government's efforts, particularly the Ministry of Justice's efforts, we were commended and shown as an example to potential EU candidate countries and other countries negotiating with the EU. So, I worked in that environment for the judiciary, and I was really satisfied with what I was doing because all the steps we were involved in, from planning to implementation, were praised in the EU and CoE reports. And this is actually the same thing Orbán did in Hungary in the first few years. Orbán and his government's efforts were also commended, applauded, and supported by the EU and the international community during those years. But it is after years we could see that they were really following a playbook.

Actually, the rules of this playbook are not invented in the twenty-first century; it was the same in the last century, actually. And I'm sure if we go back in history, we will see many other examples of this. For example, even in Shakespeare's Henry VI, you know, there's this famous quote I heard from Thomas Stadelmann, one of the iconic Swiss judges for me, where Dick the Butcher says, 'The first thing we do, let's kill all the lawyers.' So even then, it was the same. These guys are really following the same footsteps: first of all, getting international support and consolidating legitimacy inside and outside the country. Then, having strengthened their grip on power, they start implementing abusive policies. Corruption and impunity follow. Then comes authoritarianism and the only way to follow. Because this is a one-way ticket which makes the governments drift away from the rule of law and checks and balances. If you decide to go rogue, you must escape from being held responsible, so you have to erode judicial independence. To achieve this, you need to undermine the credibility of the judges, and you need to open up the independence of the judiciary to discussion. For this, you need to produce some conspiracy theories or label some judicial investigations as judicial *coups d'état*. So, they are all doing more or less the same thing. However, people in Poland, Hungary, Bulgaria, or nowadays Slovakia and some other countries are much luckier than people in Turkey in various ways, because they are EU members, and there is the burden of responsibility to Brussels. This means that despite the EU sometimes also seeming to be defenceless or at least reluctant to protect and preserve these values, it still standing up for them. So, the government of these countries, at least, were afraid of infringement procedures, conditionality clauses, and other things. They were afraid of losing many things in terms of the free trade area, Schengen privileges, etc. But Turkish people weren't so lucky. We were a country negotiating with the EU but we were not within the EU. So, the EU didn't have enough say when all these things were happening in Turkey, and the EU had already lost its leverage over Turkey at that time.

There are many things to say about this story, actually. I can say that some EU officials may have been seen as complicit in this because what they have been focusing on, and are still focusing on, is the trade relations, keeping millions of migrants and refugees in Turkey out of Europe, and realpolitik priorities; the focus was not on fundamental rights and freedoms in Turkey. So, this is what makes the story in Turkey far different from Poland, Hungary, or other countries in the EU.

At this point, ENCJ deserves to be mentioned thanks to their principled approach while suspending the observer status of the High Council for Judges and Prosecutors of Turkey, underlining the fact that it was no longer an institution which is independent of the executive and legislature ensuring the final responsibility for the support of the judiciary in the independent delivery of justice. Four years after this suspension, ENCJ issued a statement which deserves to be included in the textbooks at law faculties:

> The Council for Judges and Prosecutors is a Council in name only, as none of its actions or decisions demonstrate any concern for the independence of the judiciary. Without a Council to protect and guarantee the independent delivery of justice in Turkey, there is little hope for the Rule of Law in Turkey in general and for access to independent, fair and impartial courts for all who come before the courts including Turkish citizens.[3]

Back to your question, in 2018, when I was finally able to travel outside of Romania after two years of legal battles to obtain refugee status, one of the first places I visited was Poland. There, I found Polish judges raising awareness about the importance of judicial independence and the rule of law. They were carrying out various projects with the public to promote these values. I tried to tell them that these autocrats, these politicians with autocratic tendencies, like Erdoğan, whom I can openly call a dictator, will not stop. These autocratic governments will not stop. The next target will be the media and civil society, and silencing opponents. They will not just limit their plan to silence the judiciary. They aim to sideline and weaken the judiciary for a reason – they do not want to be subjected to a system of checks and balances. They do not want to be held responsible, criticised, or have their mistakes or failures exposed.

You should convince people that judicial independence is not just for judges – it is for the people. Eliminating the judges is just the first step of autocrats, but they intend to remove other obstacles and consolidate and further tighten their grip on power. Over time, we have seen that aspiring autocrats follow in each other's footsteps, learning from each other's experiences.

[3] ENCJ executive board statement, 8 December 2020, available at www.encj.eu/node/578.

Leonardo Puleo: You are underlining a crucial point: the relationship between judicial independence and the citizenry. In this respect, I would like to ask you how can we explain the lack of reaction from the general public to events in several countries, including Turkey?

Yavuz Aydin: To answer this question, we should compare the period before these attacks began – the so-called good old days – with the period afterward. Until 2010, Turkey was seen as a model country for the Arab Spring. This fact is often forgotten now, but Turkey was exemplified as a country that demonstrated how democracy could flourish in a Muslim-majority country. This was the soft power of Turkey at the time. Turkey's face was turned toward the West and the EU, and it was making significant progress, courageously discussing century-old problems and burdens.

For the first time, Turkey was able to openly discuss the Kurdish issue. I refrain from calling it as Kurdish 'problem' because it was actually a Turkish problem – a problem of the established Turkish state ideology vis-à-vis the rights of the Kurds. This was the first time these matters were openly addressed. The role of the military in political life and the judiciary was also being discussed, and reduced, while judicial independence was a real target for the first time, and definite steps were taken there as well. Significant progress was made in areas like freedom of expression and freedom of belief, and even in 2014 we define as the dark times when compared to the previous years, Turkey ranked 54th in the World Justice Project's Rule of Law Index.[4]

Now, however, we see a new Turkey currently ranked 117th among 145 countries in the World Justice Project's Rule of Law Index. In terms of fundamental rights and freedoms, in 2022 Turkey even ranked 133rd out of 145 countries. Turkey has also been demoted to the grey list of the Financial Action Task Force due to the country's insufficient oversight of money laundering and corruption, attributed to the lack of an independent judiciary. Turkey was the first country to be demoted to monitoring status in the CoE in 2017, a first in the organisation's history.

In terms of the situation at the ECtHR, there are already more than 25,000 cases pending before the Court about this matter, making Turkey number one in terms of applications, breaches, and unimplemented decisions across all categories. Indeed, this number corresponds to almost 37 per cent of all pending cases coming from 46 members of the CoE.

As for the implementation of ECtHR judgments, Turkey's closure rate is 67 per cent, meaning that 141 out of 430 leading cases are still unimplemented. For comparison, the absolute number is 71 for Italy, 21 for Spain, 47 for Hungary, 11 for Germany, and 8 for the UK. Thus, though the implementation rates in some other countries may seem lower in terms of percentage, Turkey is the champion both in the number of leading cases and in number of non-implementations of these decisions. Furthermore, the gravity of the cases concerning Turkey is far greater when compared to the other countries.

The most recent example which has not yet been included in the above statistics is *Yalçınkaya v Turkey* in which Turkey was found to be in breach of Article 7 of the Convention, referring to the principle of 'nullum crimen sine lege' (no crime

[4] For further information and to explore the dataset, see worldjusticeproject.org/rule-of-law-index/.

without law), which is a cornerstone of legal certainty and fairness in criminal justice. Referring also to Article 46 of the Convention, this ruling highlighted the arbitrary nature of many prosecutions in Turkey.

What makes this ruling historic and unprecedented is that the ECtHR explicitly said that the same principle is applicable to more than 8,000 cases pending in Strasbourg and to more than 100,000 cases pending before Turkish courts that are expected to reach Strasbourg in a few years. Thus, the ruling has far-reaching implications for thousands of similar cases pending in Turkish courts and before the ECtHR. It exposes the serious nature of issues affecting not only Yalçınkaya but also hundreds of thousands of other applicants who face a systemic failure to guarantee fair trial rights, legal certainty, and freedom of expression.

Turkey has also become the second country against which an infringement procedure was launched by the CoE – the first was Azerbaijan following the Ilgar Mammadov case. However, Azerbaijan released Ilgar Mammadov and closed the file, and the procedure ended, meaning that Turkey remains the only CoE Member State with an ongoing infringement procedure due to its failure to implement the decision in the Osman Kavala case. Kavala was a philanthropist who stood by those who urged the government to adhere to the rule of law and democracy during the Gezi Park events of 2013, he was charged with attempting to overthrow the government, and he is still in prison despite the ECtHR ruling and the decision of the CoE's Committee of Ministers. Furthermore, the appeal court in Istanbul has overturned a decision to acquit Mr Kavala, by ignoring the aforementioned decisions of the ECHR and the Committee of Ministers of the Council of Europe. By the way, the panel of judges who dared to acquit Mr Kavala of the baseless charges in 2019 have since been demoted and sent to different cities following a swift disciplinary proceeding conducted by the Turkish Council of Judges and Prosecutors.

Turkey was found in violation of Article 18 by the ECHR in the Osman Kavala case. The breach of Article 18 explicitly means that in these cases, the Turkish courts had a political rather than judicial motivation. Like Article 7, no violations of Article 18 have been recorded for other countries in the last 7 years, whereas Erdoğan's 'new Turkey' has managed to violate these articles a record number of times. This is setting a new low in terms of arbitrariness and lawlessness!

In the Global Crimes Index,[5] Turkey ranks 12th out of approximately 100 countries for having the most crime. There are many examples like this. In June 2023, the Council of Europe adopted Resolution 2509, condemning Turkey for transnational repression against its citizens on European soil.

This deterioration on different fronts is thanks to the government's success in removing obstacles to consolidating its power. The public's lack of reaction can be attributed to the government's effective manipulation of society: its divide-and-rule tactics, and the use of fear as a tool for populist politics. Unfortunately, the public reaction was very weak during these events, for various reasons, including cultural factors.

[5] For further information and to explore the dataset, see ocindex.net/.

Turkey was on the brink of a transformation in the early 2000s or the first decade of the 2000s, but there was not a sufficiently deep-rooted culture of democracy or judicial independence. Turkey never experienced a real democracy or a truly independent judiciary, and so people did not realise what they were missing. It is no secret that the judiciary in Turkey has always been used as an instrument or as a tool to silence dissidents at different levels. However, the situation has never previously been as bad and miserable as it is now during the history of Turkish Republic. I recall the words of Professor Kees Sterk (chapter 7) from the Netherlands, who is also a judge. During a recent conference, he said that investing in judicial independence is essential for a state, but investing in judicial culture and a democratic culture is far more critical because culture eats rules for breakfast.

The atmosphere of fear was another significant factor. After July 2016, the government repressed all critics harshly, leaving no room for any dissent. This harshness contributed to the lack of public reaction. Eventually, Turkey's drifting away from democracy contributed to the invention of the terms 'autocratic legalism' and 'electoral autocracy'. There are still some academics who call Turkey an illiberal democracy, but I agree with the European Court of Justice President Koen Lenaerts who says: 'there is no such thing as illiberal democracy, there is either democracy or not'.

Leonardo Puleo: I would like to push you a bit further to develop the concept you have just mentioned: judicial culture. During this period of dissensus over democracy and rule of law in Turkey, did you also witness tension within the judiciary?

Yavuz Aydin: Let me start with a confession: if I hadn't worked for the EU negotiation team, if I hadn't played a role in the negotiations with the EU on judiciary and fundamental rights, justice, freedom, or security, and I wouldn't be thinking this way. Furthermore, if I hadn't been sent to Brussels as the justice counsellor for the EU office, I wouldn't have had the chance to see the world differently.

In Turkey, like in Spain, Portugal, and Greece 50 years ago, or as in the new Eastern European Member States 30 years ago, we were raised in a closed society during the Cold War. We were on the front lines of the Cold War in Turkey, and it was the norm for us to live our lives in a state of exception. Turkish judges and prosecutors have been educated and come from such a world. According to an academic survey conducted in 2007, almost 90 per cent of judges and prosecutors said that they are the guardians of the state, not the guardians of freedoms and rights. This is the dominant opinion among the members of the judiciary which is rooted back many decades.

Apart from being on the front lines of the Cold War, we experienced military interventions, and coup attempts every ten years in Turkey. I remember the one in 1980 and its consequences. The militaristic state ideology was dominant, and so it wasn't difficult to manipulate the minds of judges within the judiciary by 2014. We had better times before that, but after Gezi Park and the corruption scandals, the government saw a clear and imminent danger from the judiciary. They sped up their plans to divide, rule, and manipulate the judiciary, eventually taking it over with the Association for Unity in the Judiciary.

Moreover, unfortunately, they were not alone. People often think it was only Erdoğan who did all these things, but there were colleagues who call themselves democrats, left-wing individuals, Alawites, and others in the Unity in the Judiciary Association. Even groups like YARSAV were divided: those from a real Social Democrat background diverged from those from those coming from a sort of national socialist mentality.

Turkey has been a country where different segments of society have been declared to be each other's enemies and have been fighting for many years. This is how Turkey has been ruled, and the judiciary is no exception, it is not immune from this. The same division and manipulation happened there too. People from different backgrounds supported these plans, falling into the same trap set by these *Islamofascists*. They were used as instruments, like Trojan horses, to realise government's plans.

At the end of the day, it was our colleagues who profiled us and that contributed to the purge in 2016.

Leonardo Puleo: In your opinion, this increasing dissensus over democracy and rule of law contributed to changing the ethos and the internal rules of the profession? What does it mean to be a judge, not only in Turkey but also in other contexts?

Yavuz Aydin: In today's Turkey, unfortunately, being a judge means only being a servant, essentially a slave to the governing party or ruling authority. In Turkey judges are not aware that there are no longer judges, but rather individuals who, on paper, legitimise the *raison d'être* of the government. Because in democracies, the judiciary represents the third power, right? It is the power that provides checks and balances, and these are crucial for any democracy. As Montesquieu said 300 years ago: 'There is no greater tyranny than that which is perpetrated under the shield of the law and in the name of justice'. And even 100 years before that, Thomas Hobbes tried to show this same thing in *Leviathan*: this mechanism, when it's not checked or balanced, may turn into a huge devil which destroys everything in its path. For that devil, everything is a legitimate target, because everything is lawful when there's no law to stop it. We see some implications of this as well.

Then there is Jean-Jacques Rousseau and his social contract. You know, for a healthy social contract, what is needed most is for people to have confidence in each other and in the state, and confidence that order will be restored, too. They need a mechanism which has the power to say when the government is doing something wrong, and the power to say stop to the government. So, these rules and principles have been there for 300 or 400 years. But now, unfortunately, we have just drifted away from this understanding. The judges now in Turkey do not have this understanding; indeed, it's much worse now. Not only the quantity, but the quality of this understanding is also worse because in 2016, after demonising and dividing more than 4,500 judges and prosecutors, the government purged them all. They put most of them in prison. There are still more than 500 of them in prison, including Murat Arslan, the president of YARSAV, and this is against the law, even the existing law. They are keeping him in jail, like Osman Kavala and many others.

These judges think that their role is to abide by the wishes of the president, the new 'Sultan', Erdoğan. And they are selected accordingly. There were roughly 15,000 judges in 2016. After the purge, the remaining 10,000 were terribly frightened and in this atmosphere of fear, they didn't dare say anything. Those who rejected the changes or refused to betray their colleagues were also arrested. There are still some honourable judges and prosecutors in Turkey, of course, but even they were not brave enough – they were sidelined and transferred to other courts to deal with civil cases under enormous backlog. They don't have a say in criminal cases or cases regarding rule of law, or these high-profile cases.

Now, unfortunately, the judges of Turkey are proud to not implement ECtHR. This is why Turkey ranks 133 among 145 countries in terms of fundamental freedoms. Unfortunately, Turkey has been classified as 'not free' by Freedom House for five consecutive years, and I believe judges in Turkey are not even aware of what they are doing. But at the end of the day, they will be the ones held responsible because all other civil servants or public officials will be able to say, 'I got the order from my superior, commander, or chief' or whatever. Yet according to the Turkish Constitution, judges are independent, and nobody can instruct them in their professional duties. When the tables are turned, they will not be able to say, 'I obeyed the instructions coming from the palace' or 'I did whatever the minister of justice said'. No. First of all, they will not have the chance to prove it because these politicians are intelligent enough to use judges and prosecutors to realise their plans – this is also part of the bigger plan. In this way, the politicians will be able to say: 'No, we didn't do these things. It was the courts, the judges who did this. According to the Constitution, we cannot instruct them. Show us the instructions! Did we write something to them? Did we send instructions to them? No'. And these judges will not be able to show any evidence. Another point of making changes by means of the judiciary is that, at least on paper, the government has legitimacy and legality regarding all these atrocities committed by the government. Hence, judges are to be held equally responsible for the appalling situation of the rule of law in the country. They knew what the files before them did or did not contain. They knew what the ECtHR and the UN bodies had said about their verdicts. But they chose to serve their 'Sultan' rather than the law.

Leonardo Puleo: So, what can judges do? What is the lesson that the Turkish case can provide to other countries? How can judges resist, and which strategies can they employ against this assault on the rule of law?

Yavuz Aydin: First of all, it's not only about judges, it's a matter of judicial culture. The notion of judicial independence was not invented by judges. Did we mention any judges in history in the invention of this term? No. We mentioned Jean-Jacques Rousseau, Thomas Hobbes, and Montesquieu. You learn about these things in political science courses too, not only in law faculties, because these concepts are foundational for living in harmony in a democracy. People need to have confidence, and for that, there has a system of checks and balances.

So, for this reason, it's not only a matter for judges, but also for politicians. First of all, politicians should respect these principles – they should know that whatever they do, whatever they plan, it will not be sustainable if there is no democracy. Otherwise, they will need to turn their regime into an autocracy, authoritarianism, totalitarianism, or a dictatorship. Maybe most of these politicians want to turn countries into authoritarian or totalitarian regimes provided that they are the ones ruling the country. But that approach can't last forever. Most of these politicians who have such a desire for total power deep in their souls are afraid of being held responsible at the end of the day. In the Middle East too, we saw how Gaddafi ended, how Saddam ended, how the Sudanese president ended. Now, the former Prime Minister of Nicaragua is being prosecuted in Switzerland for crimes against humanity. We have seen many examples in the past too. But like I said, when you catch the right wind behind you, when realpolitik seems to be favour of you like it is now for Erdoğan, or to an extent for Orbán or many others, they are exploiting this advantage to the utmost. But they also know that it is ultimately a one-way ticket because in this way, they are committing a lot of crimes and leaving a lot of traces by which they can be held responsible if the tables turn.

So, this is one reason for politicians to refrain from going rogue. But in the end, it is a matter of culture, as we said, not only for judges but for politicians and civil society, for media; they are all actors of democracy. But when it comes to judges, the most important thing I can say is that they should be brave, and those who cannot be brave should not be judges. Judges are the guardians of democracy, representing the checks and balances mechanism and so they should know that one day they might need to stand up against power. This should be part of the judges' job description. It's like a military job, taking the risk of dying in times of clashes or war. So, for judges, it's similar. They should take into account the fact that this job description includes standing up against power and risking many things because the executive has many powers which the judiciary does not have. They have pro-government media, they have intelligence agencies, they have mouthpieces, they have money, many things.

So, judges and candidate-judges should be aware of this. I remember now a statement from Ahmet Altan, the world-renowned novelist and intellectual. He suffered many years in prison after 2016. During an interview right after his release, he spoke about the role of judges: 'Why should I risk spending my whole life without seeing the sun just because a judge is afraid of being transferred to another city or being fired from the profession?' It is such an imbalanced situation. Judges should know that while thinking about how to protect their 'comfort zones', they are playing with the lives of multiple people – their families, their friends, as well as the democratic evolution in the country. It is such a critical and crucial role. In its decision on *Baka v Hungary*, the ECtHR explicitly underlined this fact for a judge: defending the independence of the judiciary and rule of law is not only a right, but a responsibility. So, every candidate judge and every law graduate should know that if they are ready to do this, they should become a judge or at least try to become one. We tried to do this in our country. When we needed to work, and when we had the chance to work for the good of rule of law, we did so. When we needed to stand up against tyranny, so to speak, as Montesquieu put it, we did so, and we paid the price.

I do not know anyone among my friends who regrets having stood up for what they believe in and losing everything they had – their profession, assets, and freedom – and ending up as a refugee here. For those who managed to find smugglers or pay tens of thousands of euros or dollars, not only for us to escape but for our families also, it's a big price to pay, actually. And I think now I have the right to say this. If you do not take these things into account, don't become a judge. Because you never know how things will evolve. I think we lived the best days of the world in the 1990s maybe – perhaps the early 2000s were also good. But after that, every year became worse than the last one. We saw a world with Trump, Putin, Bolsonaro, Erdoğan, Orbán, Kaczyński, and Borisov. Not only on other continents but in Western Europe and within the EU as well.

Now we are talking about France with Le Pen, Italy with Meloni; soon, the Netherlands with Wilders. So, it reminds me of something which is not good, this composition, like Europe before WWII, these rising extremisms, nationalism, and xenophobia. Things are not going in a good direction. And I believe that every judge in Europe – not only in Turkey, not only in Poland, not only in Hungary – each and every judge in Europe, especially judges who are nationals of an EU Member State, they should know. They should not forget the fact that they are not judges only of their country, but they are European judges. They are indispensable elements of this Schengen system, which is the basis of the EU project, said to be the most unique and successful project in the history of humankind. It might collapse because of these judges' the failure to act. Who knows what kind of Europe we will see in ten years?

So, if not judges, who will defend this judicial independence and rule of law? As a Turkish judge who ended up a refugee and was labelled as a terrorist in his country, I can ask: if not judges, who will act? We did it, we paid the price, and we are proud to have done so. Still, in this situation, in exile, in diaspora, we are trying to create synergy, and we are crying out that the situation in Turkey should not be accepted as the new normal. It is not normal in any way. So, the EU, the Council of Europe, the United Nations, and all individual states should say this. They should voice: 'this is not normal, and it should change'. This should not be accepted as the new normal. This is why we created an association in Belgium, Justice for the Rule of Law, comprising dozens of other judges from across Europe alongside academics. We are trying to raise these issues, but we are a baby institution – we are very new and have only some 40 members for now. But for us and for all other judiciaries and countries in Europe, the existence of umbrella institutions like MEDEL is really important. In the case of Turkey, if there is any awareness among academics or judicial institutions or even in politics, it's mostly thanks to the efforts of umbrella institutions like MEDEL or the EAJ or IAJ and AEAJ and so forth. So, these are the ones who are aware of their responsibility and who are trying to fulfil their task. It's so good that, thanks to God, these people exist and that we can voice such things and try to be the voice of the voiceless. This is the reason we established our association Justice for Rule of Law with support of prominent judges, lawyers and academics from across Europe.

21

I am not Confident that the EU Genuinely Prioritises Judicial Independence in the Serbian Case

DRAGANA BOLJEVIĆ[1]

Leonardo Puleo: Could you tell us about your professional background, outlining the reasons and motivations that led you to pursue a career as a judge?

Dragana Boljević: When I started working 40 years ago, despite living in a socialist republic viewed by Westerners as non-democratic, the judicial profession was highly respected. Judges, along with doctors and military officers, were among the most esteemed professions in our society according to polls and scholarly research. I had a deep interest in philosophy of law, and so becoming a judge offered me an excellent blend of philosophical inquiry and practical application. It allowed me to contribute to social justice and people's well-being. The combination of general principles and the specific facts of each case, where justice and equity are sought, was a profound challenge. I have never regretted becoming a judge.

Leonardo Puleo: Do you have a family tradition of relatives working as judges or lawyers?

Dragana Boljević: I am the daughter of a labourer and a housewife and the first in my family to graduate from the Faculty of Law – or, in fact, any faculty at all. I am not the only person like this – the opportunity to pursue any desired university degree had been at the disposal of everybody at that time, and it was free of charge.

Leonardo Puleo: How do you see the state of democracy, the rule of law and judicial independence, in Serbia and beyond?

Dragana Boljević: In the specific case of Serbia, the situation is somewhat paradoxical. Serbia is often perceived as having an autocratic regime, despite holding frequent democratic elections. However, we are not currently facing the same judiciary-related issues as seen, for instance, in Poland, Italy, Spain, Slovakia, Ukraine, Hungary, or Bulgaria.

[1] Interview conducted on 13 May 2024 and validated for publication on 20 January 2025.

The landscape was different 15 years ago. Back then, Europe's situation was relatively stable, while Serbia's judiciary was struggling. We experienced a *coup d'état* on the judiciary in 2009 followed by a process of 're-electing' all judges, which was a euphemism for dismissing one third of the judges without due process or legal remedies, nor any criteria for their removal. I, too, was among the judges who were dismissed, despite continuing as President of the *Drustvo sudija Srbije* (Judges' Association of Serbia, JAS) during those challenging three years. Serbia transitioned away from its socialist regime in 1990, adopting a new Constitution that established a system of separation of powers and political pluralism, and granted lifetime tenure to judges. In the 1992 general elections, all judges were elected to lifetime tenure. Following the democratic changes of 2000 and the decade that followed, more than two-thirds of judges were, let's say, scrutinised. There was no need for lustration due to the 1992 lifetime election (as not all sitting judges were elected for lifetime tenure at that time). The renewal of the judicial corps was carried out in a non-traumatic way. Until 2009, through the process the professionalism, capability, and integrity of the candidates were assessed. This involved an 80 per cent change in the composition of the Supreme Court as well. In spite of this, under the 2006 Constitution and the new politicians in the Government of democratic provenience, the 2008 law on Judges mandated a 'general election' of judges. However, this 'general election' was neither a lustration nor a vetting process. Instead, it effectively ended lifetime judicial tenure by requiring all sitting judges to reapply for their positions. Judges who failed to apply or were not reappointed lost their tenure as of 1 January 2010. For sitting judges, the process amounted to a reappointment, while those not reappointed faced dismissal. In December 2009, the High Judicial Council (HJC), operating with an incomplete membership, conducted the process in a non-transparent manner. It applied secret criteria, favouring judges without relatives in the legal profession, misused personal and classified data, and reviewed applications on average in just five minutes per case. The HJC published a list of reappointed judges that excluded 837 sitting judges – approximately one-third of the judiciary. These judges lost their positions without receiving a formal decision or access to legal remedies. The process faced decisive and persistent opposition from Serbian judges and public prosecutors' associations, supported by international judicial networks. They publicly condemned the reappointment process. The Council of Europe and European Union bodies also issued numerous critical statements. In July 2012, the Constitutional Court of Serbia annulled all HJC decisions related to the reappointment process and ordered the reinstatement of all non-reappointed judges.

We knew that similar dynamics could spread everywhere. I didn't hesitate to talk about the Serbian experience and accept frequent invitations to speak about it, especially in Turkey, where the situation turned out to be much worse as of 2016. My colleagues and I addressed the Council of Europe institutions, as well as the European Commission and the European Parliament numerous times, warning that what was happening in Serbia could spread like a virus across Europe – a prelude, perhaps, to what later unfolded in Poland and Turkey. At the time, some of my colleagues may have doubted my words, but today, the situation has indeed worsened across Europe, while in Serbia, things have taken a different turn.

With the support of partners such as MEDEL and the International Association of Judges, as well as the Consultative Council of European Judges – which is an advisory body of the CoE – and the Judges' Association of Serbia, we fought tirelessly for three years, successfully overturning the results of this so-called judiciary reform in Serbia. But the situation was different in those days. If we had to fight the same battle today, I'm not sure the outcome would be the same.

Serbia recently underwent legal changes as part of our EU integration process, in response to demands from the EU to enhance judicial independence. In 2022, a referendum was held specifically on constitutional amendments concerning the judiciary, providing a kind of legitimacy often claimed to be lacking in the judiciary's standing if we compare it to democratically elected political branches of power. Subsequently, our laws on judiciary were also revised in 2023.[2] This process, driven by EU integration efforts, was really democratic and inclusive and has significantly improved the legal framework surrounding our judiciary. This stands in stark contrast to current events for example in Italy, where attempts are being made to amend the Constitution to the detriment of the judiciary, as you may well be aware. Hence, while we do not have an ideal situation in Serbia today, we do not currently face attempts to erode judicial independence as we did before.

Leonardo Puleo: Do you think that dialogue with EU institutions can also be helpful not only in improving judicial independence but also enhancing anti-corruption laws and minorities protection?

Dragana Boljević: As I mentioned, the results of the discussions with the EU were good, but I cannot speak to the motives of EU political elites. I am not confident that the EU genuinely prioritises judicial independence in the Serbian case. I would say there is some manipulation, as they tend to emphasise their demands for the independence of the judiciary whenever there is a deadlock in some other domain (for example, in Chapter 35 in Serbia's EU accession process related to Kosovo and EU expectations of Serbian acknowledgement of Kosovo as an independent state regardless of its act of secession). I am confident that the improvement of legal framework for the judiciary is due to the unique situation in Serbia in 2018, which was, indeed, related to EU integration.

The proposals for constitutional amendments, which threatened judicial independence, faced united opposition from judicial associations, the Supreme Court, the High Judicial Council, academics, as well as constitutional law and human rights NGOs. Among other things, the 2018 proposals for constitutional amendments planned to weaken the High Judicial Council by restricting its competence and the way of functioning. The Venice Commission and the European Commission expressed support for the 2018 constitutional amendment proposals because, at that time, they believed that Serbia could make a decisive step toward acknowledging Kosovo's independence in return. However, faced with a united front of opposition from the legal profession and seeking progress in EU integration, politicians abandoned the idea of worsening the constitutional status of the judiciary or introducing provisions that could jeopardise

[2] The 2022 constitutional framework for the Serbian judiciary marks progress compared to the previous system. This view was echoed by the Venice Commission in its November 2021 Urgent Opinion, which stated that the revised constitutional amendments, if adopted, could bring about significant positive changes in the Serbian judiciary.

judicial independence, assuming that improving the judiciary's situation would benefit the EU accession process. This assumption proved correct – two chapters were subsequently opened: Cluster 4, 'Green Agenda and Sustainable Connectivity,' and Cluster 1, 'Fundamentals.'

One must acknowledge that corruption is prevalent in Serbian society and that combatting it, along with raising the standard of legal culture, is our foremost challenge. This involves instilling a belief in the rule of law among citizens.

Regarding minority rights, we do not face significant issues, particularly with national minorities. However, if you are referring to groups other than ethnic minorities, there remains an expectation for a deeper understanding and appreciation of their rights.

Leonardo Puleo: You touch on a crucial point: citizens' perceptions of the judiciary. Do you think that citizens' perception of the judiciary in Serbia has improved in the last few years after this cycle of reforms? Do you see any trend towards increasing trust in the judiciary?

Dragana Boljević: It is important to note, first and foremost, that the judicial system is inherently conservative. Sudden disruptions are not well-suited to the judiciary. Even small changes must be thoughtfully designed, carefully prepared, and meticulously enforced. Such processes take time to yield their full impact. The feasibility of any change requires not only sufficient time but also the right conditions. This means that various relevant factors must align to ensure the proper implementation of a legal provision in practice. Only when feasibility is achieved can visibility be enhanced, and, with it, public perception potentially improved.

Coming back to your question – no, I don't see any such trend, but the basis of the mistrust is very interesting. One of the aspects of the three-year project, supported by the Dutch government, which was recently finished by the Judges' Association of Serbia, focused on assessing judges' perceptions of their position and status in society. Another aspect focused on citizens' perceptions of the judiciary and corruption within it. It was truly fascinating to discover that citizens' perceptions of corruption in the judiciary have little to do with their actual experiences or success in judicial processes.

Interestingly, those who admitted to attempting bribery or who lost their cases tended to hold a more positive view of the judiciary than the others. It is paradoxical. The only real correlation we found is between the way in which the media and politicians publicly discuss the judiciary and the public's perception of it. Citizens who follow media that are critical of the government (and usually not well informed about the functioning of judiciary) tend to perceive the judiciary as more corrupt than those who do not. Therefore, we concluded that the media should be more educated and professional when reporting on the judiciary. One more thing: citizens follow what politicians say about the judiciary, and they often criticize it without good reason, even publicly attacking it in their statements. The judiciary has its flaws, but it should not be unjustly attacked. By simply refraining from publicly attacking or unjustly criticising the judiciary, politicians could likely make a significant contribution to improving public perception.

In brief, trust in the judiciary remains very low, but it is higher than trust in politicians, the national parliament, or the police. Overall, Serbians seem to trust very few institutions. As I understand it, they are not the only ones in Europe with such a lack of trust in state institutions.

Leonardo Puleo: You mentioned that you received personal threats to your independence in 2009. How did you deal with this threat both as a judge and also on a personal level?

Dragana Boljević: Firstly, when I say 'we', I refer to the judges who were/are part of the network of the Judges' Association of Serbia. We understood that as individuals, we couldn't have any relevant impact on the judicial system. In September 2009, the Judges' Association conducted strategic planning to anticipate and respond to the challenges we were facing due to the illegal and anti-European reforms planned by the Cvetković cabinet (eg the re-election of all judges) after the adoption of the 2006 Serbian Constitution. We adopted a comprehensive set of short and long-term measures. Our well-organised approach and foresight, coupled with our dedication to the cause of judicial independence, significantly contributed to our success. For instance, in December 2009, a day before the re-election results were announced, the Judges' Association made a critical decision. It stated that all judges facing dismissal would remain members of the association until the completion of their legal procedures. This decision enabled me, for example, to continue as the president of the Judges' Association even after my dismissal. Subsequently, I was re-elected in 2011 to continue leading the association, despite my status as a dismissed judge. Notably, the majority of those who voted for me were judges who had been legally elected during that period, not those who were dismissed in 2009.

The Judges' Association of Serbia is a member of MEDEL and the International Association of Judges, and we maintained continuous contact with them. We were also closely connected with the active organisation *Rechters voor Rechters* from the Netherlands. Additionally, we maintained close ties with the European Commission and Council of Europe, especially with the Consultative Council of European Judges. Fortunately, we had a competent and supportive Ombudsman and a Commissioner for Data Protection and Free Access to Public Information in Serbia. They played crucial roles in supporting us during those challenging times. Together, we fought against the illegal acts undertaken in 2009 reappointment and after that during the revision of the 2009 reappointment, till mid 2012 when Constitutional Court annulled all the decisions of the High Judicial Council and ordered the reinstatement of all judges dismissed in 2009. We are proud that the Judges' Association succeeded in counteracting the damaging results of these so-called reforms.

Leonardo Puleo: And at that time did you witness any phenomena such as, for example, polarisation within the judiciary?

Dragana Boljević: Of course, that process was truly terrifying, not only for the judiciary but also for intellectuals who were concerned about the developments in Serbian judiciary. It was a frightening process to dismiss 1,000 judges and prosecutors – essentially one third of the judiciary – overnight, without giving them the right to challenge their dismissal or even receive a formal decision on it. Normally, when you fire an employee, you provide them with a decision and compensation, but in our case, the plan was for us to receive nothing after six months. This was an act of brutal force, and it took some time for that polarisation to fade out.

We also witnessed another phenomenon during that period: the erosion of European institutions' commitment to the rule of law. They allowed our government to undertake actions against the judiciary which were clearly in violation of the rule of law in exchange for other gains, particularly in the context of sending individuals to the Hague Tribunal (ie International Criminal Tribunal for the former Yugoslavia). It was a kind of quid pro quo arrangement.

For example, in 2008, we repeatedly informed the European Commission about the regressive laws that were undermining progress towards the rule of law in Serbia. However, the Commission initially didn't pay much attention. They seemed puzzled that the Judges' Association of Serbia was addressing these concerns directly to the European Commission – such informal and assertive approach from a nongovernmental organisation of judges was quite uncommon at the time.

It was only at the beginning of 2010 that they realised the extent of the disaster unfolding in Serbia. They then became actively engaged, but unfortunately, it took too long for their actions to have a real impact. A concern arose that the lack of results might be regarded as the result of the incompetence of those who were dealing with the situation. By the autumn of 2011, officers of the European Commission decided to sweep the issue under the carpet. During this time, it happened that two EU opposite assessments of the developing in Serbian judiciary were made. EU observers closely followed the process of the review of re-election and concluded in their report that there had been a 'travesty of justice'. Yet, the 2011 Progress report on Serbia optimistically stated that everything would 'hopefully turn well' with the Serbian judiciary.

Through discussions with Tamara Trotman, the President of the Dutch *Rechters voor Rechters* we agreed on further action. It was almost like a spy movie. I managed to send to her discreetly the report of EU observers. She promptly spoke with the Minister of Foreign Affairs in the Netherlands and with MPs from the Green Party in the European Parliament (Franziska Brantner from Germany and Marije Cornelissen from the Netherlands). They raised the issue in the European Parliament not as a problem related to Serbia, which many might overlook, but as a question about the functioning of EU institutions and their mutual trust. In December 2011, they challenged Enlargement commissioner Štefan Füle, emphasising that the European Parliament relies on the integrity of the Commission's reports to make important decisions. They asked how the European Parliament could trust the European Commission when one report described a dysfunctional justice system in Serbia while another suggested all was well. Commissioner Füle was clearly alarmed by their questions and swiftly responded that the situation was under close observation and promised transparency. Along with other events, this incident marked a significant moment when we saw the erosion of the rule of law within European Commission institutions deepen further. It is worth noting that the International Association of Judges and MEDEL are currently suing the European Commission before the Court of Justice of the EU because they refused to enforce a decision of the Court regarding Poland.

Leonardo Puleo: What do you think should be the room for manoeuvre for judges when reacting to threats against their independence? To what extent can judges confront government authority when it harms democracy and liberal rights?

Dragana Boljević: Networking between judges is really important because it provides us with insights into the judicial world worldwide. We learn about ongoing developments, realising that issues we face aren't unique to our country, but part of broader processes eroding judicial independence and democracy. Initially, we identify causes at both local and global levels. Together, we wield greater collective strength. When isolated, individuals are weak, including judges. However, when working within associations that defend independence and monitor against erosion of the rule of law, judges become stronger. International connections among colleagues are a vital tool for maintaining judicial independence. Success wouldn't have been possible in Serbia without international cooperation.

Let me once again highlight the significant success, achieved by the unity of judges and the whole legal community in Serbia in 2018, which resulted in improved legal framework for the judiciary following the constitutional amendments in 2022 and subsequent 2023 adoptions of the new judicial laws. That, along with the annulment of the 2009 re-elections of judges, achieved through collaboration, were pivotal moments for judicial integrity in Serbia. We seized these fleeting opportunities judiciously.

As judges in Serbia, we cannot be affiliated with political parties. Navigating judges' dual roles as citizens and state officials, and their civil rights, is complex. On the one hand, judges are state representatives who require dignity and impartial awareness of their responsibilities. On the other hand, they may face severe attacks that require them to speak out and defend their positions. Finding equilibrium between these roles is challenging. For instance, during last December's 2023 political elections, some judges and prosecutors in Serbia, in my view, exceeded this balance and acted politically. There was actually a debate about this on a TV broadcast between myself and a one of these judges. The Judges' Association hosted a conference on judges' freedom of speech and their limitations in September 2024, emphasising that judges, while citizens, must exercise caution.

Leonardo Puleo: Considering that Serbia somewhat anticipated the trends that have subsequently emerged in Turkey and Hungary, what are the future prospects for this rule of law crisis as it stands today?

Dragana Boljević: As things stand now, there is a significant lack of commitment to democracy within EU institutions. The alienated European institutions are far away from the citizens, so it seems that if democracy is at all attainable, this will happen more easily within national countries.

I think that the erosion of the independence of judiciary is mainly the consequence of neoliberalism. Society is atomised into individuals who think primarily about themselves. And we also have a unipolar world that has led to the disappearance of more influential trade unions and the fight for people's rights to be economically independent. Individuals don't seek common interests, don't invest the efforts to fight for social rights, and don't even believe success could be possible. Financial capital is so metastasised that it pulls all the strings, not just in one country but worldwide. We are witnessing the practice of 'forum shopping', when the parties are choosing the judge or the court or jurisdiction that has the most favourable rules or laws for the position being advocated in connection with treaties based on what is signed in contracts that do not mind the national law or legal standards. It was paradigmatical with the memorandum signed with the Troika to manage the bailout of Cyprus, Greece, Ireland, Portugal, Spain. The troika-imposed measures not only went against the rule of law but were also contrary to the national constitutions and legal framework. The erosion of the rule of law is also clearly shown in Italy not only in the context of the 2008 financial and economic crisis but in the ongoing migrant crisis as well. A nineteenth-century French Jesuit philosopher, Lacordaire, said 'Between the strong and the weak, between the rich and the poor, between the lord and the slave, it is freedom which oppresses and the law which sets free'.

As I said, when you are alone in society, you are weak. We need to abandon the concept of a divided society and people as mere customers and restore their status as citizens – well aware of what is happening in their country and around the world, capable and willing to unite in order to attain justice, enhance the common good, and enable true social justice and a just rule of law.

PART V

Academic Debates

22

Liberal Democracy and its Discontents: Normative Insights from European Judges and Recent Academic Debates

LISA CONANT

Introduction

In this commentary I analyse the reflections of judges from Denmark, Hungary, Poland, and the United Kingdom in the context of literature on comparative constitutional law and politics. Judges from Denmark and the UK have both served on the Court of Justice of the European Union, including the years leading up to British withdrawal from the European Union. Lars Bay Larsen (chapter 4) and Christopher Vajda (chapter 9) have not faced challenges to their independence; yet both hail from the rare democracies that lack a domestic practice of judicial review that overturns legislation (aka strong form judicial review)[1] and express reticence about the extent to which the judiciary can or should intervene in politics. Judges from Hungary and Poland each served on their respective national Supreme Courts as the Hungarian Fidesz and the Polish PiS governments sought political control over the judiciary and reduced the scope of media freedoms and democratic competition. András Baka (chapter 14) successfully challenged his termination before the European Court of Human Rights after the Orbán government reduced judges' retirement age to replace independent apex court judges with political loyalists. Meanwhile, Małgorzata Gersdorf remained in her post despite a similar effort to capture apex courts by lowering the retirement age that 'failed thanks to resistance within the country and from international institutions' (chapter 17). These judges demonstrate a commitment to the rule of law, which holds all actors – including elected officials – accountable to the law, and their combined observations suggest that their effectiveness requires robust political support to preserve liberal democracy. Judges alone cannot protect liberal democracy from its contemporary foes.

[1] M Wind, 'The Nordics, the EU, and the Reluctance Toward Supranational Judicial Review' (2010) 48 *Journal of Common Market Studies* 1039; R Dixon and D Landau, *Abusive Constitutional Borrowing* (Oxford, Oxford University Press, 2021).

How can Democracy be Preserved against Autocratisation?

In *How to Save a Constitutional Democracy*, Tom Ginsburg and Aziz Huq[2] identify three simultaneous requirements for liberal (constitutional) democracy: a democratic electoral system, the liberal rights to speech and association, and the rule of law. Notably absent from their account is the widespread assumption that an apex court that interprets a constitution or other 'higher law,' such as a human rights treaty, is the primary – or only – means to protect democracy, rights, and the rule of law. Chronicling interwar efforts that helped preserve democracies, Ginsburg and Huq[3] observe that a coalition of moderate Danish political parties cooperated to ameliorate the impact of the Great Depression, precluding populist radicalisation on the left and right, while the Popular Front Coalition banned paramilitary groups in France, and French conservatives refused to ally with fascist groups. Meanwhile, Finnish courts' prompt punishment of political violence stymied fascist efforts. Acknowledging that properly functioning courts may obstruct autocratic aspirations, Ginsburg and Huq caution that 'It is not wise to rely exclusively on judges to be a safeguard, particularly when liberal and constitutional norms come under sustained attack. … It may be better to think of judicial safeguards of democracy as mechanisms to buy time for the popular and elite defenders of democracy to regroup for a renewed electoral challenge'.[4]

Judge Gersdorf's reflections illustrate liberal democracy's dependence on politics, where she states 'Fortunately, the elections in Poland in 2023 put an end to the devastation of democracy and the rule of law' and 'Without international support and the support of Polish citizens, little would be achieved in the fight against the "autocratic rule of law" and the opportunists and careerist who support it' (chapter 17). In responding to political attacks on the judiciary in her country, she credits the mobilisation of active resistance by Polish judges, allies in civil society, professional associations of judges, and European Commissioners, such as Frans Timmermans, for helping to defend democracy and judicial independence. Despite the electoral defeat of the PiS government, however, Gersdorf warns that

> the Constitutional Tribunal formed in the previous period [before the 2023 elections] is still a pale imitation of what it should be. The same applies to the National Council of the Judiciary and many court presidents who were appointed by PiS (chapter 17).

To address these deficits, she defends what others may characterise as a more political role for judges:

> … Judges cannot be obliged to remain silent on matters deemed to be 'political' (…) It is the duty of every judge to defend the values and principles enshrined in the Constitution and to demand the same loudly from every authority, under all circumstances. Let us therefore

[2] T Ginsburg and A Huq, *How to Save a Constitutional Democracy* (Chicago, University of Chicago Press, 2018) 10.

[3] Ginsburg and Huq (n 2) 166.

[4] ibid 166, 189.

> allow judges to be whistle-blowers of the constitutional system. A judge should not be afraid to interact with the new media and to provide reliable information about what the law says (chapter 17).

More entrenched autocratisation in Hungary provides reason to doubt reliance on legal strategies to stop democratic demise. Orbán's electoral victory in 2010 paved the way for his government to move rapidly to capture the judiciary and place Fidesz officials and supporters above the rule of law. In *Abusive Constitutional Borrowing*, Rosalind Dixon and David Landau argue that a modern constitutional design that centralises 'power and responsibility in apex courts makes them effective tools … [in] consolidating power for the regime and repressing the opposition'.[5] The ECtHR's declaration that Hungary violated the European Convention on Human Rights when it prematurely terminated Judge Baka's mandate provided an individual remedy that could not reverse the systematic destruction of judicial independence.[6] Meanwhile, the EU's addition of 'constitutional' instruments to protect democracy and other fundamental values (Articles 2, 7, 19, 21 TEU[7]) failed to result in an effective response to persistent democratic backsliding in Hungary. Judge Bay Larsen explicitly identifies the limits of judicial interventions to prevent democratic decline and rights infringements by stating

> I am afraid that this is not a situation that can be remedied by judges only; the judges, national and European alike, must obviously fully respect the limitations for judges. We can aim to be part of the solution rather than being part of the problem (chapter 4).

Observing that '… we get the cases, they are selected by the national judges. … Whether we get a case and whether that comes this year, next year or ten years from now, we do not know', Bay Larsen also exposes the gate-keeping role played by national judges in the EU legal system that can limit the extent to which bottom-up legal mobilisation against the politicisation of national courts, rights violations, and democratic deficits reaches the CJEU.

Baka holds 'the European institutions responsible for allowing the situation in Hungary to deteriorate to its present level' – a situation that he characterises as an 'authoritarian state where the separation of powers is non-existent' and where the Hungarian judiciary is 'under the influence of the ruling party in every aspect' (chapter 14). By stating that 'the European institutions seem to be relatively weak and often need to make compromises … [that hinder] their ability to act quickly and efficiently', Baka reveals the EU's response as a *political* failure. The EU's inability to stem democratic erosion does not rest with only the European Commission or Court of Justice due to deficiencies in infringement proceedings or preliminary rulings that interpret EU law referred by national judges. In 'The last soldier standing', Dimitry Kochenov and Petra Bárd laud the CJEU for its broad reading of judicial independence as a central feature of the rule of law but nonetheless argue that 'recent case law developments are insufficient … to

[5] Dixon and Landau (n 1) 19–20.
[6] *Baka v Hungary*, App no 20261/12 (ECtHR), 23 June 2016.
[7] Consolidated Version of the Treaty on European Union [2008] OJ C115/13.

deal with the sociological legitimacy crisis in tackling illiberal democracies plaguing the EU: autocratic legalism cannot be fought with legalism alone'.[8] Instead, the EU's long-standing failure to counter Orbán's authoritarianism is shared with political allies from the European People's Party and their national counterparts in the governments of Member States.[9] Democratically elected representatives in the European Parliament and national governments lacked resolve to respond to the threats that originally motivated the addition of Articles 2 and 7 TEU. By contrast, political coordination among heads of government to isolate Austria diplomatically in 2000 produced a rapid response to the potential threat that a government led by Jörg Haider could pose for liberal democracy.[10]

Cultivating a Balance between Democratic Accountability and Legal Constitutionalism

Restoring liberal democracy in Hungary and protecting it from decline in other EU Member States is a formidable task, as illustrated by Gersdorf's grim observation that 'We are living in an era of decline in the world as we know it. (…) I have no hope that the EU and its Member States will continue to function as before. The period of prosperity and of the post-war model of democracy, based on traditional party alignment and the so-called liberal consensus, is irrevocably coming to an end. It will only get more difficult from now on' (chapter 17). Moreover, Gersdorf warns that 'the "West" of the European Union should not pretend that it is not concerned, and all this is happening only in the "wild East"'. Indeed, recent volatility in the French and German governments, the rise of far-right governing parties in Italy and the Netherlands, and the populist Brexit revolt all illustrate Judge Vajda's observation that the 'social and economic background in Europe' is 'not benign' and places governments 'under pressure to deliver on their promises and to respond to the concerns of citizens' (chapter 9). Both judges emphasise the dangers of our time, where Gersdorf laments 'the skilful manipulation of public sentiment (…) through microtargeting and trolling on social media, the internet, and by reducing the diversity of traditional media' (chapter 17) while Vajda observes 'we are living in an era … of social networks, of an enormous use of the internet but also of diffusion and rapid propagation of fake news' (chapter 9).

In response to contemporary threats, these judges emphasise the need to educate the public about liberal democracy and the role of judicial independence in it. Vajda,

[8] D Kochenov and P Bárd, 'The Last Soldier Standing? Courts versus Politicians and the Rule of Law Crisis in the New Member States of the EU' in H Ballin, G Van der Schyff and M Stremler (eds), *European Yearbook of Constitutional law 2019. Judicial Power: Safeguards and Limits in a Democratic Society* (The Hague, T.M.C. Asser Press, 2020) 243.

[9] RD Kelemen, 'The European Union's Authoritarian Equilibrium' (2020) 27 *Journal of European Public Policy* 481.

[10] W Drozdiak, 'EU warns Austria of sanctions' (1 February 2000) *Washington Post Foreign Service* A01, available at: www.washingtonpost.com/wp-srv/WPcap/2000-02/01/010r-020100-idx.html.

however, does not think judges should respond to criticisms of their decisions outside the court room or academia. Instead, he argues that

> The judgment must speak for itself. However, it is important for courts to be more transparent so that citizens can be aware of what is happening. In practice, this means streaming more hearings and issuing more press releases in important cases to make cases more accessible to journalists and the general public. This would ensure that debate on a judgment is better informed (chapter 9).

Gersdorf states 'The future belongs to the young generation, and they should be educated now. Young people must know that democracy must be fought for. It is not a given, once and for all' (chapter 17). The increase in voter turn-out among Poles aged 18–29 from 46 per cent in 2019 to 70 per cent in 2023 – when PiS lost to a pro-democracy group of opposition parties led by Donald Tusk's Civic Coalition[11] – is a beacon of hope that the peaceful, electoral mobilisation of citizens can help defeat a party responsible for an eight-year period of democratic backsliding in Poland.

Drawing on political theories of constitutionalism, I suggest that investing in efforts to improve democratic accountability may be a more effective way to fortify liberal democracies than relying on dominant models of legal constitutionalism that give apex courts the last word over disputes about rights and freedoms. In *Against Constitutionalism*, Martin Loughlin observes that 'Postwar developments, touted in the name of strengthening constitutionalism, have resulted in scores of countries instituting constitutional reforms that have, in Ran Hirschl's words, 'transferred an unprecedented amount of power from representative institutions to judiciaries' … The result is that the guardian of the constitution becomes in effect its master, and arguably undermines rather than safeguards the democratic foundation of constitutional democracy'.[12]

In this context, Richard Bellamy observes that 'Efforts will go into capturing the judiciary rather than constructing a legislative majority by reaching a mutually acceptable compromise with one's political opponents'.[13] He proposes that it is 'implausible to regard judges as basing their decisions on the "correct" view of what democratic justice demands in particular circumstances' when 'there are reasonable disagreements about justice and its implications'. In circumstances of 'profound debate and conflict,' … 'ambitious schemes of judicial review'[14] … 'risk making judicial decisions appear arbitrary, thereby threatening the legitimacy of the constitution'.[15]

Speaking to these concerns, Vajda discusses critiques about 'judicial overreach' and portrayals of 'out-of-touch judges' that 'thwart the will of the people'. The elimination of his position as the British judge at the CJEU – through a popular vote in

[11] Z Papazoski, 'Major Voter Turn-Out in Poland's 2023 Parliamentary Elections' (31 October 2023) National Democracy Institute, available at: www.ndi.org/publications/major-voter-turnout-poland-s-2023-parliamentary-elections.

[12] M Loughlin, *Against Constitutionalism* (Cambridge, MA, Harvard University Press, 2022) 129.

[13] R Bellamy, *Political Constitutionalism* (Cambridge, Cambridge University Press, 2007) 44.

[14] Constitutional review that overturns legislation on the grounds it is incompatible with a charter, constitution, convention, or treaty as a form of 'higher' or 'fundamental' law.

[15] Bellamy (n 13) 16.

the Brexit referendum motivated in part by a 'Leave' campaign to 'take back control over our laws, our borders, and our money'[16] – constituted a populist rejection of (supranational) constitutionalism and the constraints it placed on national democratic decision-making. Yet Vajda's reflections seem conflicted about the tension between law and politics as judges interpret the meaning of laws and progressively develop rights in contested cases. In discussing examples, Vajda does not explain why the judicial choice to expand the rights of same-sex couples in *Coman* against the will of the 'democratic legislator' in Romania[17] is more 'technical' and less 'political' than the deference he expresses toward the 'democratic legislator' in controversies over abortion and the right to die and have an assisted death. All three issues involve cultural conflict, and 'higher law' texts open to multiple interpretations. Despite Vajda's observation of an East/West divide in interventions at the hearing for the Coman case, he does not address the arguably competing provisions in the Charter of Fundamental Rights (Articles 7, 9, 21)[18] and lack of consensus concerning same-sex marriage or even civil unions.[19] Notably, the democracies that pioneered legal rights for same-sex civil partnership (Denmark) and marriage (the Netherlands) did so through legislation and are among the few remaining countries that govern more routinely under democratic traditions that defer to 'parliamentary sovereignty' than under systems of 'constitutional democracy' that confer 'judicial supremacy'. The strong record of rights protections in the set of liberal democracies where this more political form of constitutionalism prevails[20] justifies renewed attention to how the rule of law and democracy 'only survived and developed in those societies where the democratic control of power and the socio-economic conditions that support it persist'.[21] Politically mobilising the broad coalitions necessary to succeed in democratically representative institutions is more demanding than mobilising legally to secure favourable legal interpretations from a small set of appointed judges. Building a consensus that extends far beyond the courtroom is, however, the most promising response to an era of rising inequality and growing insecurity that has inspired widespread backlash that simultaneously threatens democracy, human rights, and the rule of law.

[16] L Conant, 'Failing Backward? EU Citizenship, the Court of Justice, and Brexit' (2021) 28 *Journal of European Public Policy* 1592.

[17] Case C-673/16 *Coman and others* ECLI:EU:C:2018:385, [2019] 1 WLR 425.

[18] Article 9 states 'The right to marry and the right to found a family shall be grounded in accordance with the national laws governing the exercise of these rights' while Article 7 confers a right to respect for private and family life, and Article 21 prohibits discrimination on the ground of sexual orientation. Charter of Fundamental Rights of the European Union [2010] OJ C202/389.

[19] P Duncan, 'A History of Same-sex Unions in Europe' (24 January 2016) *The Guardian*, www.theguardian.com/news/datablog/2016/jan/24/a-history-of-same-sex-unions-in-europe; 'Romania Condemned by European Court for Violating Rights of LGBT Couples' (23 May 2023), *Le Monde*, www.lemonde.fr/en/european-union/article/2023/05/23/romania-condemned-by-european-court-for-violating-rights-of-lgbt-couples_6027759_156.html; Human Rights Campaign, 'Marriage equality around the world' (2024), available at: www.hrc.org/resources/marriage-equality-around-the-world; *Buhuceanu and others v Romania*, App no 20081/19 (ECtHR, 23 May 2023).

[20] Including also Finland, Norway, Sweden, and the UK, who appear to protect fundamental rights as well as countries where legal constitutionalism prevails, such as Austria, Italy, Spain, and Germany. See 'civil liberties' and 'political rights' scores in Freedom House's 'Freedom in the World' reports and percentile ranks for the 'rule of law' and 'voice and accountability' in the World Bank's 'Worldwide Governance Indicators' for commonly used quantitative indicators of liberal democratic performance.

[21] Bellamy (n 13) 2.

23

Judges' Resilience in the Face of Attacks on Judicial Independence: Some Reflections on the German, Italian, and Hungarian Contexts

GÁBOR HALMAI

Introduction

The four highly interesting interviews that I will comment on – from German, Italian, and Hungarian judges – provide a partial picture of the different approaches to resilience and resistance of courts operating in three distinct EU Member States and of their respective judges as individuals in the face of attacks on judicial independence. By resilience I mean here the capacity of courts and judges to resist such threats. If one divides the factors conditioning judicial resilience into structural (political power relations) and institutional (appointment procedure, jurisdiction, etc) conditions,[1] the three countries – Germany, Italy and Hungary – of the four interviewees represent distinct categories. In Germany, both the structural and the institutional requirements of judicial independence seem to be guaranteed by constitutional rules and practices based on a strong constitutional culture. Therefore, the judges' associations can limit their activity to the traditional work of protecting the rights of their members. In Italy, both the structural and institutional conditions are more fragile, and hence it is important to use different modes of resistance to keep judicial independence alive. In contrast, in Hungary, as an electoral autocracy, judicial independence has been

[1] For more on this categorisation in the political science literature, see W Merkel and A Lührmann, 'Resilience of Democracies: Responses to Illiberal and Authoritarian Challenges' (2021) 28 *Democratization*, 871. Also about the structural and institutional factors of resilience against democratic backsliding, see RB Riedl, P Friesen, J McCoy and K Roberts, 'Democratic Backsliding, Resilience, and Resistance' (2024) 75 *World Politics* 1; AT Little and A Meng, 'What We Do and Do Not Know about Democratic Backsliding' (2024) 57 *Political Science & Politics* 1. See also S Levitsky and L Way, 'The Resilience of Democracy's Third Wave' (2024) 57 *Political Science & Politics* 198.

almost entirely dismantled making resistance by courts and judges nearly impossible.[2] However, besides demonstrating the structural and institutional aspects of their countries' state of judicial resilience, the interviews also indicate a third factor of judicial resilience, namely the personal and behavioural attitude of judges towards their own and their courts' independence.[3]

Insights from Germany

In chapter 6, Dieter Grimm emphasises the importance of the cultural preconditions for constitutionalism contributing to the resilience of the rule of law, including the independence of the judiciary, which is not questioned even by the radical right-wing populist party, AfD. This is the reason why Professor Grimm did not experience any political pressure during his tenure as a judge, despite the partisan procedure for appointing the members of the Federal Constitutional Court. The same reason explains the lack of significant political influence at entry level within the ordinary judiciary. This is despite the fact that Germany lacks a system of independent judicial self-government since organising the judiciary is a competence of the *Länder* whereby the Minister of Justice has ultimate authority over all members of the judiciary – as Andrea Titz asserts in chapter 8. Titz' assessment of the need to fight for judicial independence in Germany is similar to that of Judge Grimm: 'It is not always a battle' (chapter 8). This is another proof that judicial self-government cannot be viewed as a panacea for all problems of court administration in Europe.[4] As Judge Titz argues, in Germany 'Every Minister of Justice is already theoretically able to appoint whomever he or she likes as a judge' (chapter 8). Nevertheless, she asserts that 'the independence of the judiciary remains unaffected by political controversies' despite the fact that judges in Germany are allowed to be involved in political movements or demonstrations and even be members of a political party, unlike in most of the 'backsliding' East-Central European countries. The German Judges' Association is allowed to participate in the law-making process, and judges have the right to express their concerns regarding legislative changes, without facing sanctions. This stands in contrast with what happened to the former President of the Hungarian Supreme Court, Judge Baka (see chapter 14), whose mandate was terminated prematurely due to his criticism of the Hungarian judicial reform in 2011.[5] In other words, the tendency to maintain the rule of law as a cornerstone of a country's political/constitutional culture on which there is consensus in society, as Judge Titz puts

[2] A more detailed analysis of the lack of checks and balances can be found in M Bánkuti, G Halmai and KL Scheppele, 'From Separation of Powers to a Government without Checks: Hungary's Old and New Constitutions' in GA Tóth (ed), *Constitution for a Disunited Nation. On Hungary's 2011 Fundamental Law* (New York, CEU Press, 2012).

[3] For more about this 'agentic' factor of judicial resilience, see L Epstein and J Knight, *The Choices Justices Make* (Washington, D.C., CQ Press, 1998); JA Segal and HJ Spaeth, *The Supreme Court and the Attitudinal Model*, (Cambridge, Cambridge University Press, 1993).

[4] This is the main conclusion of David Kosař's, seminal book, comparing the experiences of the Czech and the Slovak judicial councils. D Kosař, *Perils of Judicial Self-Government in Transitional Societies* (Cambridge, Cambridge University Press, 2016).

[5] *Baka v Hungary*, App no 20261/12 (ECtHR, 23 June 2016).

it, can be more effective than the formal legal tools of militant democracy, which were widely promoted and used in democratic Germany after Nazism (chapter 8).

Insights from Italy

Judge Titz compares the rosy situation of judicial resilience in Germany to that in Italy, 'where the Minister of Justice is openly confronting judges and public prosecutors with whom he had disagreements when he was a lawyer' (chapter 8). Indeed, Luca Perilli echoes the opinion of the European Association of Judges when he states (chapter 12), that the draft constitutional amendment of June 2024 for changing the governance of the judiciary, together with the composition and means of the functioning of the Supreme Council of the Judiciary represents a 'serious attack on the independence of the judiciary, and undermining the existing balance of powers in Italy, and a clear infringement of the European standards'. Perilli argues that in a place like Italy, the country with the highest number of disciplinary proceedings against judges and prosecutors of all Member States of the Council of Europe, there is a real danger that the government will dismantle the previous system which complied with European Union standards and instead create a new disciplinary body that is separate from the judicial system, as a sort of special court. Judge Perilli, along with the large majority of judges and prosecutors, as well as the *Associazione Nazionale Magistrati*, is very critical of the reform. Yet in order to legitimise its plans, the government has invoked the citizens' negative perception on judicial independence and impartiality. Depiction of judges in the media, in particular those dealing with migration, also plays a role, as illustrated in chapter 12. In relation to the appointment scandal in 2020,[6] Judge Perilli describes how judges in Catania refused to validate the detention of migrants based on the argument that the new regulation violated the Italian constitution as well as the EU Charter of Fundamental Rights and the European Pact on Migration. In reaction, members of the governing parties accused the judges of blocking an act of Parliament. This populist attack on certain judges certainly undermined the social resilience of the judiciary, and as Perilli predicts, it also endangers the future activity of young judges, as can already be observed in the increasing passivity of judicial associations in Italy. One of the tactics of the current Italian government against judges who apply the EU Pact on Migration, similarly to the abusive practice of the Hungarian government, is to invoke the country's national constitutional identity to legitimise the non-application of EU law. On this matter, like Professor Grimm, Judge Perilli also blames the EU for not being always fully committed to the European values entrenched in Article 2 TEU. While Grimm suggests that it might one day be possible to amend the Treaty in order to expel any Member State that consistently and systematically deviates from the Union's values (as Hungary has been doing since 2010), Perilli advocates a more significant use of the value conditionality mechanism that has already been tested in the case of Hungary.

[6] See A Sallusti and L Palamara, *Il Sistema. Potere, Politica, Affari: Storia Segrata della Magistratura italiana* (Milan, Rizzoli, 2021).

Insights from Hungary

Based on the narratives discussed so far, Hungary is an outlier in terms of the resilience of the rule of law, and it represents the most serious dismantlement of judicial independence within the EU.[7] The interview with Hungarian Judge Tamás Matusik (chapter 19), perfectly proves the sad state of judicial resilience in his – and also my own – home country. In the interview, Matusik tells his story as a member of the Judicial Council, elected in 2018. Along with other judges, Matusik faced attacks in the media loyal to the government (with 400 critical articles published in a single month!) and also from the Head of the Judicial Office, a body which was formally subordinated to the Council which, in turn, had no effective supervisory competences. This conflict resulted in the shut-down of any cooperation between the Judicial Office and the Council for one and a half years, causing a constitutional crisis. Due to the EU's decision to withhold funds over concerns about the rule of law, the Council was able to force the Hungarian Government to remove the Head of the Judicial Office, the wife of a prominent member of the governing Fidesz party, and 'demote' her to the position of a judge at the politically captured Constitutional Court. However, such instances of EU-led mitigation of corruption were rare during the 15 year-long history of the authoritarian Orbán-regime.

But this turned out to be a very short-lived success for the Judicial Council and its then President, Judge Matusik, who – as explained in chapter 19 – did not run for office again after his mandate finished. The 2024 election process resulted in a new body, the majority of whom were once again loyal to the government. One early sign of the betrayal of judicial independence by the newly elected Judicial Council was their recent agreement with the Minister of Justice to link the long-awaited increase in judicial salaries to new judicial reforms, thereby further dismantling the remainders of judicial independence. On 21 November 2024 Judge Matusik published his reaction to this decision on X: 'JUSTICE FOR SALE? The Hungarian National Council has given up its independence when bowing to the pressure of the Minister of Justice and deciding to sign an agreement linking judicial pay rise to dangerous court reforms after secret fast-track negotiations.'[8] As Amnesty International Hungary reported, the election of the members of the Judicial Council was partly rigged,[9] but Judge Matusik points out two other possible reasons for the behaviour of the recently elected judges. One is that many judges who elected the new Council members 'do not consider it important to participate in the process of safeguarding the separation of powers', while the other reason is that 'the mindset of the Hungarian judges and people. The public mindset in Hungary is different, and it may lead us to accept certain deals within the community'.[10] However, instead of blaming the judges themselves, I would rather emphasise that the judges'

[7] The Resilio Monitor project assesses the resilience of the rule of law in the EU. In 2024 among the 27 EU Member States Hungary's resilience was ranked the lowest. See: M Skóra, D Nonhoff and Y Albrecht, *What makes the rule of law resilient? Evidence from EU27. RESILIO Monitor Full Report* (Berlin, Institut für Europäische Politik, 2024).

[8] Judge Matusik's post is available at: x.com/TamasMatusik/status/1859490126155427965.

[9] For more about the irregularities of the election proceedings see the report of Amnesty International Hungary: www.amnesty.hu/election-of-the-new-national-judicial-council-of-hungary/.

[10] On 26 November Judge Matusik also gave an interview on the Partizan YouTube channel: x.com/TamasMatusik/status/1861820854696309241 (quotes translated by author).

existential fear of retribution can also be a decisive factor in the system. An example of this is the initiation of disciplinary proceedings against a judge who referred preliminary questions to the Court of Justice of the European Union.[11] Additionally, a well-respected Supreme Court judge was suspended from his leadership position by the President of the Supreme Court after he signed a protest letter against the above-mentioned agreement between the Ministry of Justice and the Judicial Council.[12] I assume that some of those judges, who may have been afraid of sanctions, are the ones mentioned by Judge Matusik, and who are now leaving the judiciary.[13]

One possible reason why Viktor Orbán's government in Hungary eliminated the independence of constitutional review and the judiciary altogether is mentioned in the interview with Judge Grimm. This is, namely, the very active jurisprudence of the Constitutional Court led by President László Sólyom in the first nine years of the democratic transition (1990–1998). Professor Grimm argues that 'Parliament must enjoy a certain degree of autonomy in determining political goals and the means to reach them'. Grimm also refers to the modern understanding of the rule of law as not only a formal, but a material concept as well: 'Not any law that was passed in due form can claim binding force. It can only do so if it is also compatible with certain fundamental legal principles or values' (see chapter 6). These words refer to the 1992 decision of the Sólyom Court[14] which invalidated the law on retroactive justice targeting perpetrators who had not been prosecuted under the Communist regime for political reasons. The court based its decision on a formal understanding of the rule of law, stating that extending the statute of limitations would violate the principle that the rule of law cannot be restored through its own violation. The German Federal Constitutional Court did not apply the statute of limitation in similar cases, precisely because those crimes had not been prosecuted for political reasons. I do agree that such formalistic interpretations of legal constitutionalism, or the perception of them as such, may have estranged people from the very idea of liberal constitutionalism.[15] Maybe more deference on the side of the courts vis-á-vis Parliament, as Judge Grimm argues, will also be instrumental when the restoration of the rule of law and judicial resilience comes back onto the agenda in Hungary and in other backsliding countries. But this cannot happen unless we build a constitutional culture in which the people understand the importance of judicial independence. Courts and judges have a vital role to play in this endeavour, as illustrated by the interviews brought together in this volume.

[11] See the case of Judge Vasvári, 'Hungary: Disciplinary Action Judge for Recourse to EU Court Must Cease' (18 November 2019) International Commission of Jurists, www.icj.org/hungary-disciplinary-action-against-judge-for-recourse-to-eu-court-must-cease/.

[12] Declaration by Judge András Kovács, available at mabie.hu/images/LEVELEK%202024/1128/Kovacs%20Andras%20levele.pdf.

[13] In November 2024, the head of the Criminal Senate at the Metropolitan Appeal Court, one of the leaders of Res Iudicata, one of the Judges Associations, resigned in protest against the same agreement. S Viktória, '"Az én értékrendemmel ez már nem fér össze" – lemondott bírói tisztségéről a Fővárosi Törvényszék Büntető Kollégiumának tanácselnöke' (29 November 2024) *hvg.hu*, hvg.hu/itthon/20241129_lemondott-biro-laczo-adrienn.

[14] Decision of 5 March 1992, Hungarian Constitutional Court, No 11/992 (III.5.).

[15] See my similar assessment of such impact of certain early decisions of the first Constitutional Court I had the privilege to contribute to as chief advisor to President Sólyom, and I still agree with G Halmai, 'From Liberal Democracy to Illiberal Populist Autocracy: Possible Reasons for Hungary's Autocratization' (2024) 16 *The Hague Journal on the Rule of Law* 439.

24

Activism and the Evolving Role of European Judges: Defending Rights in an Age of Democratic Dissensus

AGNIESZKA KUBAL

Introduction

This collection of interviews with judges from Poland, Hungary, Italy, and Portugal offers profound insights into the evolving role of European judges. Drawing on the conversations with figures such as Małgorzata Maria Gersdorf (chapter 17), Monika Frąckowiak (chapter 16), José Igreja Matos (chapter 11), and Luca Perilli (chapter 12), as well as broader socio-legal scholarly insights,[1] this commentary examines the transformation of the judiciary amid threats to democratic norms and explores whether these changes are likely to endure.

The main argument I advance is as follows: judicial activism has long been a feature of legal systems in Europe and beyond.[2] In recent years, the challenges posed by democratic backsliding have brought to light various strategies employed by judges to safeguard their independence. Notably, many judges have increasingly turned to international apex courts as a countermeasure, marking a shift from the traditionally dominant approach of legal formalism.[3] While the immediate judicial crises in some countries – such as Poland – may have subsided, the reliance on European apex courts and the cultivation of transnational judicial solidarity present opportunities to address the broader and more persistent issue of expanding legal dualism.

[1] A Kubal, 'Judicial Relational Legal Consciousness: Authoritarian Backsliding as a Catalyst of Change' (2024a) 51 *Journal of Law and Society* S45; L Puleo and R Coman, 'Explaining Judges' Opposition when Judicial Independence is Undermined: Insights from Poland, Romania, and Hungary' (2024) 31 *Democratization* 47; K Hendley, 'Varieties of Legal Dualism: Making Sense of the Role of Law in Contemporary Russia' (2011) 29 *Wisconsin International Law Journal* 233; K Hendley, *Everyday Law in Russia* (Ithaca, Cornell University Press, 2017).

[2] C Green, 'An Intellectual History of Judicial Activism' (2009) 58 *Emory Law Journal* 1195; JS Schacter, 'Putting the Politics of "Judicial Activism" in Historical Perspective' (2018) 2017 *The Supreme Court Review* 209; R Hoque and MMM Khan, 'Judicial Activism and Islamic Family Law: a Socio-Legal Evaluation of Recent Trends in Bangladesh' (2007) 14 *Islamic Law and Society* 204.

[3] Kubal (n 1).

The concept of legal dualism, first articulated by Kathryn Hendley in her analysis of the Russian legal system, offers a valuable lens through which to understand the politicisation of justice in the context of democratic dissensus. Hendley describes legal dualism as the coexistence of two legal realms: a predominant one that adheres to principles of justice and legality for everyday cases, and a smaller, high-profile sphere where political interests distort judicial outcomes.[4] This dualism reflects a broader undermining of democratic principles, especially in contexts where political interference in the judiciary is designed to erode democratic norms and institutions.

Hendley's insights into the varieties of legal dualism underscore a trend in which political interference is deployed to challenge the liberal democratic consensus. In response, I propose that strategies of judicial activism honed during the period of the crisis of democracy – including turning to international apex courts, fostering transnational solidarity,[5] and engaging in collective resistance[6] – serve as critical tools to counteract the detrimental effects of expanding legal dualism. These strategies not only reinforce judicial independence but also help to safeguard democratic principles in increasingly polarised and contentious political landscapes.

The Crisis of Democracy as a Catalyst for Change in Central Eastern Europe

Authoritarian backsliding in Poland and Hungary has profoundly altered the judicial landscape. Judges who once adhered strictly to national legal frameworks have increasingly turned to European law and human rights instruments as tools of resistance. The crisis, as I argued elsewhere[7] has been 'productive' in shaping a new relational legal consciousness,[8] whereby judges no longer see themselves as mere arbiters of national law but as active participants in a broader European legal order, turning not only to the CJEU but also to the ECtHR. This shift is vividly illustrated by the words of a Polish district court judge:

> Only five years ago, I treated the European Court of Human Rights (ECtHR) as a court from a galaxy far, far away. There were some cases regarding pre-trial detention, and excessive length of proceedings. Something was going on there, but I thought it was all resolved [in Polish law] … I thought: 'We have a sound legal system – why go so far?[9]

[4] Hendley (n 1).

[5] Puleo and Coman (n 1).

[6] M Mrowicki, *All Rise – Judicial Resistance in Poland* (Washington, D.C., International Center on Nonviolent Conflict 2024); B Grabowska-Moroz and O Śniadach, 'The Role of Civil Society in Protecting Judicial Independence in Times of Rule of Law Backsliding in Poland' (2021) 17 *Utrecht Law Review* 56; Ł Bojarski, 'Civil Society Organizations for and with the Courts and Judges – Struggle for the Rule of Law and Judicial Independence: The Case of Poland 1976–2020' (2021) 22 *German Law Journal* 1344; CY Matthes, 'Judges as Activists: How Polish Judges Mobilise to Defend the Rule of Law' (2022) 38 *East European Politics* 468.

[7] Kubal (n 1).

[8] Legal consciousness is defined as 'ways in which people understand, experience, or act in response to law', LJ Chua and DM Engel, 'Legal Consciousness Reconsidered' (2019) 15 *Annual Review of Law and Social Science* 335.

[9] Quoted in Kubal (n 1) 52.

Initially, the judge's perception of the ECtHR as a distant and irrelevant institution underscores the dominance of legal formalism within national contexts. This mindset reflects a time when judges viewed their primary duty as upholding domestic legal frameworks, assuming these systems were robust and self-sufficient. However, the erosion of judicial independence and the manipulation of legal structures by authoritarian governments exposed the limitations of this insular approach.

The realisation that national systems are vulnerable to political interference has prompted judges to re-evaluate their roles. The embrace of European jurisprudence is not merely a defensive strategy but a conscious redefinition of judicial identity. Prof. Gersdorf, in her interview for this volume (see chapter 17), captures this transformation succinctly:

> judges cannot be obliged to remain silent on matters that are deemed to be 'political'. The world is changing dynamically, and even the British no longer support Lord Kilmuir's once famous 1955 rules, which banned all statements to the media outside the courtroom. This does not mean that those entrusted with the power of adjudication should undertake normal political engagement, because, after all, the separation of powers and the impartiality of the judiciary should be taken seriously. However, there are issues of principle about which one must not be silent, and the statements formulated in legal judgments do not have sufficient resonance in society. It is the duty of every judge to defend the values and principles enshrined in the Constitution and to demand the same loudly from every authority, under all circumstances. Let us therefore allow judges to be whistle-blowers of the constitutional system (chapter 17).

Gersdorf's call for judges to act as 'whistle-blowers of the constitutional system' (chapter 17) underscores the ethical dimension of this transformation. It moves beyond the traditional notion of judges as passive interpreters of law and assigns them a more active role as defenders of constitutional values. This redefinition aligns with a judicial philosophy that prioritises principles over procedural constraints. The invocation of whistleblowing suggests that judges have a duty not only to interpret the law but also to expose and challenge legal violations, even at the risk of suffering personal and professional consequences.

In embracing European jurisprudence, judges are also fostering a sense of solidarity across borders. The turn to supranational courts like the ECtHR and the European Court of Justice represents more than a legal strategy; it is a statement of shared values and mutual accountability. This emerging transnational judicial consciousness could strengthen the judiciary's collective capacity to resist authoritarian encroachments, offering a model of resilience that extends beyond national boundaries.

The Dilemma of Judicial Activism

The evolution of judicial roles in Poland and Eastern Europe can serve as a shared exercise in identity-building with Western judges facing similar threats. Judicial independence is increasingly at risk, not only in the democratically backsliding countries of Eastern Europe but also in Western beacons of democracy like Germany (see chapter 8), where the rise of *Alternative für Deutschland* is challenging democratic norms, and Italy, with its populist governments led by the Brothers of Italy (*Fratelli d'Italia)* undermining judicial autonomy. This new judicial role blurs traditional boundaries. The ability to defend judicial independence, as Luca Perilli succinctly observes in chapter 12, is both essential and vulnerable:

> Judicial independence is the key value for the protection of the rights of individuals, especially in times of change and constitutional transitions, and judges are those who can and must protect those rights. However, this requires that their independence from political power is guaranteed. Judges can be a big obstacle for authoritarian regimes. This is why the independence of the judiciary is the first target of autocrats (chapter 12).

Historically, judges were expected to maintain a degree of detachment from political controversies. However, as Gersdorf suggests (chapter 17), silence in the face of democratic backsliding can no longer be defended as neutrality. Judges must now navigate a delicate balance between activism and impartiality, fulfilling their duty to uphold the law while also safeguarding democratic values. This recalibration of judicial identity is not just a response to external pressures but a reflection of an evolving understanding of what judicial independence truly entails in a contested political landscape.

This sentiment resonates throughout the interviews, reflecting a common thread across different legal systems. As authoritarian regimes in Poland and Hungary have demonstrated, undermining judicial independence is a strategic move aimed at consolidating power. The role of the judiciary to serve as a check on executive overreach makes it a prime target for autocrats seeking to erode democratic institutions. Perilli's insight is echoed by José Igreja Matos (chapter 11), a Portuguese judge who similarly emphasises the precarious nature of judicial independence:

> Judicial independence is never a given. It is always a fight; it is always something that could collapse (…) Autocrats use the same approach to attack the judges, the media, the opposition … Controlling the judges and the media makes it inevitable that such leaders will also be able to control societies to perpetuate their power (chapter 11).

This warning underscores the idea that judicial independence must be actively safeguarded, not passively assumed. As argued by Claudia Matthes, Marcin Mrowicki, or Łukasz Bojarski[10] judicial resistance often emerges through networks of solidarity, both domestic and transnational. Professional associations and judicial networks play a critical role in mobilising judges against threats.[11] In Poland and Hungary, these associations have become focal points of opposition, organising legal challenges and public campaigns to defend judicial autonomy.[12] These reflections underscore a critical insight: judicial independence must be actively defended, not taken for granted. The interviews suggest that this defence requires not only legal acumen but also a willingness to engage in public discourse – a departure from traditional judicial passivity.

However, the interviews also reveal that defending judicial independence requires more than legal expertise; it demands public engagement. This marks a significant departure from the traditional notion of judicial passivity. Judges like Gersdorf and Frąckowiak articulate a growing recognition that we can no longer justify silence in

[10] Bojarski (n 6); Matthes (n 6); Mrowicki (n 6).

[11] R Coman and L Puleo, 'Opposition and Resistance: How Judges and Professional Associations in Poland, Hungary, and Romania Defend their Independence' (2025) 41 *East European Politics* 24.

[12] Puleo and Coman (n 1).

the face of democratic backsliding. A central tension explored in the interviews is the balance between judicial activism and legal formalism. Monika Frąckowiak explains this challenge in the Polish context:

> we cannot go back to the situation we had in 2015. We need to learn from what happened in Poland. That means that judges cannot only speak through their judgments. It is something what we know to be 100 per cent true. Magistrates need to be active and open to society. But, at the same time, it is difficult to find the right balance between being simply a judge and being an activist, because a judge should always be limited by the position they hold (chapter 16).

This tension between activism and impartiality mirrors the broader challenges of judicial resistance. As I argued in my analysis of resistance coalitions in Poland, judges are increasingly compelled to engage with broader social movements.[13] This reflects the dynamic alliances that emerge between marginalised groups and legal actors, driven by a shared need to defend fundamental rights.[14] Similarly, in the judicial context, activism is not an ideological choice but a practical necessity in the face of systemic threats. Judge Tuleya's reflections on the evolving perception of Polish judges underscore this shift from distant sympathy to active collaboration:

> The Dutch, the Germans, the French, etc. – now it's not sympathy, it's full understanding … What you are doing here in Poland can be a kind of lesson because we can learn from it and somehow try to use it at home.[15]

This nuanced understanding of judicial activism acknowledges the complexities of modern judicial roles. Judges are increasingly called upon to navigate politically charged cases involving human rights, environmental protection, and social justice. The evolving political landscape demands a recalibration of judicial responsibilities, balancing adherence to legal formalism with a commitment to broader constitutional principles. The interviews suggest that transnational solidarity, fostered through professional networks, is crucial in sustaining judicial independence across Europe.

Activism as a Measure of Judicial Resilience against Legal Dualism

Yet the interviews contained in this book aptly demonstrate that the activism, resistance, solidarity and other practical toolkits developed by judges during the authoritarian backsliding have further, more pressing applications today. The notion of legal dualism, originally articulated by Kathryn Hendley in the Russian context,[16] refers to a bifurcated legal system where the vast majority of cases adhere to established legal norms, but a politically sensitive subset is manipulated or selectively enforced by authoritarian regimes. This concept takes on heightened relevance in Europe amidst

[13] A Kubal, 'Queer Coalition? Rule of Law Crisis and LGBTQ+ Rights in Polish Courts' (2024b) 76 *Europe-Asia Studies* 1347.
[14] ibid. See also Grabowska-Moroz and Śniadach (n 6).
[15] Quoted in Kubal (n 1) S57.
[16] Hendley (n 1).

the growing phenomenon of democratic dissensus, where the foundational consensus that democracy is the 'only game in town' has fractured. In this context, legal dualism transcends isolated cases of corruption or political interference, signalling a more systemic erosion of the rule of law. As judicial systems become battlegrounds for contested visions of governance, the selective enforcement of legal norms threatens to undermine the very principles of democracy, turning legal systems into tools for consolidating authoritarian control and deepening societal divisions.

Judges in countries like Poland, Hungary but also those in Western European jurisdictions are not only adjudicating ordinary cases but also navigating politically charged cases that test the boundaries of their independence and integrity. The concept of legal dualism poses a direct challenge to judicial impartiality. As Alexei Trochev and Rachel Ellet explained in the context of hybrid regimes, 'the judiciary is progressively more politicised, politics are increasingly judicialized, and key political questions are regularly framed as legal questions or disputes'.[17] Igreja Matos's comments on the emerging challenges for the judiciary highlight the breadth of these issues, extending well beyond cases concerning the legal constitutional order per se:

> I think environmental protection will be a major issue for judiciary over the next ten years (…) Another topic is migration (…) We could mention here all the cases that deal with challenges for modern societies such as abortion, discrimination against minorities, and the use of technology in the workplace, for instance. You see the latter in Asia, for instance, in China, where there is an attempt to control the private and the professional life of citizens now and we also have the technological tools to effectively do so (chapter 11).

These issues, while ostensibly legal matters, carry significant political implications. The enforcement of environmental regulations, for example, often pits judges against powerful corporate interests and government policies. Similarly, cases involving migration and minority rights are deeply politicised, reflecting broader societal debates about national identity and social cohesion. This highlights a significant shift in judicial responsibilities. Judges are no longer confined to the interpretation and application of national laws but must increasingly engage with European legal frameworks due to creeping legal dualism. The requirement to disapply national laws in cases of conflict with EU law places judges in a precarious position, especially when these conflicts involve politically sensitive issues like human rights and civil liberties.

In such contexts, judicial resilience and outspokenness become essential. The techniques of resistance honed in the context of judicial independence must now be applied to a broader array of human rights and civil liberties issues. Judges are increasingly called upon to adopt a proactive stance, leveraging European legal frameworks to safeguard fundamental rights. This shift challenges traditional notions of judicial neutrality. As Igreja Matos aptly notes, the role of a judge is to navigate the complexities of truth and to appreciate nuance:

> And that is the role of a judge – our role is to listen to the different sides of the same story, to be aware of subtility and nuances. The truth is not black and white … (chapter 11).

[17] A Trochev and R Ellett, 'Judges and their Allies: Rethinking Judicial Autonomy through the Prism of Off-Bench Resistance' (2014) 2 *Journal of Law and Courts* 67, 82.

The increasing legal dualism forces judges to confront ethical dilemmas. Silence or inaction in the face of human rights violations can be tantamount to complicity. The ethical imperative to 'speak up', as articulated by Gersdorf and others, is not merely a matter of personal conviction but a professional duty. Judges must find ways to assert their independence and uphold the rule of law without compromising their impartiality.

The concept of legal dualism also underscores the importance of judicial discretion and integrity. In systems where politically sensitive cases are treated differently, the onus falls on judges to ensure that the rule of law prevails. This requires a nuanced understanding of legal principles and a willingness to engage with supranational legal frameworks. The interviews suggest that judges are increasingly prepared to take on this role, viewing themselves as custodians of democratic values. As Perilli notes, the application of EU law often serves as a critical mechanism for safeguarding fundamental rights:

> the application of EU Law often triggers the Charter of Fundamental Rights of the European Union (…) This operation often implies the interpretation of national law consistently with the national constitution or supranational sources of law. Sometimes it even implies the disapplication of the national law in cases where non-compliance with EU law has a direct effect (chapter 12).

As I have demonstrated elsewhere,[18] this shift towards broader societal responsibility vis-à-vis expanding legal dualism represents a new relational legal consciousness, capturing 'the multiple and shifting relations of co-determination among politics and law, without collapsing them into one another'.[19] Judges no longer see themselves as mere interpreters of national law but as active participants in a broader legal order. This consciousness is essential in combating the creeping politicisation of law and ensuring that legal dualism does not undermine the rule of law. The interviews in this book illustrate a judiciary in flux, grappling with its role in an increasingly authoritarian world. While the crisis has been productive in fostering a sense of European judicial solidarity, the future remains uncertain – judicial activism might become one of the measures of legal systemic resilience and restraint against expanding legal dualism.

[18] Kubal (n 1).

[19] C Boukalas, 'Politics as Legal Action/Lawyers as Political Actors' (2013) 22 *Social & Legal Studies* 395, 415.

25

The Fertile Fear of the Abyss: Or, How the Rule of Law Crisis Spurred Judges to Mobilise European Law

TOMMASO PAVONE

Out of the Courthouses and into the Streets

Sifting through this volume's fascinating interviews with European judges, I could not help but reminisce about the many interviews with lawyers and judges that I completed for my 2022 book, *The Ghostwriters*.[1] I have been itching for an opportunity to pen an addendum to my argument therein that lawyers have been the primary and underappreciated catalysts of 'the judicial construction of Europe'.[2] This commentary is my addendum.

I concluded *The Ghostwriters* by grappling with the threats to the rule of law (RoL) plaguing the European Union (EU). Seeking to strike an optimistic note in a time of crisis, I suggested that the protagonists of my book might mobilise anew to rescue the RoL. Those protagonists were what I and others[3] call 'Euro-lawyers', or entrepreneurial attorneys across EU Member States who advanced European legal integration by mobilising EU law before national courts and soliciting preliminary references to the Court of Justice of the EU, often behind-the-scenes. With eyes squarely fixed on Budapest and Warsaw, I suggested that Euro-lawyers could now embrace a more public-facing role to

> expos[e] repression masked as law by representing dissident academics and publicizing the sham trials brought against them … ban[d] together into transnational associations to defend journalists and public watchdogs against legal harassment and intimidation … identify hooks to European law that can be publicized in the streets, invoked in the courts … [and] complemen[t] public advocacy with behind-the-scenes lobbying campaigns, supplying

[1] T Pavone, *The Ghostwriters: Lawyers and the Politics Behind the Judicial Construction of Europe* (Cambridge, Cambridge University Press, 2022).

[2] A Stone Sweet, *The Judicial Construction of Europe* (New York, Oxford University Press, 2004).

[3] A Vauchez, *Brokering Europe: Euro-Lawyers and the Making of a Transnational Polity* (Cambridge, Cambridge University Press, 2015).

European institutions with rapid legal analyses and situation reports that cut through the fog of state disinformation.[4]

It turns out that all the above strategies have indeed been mobilised to defend the RoL, judicial independence, and the EU legal order. Yet it has been *judges*, more so than lawyers, who are at the *avant-garde* of this legal mobilisation campaign. To be sure, crises (like the RoL crisis) 'have a way of bringing to light previously hidden possibilities for agency and institutional change' to a wide array of actors.[5] But it has been judges who have seized these possibilities, perhaps because they did not interpret them as mere choices to be freely made, but as imperatives without escape. When your colleagues are being fired, disciplined, politically attacked, and cowed into obeisance by illiberal governments (and when you might soon be next), then abandoning the trudge of daily work to pursue 'off-bench mobilisation' begins to feel like a professional duty and a moral obligation.[6]

In this chapter's brief commentary, I want to elaborate how the RoL crisis in Europe has catalysed a mechanism of judge-driven legal mobilisation that is novel to the post-war EU context: 'the fertile fear of the abyss'. In conversation with the interviews in this volume, I trace how the rise of illiberal governments attacking the RoL has jolted many European judges out of their entrenched bureaucratic routines into exploring new, public, transnational, and uncomfortable avenues of European legal mobilisation. Although this EU-wide galvanisation of judges should not be overstated and its capacity to reverse RoL backsliding is dubious, it undeniably constitutes a remarkable new chapter in the history of European legal integration.

The Fertile Fear of the Abyss

To wit: what the interviews in this volume highlight is what we might call the 'fertile fear of the abyss': the ways that a diffusing threat and sense of crisis can shake judges out of the bureaucratic status-quo towards more active and public forms of European legal mobilisation.[7]

In proposing this phrase, I build on Charles Epp's perceptive study of how litigation pressures in the United States fomented a 'fertile fear of liability' within some police departments that induced these bureaucracies to embrace reform.[8] Like police

[4] Pavone (n 1) 318–19.

[5] ibid 317.

[6] CY Matthes, 'Judges as Activists: How Polish Judges Mobilise to Defend the Rule of Law' (2022) 38 *East European Politics* 468; R Coman and L Puleo, 'Opposition and Resistance: How Judges and Professional Associations in Poland, Hungary, and Romania Defend Their Independence' (2025) 41 *East European Politics* 24; P Cebulak, 'Mapping the Potentials and Pitfalls of using European Law for Strategic Litigation against Illiberal Reforms' (2024) 20 *International Journal of Law in Context* 379.

[7] JA Mayoral and AT Pérez, 'On Judicial Mobilisation: Entrepreneuring for Policy Change at Time of Crisis' (2018) 40 *Journal of European Integration* 719; Coman and Puleo (n 6); L Puleo and R Coman, 'Explaining Judges' Opposition When Judicial Independence is Undermined: Insights from Poland, Romania, and Hungary' (2024) 31 *Democratization* 47.

[8] C Epp, *Making Rights Real: Activists, Bureaucrats, and the Creation of the Legalistic State* (Chicago, University of Chicago Press, 2010).

departments, judiciaries are entrenched bureaucracies: much of my previous research traced how the pressures of daily work and entrenched bureaucratic routines within civil service judiciaries render most national judges reluctant to break the status-quo and mobilise European law. To this day, lacklustre training in European law, onerous workloads, and conformist career pressures within judicial hierarchies dissuade most judges from seeking creative points of contact with European law and supranational courts.[9] Under these conditions of institutional 'path dependence',[10] it usually takes an exogenous push or existential crisis to prompt judges to recognise that they have a problem that cannot be absorbed by business-as-usual.[11] In the past, under more stable conditions of 'normal politics', the exogenous pushes were gradual and haphazardly mobilised by Euro-lawyers targeting individual judges with strategic litigation campaigns. But as Euro-lawyers increasingly agglomerated into corporate law firms and set their sights on specialised niches of EU economic law,[12] they left behind a latent space for legal mobilisation that judges are increasingly occupying. For today's European judges who have been jolted into mobilising EU safeguards of democracy, human rights, and the RoL (enshrined in Article 2 TEU) alongside the European Convention on Human Rights, the catalyst is an existential crisis threatening to spill across borders: government attacks that are putting their livelihoods, vocation, and authority at risk.

The greater the on-the-ground politicisation and contestation of European law, the greater the need for Euro-lawyers past and judges present to exit the courthouse and mobilise in the public sphere.[13] This does not mean that 'on-bench' mobilisation and institutional resistances – such as defiant preliminary references to the CJEU – do not matter.[14] Such acts of rebellious judicial dialogue can spur innovative rulings that expand national judges' legal toolkit to defend the RoL, particularly when the Commission fails to act as a supranational 'guardian of the Treaties'.[15] But when the RoL and liberal democracy are threatened and governments attack judges to silence

[9] T Pavone, 'Revisiting Judicial Empowerment in the European Union: Limits of Empowerment, Logics of Resistance' (2018) 6 *Journal of Law & Courts* 303; Pavone (n 1) 317; T Pavone, '"In this Bureaucratic Silence EU Law Dies": Fieldwork and the (Non)-Practice of EU law in National Courts' in M Rask Madsen, F Nicola and A Vauchez (eds), *Researching the European Court of Justice: Methodological Shifts and Law's Embeddedness* (Cambridge, Cambridge University Press, 2022).

[10] J Mahoney, 'Path dependence in historical sociology' (2000) 29 *Theory and Society* 507; S Page, 'Path dependence' (2006) 1 *Quarterly Journal of Political Science* 87.

[11] E González-Ocantos, *Shifting Legal Visions: Judicial Change and Human Rights Trials in Latin America* (New York, Cambridge University Press, 2016).

[12] L Avril, 'Le Costume Sous la Robe: Les avocats en professionnels multi-cartes de l'État régulateur européen', PhD thesis, Université Paris 1 Panthéon-Sorbonne 2019; Pavone (n 1) 197–238.

[13] T Pavone, 'From Marx to Market: Lawyers, European Law, and the Contentious Transformation of the Port of Genoa' (2019) 53 *Law & Society Review* 851; T Pavone, 'Like Oil Floating on Water: Italy's Olive Crisis and the Politics of Backlash against Transnational Legal Orders' (2021) 14 *FIU Law Review* 633; Pavone (n 1) 241–306.

[14] Coman and Puleo (n 6).

[15] C Closa, 'The Politics of Guarding the Treaties: Commission Scrutiny of Rule of Law Compliance' (2019) 26 *Journal of European Public Policy* 696; C Emmons and T Pavone, 'The Rhetoric of Inaction: Failing to Fail Forward in the EU's Rule of Law Crisis' (2021) 28 *Journal of European Public Policy* 1611; RD Kelemen and T Pavone, 'Where Have the Guardians Gone? Law Enforcement and the Politics of Supranational Forbearance in the European Union' (2023) 75 *World Politics* 779; M Mandujano Manriquez and T Pavone, 'Follow the Leader: The European Commission, the European Court of Justice, and the EU's Rule of Law Revolution' (2024) 32 *Journal of European Public Policy* 444.

the on-the-ground sentinels of European law,[16] formal judicial procedures are insufficient. Rather, brokering public support and civil society mobilisation across borders becomes essential to resist democratic and RoL backsliding.[17] Judges have to disenchant themselves and explain, in plain speak, why judicial independence matters to citizens and their freedoms: in other words, why non-judges should care that judiciaries are under attack and then rally to their defence.[18] And they must network across borders with colleagues that are not yet threatened, but who can appreciate the moral bankruptcy of silence and recognise that the RoL crisis risks spreading beyond the usual suspects of Hungary, Poland, Romania, and Slovakia.

The interviews with judges recurrently highlight the fertile fear of the abyss and the consequent sense that judges across Europe should band together by doing something (uncomfortably) new: mobilising in the public sphere. Consider the strikingly parallel views of two different judges located in two different contexts. The first, Tamás Matusik (see chapter 19), is a Hungarian judge, who as President of the National Judicial Council faces a barrage of political attacks from the government-controlled press. From his perspective, going public is an existential necessity, a last-ditch means to forge transnational alliances to resist an illiberal government. This same imperative of going public and brokering transnational solidarity is echoed by the second judge, Kees Sterk (see chapter 7), whose presidency of the ENCJ was marked by the much-publicised suspension of the Polish Judicial Council due to its subservience to the executive. While Judge Sterk is under no immediate personal threat, he recognises that because illiberal 'scripts' can rapidly diffuse,[19] an attack on one European judge is an attack on all:

> Judge Matusik: 'When your independence and integrity are called into question, you must be prepared to respond (…)
>
> The point that I always emphasize in interviews and conferences is the importance of judicial solidarity. This is not my original idea; it was also a topic of the ENCJ. Solidarity among judges can prevent the decline of independent judiciary. When we share knowledge, challenges, and solutions, and show solidarity with each other (…) we can convey information to the European Commission more effectively' (see chapter 19).
>
> Judge Sterk: 'For the first time, I must say that we, the judiciaries in Europe, are really working together … There is a sense of urgency among European judges because of the threats from politicians against their independence … I don't like to get involved in politics. But when it comes to the independence of the judiciary, I have learned to be vocal in the press and in parliaments, including the European Parliament. It is not enough to have laws protecting you;

[16] KL Scheppele, 'Autocratic Legalism' (2018) 85 *University of Chicago Law Review* 545; R Coman, *The Politics of the Rule of Law in the EU Polity* (Cham, Palgrave Macmillan, 2022).

[17] M Blauberger and RD Kelemen, 'Can Courts Rescue National Democracy? Judicial Safeguards Against Democratic Backsliding in the EU' (2017) 24 *Journal of European Public Policy* 321; L Gamboa, *Resisting Backsliding: Opposition Strategies Against the Erosion of Democracy* (Cambridge, Cambridge University Press, 2022); B Garcia-Holgado, 'Overruling the Executive: Judicial Strategies to Resist Democratic Erosion' (2025) *Journal of Law and Courts* (first view) 1.

[18] Scheppele (n 16) 581–83.

[19] ibid 548–49.

judges must reach out to the public and politicians, work together and support each other. This is quite different from the traditional way in which I, and many judges in Europe, were trained' (see chapter 7).

The interviews also underscore that judges are under no illusion that the public will automatically rally to their defence when illiberal governments go after the courts. Rather, judges need to roll up their sleeves, leave their courthouses, and identify concrete ways to link their own fate to that of ordinary citizens. In the words of judge Zdeněk Kühn (see chapter 18) in Czechia and judge Manuela Cadelli (see chapter 5) in Belgium:

> Judge Kühn: 'do I believe that we will gather the support from ordinary people? I don't think that we will get the support unless we are able to link this to some future dramatic situation, such as an assault on the independence of the judiciary, with something more concrete, something more visible to the people. I don't believe that people will take to the streets just to protect the independence of judiciary, because for them it's too abstract' (chapter 18).
>
> Judge Cadelli: 'The case of the Polish Judge, Igor Tuleya, is very revealing. As a judge in Warsaw, he was one of those who openly criticised the Polish government and its measures and he suffered the consequences. A march was organised in Poland with the participation of judges from several European countries. This march left its mark on the public (…)
>
> Judges always think they have too much work, so they prefer to stay at home and make judgments. We need to get out – the judge in the city' (chapter 5).

What we are witnessing, in short, is a tectonic shift in many European judges' 'legal consciousness',[20] which in turn is catalysing greater openness to transnational networking and to novel avenues of legal mobilisation. The concrete results of this cognitive and behavioural shift by judges are many, including:

- The newfound sense of urgency and purpose that is galvanising European judges' associations (ex. ENCJ, MEDEL, *Rechters voor Recthers*) to organise media interviews and open letters supporting threatened judges and to lobby the European Commission to open infringement proceedings against recalcitrant governments.[21]
- The innovative supranational lawsuits that judges' associations and their members are pioneering, from seeking to annul the European Council's decision to disburse COVID-19 recovery funds of the Recovery and Resilience Facility to Poland despite the government's continued attacks on the judiciary (*MEDEL v Council*[22]), to lawsuits at the ECtHR that established national judges' right under

[20] S Silbey, 'After Legal Consciousness' (2005) 1 *Annual Review of Law and Social Science* 323.

[21] MEDEL, 'MEDEL statement on the new infringement procedure against Poland (April 29 2019) available at: medelnet.eu/medel-statement-on-the-new-infringement-procedure-against-poland-3/; ENCJ, 'Letter to President-Elect of the European Commission, Frau Dr. Ursula von der Leyen' (20 September 2019), available at: pgwrk-websitemedia.s3.eu-west-1.amazonaws.com/production/pwk-web-encj2017-p/News/letter%20to%20President%20Elect%20Mrs.%20Ursula%20Von%20der%20Leyen%2020%20september%20pub.pdf.

[22] Case T-530/22 *MEDEL v Council* ECLI:EU:T:2024:363.

the ECHR to protest and mobilise in public when their independence is threatened (*Juszczyszyn v Poland* (2022) and *Tuleya v Poland* (2023)).[23]

- The embrace of tried-and-true repertoires of 'contentious politics',[24] such as the Romanian Judges' Forum's organisation of several protests between 2017 and 2019 against judicial repression that 'were widely supported by mass demonstrations in different cities in the country',[25] or MEDEL's organisation of multiple online demonstrations to support Judge Igor Tuleya during his criminal trial in Poland.[26]

Quo Vadis?

It is too early to assess whether judges' European campaign in defence of the RoL will ultimately succeed. Judicial mobilisation surely inspired some Polish voters to 'revers[e] the tide of autocracy' in the October 2023 elections, 'but the RoL is on life support in Hungary and there are worrying signs of an authoritarian turn in Slovakia and Italy'.[27] Judges' opposition to backsliding governments also risks going too far and becoming counterproductive. For instance, it might seem appealing for judges to resist RoL backsliding by targeting the systemic corruption of illiberal governments. But political scientists warn us that when judges launch anti-corruption campaigns in a context of democratic backsliding, they can unwittingly reinforce populist calls to burn down a corrupt 'system' and invite massive backlash from threatened political elites.[28] Judges can avoid these risks by mobilising around moderate goals – the RoL, judicial independence, the separation of powers – while forbearing from the more radical and adversarial objective of toppling ruling elites. Yet the recognition that judges cannot topple the likes of Viktor Orbán brings us back to the elephant in the room: judges cannot act alone. So long as European voters gravitate towards far-right parties and do not penalise politicians with illiberal agendas,[29] and so long as the European Commission remains politically hamstrung as 'guardian of the Treaties', the EU's 'authoritarian equilibrium' will endure.[30]

[23] *Juszczyszyn v Poland*, App No 35599/20 (ECtHR, 6 October 2022); *Tuleya v Poland*, App nos 21181/19 and 51751/20 (ECtHR, 6 July 2023); M Szwed, 'Protecting the Rights of Judges: the Judgments of the European Court of Human Rights in Juszczyszyn v Poland and Tuleya v. Poland' (2024) 25 *ERA Forum* 141.

[24] C Tilly and S Tarrow, *Contentious Politics*, 2nd edn (New York, Oxford University Press, 2015).

[25] Coman and Puleo (n 6) 34–35.

[26] MEDEL, 'Protests co-organized by MEDEL and other institutions in Poland and Europe' (6 June 2020) available at: medelnet.eu/protests-co-organized-by-medel-and-other-institutions-in-poland-and-europe/.

[27] T Pavone, 'Is the EU's Rule of Law Crisis a Byproduct of Dissensus and Disunion?' (2024) 46 *Journal of European Integration* 963, 970.

[28] L Gamboa, B García-Holgado and E González-Ocantos, 'Courts Against Backsliding: Lessons from Latin America' (2024) 46 *Law & Policy* 358.

[29] V Valentim, *The Normalization of the Radical Right: A Norms Theory of Political Supply and Demand* (New York, Oxford University Press, 2024).

[30] RD Kelemen, 'Will the European Union Escape its Autocracy Trap?' (2025) 32 *Journal of European Public Policy* 341.

Yet, being stuck with the RoL crisis for the foreseeable future does not imply that the efforts of judges testified in this volume are for naught. If there is one recurrent takeaway from decades of socio-legal research, it is that legal mobilisation can bolster participants' sense of dignity, self-respect, and empowerment even when they fail to achieve their broader political and policy agenda.[31] From the depths of their sudden vulnerability, European judges are rediscovering just how much they matter for the fate of liberal democracy and the future of the EU, and they are acting upon this newfound sense of agency. They are giving us reason to be biased for hope.

[31] M McCann, *Rights at Work: Pay Equity Reform and the Politics of Legal Mobilization* (Chicago, University of Chicago Press, 1994); EA Andersen, *Out of the Closets and into the Courts: Legal Opportunity Structure and Gay Rights Litigation* (Ann Arbor, University of Michigan Press, 2006); L Vanhala, *Making Rights a Reality? Disability Rights Activists and Legal Mobilization* (Cambridge, Cambridge University Press, 2010); S Hermansen and T Pavone, 'EU Law Litigation: Who Litigates, Who Influences Judges, What Downstream Effects?' in D Naurin, U Sadl and J Zglinski (eds), *Empirical Legal Studies of EU Law* (Cambridge University Press, Forthcoming 2025).

26

The Twilight of Resilience? Reflections on the Limits of Judicial Activism in the Face of Democratic Decline

KATARÍNA ŠIPULOVÁ

As nightfall does not come at once, neither does oppression. In both instances, there is a twilight when everything remains seemingly unchanged, and it is in such a twilight that we all must be most aware of change in the air – however slight – lest we become unwitting victims of darkness. [William O Douglas][1]

Introduction

Should judges be indifferent to the pressures of time? The past decade has been one of moral and professional reckoning for many judiciaries. Once expected to embody neutrality and restraint,[2] many judges have been thrust into roles they never envisioned – public speakers, guardians of democracy, and dissidents mobilising (in) the streets. This shift has raised fundamental questions: Should judges remain silent in the face of political encroachment and trust in institutional safeguards? Or must they step outside the courtroom, resisting through activism, media engagement, and transnational alliances? These dilemmas are not merely theoretical – they shape the fate of judicial institutions and, by extension, the rule of law itself. Comparative research across continents reinforces the need to understand judicial behaviour under stress.

[1] W O Douglas (ed), *The Douglas letters: Selections from the private papers of Justice William O. Douglas* (Adler & Adlers, Bethesda MD, 1987).

[2] JA King, 'Institutional Approaches to Judicial Restraint' (2008) 28 *Oxford Journal of Legal Studies* 409; RA Posner, 'The Meaning of Judicial Self-Restraint' (1983) 59 *Indiana Law Journal* 59; RA Posner, 'The Rise and Fall of Judicial Self-Restraint' (2012) 100 *California Law Review* 519; K Lachmayer, 'Formalism and Judicial Self/restraint as Tools Against Populism?' in F Gárdos-Orosz and Z Szente (eds), *Populist Challenges to Constitutional Interpretation in Europe and Beyond* (London, Routledge, 2021); JP Dawson, *The Oracles of the Law* (Ann Arbor, The University of Michigan Law School, 1968).

While legal scholars and policymakers have largely focused on institutional safeguards of judicial independence,[3] the role of judicial culture in resistance to democratic backsliding remains undertheorised,[4] particularly so in the post-communist area. In this chapter, I offer a reflection on how judicial culture[5] – that is the internalised norms, attitudes, beliefs, and values that shape how judges understand their function and agency – shapes judges' reactions under pressure. The conversations with actors of judicial resistance show us that judges who stood up are aware of the limitations which their judicial role places on their resistance and engagement in civil society. I therefore argue that if judges are to protect democracy, they need to be understood as a self-standing political actor with agency and legitimacy separate from their traditional judicial role. I further theorise that the ability to fulfil this second role depends on a particular judicial culture and that a failure to cultivate a robust judicial culture compatible with formal designs of democratic institutions in post-communist transitions has left many Central and Eastern European judiciaries vulnerable to easy political capture,[6] political compliance, and internal polarisation.

The importance of judicial perspectives cannot be overstated. Judges do not operate in a vacuum; they interpret and apply the law through the lens of their professional experiences, historical context, and ideological dispositions.[7] The culture they appropriate however does not emerge as a mere by-product of formal constitutional guarantees. Instead, it is inherently relational,[8] actively forged through professional socialisation,[9] and constant internalisation of new norms and across different internal and external

[3] T Ginsburg, *Judicial Review in New Democracies. Constitutional Courts in Asian Cases* (Cambridge, Cambridge University Press, 2003); T Ginsburg and N Garoupa, 'Judicial Audiences and Reputation: Perspectives from Comparative Law' (2009) 47 *Columbia Journal of Transnational Law* 451.

[4] R Dixon and S Issacharoff, 'The Resilience of the Rule of Law' in RL Abel (ed), *Law's Wars: The Fate of the Rule of Law in the US 'War on Terror'* (Cambridge, Cambridge University Press, 2016) 45; L Puleo and R Coman, 'Explaining Judges' Opposition when Judicial Independence is Undermined: Insights from Poland, Romania, and Hungary' (2024) 31 *Democratization* 47.

[5] AA Aguiar-Aguilar, 'Understanding the Judiciary from the Inside. The Legal Culture of Judges in Mexico' (2022) 43 *Justice system Journal* 576; L Hilbink, 'Agents of Anti-Politics: Courts in Pinochet's Chile' in T Ginsburg and T Moustafa (eds), *Judges Beyond Politics in Democracy and Dictatorship* (Cambridge, Cambridge University Press, 2007); J Couso, 'Models of Democracy and Models of Constitutionalism' (2011) 89 *Texas Law Review* 1517; J Couso and L Hilbink, 'From Guietism to Incipient Activism: the Institutional and Ideological Roots of Rights Adjudication in Chile' in G Helmke and J Ríos Figueroa (eds), *Courts in Latin America* (Cambridge, Cambridge University Press, 2011) 99; M Ingram, *Crafting Courts in New Democracies. The Politics of Subnational Judicial Reform in Brazil and Mexico* (Cambridge, Cambridge University Press, 2016a); M Ingram, 'Networked Justice: Judges, the Diffusion of Ideas, and Legal Reform Movements in Mexico' (2016b) 48 *Journal of Latin American Studies* 739; E González-Ocantos, *Shifting Legal Visions: Judicial Change and Human Rights Trials in Latin America* (New York, NY, Cambridge University Press 2016); R Robinson and B Swedlow, 'Beyond Liberal and Conservative: Advancing the Study of Judicial Behavior with a Cultural Theory of Political Values' (2018) 6 *Journal of Law and Courts* 263; A Huneeus, J Couso and R Sieder, *Cultures of Legality: Judicialization and Political Activism in Latin America* (Cambridge, Cambridge University Press, 2010).

[6] K Šipulová and S Spáč, '(No) Ghost in the Shell: The Role of Values Internalization in Judicial Empowerment in Slovakia' (2023) 24 *German Law Journal* 1412.

[7] T Ginsburg and T Moustafa, *Rule by Law: The Politics of Courts in Authoritarian Regimes* (New York, Cambridge University Press, 2008) 22; González-Ocantos (n 5).

[8] A Kubal, 'Judicial Relational Legal Consciousness: Authoritarian Backsliding as a Catalyst of Change' (2024) 51 *Journal of Law and Society* S45.

[9] Aguiar-Aguilar (n 5).

judicial networks.[10] Building on these relational perspectives and a set of interviews with judges from Serbia, Romania, Poland, and Bulgaria, this chapter adds to a new literature filling the void and transposing the concept of judicial culture to studies of judicial resistance. It reflects on how these judges acted and reacted under pressure, how they interpreted the rule of law crisis and its effects, and, most importantly, how the democratic decline and political pressure shaped their perception of the judicial role. The interviews reveal not only their attitudes, but also their frustrations, motives, and ethical dilemmas they faced when calculating their actions under duress. The insights gained from these conversations deepen our understanding[11] of why some judiciaries resist political capture, while others remain passive or fragmented.

The interviewed judges bring forward distinct perspectives shaped by their experiences within national judicial systems that have faced substantial political interference. Monika Frąckowiak is a district court judge in Poland and a member of the association Iustitia, which has been at the forefront of resistance against government-led judicial reforms since 2015 (chapter 16). Dragoş Călin is a Court of Appeal judge and co-president of the *Romanian Judges' Forum*, an association advocating for judicial independence in a politically volatile Romanian situation, active also in academia (chapter 15). Dragana Boljević has served as a senior judge and was a long-time leader of the Judges' Association of Serbia, actively opposing judicial appointments manipulated by political authorities (chapter 21). Yavuz Aydin, originally a Turkish judge, sought asylum in Romania after being purged following the events of the 2016 coup attempt (chapter 20). All of them share a path of career judges, having entered their respective judiciaries at a relatively young age after finishing their university education. All of them experienced shorter or longer periods of political oppression, some with a more and some with a less fortunate ending.

The interviews obviously provide only a snippet of how judges in jurisdictions with different institutional structures, career incentives and personal beliefs think about their role in the protection of democracy. The conversations reflected in this chapter do not represent the judiciary as a whole, or the mindsets of judges of any particular country. Instead, they offer us a sneak-peak into the contemplations of those judges who stood up to the pressure. Instead of attempting to overgeneralise, I use the conversations to offer a few remarks on limitations, flaws and stereotypical beliefs we often have about judicial resistance, and show how the vulnerability of judiciaries interacts with judicial culture. While some judges have embraced activism and resistance as a necessary defence against political encroachment, others have expressed scepticism both towards the glorified alliance with supranational institutions, including the EU, and towards the normative heroisation of the judiciary. In other words, these reflections expose potential the limits of judicial resistance and raise an unsettling question: Can courts effectively safeguard democracy without becoming too political?

[10] Kubal (n 8).

[11] Y Kureshi, 'When Judges Defy Dictators' (2021) 53 *Comparative Politics* 233; Sd Schaaf, 'When Do Courts Constrain the Authoritarian State? Judicial Decision-Making in Jordan and Palestine' (2022) 54 *Comparative Politics* 375; J Yam, 'Judging Under Authoritarianism' (2024) 87 *Modern Law Review* 894.

When Culture Eats Rules for Breakfast:[12] The Missing Piece of Puzzle in Post-communist Transitions

It is well known and frequently criticised by the political science literature that reforms in Central and Eastern Europe in the immediate aftermath of communism prioritised formal guarantees of constitutional democracy, while neglecting the cultural change. Transitional processes targeting judges therefore rarely focused on the effective personnel purges, transformation of mindsets, and entrenchment of a new system of beliefs.[13] In the area of justice, this process was demonstrated by a focus on entrenchment of constitutional courts, judicial councils to the detriment of processes of accountability and new professional socialisation of judges.[14]

Interviewed judges, although they themselves participated in an active resistance, seem to be aware of this limit. They typically interpreted the subservience of the judicial majority in backsliding democracies as a combination of the chilling effect (harsh backlash against recalcitrant colleagues) and hierarchical obedience inherent to post-communist judicial regimes. As Dragoş Călin (Romania) observed in his interview, early reforms created a new institutional architecture but left intact judges accustomed to hierarchical obedience:

> In Romania, the judiciary laws were changed in 2022 due to forceful reactions from judges at that time. However, we still face many problems. For example, one major issue is the subordination of judges to court presidents, leading to processes for promoting judges to higher functions that lack meritocracy. The High Court of Cassation only promotes certain judges who are comfortable with members of the Superior Council of Magistracy (chapter 15).

In some CEE judiciaries, the large-scale political backlash and decline of judicial independence catalysed certain ideational shift in this hierarchical understanding. Similarly to how Yam proposed a normative adjudicative framework for judging under authoritarianism,[15] some courts eventually moved from positive legal formalism to more normative argumentative legal culture.[16]

> What most judges in Poland understood is that we must change our language to be much more comprehensive and understood. We need to drop the tendency of using our typical

[12] Interview with Aydin, ch 20 in this volume. Interestingly, see MA Dichio and I Logvinenko, 'Culture and Practice Eat Documents for Lunch: Norms and Procedures in the 2020 Election Cases' (2025) 46 *Law and Policy* 298, reporting a very similar statement of one of the US state Supreme Court judges, remarking on the meaningless of formal rules without dedicated informal norms and practices.

[13] M Popova, 'Can a Leopard Change its Spots? Strategic Behaviour versus Professional Role Conception During Ukraine's 2014 Court Chair Clections' (2020) 42 *Law&Policy* 365; L Hilbink, 'The Origins of Positive Judicial Independence' (2012) 64 *World Politics* 587; D Kapiszewski, *High Courts and Economic Governance in Argentina and Brazil* (Cambridge, Cambridge University Press, 2012), K Šipulová and D Kosař, 'Purging The Judiciary After a Transition: Between the Rock and the Hard Place' (2025) 17 *Hague Journal on the Rule of Law* 61.

[14] D Piana, *Judicial Accountabilities in New Europe. From Rule of Law to Quality of Justice* (Farnham, Ashgate, 2010) 101; Šipulová and Kosař (n 13); N Garoupa, 'Purging Disloyal Courts in Democratic Transitions and Judicial Preferences' (2024) 18 *International Journal of Transitional Justice* 474; K Šipulová and H Smekal, 'Between Human Rights and Transitional Justice: The Dilemma of Constitutional Courts in Post-Communist Central Europe' (2021) 73 *Europa-Asia Studies* 1010.

[15] Yam (n 11).

[16] Aguiar-Aguilar (n 5).

> patronizing tone. And, within the court, we must open the institution to some other activities than just delivering justice. Courts should be open to students, pupils, society in general (Frąckowiak, chapter 16).

In other countries, extreme pressure however further closed judges to ideational shifts. Aydin interpreted the decline of internal, mental judicial independence as a result of fear and weakly embedded democratic institutions, which allowed judges and prosecutors to perceive themselves as 'guardians of the state, not the guardians of freedoms and rights'.

> Turkey was on the brink of a transformation in the early 2000s or the first decade of the 2000s, but the deep-rooted culture of democracy and judicial independence was insufficient. Turkey never had a real democracy or a truly independent judiciary, and people did not know what they were missing. (…) In today's Turkey, unfortunately, being a judge means only being a servant, essentially a slave to the governing party or ruling authority. In Turkey judges are not aware that there are no longer judges, but rather individuals who, on paper, legitimise the raison d'être of the government. (…) These judges think that their role is to abide by the wishes of the president, the new 'Sultan', Erdogan (Aydin chapter 20).

Interviewed judges also acknowledged that the lack of ideational independence plays well in the hands of the governments that use the capture of courts to cleverly shift the blame and accountability to a different actor, as well as utilise loyal decision-making to increase the legitimacy of their own policies.

Whether democratic backsliding triggered a shift in judicial legal consciousness and culture depended, at least in the case of interviewed judges, mostly on relational aspects of judicial resistance.[17] Social pressure, particularly the one coming from legal professional groups, can impact the directionality of judicial resistance.[18] Judges who stood up therefore consistently highlighted the role of networks – not only among judicial associations at the international level, but also with actors outside the judicial arena, NGOs, media, or the public. These networks offered judges not only support, but also a 'better insight' and better awareness of the gravity of democratic threats, and of the role of judicial resistance that goes outside of formalist legal interpretation. Formal legal safeguards mean little when judges themselves do not embrace their democratic role, but stick to positivist legal culture accustomed to present judiciary as the hand of the state power.

The Leaky Umbrella of European Democratic Protection

Not surprisingly, one of the key alliances forged during democratic backsliding in the CEE region was the cooperation of judges with European supranational institutions, both at the level of the Council of Europe and the EU. However, interviewed judges were unified in scepticism about the EU's actual commitment to protecting judicial independence. While they typically acknowledged the importance of CJEU rulings and

[17] Echoing Kubal's work in 'Judicial Relational Legal Consciousness' (n 8).

[18] P Leisure and D Kosar, 'Court-hoarding: Another Method of Gaming Judicial Turnover' (2025) 46 *Law and Policy* 328.

jurisprudential development, they remained cautious when reflecting on the EU's general role in fighting constitutional decline. The disillusionment was starkest in Serbia, Romania and Turkey. Judge Călin, for example, highlighted the contrast between the 'steadfast' alliance of the CJEU and political imprudence of the European Commission which seems to be easily paralysed by internal politics. In particular, he criticised the Commission's decision to lift the CVM, one of the strongest compliance tools the EU had against Romania:

> We had a problem with the European Commission because it abandoned the honest judges and prosecutors in Romania who stand up for the independence of the judicial system. We are constantly humiliated, harassed, and blocked in terms of promotion and career advancement within the judicial system … Regrettably, Romanian judges were compelled to pursue actions to safeguarding their independence which were not supported by the European Commission. No infringement procedure has been completed, no action by the European Commission for the application of the CVM has ever been before the CJEU. The CVM had a scope of application that was wider than EU law generally, as it also applied to purely national corruption cases (without EU funds being involved). This passivity on the part of the European Commission sets a dangerous precedent, gradually eroding judicial independence, and it may serve as a troubling example for other EU Member States. Currently, Slovakia faces a similar situation, and it's conceivable that other countries in Eastern Europe may follow this path in the future (chapter 15).

Călin further hinted that although there is a daily cooperation between the European Commission and Romanian judges, the Commission keeps refraining from initiating infringement cases against Romania. This sentiment reflects quite well very recent political science scholarship that provided empirical evidence of the Commission's reluctance to be a committed rule of law actor.[19] The perceptions of the interviewed judges however go even further and question the long-held belief that while the EU lacks strong compliance tools against its own Member States, it is capable of triggering substantial systemic changes in candidate countries.[20] Serbian Judge Boljević noted a surprising development of the European Commission's position. In the course of the first wave of political attacks against the judiciary in 2008, the Commission, repeatedly informed about the development, did not pay much attention, which Boljević interpreted as a puzzlement and lack of established channels between Commission and domestic NGOs. However, a decade later, the commitment seemed to further weaken due to other political interests:

> I am not confident that the EU genuinely prioritises judicial independence in the Serbian case. I would say that they tend to manipulate their demands for the independence of the judiciary whenever there is a deadlock in some other domain … We also witnessed another

[19] RD Kelemen and T Pavone, 'Where Have the Guardians Gone? Law Enforcement and the Politics of Supranational Forbearance in the European Union' (2023) 75 *World Politics* 779; RD Kelemen, 'Will the European Union Escape its Autocracy Trap?' (2024) 32 *Journal of European Public Policy* 341; R Coman and A Buzogány, 'The European Union's Response to the Rule of Law Crisis and the Making of the New Conditionality Regime' (2024) 62 *Journal of Common Market Studies* 102.

[20] U Seddelmeier, 'Anchoring Democracy from Above? The European Union and Democratic Backsliding in Hungary and Romania after Accession' (2014) 52 *Journal of Common Market Studies* 105; U Sedelmeier, 'Is Europeanisation through Conditionality Sustainable? Lock-in of Institutional Change after EU Accession' in T Borzel and T Risse (eds), *From Europeanisation to Diffusion* (London, Routledge, 2014).

> phenomenon during that period: the erosion of European institutions' commitment to the rule of law. They allowed our government to undertake actions against the judiciary which were clearly in violation of the rule of law in exchange for other gains, particularly in the context of sending individuals to the Hague Tribunal (ie International Criminal Tribunal for the former Yugoslavia). It was a kind of quid pro quo arrangement (chapter 21).

This sentiment was echoed by Aydin, who also criticised the EU for turning a blind eye to judicial repression in exchange for geopolitical stability:

> Some EU officials may have been seen as complicit in this because what they have been focusing on, and are still focusing on, is the trade relations, keeping millions of migrants and refugees in Turkey out of Europe, and realpolitik priorities; the focus was not on fundamental rights and freedoms in Turkey (chapter 20).

Thus, while European institutions play an important role in providing legal precedents and symbolic support, judges across the region remain sceptical about whether these mechanisms can meaningfully protect judicial independence without sustained domestic activism and political will. This finding might be surprising in the face of largely optimistic European legal scholarship, but resonates well with more empirically oriented political science research on EU's role in democratic backsliding.

The Risks of Heroising the Judiciary: The Thin Red Line between Activism and Overreach

> But when it comes to judges, the most important thing I can say is that they should be brave, and those, who cannot be brave should not be judges. Judges are the guardians of democracy, representing the checks and balances mechanism and so they should know that one day they might need to stand up against power … If not judges, who will defend this judicial independence and rule of law? As a Turkish judge who ended up a refugee and was labelled a terrorist in his country, I can ask: if not judges, who will act? (Aydin chapter 20).

Are then judges the proverbial last and only soldier standing in the face of the rule of law decline?[21] This portrayal, combined with powerful imaginaries of judges dressed in black robes marching in the streets, attracted a lot of attention and eventually became the defining narrative of the European wave of de-democratisation. Kubal observed that in Poland, the massive resistance combined with frontal attacks against courts shifted the essence of judicial legal consciousness,[22] and allowed judges to embrace activism and resistance, perhaps sometimes more political than legal, as a necessary defence against populist attacks. As Judge Călin noted:

> A judge is a member of civil society and cannot be expected to live in isolation from reality. In some post-communist societies, civic attitudes may not yet be fully developed, and the

[21] D Kochenov and P Bárd, 'The Last Soldier Standing? Courts Versus Politicians and the Rule of Law Crisis in the New Member States of the EU' in H Ballin, G Van der Schyff and M Stremler (eds), *European Yearbook of Constitutional law 2019. Judicial Power: Safeguards and Limits in a Democratic Society* (The Hague, T.M.C. Asser Press, 2020) 243.

[22] Kubal (n 8).

> public may not immediately react to abuses of power. Judges and prosecutors should be allowed to express their opinions publicly as long as their impartiality is not compromised. The judiciary should not be envisioned as a silent entity where only heads of courts or prosecutor offices can speak out, leaving others condemned to perpetual silence (chapter 15).

The deeper dimension of this shift is a slow change of how judges (and other actors) think of their role in the political system. Generally, the increased activism always triggers criticism over potential abuse of power and balances on the thin line between resistance and overreach. It carries an inherent risk of judges being blamed for overstepping their role and entering the political arena. But what exactly is this role? Judge Boljevic summarised the sentiment frequently present in bureaucratic judiciaries with deeply hierarchical structure with the following words:

> As judges, we cannot be affiliated with political parties. Navigating judges' dual roles as citizens and **state officials** [emphasis added], and their civil rights, is complex. On the one hand, judges are **state representatives** [emphasis added] who require dignity and impartial awareness of their responsibilities. On the other hand, they may face severe attacks that require them to speak out and defend their positions. Finding equilibrium between these roles is challenging (chapter 21).

Courts, naturally, represent the state and issue judgments in the name of the state. Yet, they are also a separate branch of the state power. The problem of self-identification of judges as state officials is most visible in communist regimes that effectively erased the borders between the political apparatus of the executive power and the judges. Aside perhaps from constitutional courts, many post-communist judiciaries still struggle to abandon this role-conception.[23] This dimension of judicial culture, largely overlooked by scholarship, has some implications on how resistant different levels of domestic courts truly are and how readily they defer to or rubber-stamp policies of non-democratic leaders. Empirical studies of decision-making of Latin American courts support this narrative, suggesting that personnel composition (courts staffed by insiders – ie career judges – or outsiders) explains the distance of individual courts from the in-ward looking judicial passivity. Courts that were open to outsiders unaffiliated with traditional career judicial networks seem to be more resistant. Their judges have developed a new institutional identity that, next to the self-preservation agency, motivates them to execute their role properly.[24]

On the other hand, both judicial deference and judicial activism come with a set of problems. Many courts consciously avoid being portrayed as political actors.[25] When judges assume activist roles, they may inadvertently justify governmental crackdowns on judicial independence, reinforcing the narrative that courts are politically motivated. Some Latin American courts that openly confronted executive overreach often suffered

[23] Šipulová and Kosař (n 13).

[24] D Zambrano, LM da Silva, R Garcia Miron and S Rodríguez, 'How Latin America's Judges are Defending Democracy' (2024) 35 *Journal of Democracy* 118.

[25] JK Staton, *Judicial Power and Strategic Communication in Mexico* (Cambridge: Cambridge University Press, 2010).

institutional weakening and credibility loss.[26] Excessive judicial activism can trigger counter-mobilisation by illiberal political actors, leading to further repression of courts and the rule of law.[27]

Yam, Schaaf, Jakab and Graver therefore warn that judges in hybrid regimes face a constant balancing between asserting their independence and avoiding political retaliation.[28] While courts with high public trust tend to push back against governments on illiberal policies,[29] unpopular courts are hesitant to effectively conduct judicial review on publicly salient topics.[30] Moreover, as I suggested in my previous work, even off-bench judicial resistance can have a dark side. If it relies on methods incompatible with the rule of law, it inadvertently risks further polarisation, alienation of the public, and, in turn further executive backlash.[31] Polish judges facing the process of re-democratisation seem to be most aware of this paradox, struggling to undo populist legislation without using the same instruments PiS was using.[32] Judge Frąckowiak candidly reflected on this tension while warning against the heroisation of judges and their behaviour outside of the judicial arena:

> I have realized for myself that we cannot go back to the situation we had in 2015. We need to learn from what happened in Poland. That means that judges cannot speak only through their judgments. It is something what we know for 100 per cent. Magistrates need to be active, be open to the society. But, at the same time, it is difficult to find the balance between being simply a judge and an activist, because a judge should always be limited by the position he or she is having. There are some limits, some boundaries he or she cannot cross. *We must keep our integrity, remembering that we are judges, not pop stars* (chapter 16).

While judicial resistance is often necessary in the face of democratic erosion, its effect must be carefully calibrated to avoid reinforcing authoritarian narratives that courts are obstacles to 'popular sovereignty'. In this sense, judicial heroisation may be a double-edged sword, fostering public support for courts in the short term while providing ammunition for illiberal leaders to undermine judicial institutions in the long run.

[26] M Gandur,' Public Partisan Reactions to Judicial Checks: Evidence from Argentina' (2023) American Political Science Association Working Paper, www.derecho.unt.edu.ar/comp/archivos/1685106606476549171.pdf.

[27] HP Graver, *Judges Against Justice: On Judges When the Rule of Law is Under Attack* (Berlin, Springer, 2015).

[28] Yam (n 11); Schaaf (n 11); A Jakab, 'What Can Constitutional Law Do Against the Erosion of Democracy and the Rule of Law? On the Interconnectedness of the Protection of Democracy and the Rule of Law' (2020) 6 *Constitutional Studies* 5; Graver (n 27).

[29] Zambrano et al (n 24).

[30] JN Krehbiel, 'Public awareness and the Behaviour of Unpopular Courts' (2020) 51 *British Journal of Political Science* 1601.

[31] K Šipulová, 'The Light and the Dark Side of Judicial Resistance' (2025) 47 *Law & Policy* 1; D Kosař and K Šipulová, 'Court-Unpacking: A Preliminary Inquiry' in M Bobek, A Bodnar, A von Bogdandy and P Sonnevend (eds), *Transition 2.0 Re-establishing Constitutional Democracy in EU Member States* (Baden-Baden, Nomos, 2023).

[32] Frąckowiak, ch 16 in this volume.

Conclusion: Beyond Courts – The Need for Societal and Institutional Resilience

The experiences of judges who actively stood up to attacks at courts in Poland, Romania, Serbia, and Bulgaria underscore a critical reality: judicial independence cannot survive on institutional safeguards alone. Conversations encompassed in this manuscript demonstrate three limitations judges who resisted experienced. First, cultural subservience to the state limits not only the ability of judges to resist, but also prevents them from gaining social legitimacy. Second, the supranational alliances have many pragmatic limits. They may motivate judges to resist, but they are not always reliable. The European Commission is an important partner for judicial resistance, but not always acts in domestic judges' best interest. Third, judges are aware of the multi-layered nature of their role inside and outside the courtroom and of the limitations it brings. Judicial culture might be one of the variables explaining the variance in judicial reactions under political pressure. But even more importantly, it is worth theorising that judicial culture plays a role in a broader democratic resilience, especially in finding the balance between the political and legal agency of judges. The stories of post-communist judiciaries are full of suggestions that culture and professional self-perception of judges who self-identify with the state, who narrow down their social and political role to the mere application of formal legal norms, prevent successful transposition of democratic political designs that ought to re-establish the rule of law. Socialist regimes successfully stripped the judiciaries of their identity and function within the separation of powers. Transitional processes attempted to restore the institutional independence and autonomy of judiciary but failed to reshape its internal culture and self-understanding. This brief chapter obviously cannot aspire to any causal claims, however, it seeks to open a deeper, theoretical and fact-based discussion on the role and function of judges in democracy and on the relationship of their culture in democratic resilience.

27

Law, Politics and Society. Europeanisation Amid Dissensus over Liberal Democracy, Institutions and Values

RAMONA COMAN

Introduction

How do judges conceive their roles when their independence is under strain? The book offers contrasting reflections. As judge Grimm put it, 'normally, it is not seen as virtuous for judges to go public outside of their rulings' (chapter 6). 'The role of the judge is to stay inside the court', stated Judge Vajda (chapter 9). This role is rooted in the 'genetic code' or in the way judges are trained to be 'silent' and 'to be prepared more to listen than to speak', as emphasised by Judge Igreja Matos (chapter 11). When the core pillars of liberal democracy were dismantled in some EU Member States, such as Poland and Hungary, some judges believed that 'simply doing their job and being protected by the law was enough to protect their independence', as underlined by Judge Sterk (chapter 7). In contrast, others have engaged in a broader collective and pan-European reflection not only about their role in relation to politics but also in society.

The 18 interviews in this book shows that judges' responses to the rule of law crisis have taken various forms, both *within* and *outside* judicial institutions. The use of legal mechanisms including strategic litigation, judicial cooperation, and consultation / corporatist interest representation prevailed. But new and more extensive forms of social mobilisation and resistance have also taken shape, contributing to strengthening the bonds of solidarity between judges, and building and boosting networks[1] of national, European, and international professional associations.

Like the previous commentaries, my reading of the interviews is informed by my previous work on European integration and, more specifically, Europeanisation. The 18 narratives offer insights into four avenues of research. For scholars in political science and political theory, they provide insights into the interplay between political and legal

[1] C Dallara and D Piana, *Networking the Rule of Law. How Change Agents Reshape Judicial Governance in the EU* (London, Routledge, 2015).

constitutionalism, or the role of judges in political regimes (Section 1). For scholars in European studies, they not only point to a new stage in the process of EU integration through law – highlighting the increasing engagement of judges from Central and Eastern European countries in dialogue with the Court of Justice of the European Union (Section 2) – but also attest to new forms of horizontal Europeanisation (Section 3). Ultimately, they invite the reader to reflect on the role of judges in their relationship with citizens and society (Section 4).

Law and Politics: Government 'With Judges', 'By Judges' and/or 'Against Judges'?

Nothing is simple when it comes to the role of judges in political regimes, whether in national or supranational polities beyond the state such as the EU. Their place in democracy has long been disputed, a debate that intensified during the creation of modern states and the drafting of the first constitutions. The role of judges is rooted in specific political and judicial cultures, and is shaped in different national social, political and economic contexts. In recent decades, the state of democracy in Europe and beyond has brought back into focus this debate about government 'with judges', 'by judges' or 'against judges'. Yet, what is really at stake here?

'Governing With Judges' vs 'Government By Judges'

The empowerment of judges emerged as one of the defining features of the democratisation wave in Western Europe in the aftermath of World War II. While most of the democracies established after World War I rejected the control of courts perceived as incompatible with the power of the people, after World War II constitutionalism developed rapidly to ensure the respect of rights, the separation of powers, and the independence of the judiciary. Yet this happened without altering the idea that democracy is the power of the people, but rather implying that the people is only one it its components.[2] On the ruins of the war and motivated by the *never-again* ethos, the idea of governing *with judges*[3] was no longer seen as a heresy.[4] Constitutions empower states, embody political values, ideals and goals, provide institutional stability, protect fundamental rights and above all legitimise regimes.[5] In this framework, the judiciary plays a key role deciding legal disputes between major institutions of the state or between the state and the individual. To this end, the independence of the judiciary – principle which is not an invention of judges, as underlined by Yavuz Aydin (chapter 21) – is protected as discussed in chapter 3.

[2] Y Mény and Y Surel, 'The Constitutive Ambiguity of Populism' in Y Mény and Y Surel (eds), *Democracies and the Populist Challenge* (New York, Palgrave, 2002) 10.

[3] A Stone Sweet, *Governing with Judges: Constitutional Politics in Europe* (Oxford, Oxford University Press, 2000).

[4] P Magnette, *L'Europe, l'Etat et la démocratie* (Bruxelles, Editions Complexe, 2000).

[5] A Heywood, *Politics* (London, Macmillan International, 2019) 301.

In liberal democracies, judges' interactions with politics take many forms. On the one hand, judges are entrusted with the responsibility of applying the law in line with constitutional principles and international law, as well as upholding the law.[6] They safeguard individual rights and provide impartial resolutions of conflicts. In states with codified constitutions, constitutional courts interpret the constitutions itself, although their power can vary regarding their capacity to constrain the authority of those who make and enforce the law. Against this backdrop, two contrasting images of the judge have evolved in continental Europe: one portraying the judge as the *bouche de la loi* (a mere 'applier of the law') and another encapsulating the idea of the judge as giving meaning to the law, in the sense that all law is 'judge-made law',[7] resulting into a 'government by judges'.[8]

Liberal democracy is rooted in an intrinsic tension between the power of the people on the one hand (the popular will) and, on the other, the constitutionalist provisions which protect the citizen from the government and the arbitrary exercise of power.[9] The former pertains to the power of parliaments, as representatives of the people, and the latter to the power of courts, as defenders of constitutions. When it comes to 'who should have the last word', political constitutionalism underlines parliamentary supremacy and an interaction between law and politics.[10] In contrast, legal constitutionalism presupposes that the dominant legislature does not have the right to override or compromise individual legal rights.[11]

Tensions between these two traditions have always been latent in every political system. As Gamboa et al put it, 'existing checks and balances exist in an equilibrium that is often quite tense'.[12] While 'making the law is the task of the democratic legislator', as argued by Judge Vajda (chapter 9), 'the judiciary has the power over the meaning of the law', as emphasised by Judge Baka (chapter 14). In some cases, tensions occur because those in power 'need to make compromises, so they make vague laws', as illustrated by Judge Sterk (chapter 7) or because laws are 'harsh', as exemplified by Judge Cadelli (chapter 5). In other contexts, tensions occur due to the tendency for politics to become increasingly judicialised and or because 'politicians are very interested in meddling with judges'.[13] Abuses of the law are not specific to non-democratic regimes. Even in liberal democracies political actors and courts can abuse the law[14] and the ideal of the rule of law.

[6] HP Graver, *Valiant Judges, Iniquitous Law. Thirteen Stories of Heroes of the Law* (London, Routledge, 2024) 3.

[7] Heywood (n 5) 301.

[8] S Saurugger and F Terpan, *The Court of Justice of the European Union and the Politics of the Law* (London, Palgrave, 2017) 41.

[9] J Leca, 'La démocratie à l'épreuve des pluralismes' (1996) 46 *Revue française de science politique* 225.

[10] R Bellamy, *Political Constitutionalism* (Cambridge, Cambridge University Press, 2007).

[11] P Blokker, *New Democracies in Crisis? A Comparative Constitutional Study of the Czech Republic, Hungary, Poland, Romania and Slovakia* (Milton Park, Routledge, 2014).

[12] L Gamboa, B García-Holgado and E González-Ocantos, 'Courts against Backsliding: Lessons from Latin America' (2024) 46 *Law & Policy* 358, 361.

[13] Gamboa, García-Holgado and González-Ocantos (n 12).

[14] A Sajó, *Ruling by Cheating Governance in Illiberal Democracy* (Cambridge, Cambridge University Press, 2020) 292.

'Governing Against Judges'

The judge is under pressure when the legislator attacks the law.[15] In addition, when a political regime changes its nature, transitioning from democracy to something else, executives and parliaments use courts to reinforce their rule.[16] Historical examples show how judges in the past have been at the service of a repugnant moral ideology.[17] 'Loyal judges' engaged in an 'abusive judicial review', helping executives attack democracy by validating contested laws and degrees and often interpreting the constitution with the goal of undermining liberal democracy.[18] In these contexts, judges become instruments or 'the pawns of their rulers',[19] being not only complicit in dismantling democracy and the rule of law but also in instating oppression and tyranny.[20] Yet, there have been also other examples showing that 'judges do not always participate in oppression by authoritarian regimes', but that they have also engaged in 'activities seeking to defend the basic legal freedoms of liberal society'.[21] In Nazi Germany, while some judges were complicit with the atrocities of the regime, others did try to limit its inhuman excesses and atrocities.[22]

In recent years, populist radical right parties (chapter 2) have challenged liberal democracy in many ways. As Krygier underlined, populists have created 'paradoxical relationships with pivotal elements of democracy and the rule of law.'[23] While some populist parties devote particular attention to constitutions, their activities are anti-constitutional, in the sense that 'they are hostile to underlying values and principles of constitutionalism, and to institutional practices and principles that have been developed to serve these values'.[24] Being against pluralism and multiculturalism, radical right populists target courts, media, civil society, and academia, all actors whose opinions and action might limit their power,[25] as discussed in chapter 2. Through different strategies of delegitimisation[26] those in power portray judges as corrupt, incompetent, and immoral,[27] as being communists, or as acting as a cast, and therefore seeking to remove judges from their functions and replace them. Judges' decisions 'are often presented by the media and politicians as political decisions', 'against the government', with a clear

[15] HP Graver, *Judges against Justice on Judges when the Rule of Law is under Attack* (Berlin, Springer, 2015).

[16] AW Pereira, *Political (In)Justice. Authoritarianism and the Rule of Law in Brazil, Chile and Argentina.* (Pittsburgh, University of Pittsburgh Press, 2005); T Moustafa, *The Struggle for Constitutional Power. Law Politics and Economic Development in Egypt* (Cambridge, Cambridge University Press, 2007); L Hilbink, *Judges beyond Politics in Democracy and Dictatorship. Lessons from Chile* (Cambridge, Cambridge University Press, 2007).

[17] M Cadelli, *Nuremberg 1947: Le poignard de l'assassin sous la toge du magistrat* (Limal, Anthemis, 2023).

[18] Gamboa, García-Holgado and González-Ocantos (n 12).

[19] Moustafa (n 16) 15.

[20] Graver (n 15).

[21] ibid 3.

[22] ibid.

[23] M Krygier, 'Introduction: Anti-constitutional Populism' in M Krygier, A Czarnota and W Sadurski (eds), *Anti-Constitutional Populism* (Cambridge, Cambridge University Press, 2022).

[24] DV Kochenov and B Grabowska-Moroz, 'Constitutional Populism versus EU law: A much more Complex Story than You Imagined' in Krygier, Czarnota and Sadurski (n 23).

[25] Kochenov and Grabowska-Moroz (n 24) 467.

[26] R Coman and C Volintiru, 'Anti-liberal Ideas and Institutional Change in Central and Eastern Europe' (2021) 24 *European Politics and Society* 5.

[27] Kochenov and Grabowska-Moroz (n 24) 468.

impact on the perception of judges' impartiality', as discussed by European delegated prosecutor Guglielmi (chapter 10).

Nonetheless, radical right populist governments do not abolish judicial institutions; rather they are 'restuffed and re-purposed',[28] as illustrated by Yavuz Aydin:

> On 15 July 2016, the day of the attempted coup, there were around 14,500 judges/prosecutors in Turkey. After the suspension of the first 2,800, this number climbed to 4,560 in the following weeks. Currently there are around 21,000 judges and prosecutors in Turkey. This means that, having 'cleared the way' by sacking and imprisoning thousands of judges while sowing fear among those remaining, the Erdoğan government hired 11,000 'accredited' new judges over a period of four years and consolidated power through the judiciary from 2020 onwards. (chapter 20).

In many ways, the interviews in this book can be seen as evidence of judges' strategies to self-legitimise their role, illustrating a rhetoric of normative justification for their action. By the same token, these narratives also illustrate how different forms of political dissensus over liberal democracy – ranging from dismantling core pillars of liberal democracy to more constructive debates about rights and values (chapters 4, 5, 7, and 9), specific policies such as migration or environment (chapter 11), or migration (chapters 7 and 12) – give rise to the need for judges to balance their relation not only with politics but also with society.

From Top-down to Bottom-up Europeanisation. National Low Court Judges as Key Actors in the Process of Legal Integration

Over the past six decades or so, the role of judges has been strengthened at the national and supranational levels by the dynamics of the European political and legal integration. Against this backdrop, the transformation of courts has been examined in terms of Europeanisation, and also understood as an *adaptative process* triggered by the EU with varying impacts on domestic politics, policies, and polity. Following a top-down perspective, a vast body of literature has highlighted the potential impact of EU law and institutions on national courts. It has been argued that legal integration has been shaped both from the top – through the 'proactive' role of the CJEU – and from the bottom, through the role of Euro-lawyers and national judges.[29]

On the one hand, the CJEU has become a pivotal institutional actor by interpreting treaties and ruling on key policy areas.[30] In so doing, the Court put forth a 'pro-integration agenda' and built a new legal order in the 1960s, then protecting fundamental rights in the 1970s, and completing the internal market in the 1970/80s. At the same time, it was also attempting to making the first moves to establishing the initial

[28] Krygier (n 23).
[29] A Vauchez (ed), *Brokering Europe. Euro-Lawyers and the Making of a Transnational Polity* (Cambridge, Cambridge University Press, 2015).
[30] Saurugger and Terpan (n 8).

elements of a Europe-wide social policy and proclaiming the constitutional role of EU treaties.[31] The CJEU also promoted the language of rights which gained prominence in many areas of EU case law,[32] as discussed by judges Bay Larsen (chapter 4) and Hernández García (chapter 13). On the other hand, with the bottom-up approach, national judges ensure that European law in applied uniformly and effectively. When courts and judges have doubts about interpreting the validity of EU law, they can interact with the CJEU through the preliminary ruling procedure.[33]

When they engage with the CJEU, national judges enter into 'a relationship that has taken on a life of its own'.[34] Judicial cooperation through preliminary rulings has often been seen as an instrument that national judges use not only to solve disagreements or ensure uniform interpretation but also to empower themselves through European law. Recent studies have shown however that, for many reasons, judges use these avenues of dialogue with caution, 'resisting their own empowerment' as explained by Tommaso Pavone in *The Ghostwriters: Lawyers and the Politics Behind the Judicial Construction of Europe*.[35] While some judges engaged in what Haas conceptualised as a process of transfer of loyalty to a new centre of supranational power – being loyal to a set of symbols, values and institutions – others have maintained their loyalty to national power. In other words, judges' legal mobilisation depends on many factors, including institutional and cultural rules internal to the judiciary, which limit the opportunities to express dissent. In the same vein, judges' ideological beliefs, attitudes towards the EU, and preferences explain their propensity to engage in forms of legal mobilisation.[36]

As a result, the process of legal integration has strengthened the bonds between the different levels of jurisdiction, enhancing opportunities for cooperation but also increasing the potential for tension. More than once, national constitutional courts have questioned the role of the CJEU,[37] and more specifically the primacy of EU law over national law on democratic grounds, to give one example. Some courts have accepted European law on their own terms. At the same time, in the decade of the Eurozone,[38] rule of law, or migration crises, national judges turned to the CJEU to challenge national legislation, without overlooking the role of the ECtHR jurisprudence relating to the protection of fundamental rights.

The 18 narratives in this volume show that the use of the law is the most common *repertoire d'action*. When the PiS government in Poland and the Romanian Social Democrat government adopted measures weakening or dismantling the rule of law, both

[31] ibid 19–32.

[32] ibid 40.

[33] T Pavone, *The Ghostwriters: Lawyers and the Politics Behind the Judicial Construction of Europe* (Cambridge, Cambridge University Press, 2022).

[34] R Ladrech, *Europeanization and National Politics* (Basingstoke, Palgrave, 2010) 119.

[35] Pavone (n 33).

[36] L Puleo and R Coman, 'Explaining Judges' Opposition when Judicial Independence is Undermined: Insights from Poland, Romania, and Hungary' (2024) 31 *Democratization* 47.

[37] Ladrech (n 34).

[38] JA Mayoral and AT Pérez, 'On Judicial Mobilization: Entrepreneuring for Policy Change at Times of Crisis' (2018) 40 *Journal of European Integration* 719.

Polish and Romanian judges and associations such as Themis or Iustitia or the *Asociaţia Forumul Judecătorilor din România* (Romanian Judges' Forum Association) turned to the CJEU with a growing number of preliminary questions.[39] Others turned to the ECtHR, as illustrated by Yavuz Aydin in the case of Turkey: '25,000 cases' were pending before the Court, 'making Turkey number one in terms of applications, breaches, and unimplemented decisions across all categories' (chapter 20).

Faced with these challenges, some judges remained rather silent[40] as explained by Judge Matusik (chapter 19). Others turned to supranational courts, despite disciplinary sanctions like in the case of Judge Călin (chapter 15), or defamation campaigns, like the ones faced by Judge Gersdorf (chapter 17), and harassment as experienced by Judge Matusik (chapter 19), thus lending their actions an appearance of resistance. Resistance here refers to 'the capacity of actors to challenge and defy the power of the government and to stand against it as an act of transgression while facing or taking the risk of facing the consequences of this act'.[41]

Some of the cases brought to the CJEU were related to disciplinary measures concerning magistrates, others related to the principle of judicial independence and effective judicial protection or equal treatment and non-discrimination. In addition to preliminary rulings, Judge Sterk also recounted how, in 2024, four professional associations of judges – the Association of European Administrative Judges, the European Association of Judges, MEDEL, and *Rechters for Rechters* – brought to the CJEU the Council's decision to disburse EU funds to Poland as part of the Recovery and Resilience Facility despite rule of law concerns in the country (chapter 7).

As stated by Judge Călin, 'The CJEU has traditionally been a steadfast ally of Romanian judges, indeed perhaps the only reliable one' (chapter 15). However, in a few of the interviews, albeit not the majority, judges were more nuanced in their opinions of the role of the European Commission in safeguarding or promoting the independence of judges in EU and non-EU Member States (see also chapter 28). Some deplored how the 'Commission has often inexplicably neglected its role outlined in the founding treaties' (chapter 15), others like Judge Sterk (chapter 7) and Judge Perilli (chapter 12) pointed to the EU's inability to protect its own values. But even if the EU seem to 'be defenceless or at least reluctant to protect and preserve these values', the former Turkish Judge Yavuz Aydin contends that 'people in Poland, Hungary, Bulgaria, or nowadays Slovakia and some other countries are much luckier than people in Turkey in various ways, because they are EU members, and there is the burden of responsibility to Brussels' … In his opinion, at least the EU is 'still standing up for them' (chapter 20).

[39] A list of preliminary rulings is provided in the article R Coman and L Puleo, 'Opposition and Resistance: How Judges and Professional Associations in Poland, Hungary and Romania Defend their Independence' (2025) 41 *East European Politics* 24.

[40] Puleo and Coman (n 36) 47–69.

[41] Coman and Puleo (n 39) 29.

Horizontal Europeanisation of Judicial Culture: Ethics, Identity and Solidarity

While previous research devoted attention to top-down or bottom-up dynamics of Europeanisation, recent developments provide insights that shed light on horizontal effects such as increased cooperation between judicial actors.[42] Domestic actors – in this case judges – are filters and users of European norms and rules. The 18 narratives show how formal and informal interactions – which can be conceptualised as mechanisms of horizontal Europeanisation – have given rise to different outcomes such as ethics for judges, a sense of collective identity as European judges, and bonds of solidarity, all important factors in the emergence of a judicial culture.

Ethics for Judges

Several judges underline how the measures adopted by the Hungarian Fidesz and the Polish PiS parties put the question of the independence of the judiciary on the agenda of judicial networks such as ENCJ (chapter 7) or professional associations such as MEDEL (chapter 10), the IAJ (chapter 11), or the EAJ. After two years of reflections, in June 2010, the General Assembly of ENCJ in London, in its Working Group of Judicial Ethics 2009–2010, adopted the report entitled 'Judicial Ethics – Principles, Values and Qualities' as guidelines for the conduct of European judges. Independence, integrity, impartiality, reserve and discretion both in public and in private life, diligence, respect and the ability to listen, competence, and transparency are all meant to govern judges' work. For justice to be done, values and qualities matter too, including: wisdom, loyalty to the Constitution of one's country and to its democratic institutions, and to fundamental rights, as well as humanity. Courage is another important quality which is needed 'to conduct certain procedures, to cope with various pressures, political, social, and of public opinion, as well as from media and vested interests'.[43]

In the same vein, in 2022, the Consultative Council of European Judges of the Council of Europe adopted an Opinion No. 25 (2022) which addresses 'the legal and ethical duty of a judge to speak out in order to safeguard the rule of law and democracy at the domestic, but also at the European and international level'.[44] The Opinion underlines the fact that a judge enjoys the right to freedom of expression like any other citizen. It sets a series of limitations on the freedom of expression either in relation to judicial disputes or regarding public debates. The Opinion also states that 'judges have the right to make comments on matters that concern fundamental human rights, the rule of law, matters of judicial appointments or promotion, and the proper functioning of the

[42] MP Vink and P Graziano, 'Challenges of a New Research Agenda' in P Graziano and MP Vink (eds), *Europeanization. New Research Agendas* (New York, Palgrave Macmillan, 2008) 10.

[43] European Network of Judicial Councils, 'Judicial Ethics – Principles, Values and Qualities', www.encj.eu/images/stories/pdf/ethics/judicialethicsdeontologiefinal.pdf 13.

[44] Consultative Council of European Judges, Opinion No. 25 (2022) on freedom of expression of judges, rm.coe.int/opinion-no-25-2022-final/1680a973ef%0A%0A, 3.

administration of justice, including the independence of the judiciary and separation of powers'.[45] By the same token, judges have the right to make demands concerning their professions' working conditions and other professional interests as expressed by their professional associations. In its opinion, the CCJE also devoted particular attention to the 'educative role of courts and the associations of judges' and the importance of judges explaining the functioning and values of the judiciary.[46] As judge Kühn emphasised (chapter 18), 'every judge in Europe today must recognise their duty to uphold democracy, the rule of law, and the judicial system they serve, as well as the system they are entrusted to protect'.

European Identity and Transnational Solidarity

Developments in Hungary, in Poland, in Romania, but also in Turkey and other countries have intensified formal and informal cooperations between judges. As underlined by Judge Sterk 'for the first time, I must say that we, the judiciaries in Europe, are really working together' (chapter 7). In the first half of the 2010s many European judges were very sympathetic not only to the state of the judiciary in Poland and Hungary, but also to the coup in Turkey, when 'almost 3,000 judges and prosecutors were arrested and detained and more than 3,000 were fired' (chapter 12). While the *Associazione Nazionale Magistrati* in Italy organised protests in Milan and Rome (chapter 12), the 'EAJ created a solidarity fund' and 'more than €300,000' was raised to support Turkish judges and prosecutors who were in prison or exile, as recalled by Judge Igreja Matos (chapter 11) or to support judges in Columbia, as mentioned by Judge Titz (chapter 8). Solidarity has strengthened the bonds between judges and associations and served as an important supporting factor. As Judge Grimm argued 'Manifestations of solidarity … might encourage judges to resist to the extent possible, and it may also make an impression on the general public (chapter 6); solidarity, as Judge Matusik contended, 'can prevent the decline of independent judiciary' (chapter 19). These interactions have given meaning to the notion and the implications of being a *European judge*.

Law and Politics: National and European Forms of Interest Representation

Professional associations of judges have received little attention in the literature, either because they are less active or because their activity remains confined to this specific milieu. The narratives in this volume underline the role of professional associations as an arena where interests crystalise through debates and interactions. Depending on national traditions, in some countries judges are represented by a single professional association. In others, their different sensibilities are represented by a plurality of associations.

[45] Consultative Council of European Judges, Opinion No. 25 (2022).
[46] ibid.

At the national level, associations represent the interests of the profession; they are often consulted in national decision-making processes on legislation concerning the organisation, career, and administration of the judiciary. As stated by Judge Titz, it is 'also the duty of the Judges Association to voice concerns and to contribute to the formation of laws, which we are committed to doing diligently' (chapter 8). Professional associations are not immune to budget cuts or measures aimed at reorganising the work of judges, to measures reducing the time judges need to write their decisions to increase the efficiency of justice (chapter 5), to measures concerning the resources allocated to the system such as the number of places available, and the objectives of making the justice system more efficient or digitalising it, to give just a few examples. These forms of consultation or corporatist interest representation are more or less institutionalised, whether formally or informally. Therefore, professional associations of judges' draft opinions and memoranda on legislative proposals concerning matters related to their organisation and functioning, either as collective actors or in individual statements.

At the European level, professional associations are also active in consultations organised by EU institutional actors, such as the European Commission. They participate either in broad discussions addressed to other stakeholders or in more specific informal consultations. Some of these formal consultations are instigated by political actors (governments in EU Member States or the European Commission), while others are more informal and can take either top-down forms or emanate from bottom-up initiatives by judges. Formally and informally, they participated in discussions and consultations with EU institutions, mainly with the European Commission (chapters 15, 21 and 11) to provide opinions on the state of the rule of law. While the Commission has often been seen as an ally in these processes of transferring loyalty from the national to the supranational level, the interviews in this book illustrate a more critical picture not only of the Commission's support in its interactions with trade associations (chapter 15), but of the EU's role more generally in defending EU's values (chapter 12).

Law and Society

Beyond the relationship between judges and politics, the interviews in this book provide broader reflections on the role of judges in society and the role of the judiciary as a service, not only as a power in the state (chapter 12). As Judge Cadelli put it, 'When people enter a courthouse, they are not looking for the law, they are looking for human contact' (chapter 5). Judge Perilli similarly asserted, 'If a court is not able to provide a proper and timely service for these citizens, then the citizens will have the perception that judges do not do enough to protect their rights. Changing behaviour, attitude, and organisation is a key. To do so, judges need to change their way of thinking about their role as a service, and not only as a power' (chapter 12).

These reflections seem to influence the way some judges preform their roles. How judges speak through their judgments matters, Judge Cadelli argued (chapter 5). Yet judges are not limited to speaking only through their judgments, maintained Judge

Frąckowiak (chapter 16). Over the past decade, many judges sought to make their voice heard, some through conferences in schools and universities (chapter 9), others in gatherings with civil society (chapter 5), at music festivals (chapter 16) or in the streets (chapter 15). While in the past, judges' protests 'were typically associated with issues such as working conditions and salaries, as seen in Romania during the 1990s, where many judges faced precarious working environments,[47] recent years have seen an increase in the number of instances when judges have expressed dissent off-bench.[48] The action of judges did not take place in a vacuum. It received support from citizens on many occasions. In Romania between 2017 and 2019, numerous protests took place against measures adopted by the Romanian Social Democrat government, with some judges demonstrating not only in Bucharest but also in Brussels, in front of the *Palais de Justice*. In the same vein, protests erupted in Poland against restrictive abortion laws and the violation of the Constitution, among others. Polish judges received support from a wide range of civil society associations, including *KOR* but also Free Courts (*Wolne Sądy*), the Citizens of the Republic of Poland (*Obywatele RP*), Amnesty International, and many other national and European associations (chapter 17). It is important to note that many judges are also academics, therefore their actions have received support not only from lawyers but from scholars across various disciplines, who chose to step out of their 'ivory towers' to shed light on the critical issues at stake. Judges from many European countries left their courtrooms to participate in the March of a Thousand Robes held on 11 January 2020, in Warsaw, in solidarity with Polish judges and citizens, marching in defence of judicial independence in an event organised under the slogan: *Right to Independence. Right to Europe.* The March was the largest professional gathering of judges in Europe. It saw 30,000 participants and hundreds of judges from 22 European countries including Austria, Germany, Portugal, Denmark, France, Croatia, Greece, Slovenia, Spain, Hungary, Ireland, Italy, Norway, Romania, the Netherlands, Czechia, Latvia, Bulgaria, Turkey, Estonia, Belgium, and Slovakia.[49] For several hours, judges and citizens marched through the streets of Warsaw, starting at the Supreme Court, passing by the Presidential Palace, and concluding at the Polish Parliament. The March fostered a new sense of identity and solidarity among judges, giving substance to the expression *European judges*. The contact with society emerges as a central point of reflection because, as Judge Perilli underlined, even if guarantees of independence are in place, if 'this independence is not strongly rooted in society' it 'makes the judiciary weak vis-à-vis the political power' (chapter 12).

[47] R Coman, *Réformer la justice dans un pays post-communiste. Le cas de la Roumanie* (Bruxelles, Éditions de l'Université de Bruxelles, 2009).

[48] CY Matthes, 'Judges as Activists: How Polish Judges Mobilise to Defend the Rule of Law' (2022) 38 *East European Politics* 468.

[49] International Association of Judges, www.ekou.ee/doc/2024-01-11_IAJ-UN-1000-Robes-March.pdf.

28

Learning from Judges. Looking Forward

ANDREW BRADLEY

'There can be no justice without a strong independent judiciary. The judiciary can do little without the support of a strong legal profession'.

Nelson Mandela[1]

Introduction

Liberal democracy and the rule of law are being challenged globally, and democratic backsliding has become a real concern shared not only by those who govern democracies, but also for national and international democracy support organisations, including civil society.[2] Citizens and defenders of liberal democracy see and experience that their efforts to safeguard and enhance liberal democracy are being challenged or dismissed. With only limited options at their disposal, and in some cases as the last and only resort, have led citizens and democracy defenders to increasingly rely on national constitutions and the legal interpretation thereof by judges to defend democracy and the rule of law. Member States of the EU are not shielded from challenges to liberal democracy and the erosion of the essential importance of the rule of law, as outlined in the annual Rule of Law Report[3] of the European Commission and annual World Justice Project (WJP) Rule of Law Index.[4] Commentators, including academics, lawyers, and democracy practitioners, are in unison that democratic backsliding, including challenges to the rule of law, are occurring in several EU Member States. Many democratic freedoms are being questioned and challenged, including one of the main pillars of liberal democracy, the

[1] Opening address by Nelson Mandela to the Law Society of the Transvaal (29 October 1993), available at: www.mandela.gov.za/mandela_speeches/1993/931029_law.htm#:~:text=There%20can%20be%20no%20justice,Africa%2C%20is%20likely%20to%20prosper.

[2] IT Cameron, 'The Role of the Venice Commission in Strengthening the Rule of Law' in AB Engelbrekt, A Moberg and J Nergelius (eds), *Rule of Law in the EU 30 Years After the Fall of the Berlin Wall: Taking Stock and Looking Ahead* (Oxford, Hart Publishing, 2021).

[3] European Commission, Annual Rule of Law Cycle, commission.europa.eu/strategy-and-policy/policies/justice-and-fundamental-rights/upholding-rule-law/rule-law/annual-rule-law-cycle_en.

[4] World Justice Project, *Rule of Law Index*, worldjusticeproject.org/rule-of-law-index/.

independence of the judiciary, which in any liberal democracy, should be free from any political interference.[5]

The assault on the independence of the judiciary is well articulated by judges in this volume. While the phenomenon is global, national situations vary considerably. In some cases, there is a phenomenon of autocratisation at stake, including autocratic capture and the disregard for the rule of law. In others, there is a sense of dissatisfaction with the functioning of the judiciary amid inherent tensions between law and politics. Dissensus over liberal democracy encapsulates all these phenomena which are some of the key reasons for the evolving role and consciousness of judges in society. Interviews conducted provide insights into the various strategies, mechanisms and means used by judges at the national and supranational levels to defend, safeguard, and promote the independence of the judiciary, including the reliance on EU law and rulings by the CJEU and the ECtHR. As recounted by the judges' interviews and expert commentaries in this volume, these mentioned legal avenues available to them as individuals or via their representative professional associations to challenge national disputed measures before the CJEU and ECtHR, as well as cross-border support and solidarity from their peers, provide national judges with a toolkit to mobilise for the defence of liberal democracy in EU Member States and beyond.

The challenge posed to judges, as mentioned by several interviewees, is to navigate the delicate and important reasonable balance 'between the degree to which judges may be involved in society and the need for them to be, and to be seen as independent and impartial in the discharge of their duties', as also underlined in Opinion No. 3 of the CCJE.[6]

This chapter analyses the legal and societal avenues available for judges to support the independence of the judiciary and includes a section on lessons learned from judges and commentators. To this end, derived from the interviews and commentaries, a summary of key practical and implementable takeaways to contribute to the safeguarding of the independence of the judiciary and to ensure the optimum functioning of the judicial system, are captured in the concluding section of this chapter.

Legal Avenues

Compliance with the founding values of the EU is prescribed in its law. Disregard of these values, and especially the adherence to the rule of law and the safeguarding of the independence of the judiciary, is however taking place. Existing mechanisms to safeguard the rule of law, such as Article 7 TEU, were deemed insufficient to address these challenges. As the rule of law is enshrined in both the ECHR and EU treaties, the jurisdictions of the ECtHR and the CJEU provide important legal avenues to challenge national measures or practices related to the organisation of the judiciary. The interviews in this volume illustrate individual applications to the ECtHR

[5] WA Galston, 'The populist challenge to liberal democracy' (2018) 29 *Journal of Democracy* 5.

[6] Opinion No. 3 of the CCJE to the attention of the Committee of Ministers of the Council of Europe on the principles and rules governing judges' professional conduct, in particular ethics, incompatible behaviour and impartiality (November 2002).

(such as *Baka v Hungary* discussed in chapter 14) or challenging EU measures through preliminary rulings at the CJEU.

As so aptly expressed in this volume by judges, judicial mobilisation[7] refers to the practice when the parameters of the law are used to realise claims and wishes to achieve change or protect and maintain interests. This mobilisation can be carried out by individuals or by professional national and European associations of judges, represented in this volume. As captured in this volume, judges became creative through networks, peer support, and active civic involvement to ensure the application of EU law at the national level in cases when Member States transgressed. These mechanisms and strategies used to seek policy change and the adherence to the rule of law at the national level, were engineered in- and outside legal systems and institutions, and in the latter case, especially through civil society organisations and networks.

Societal Avenues

When fundamental rights and civil liberties are at stake, judges may be called upon to act beyond their traditional role of interpreters of law, and to rather become defenders of the constitution, fulfilling their duty to uphold the law while also safeguarding democratic values. The evolution of the role of judges stems from a legal consciousness to balance the intricate interplay between law and politics within an interconnected and constant changing context.[8] Judicial mobilisation is described as an action that involves more than going to court to litigate disputes, as this action may prove ineffective or even irrelevant in some contexts. In addition to litigation, judicial mobilisation may take place in many ways – the articulation of an issue, by supporting a cause, or through the expression of solidarity, including through group action or group mobilisation. Through the transformation of the role of judges and the evolution of judges' consciousness, judicial mobilisation is taking place not only in national or supranational courts, but also in other arenas – such as civic platforms, judicial associations and within other interest groups.[9] Legal consciousness can be described as one of the core elements of the legitimacy of any legal system.[10] Therefore, it is the critical awareness of injustices within the parameters of any legal system, motivating social action with the objective to safeguard or reform laws in accordance with democratic norms.[11] In EU Member States, national judges are seen to be also EU judges when applying EU law. The profile of judges, their interests and values, and the policy/legal context in which they operate, determine their engagement with EU law. In addition, exchanges and interactions of

[7] J Handmaker, 'Introduction to the legal mobilization special focus' (2023) 15 *Journal of Human Rights Practice* 1.

[8] L Epstein and N Waterbury, 'Judicial Behavior' in WR Thompson (ed), *Oxford Research Encyclopedia of Politics* (Oxford, Oxford University Press, 2020).

[9] LJ Chua, DM Engel and S Liu, 'Legal Mobilization' in LJ Chua, DM Engel and S Liu (eds), *The Asian Law and Society Reader* (Cambridge, Cambridge University Press, 2023).

[10] A Kubal, 'Judicial Relational Legal Consciousness: Authoritarian Backsliding as a Catalyst of Change' (2024a) 51 *Journal of Law and Society* S45.

[11] F Horák, D Lacko, and A Klocek, 'Legal Consciousness: A Systematic Review of its Conceptualization and Measurement Methods' (2021) 31 *Anuario de Psicología Jurídica* 9.

national judges with their peers and activists in other EU Member States, as highlighted in interviews conducted for this volume, shape the propensity to mobilise EU law at the national level in defence of liberal democracy and the rule of law.

Learning from Judges: Towards a Culture for the Rule of Law within the Judiciary and Society

What lessons for the future can be learned from the judges interviewed and expert commentaries in this volume? Within the framework of the judiciary, it will be important to consider which past experiences could be relevant in new and specific circumstances or adapted for purpose in future. The importance of commitment, patience, persistence, vision, the ability to dialogue with a view to build convergence and consensus, peer support, and the conscience to always act in accordance with the law, are important requisites for maintaining the checks and balances of liberal democracy.

It is not the objective of this chapter to take a stand in support of any action taken by, or inaction of judges in the face of challenges to liberal democracy, including the assault on the independence of the judiciary. While some judges are in support of increased judicial resistance or mobilisation, several interviewees also articulate a clear preference for being rather in favour of using traditional legal avenues, and revisiting the role of judges and their roles in society to address challenges. It could be seen that the different stances taken by judges are either shaped by experiences of political interference and direct political attacks, or no experiences at all of interference or attacks.

Legal mobilisation has a role to play, it has also evolved over time with more cases brought by judges and associations to the ECtHR and the CJEU, and will continue to reinvent itself. The interviews in this volume offer also insights on how to strengthen the culture for the rule of law within the judiciary and in society. Some of the interviews also mark an awareness of how judges can break with their older practices that keep them far from society and its realities. Key practical and implementable takeaways to contribute to the safeguarding of the independence of the judiciary and to ensuring the optimum functioning of the judicial system, can be summarised as follows:

Make cases more accessible to journalists and the general public

To the question as how to address the current challenges, Judge Vajda argues that: 'It is important for courts to be more transparent so that citizens can be aware of what is happening. In practice, this means streaming more hearings and issuing more press releases in important cases to make cases more accessible to journalists and the general public. This would ensure that debate on a judgment is better informed'.

He continues with his reflection and emphasises that, 'it was of great interest in these high-profile cases that could easily be followed by everyone via a computer screen', and that, 'courts can issue a press release that summarises what the judgment is about. The European courts do this, the UK Supreme Court does this, and I think the German courts and possibly other courts in the EU do as well. Unfortunately, if you are not a lawyer, you may not feel inclined to read, or be able to understand, a long judgment.

So it is very important to have a press release that sets out clearly what is at stake and that summarises the judgment. This means that citizens can be much better informed as to what the Court has said, rather than just getting that information from some clip on the Internet, which may be inaccurate' (see chapter 9).

Judge Kühn is of the view in chapter 18 that judges, 'should write judgments in a way which will be accessible and understood by the people'.

These reflections are in line with the Bengalore Principles of Judicial Conduct[12] adapted in 2002 which state that 'a judge shall be independent in relation to society in general and in relation to the particular parties to a dispute which the judge has to adjudicate' (Article 1.3) but at the same time, to ensure equality 'a judge shall be aware of, and understand, diversity in society and differences arising from various sources, including but not limited to race, colour, sex, religion, national origin, caste, disability, age, marital status, sexual orientation, social and economic status and other like causes ("irrelevant grounds")' (Article 5.1).

Takeaways:

Improve communication to the public by issuing accessible statements in not too technical language that summarize the main elements of a judgment.

Identify and address the deeper social challenges of society that contribute to the crisis of liberal democracy in Europe.

Public Engagement, Capacity Building, Trust and Role of Civil Society

Defending the rule of law is not only a matter of judges. As Aydin mentions, '… judicial independence is not just for judges – it is for the people', and that 'judicial independence is essential for a state, but investing in judicial culture and a democratic culture is far more critical because culture eats rules for breakfast' (see chapter 20).

Several judges argued in this volume the importance of reaching out to the public to maintain 'the trust of the public', as stated by Judge Sterk (chapter 7), 'because at the end of the day, it is the trust of the public that will be decisive in whether you lose your independence or not, when attacked by (populist) governments'. And this engagement marks a break with the past and with the way many judges were trained on continental Europe. Judge Grimm is of the view that, 'you must also reach out to the public, and you must try to gain and maintain the trust of the public. Because at the end of the day, it is the trust of the public that will be decisive in whether you lose your independence or not, when attacked by (populist) governments' (see chapter 6).

For many judges, the way forward lies in a stronger culture of democratic values and standards in society, as stated by Judge Guglielmi in chapter 10, 'a stronger civil society acting in defence of the rule of law, values, and democracy: this is my feeling and my hope'.

How to reconnect with society is discussed in different ways in this volume. Some of the interviews focus on the way in which judges write their judgments, such as Judge

[12] United Nations, 'Bangalore Principles of Judicial Conduct' (2002) UN Doc E/CN.4/2003/65.

Cadelli, 'We must give reasons (this is about legal reasoning)' (see chapter 5). Other have also underlined the importance of being present in schools, universities and public debates. This is a two-way process. It is not just a question of citizens learning more about the role of judges, but also of judges learning more about the societies in which they live. As underlined by Judge Igreja Matos, 'The main issues are education about justice to help build closer ties with civil society as well as communication challenges' (see chapter 11).

Judge Perilli mentions: 'Being a judge today is a very difficult and challenging task. It requires high professional and ethical skills. It is not sufficient to simply have knowledge of the national law, even if this is a precondition to becoming a judge and is the main focus of national competition to access the judiciary in Italy. The judge must also have consistent knowledge of the European Union law that governs cases that falls into its scope of application, and the scope of application of EU Law is becoming broader and broader' (chapter 12).

In addition, he adds that, 'To perform her/his work the judge needs therefore broad legal knowledge and clear awareness of her/his role, but also a strong independence from political power'. Concluding on skills, Judge Perilli states, 'The task of the judge is very difficult because to be fully professional, judges must also develop soft skills, the capacity to communicate with the parties, the ability to identify and prevent bias, and to manage time. Improving these skills takes training and time'.

Takeaways:

Increase strategic engagement with the public, including the media, to explain the role of judges and the necessity of an independent judicial system.

Advocate for and build societal trust in judges and institutions of governance.

Scale up the professionalisation of the judicial profession by, inter alia, encouraging judges to develop and acquire soft skills, to develop capacities to communicate and engage with all levels of society, and to manage time more effectively and efficiently. To this end, opportunities for training and peer exchanges, and the provisions of resources, including financial, for professionalisation should be facilitated.

Develop and provide civic and civil education for citizens to understand the roles and functions of judges, the CJEU and the ECtHR, as well as liberal democracy and the importance of judicial independence.

Judges and Political Actors: Participation in Law Making

As the European Charter[13] on the statute for judges points out, judges are encouraged to defend their rights as a profession through professional organisations and to be consulted by political actors over plans that modify their status, remuneration or their social welfare as stated in Articles 1.7 and 1.8 below:

> 1.7. Professional organizations set up by judges, and to which all judges may freely adhere, contribute notably to the defence of those rights which are conferred on them by their

[13] Council of Europe, 'European Charter on the Statute for Judges' (1998) DAJ/DOC (98)23.

> statute, in particular in relation to authorities and bodies which are involved in decisions regarding them.
>
> 1.8. Judges are associated through their representatives and their professional organizations in decisions relating to the administration of the courts and as to the determination of their means, and their allocation at a national and local level. They are consulted in the same manner over plans to modify their statute, and over the determination of the terms of their remuneration and of their social welfare.

The interviews in this book also emphasise this dimension – namely the involvement of judges in defining the policies that affect their careers or operating methods. As highlighted by Judge Titz, 'The Judges Association bears the primary responsibility for shaping the law. It is crucial for us to participate actively in the law-making process and to express our concerns about significant societal changes from a judicial standpoint. While an individual judge cannot impose personal morals in his or her rulings, he or she must conscientiously apply the law ethically. However, it is also the duty of the Judges Association to voice concerns and to contribute to the formation of laws, which we are committed to doing diligently. We have the right to be heard when new laws are being formulated, and we strive to use our influence in this regard' (see chapter 8).

This participation becomes even more important when resources are at stake. For Judge Igreja Matos, one of the main concerns in EU Member States is, 'the lack of means. It is not popular for the state to give resources to the justice system, and it doesn't get anyone votes. It is better to open a hospital or to build a road than to have modern courts, and to have proper resources for the justice system. The lack of resources is a key problem, and indeed a transversal problem' (see chapter 11).

> Takeaways:
>
> **Strengthen** the democratic legitimacy of the judiciary as judges make consequential decisions that could have important political and social implications.
>
> **Secure** judicial independence, especially from political power, to allow judges to protect the rights of individuals, especially in times of change and constitutional transitions.
>
> **Ensure**, as the law requires, sufficient budgetary provisions, including adequate salaries, for judges, clerks, and employees in the justice system.

Strengthening Judicial Culture of the Rule of Law Through Networking and Cooperation

Judge Bay Larsen argued that 'a way forward is judicial cooperation' (see chapter 4). For Judge Baka, 'I was invited to Poland in 2016 to attend the inaugural Congress of Polish Judges. It turned out to be a critical gathering for the Polish judiciary to protect its independence, and I am convinced that such meetings are incredibly valuable and efficient' (see chapter 14).

Networking and cooperation nature solidarity among judges which is important when the independence of the judiciary is under attack. Judge Matusik states, 'Solidarity among judges can prevent the decline of independent judiciary. When we share knowledge, challenges, and solutions, and show solidarity with each other – and examples here include both the EAJ and the IAJ, we can convey information to the European Commission more effectively'. He adds, 'By joining forces and sharing our thoughts and results, we can find higher-level solutions to these common challenges' (see chapter 19).

Takeaways:

Encourage greater participation in Judges Associations that primarily bears the responsibility for shaping the law and allow judges to express their opinions publicly as long as their impartiality is not compromised.

Change the mindset of the judiciary in relation to the role of judges that would allow for their active participation in society, judges' associations, and peer exchanges, as well as to embrace an openness to transnational networking.

EU Values and Democracy

The interviews in this volume offer insights into judges' mixed perceptions of the EU's role in defending its values. While the EU seems to be a solution, there is also dissatisfaction with regards to its ability to stand for its own values.

Judge Titz is of the view that, 'The European institutions have the potential to play a constructive role in addressing certain issues. For instance, they can decide to withhold the substantial funds they typically provide from countries that no longer maintain stable democracies or uphold the rule of law, as in the case of Hungary. This approach could be effective in certain cases. However, it is essential to recognise that dealing with European institutions is not straightforward. Their decision-making process is often slow due to their dependency on member states and the requirement for either a majority or a unanimous vote to enact measures. Despite these challenges, I believe that the European Union and its institutions can be part of the solution' (see chapter 8).

Political actors also have a role to play in safeguarding EU's common values, and judges are concerned that relying solely on the courts may be counterproductive, as illustrated by Judge Kühn, 'it is dangerous is if we concentrate too much of our attention on constitutional court judges'. He further states: 'That's why not only Constitutional Court judges, but all judges in Europe today must be aware of their responsibility to democracy and the rule of law, and to the system they were appointed to as well as the system they are supposed to defend' (see chapter 18).

The EU needs reforms to strengthen democracy at the supranational level, as discussed by judges Gersdorf and Grimm. For Judge Grimm, recent developments have 'shown the necessity of a means to expel Member States that consistently and seriously deviate from the Union's values. However, creating such a means would be very challenging, as it requires the consent of the countries in question. It is unlikely that this can be secured in times of crisis. But one should be mindful if a window of opportunity opens'. Further Judge Grimm proposes that, 'the European Union enhance its own democratic foundations' (see chapter 6).

For Judge Gersdorf, 'The guarantees of the tripartite division of power are too weak in the face of a genuinely unchecked executive power, which is becoming increasingly widespread'. She adds, 'the selection of judges should be recognised as a huge responsibility', and believes that, 'ensuring the autonomy of judges and courts will require rethinking some minimum requirements for them at the EU level and, arguably, may require constitutional changes in many Member States' (see chapter 17).

> Takeaways:
>
> **Address** the façade of democracy by making elections more transparent, competitive, and fair.
>
> **Enhance** the democratic foundations of the EU by empowering EU institutions through a reform process, including the improved application of the subsidiarity principle between the supranational and national levels to improve effective and efficient decision-making that is enforced. Harmonisation of national law among EU Member States, in accordance with EU law and based on a balanced approach between the application of the primacy of EU law and respect for the Member States' national constitutional identity, is required.
>
> **Develop** minimum requirements and standards for judges and courts at the EU-level, including a system where government cannot exercise undue political influence on the appointment of judges, to ensure the autonomy of judges and courts at the national level.

The listed takeaways, derived from interviews and commentaries, while not exhaustive, are presented for follow up by, inter alia, judiciaries, EU institutions, EU Member States, and civil society organisations.

BIBLIOGRAPHY

Aguiar-Aguilar, AA, 'Understanding the Judiciary from the Inside. The Legal Culture of Judges in Mexico' (2022) 43 *Justice system Journal* 576.

Akkerman, T, Lange, S de and Rooduijn, M (eds), *Radical Right-Wing Populist Parties in Western Europe: Into the Mainstream?* (London, Routledge, 2016).

Andersen, EA, *Out of the Closets and into the Courts: Legal Opportunity Structure and Gay Rights Litigation* (Ann Arbor, University of Michigan Press, 2006).

Avril, L, 'Le Costume Sous la Robe: Les avocats en professionnels multi-cartes de l'État régulateur européen' (PhD thesis, Université Paris 1 Panthéon-Sorbonne 2019).

Baldini, G, 'From "Anomaly" to "Laboratory"? Fratelli d'Italia, Illiberalism and the Study of Right-Wing Parties in Western Europe' (2024) 22 *Political Studies Review* 402.

Bánkúti, M, Halmai, G and Scheppele, KL, 'From Separation of Powers to a Government without Checks: Hungary's Old and New Constitutions' in GA Tóth (ed), *Constitution for a Disunited Nation. On Hungary's 2011 Fundamental Law* (New York, CEU Press, 2012) 237–68.

Bánkúti, M, Halmai, G and Scheppele, KL, 'Hungary's Illiberal Turn: Disabling the Constitution' (2012) 23 *Journal of Democracy* 138.

Bedner, A, 'An Elementary Approach to the Rule of Law' (2010) 2 *Hague Journal on the Rule of Law* 48.

Behr, V, 'Towards a Transnational and Social History of Anti-Liberalism. Insights from the Trajectory of Ryszard Legutko' (2023) 24 *European Politics and Society* 22.

Bellamy, R, *Political Constitutionalism* (Cambridge, Cambridge University Press, 2007).

Bermeo, N, 'On Democratic Backsliding' (2016) 27 *Journal of Democracy* 57.

Bill, S, 'PiS's Strategies of Elite Replacement' (2022) 36 *East European Politics and Societies* 118.

Blauberger, M and Kelemen, RD, 'Can Courts Rescue National Democracy? Judicial Safeguards Against Democratic Backsliding in the EU' (2017) 24 *Journal of European Public Policy* 321.

Bluhm, K and Varga, M, *New Conservatives in Russia and East Central Europe* (London, Routledge, 2019).

Blokker, P, *New Democracies in Crisis? A Comparative Constitutional Study of the Czech Republic, Hungary, Poland, Romania and Slovakia* (Milton Park, Routledge, 2014).

Bobbio, N, *Liberalism e Democrazia* (Roma, Franco Angeli, 1988).

Bojarski, Ł, 'Civil Society Organizations for and with the Courts and Judges – Struggle for the Rule of Law and Judicial Independence: The Case of Poland 1976–2020' (2021) 22 *German Law Journal* 1344.

Börzel, TA, Risse, T, Anderson, SB and Garrison, JA (eds), *Polarization and Deep Contestations. The Liberal Script in the United States* (Oxford, Oxford University Press, 2024).

Boukalas, C, 'Politics as Legal Action/Lawyers as Political Actors' (2013) 22 *Social & Legal Studies* 395.

Briquet, J-L, 'La crise politique en Italie. Les analyses de la science politique italienne' (1995) 8 *Revue française de science politique* 127.

Briquet, J-L, 'Juges rouges ou Mains propres ?' (2002) 15 *Critique internationale* 45.

Brug, W van der, Popa, S, Hobolt, SB and Schmitt, H, 'Democratic Support, Populism, and the Incumbency Effect' (2021) 32 *Journal of Democracy* 131.

Bugaric, B and Ginsburg, T, 'The Assault on Post-Communist Courts' (2016) 27 *Journal of Democracy* 69.

Buzogány, A, 'Illiberal Democracy in Hungary: Authoritarian Diffusion or Domestic Causation?' (2017) 24 *Democratization* 1307.

Cadelli, M, *Nuremberg 1947: Le poignard de l'assassin sous la toge du magistrat* (Limal, Anthemis, 2023).

Cameron, IT 'The Role of the Venice Commission in Strengthening the Rule of Law' in AB Engelbrekt, A Moberg and J Nergelius (eds), *Rule of Law in the EU 30 Years After the Fall of the Berlin Wall: Taking Stock and Looking Ahead* (Oxford, Hart Publishing, 2021) 147–80.

Canihac, H, 'Illiberal, Anti-liberal or Post-liberal Democracy? Conceptualizing the Relationship between Populism and Political Liberalism' (2022) 4 *Political Research Exchange* 1.
Cebulak, P, 'Mapping the Potentials and Pitfalls of using European Law for Strategic Litigation against Illiberal Reforms' (2024) 20 *International Journal of Law in Context* 379.
Chua, LJ and Engel, DM, 'Legal Consciousness Reconsidered' (2019) 15 *Annual Review of Law and Social Science* 335.
Chua, LJ, Engel, DM and Liu, S, 'Legal Mobilization' in LJ Chua, DM Engel and S Liu (eds), *The Asian Law and Society Reader* (Cambridge, Cambridge University Press, 2023) 183–226.
Closa, C, 'The Politics of Guarding the Treaties: Commission Scrutiny of Rule of Law Compliance' (2019) 26 *Journal of European Public Policy* 696.
Collier, D, Hidalgo, D and Maciuceanu, O, 'Essentially Contested Concepts: Debates and Applications' (2006) 11 *Journal of Political Ideologies* 211.
Coman, R, *Réformer la justice dans un pays post-communiste. Le cas de la Roumanie* (Bruxelles, Éditions de l'Université de Bruxelles, 2009).
Coman, R, *The Politics of the Rule of Law in the EU Polity* (Cham, Palgrave Macmillan, 2022).
Coman, R and Brack, N, 'Dissensus over Liberal Democracy: Concept-Building and Typology' (forthcoming) *European Political Science.*
Coman, R and Buzogány, A, 'The European Union's Response to the Rule of Law Crisis and the Making of the New Conditionality Regime' (2024) 62 *Journal of Common Market Studies* 102.
Coman, R, Paulis, E, Puleo, L and Trino, N, 'Building and Legitimizing an Illiberal Transnational Field: Illiberal Think Tanks' Struggle for Cultural Hegemony in Poland and Hungary' (forthcoming) *European Political Science.*
Coman, R, and Puleo, L, 'Opposition and Resistance: How Judges and Professional Associations in Poland, Hungary, and Romania Defend their Independence' (2025) 41 *East European Politics* 24.
Coman, R and Volintiru, C, 'Anti-liberal Ideas and Institutional Change in Central and Eastern Europe' (2021) 24 *European Politics and Society* 5.
Conant, L, *Justice Contained: Law and Politics in the European Union* (Ithaca, N.Y., Cornell University Press, 2002).
Conant, L, 'Failing backward? EU citizenship, the Court of Justice, and Brexit' (2021) 28 *Journal of European Public Policy* 1592.
Corstens, G, *Understanding the Rule of Law* (Oxford, Hart Publishing, 2017).
Couso, J, 'Models of Democracy and Models of Constitutionalism' (2011) 89 *Texas Law Review* 1517.
Couso, J and Hilbink, L, 'From Guietism to Incipient Activism: The Institutional and Ideological Roots of Rights Adjudication in Chile' in G Helmke and J Ríos Figueroa (eds), *Courts in Latin America* (Cambridge, Cambridge University Press, 2011) 99–127.
Dallara, C, 'Powerful Resistance against a Long-running Personal Crusade: the Impact of Silvio Berlusconi on the Italian Judicial System' (2015) 20 *Modern Italy* 59.
Dallara, C and Piana, D, *Networking the Rule of Law. How Change Agents Reshape Judicial Governance in the EU* (London, Routledge, 2015).
Dawson, JP, *The Oracles of the Law* (Ann Arbor, The University of Michigan Law School, 1968).
Dichio, MA and Logvinenko, I, 'Culture and Practice Eat Documents for Lunch: Norms and Procedures in the 2020 Election Cases' (2025) 46 *Law and Policy* 298.
Dixon, R and Issacharoff, S, 'The Resilience of the Rule of Law' in RL Abel (ed), *Law's Wars: The Fate of the Rule of Law in the US 'War on Terror'* (Cambridge, Cambridge University Press, 2016) 650–86.
Dixon, R and Landau, D, *Abusive Constitutional Borrowing* (Oxford, Oxford University Press, 2021).
Donovan, T, 'Authoritarian Attitudes and Support for Radical Right Populists' (2019) 29 *Journal of Elections, Public Opinion and Parties* 448.
Emmons, C and Pavone, T, 'The Rhetoric of Inaction: Failing to Fail Forward in the EU's Rule of Law Crisis' (2021) 28 *Journal of European Public Policy* 1611.
Engler, S, Gessler, T, Abou Chadi, T and Leemann, L, 'Democracy Challenged: How Parties Politicize Different Democratic Principles' (2023) 30 *Journal of European Public Policy* 1961.
Enyedi, Z, 'Concept and Varieties of Illiberalism' (2024) 12 *Politics and Government* 1.
Epp, C, *Making Rights Real: Activists, Bureaucrats, and the Creation of the Legalistic State* (Chicago, University of Chicago Press, 2010).
Epstein, L and Knight, J, *The Choices Justices Make* (Washington, D.C., CQ Press, 1998).

Epstein, L and Waterbury, N, 'Judicial Behavior' in WR Thompson (ed), *Oxford Research Encyclopedia of Politics* (Oxford, Oxford University Press, 2020).
Foa, RS and Mounk, Y, 'The Danger of Deconsolidation: The Democratic Disconnect' (2016) 27 *Journal of Democracy* 5.
Foa, RS and Mounk, Y, 'The Signs of Deconsolidation' (2017) 28 *Journal of Democracy* 5.
Frederiksen, KVS, 'Do Partisanship and Policy Agreement Make Citizens Tolerate Undemocratic Behavior?' (2024) 86 *Journal of Politics* 766.
Freeden, M, 'Democracy Dis-integrated: The Current Conceptual Confusion' (2020) 25 *Journal of Political Ideologies* 1.
Fukuyama, F, *The End of History and the Last Man* (London, Penguin, 1993).
Gallie, WB, 'Essentially Contested Concepts' (1956) 56 *Proceedings of the Aristotelian Society* 167.
Galston, WA, 'The Populist Challenge to Liberal Democracy' (2018) 29 Journal of Democracy 5.
Gamboa, L, *Resisting Backsliding: Opposition Strategies Against the Erosion of Democracy* (Cambridge, Cambridge University Press, 2022).
Gamboa, L, García-Holgado, B and González-Ocantos, E, 'Courts against Backsliding: Lessons from Latin America' (2024) 46 *Law & Policy* 358.
Gandur, M, 'Public Partisan Reactions to Judicial Checks: Evidence from Argentina' (2023) American Political Science Association Working Paper.
Garcia-Holgado, B, 'Overruling the Executive: Judicial Strategies to Resist Democratic Erosion' (2025) *Journal of Law and Courts* (first view) 1.
Garoupa, N, 'Purging Disloyal Courts in Democratic Transitions and Judicial Preferences' (2024) 18 *International Journal of Transitional Justice* 474.
Giannoulopoulos, D and McDermott, Y (eds), *Judicial Independence Under Threat* (The British Academy by Oxford University Press, 2022).
Ginsburg, T, *Judicial Review in New Democracies. Constitutional Courts in Asian Cases* (Cambridge, Cambridge University Press, 2003).
Ginsburg, T and Garoupa, N, 'Judicial Audiences and Reputation: Perspectives from Comparative Law' (2009) 47 *Columbia Journal of Transnational Law* 451.
Ginsburg, T and Huq, A, *How to Save a Constitutional Democracy* (Chicago, University of Chicago Press, 2018).
Ginsburg, T and Moustafa, T, *Rule by Law: The Politics of Courts in Authoritarian Regimes* (Cambridge, Cambridge University Press, 2008).
González-Ocantos, E, *Shifting Legal Visions: Judicial Change and Human Rights Trials in Latin America* (New York, Cambridge University Press, 2016).
Grabowska-Moroz, B and Śniadach, O, 'The Role of Civil Society in Protecting Judicial Independence in Times of Rule of Law Backsliding in Poland' (2021) 17 *Utrecht Law Review* 56.
Graham, GMH and Svolik, W, 'Democracy in America? Partisanship, Polarization, and the Robustness of Support for Democracy in the United States' (2020) 114 *American Political Science Review* 392.
Graver, HP, *Judges against Justice on Judges when the Rule of Law is under Attack* (Berlin, Springer, 2015).
Graver, HP, *Valiant Judges, Iniquitous Law. Thirteen Stories of Heroes of the Law* (London, Routledge, 2024).
Green, C, 'An intellectual history of judicial activism' (2009) 58 *Emory Law Journal* 1195.
Guasti, P and Bustikova, L, 'Varieties of Illiberal Backlash in Central Europe' (2023) 70 *Problems of Post-Communism* 130.
Guarnieri, C, 'The judiciary in the Italian political crisis' (1997) 20 *West European Politics* 157.
Guarnieri, C and Pederzoli, P, *La puissance de juger* (Paris, Editions Michalon, 1996).
Halmai, G, *Perspectives on Global Constitutionalism* (The Hague, Eleven International Publishing, 2014).
Halmai, G, 'The Coup Against Constitutional Democracy. The Case of Hungary' in M Graber, S Levinson and M Tushnet (eds), *Constitutional Democracy in Crisis?* (Oxford, Oxford University Press, 2018) 243–56.
Halmai, G, 'From Liberal Democracy to Illiberal Populist Autocracy: Possible Reasons for Hungary's Autocratization' (2024) 16 *Hague Journal on the Rule of Law* 439.
Hamilton, A, 'Federalist no 78 (1788)' in GW Carey and J McClellan (eds), *The Federalist* (Indianapolis, Liberty Fund, c2001).
Handmaker, J, 'Introduction to the Legal Mobilization Special Focus' (2023) 15 *Journal of Human Rights Practice* 1.

Hendley, K, 'Varieties of Legal Dualism: Making Sense of the Role of Law in Contemporary Russia' (2011) 29 *Wisconsin International Law Journal* 233.
Hendley, K, *Everyday Law in Russia* (Ithaca, Cornell University Press, 2017).
Hermansen, S and Pavone, T, 'EU Law Litigation: Who Litigates, Who Influences Judges, What Downstream Effects?' in D Naurin, U Sadl and J Zglinski (eds), *Empirical Legal Studies of EU Law* (Cambridge University Press, forthcoming 2025).
Heywood, A, *Politics* (London, Macmillan International, 2019).
Hilbink, L, 'Agents of Anti-Politics: Courts in Pinochet's Chile' in T Ginsburg and T Moustafa (eds), *Judges Beyond Politics in Democracy and Dictatorship* (Cambridge, Cambridge University Press, 2007) 102–31.
Hilbink, L, *Judges beyond Politics in Democracy and Dictatorship. Lessons from Chile* (Cambridge, Cambridge University Press, 2007).
Hilbink, L, 'The Origins of Positive Judicial Independence' (2012) 64 *World Politics* 587.
Hirschl, R 'The Judicialization of Politics' in RE Goodin (ed), *The Oxford Handbook of Political Science* (Oxford and New York, Oxford University Press, 2011) 253–74.
Hoque, R and Khan, MMM, 'Judicial Activism and Islamic Family Law: A Socio-legal Evaluation of Recent Trends in Bangladesh' (2007) 14 *Islamic Law and Society* 204.
Horák, F, Lacko, D and Klocek, A, 'Legal Consciousness: A Systematic Review of its Conceptualization and Measurement Methods' (2021) 31 *Anuario de Psicología Jurídica* 9.
Huneeus, A, Couso, J and Sieder, R, *Cultures of Legality: Judicialization and Political Activism in Latin America* (Cambridge, Cambridge University Press, 2010).
Ingram, M, *Crafting Courts in New Democracies. The Politics of Subnational Judicial Reform in Brazil and Mexico* (Cambridge, Cambridge University Press, 2016).
Ingram, M, 'Networked Justice: Judges, the Diffusion of Ideas, and Legal Reform Movements in Mexico' (2016) 48 *Journal of Latin American Studies* 739.
Issacharoff, S, *Fragile Democracies. Contested Power in the Era of Constitutional Court* (Cambridge, Cambridge University Press, 2015).
Jakab, A, 'What Can Constitutional Law Do Against the Erosion of Democracy and the Rule of Law? On the Interconnectedness of the Protection of Democracy and the Rule of Law' (2020) 6 *Constitutional Studies* 5.
Kafka, F, *The Trial* (I Parry trans, Penguin Group, 2019).
Kapiszewski, D, *High Courts and Economic Governance in Argentina and Brazil* (Cambridge, Cambridge University Press, 2012).
Katsambekis, G, 'Mainstreaming Authoritarianism' (2023) 94 *The Political Quarterly* 428.
Kauth, JT and King, D, 'Illiberalism' (2020) 61 *European Journal of Sociology* 365.
Kazai, V, 'Constitutional Adjudication under Political Pressure – Judicial Review in Illiberal Political Regimes', paper presented at ICON-S CEE conference held in Prague in 2019.
Kelemen, RD, 'The European Union's Authoritarian Equilibrium' (2020) 27 *Journal of European Public Policy* 481.
Kelemen, RD, 'Will the European Union Escape its Autocracy Trap?' (2025) 32 *Journal of European Public Policy* 341.
Kelemen, RD and Pavone, T, 'Where Have the Guardians Gone? Law Enforcement and the Politics of Supranational Forbearance in the European Union' (2023) 75 *World Politics* 779.
King, JA, 'Institutional Approaches to Judicial Restraint' (2008) 28 *Oxford Journal of Legal Studies* 409.
Kingzette, J, Druckman, JN, Klar, S, Krupnikov, Y, Levendusky, M and Ryan, JB, 'How Affective Polarization Undermines Support for Democratic Norms' (2021) 85 *Public Opinion Quarterly* 663.
Kochenov, D and Bárd, P, 'The Last Soldier Standing? Courts versus Politicians and the Rule of Law Crisis in the New Member States of the EU' in H Ballin, G Van der Schyff and M Stremler (eds), *European Yearbook of Constitutional law 2019. Judicial Power: Safeguards and Limits in a Democratic Society* (The Hague, T.M.C. Asser Press, 2020) 243–87.
Kochenov, DV and Grabowska-Moroz, B, 'Constitutional Populism versus EU law: A much more Complex Story than You Imagined', in M Krygier, A Czarnota, W Sadurski (eds), *Anti-Constitutional Populism* (Cambridge, Cambridge University Press, 2022).
Kosař, D, *Perils of Judicial Self-Government in Transitional Societies* (Cambridge, Cambridge University Press, 2016).

Kosař, D and Šipulová, K, 'Comparative Court-Packing' (2023) 21 *International Journal of Constitutional Law* 80.

Kosař, D and Šipulová, K, 'Court-Unpacking: A Preliminary Inquiry' in M Bobek, A Bodnar, A von Bogdandy and P Sonnevend (eds), *Transition 2.0 Re-establishing Constitutional Democracy in EU Member States* (Baden-Baden, Nomos, 2023) 323–60.

Kovács, K and Scheppele, KL, 'The Fragility of an Independent Judiciary: Lessons from Hungary and Poland–and the European Union' (2018) 51 *Communist and Post-Communist Studies* 189.

Krehbiel, JN, 'Public Awareness and the Behaviour of Unpopular Courts' (2020) 51 *British Journal of Political Science* 1601.

Krishnarajan, S, 'Rationalizing Democracy: The Perceptual Bias and (Un)Democratic Behavior' (2023) 117 *American Political Science Review* 474.

Krygier, M, 'Rule of Law (and Rechtsstaat)' in JR Silkenat, JE Hickeyand and PD Barenboim (eds), *The Legal Doctrines of the Rule of Law and the Legal State (Rechtsstaat)* (Cham, Springer, 2014) 45–61.

Krygier, M, 'Illiberalism and the Rule of Law' in A Sajó, R Uitz and S Holmes (eds), *Routledge Handbook of Illiberalism* (New York, Routledge, 2021) 533–53.

Krygier, M, 'Introduction: Anti-constitutional Populism' in M Krygier, A Czarnota and W Sadurski (eds), *Anti-Constitutional Populism* (Cambridge, Cambridge University Press, 2022).

Kubal, A, *Immigration and Refugee Law in Russia* (Cambridge, Cambridge University Press, 2019).

Kubal, A, 'Judicial Relational Legal Consciousness: Authoritarian Backsliding as a Catalyst of Change' (2024) 51 *Journal of Law and Society* S45.

Kubal, A, 'Queer Coalition? Rule of Law Crisis and LGBTQ+ Rights in Polish Courts' (2024) 76 *Europe-Asia Studies* 1347.

Kühn, Z, 'The Judiciary in Illiberal States' (2021) 22 *German Law Journal* 1231.

Kureshi, Y 'When Judges Defy Dictators' (2021) 53 *Comparative Politics* 233.

Lachmayer, K, 'Formalism and Judicial Self-restraint as Tools Against Populism?' in F Gárdos-Orosz and Z Szente (eds), *Populist Challenges to Constitutional Interpretation in Europe and Beyond* (London, Routledge, 2021) 75–94.

Ladrech, R, *Europeanization and National Politics* (Basingstoke, Palgrave, 2010).

Laruelle, M, 'Illiberalism: A Conceptual Introduction' (2022) 38 *East European Politic* 303.

Latour, B, *La fabrique du droit. Une ethnographie du Conseil d'État* (Paris, La Découverte, 1999).

Leca, J, 'La démocratie à l'épreuve des pluralismes' (1996) 46 *Revue française de science politique* 225.

Leisure, P and Kosař, D, 'Court-hoarding: Another Method of Gaming Judicial Turnover' (2025) 46 *Law and Policy* 328.

Levitsky, S and Way, L, 'The Resilience of Democracy's Third Wave' (2024) 57 *Political Science & Politics* 198.

Levitsky, S and Ziblatt, D, *How Democracies Die* (New York, Crown, 2018).

Lewandowsky, M and Jankowski, M, 'Sympathy for the Devil? Voter Support for Illiberal Politicians' (2023) 15 *European Political Science Review* 39.

Linz, J and Stephan, A, *The Breakdown of Democratic Regimes: An Introduction* (Baltimore, The Johns Hopkins University Press, 1978).

Little, AT and Meng, A, 'What We Do and Do Not Know about Democratic Backsliding' (2024) 57 *Political Science & Politics 1.*

Losurdo, D, *Controstoria del liberalismo* (Bari-Roma, Laterza, 2005).

Loughlin, M, *Against Constitutionalism* (Cambridge, MA, Harvard University Press, 2022) 129.

Lührmann, A and Lindberg, SI, 'A Third Wave of Autocratization is Here: What is New about it?' (2019) 26 *Democratization* 1095.

Magalhaes, P, Guarnieri, C and Kaminis, Y, 'Democratic Consolidation, Judicial Reform and the Judiciarisation of Politics in Southern Europe' in R Gunther, N Diamandouros and D Sotiropoulos (eds), *Democracy and the State in the New Southern Europe* (Oxford, Oxford University Press, 2006) 139–96.

Magnette, P, *L'Europe, l'Etat et la démocratie* (Bruxelles, Editions Complexe, 2000).

Mahoney, J, 'Path Dependence in Historical Sociology' (2000) 29 *Theory and Society* 507.

Malka, A, Lelkes, Y, Bakker, BN and Spivack, E, 'Who Is Open to Authoritarian Governance within Western Democracies?' (2022) 20 *Perspectives on Politics* 807.

Mandujano Manriquez, M and Pavone, T, 'Follow the Leader: The European Commission, the European Court of Justice, and the EU's Rule of Law Revolution' (2024) 32 *Journal of European Public Policy* 444.

Martinez, JS, 'Horizontal Structuring' in A Sajó and M Rosenfeld (eds), *The Oxford Handbook of Comparative Constitutional Law* (Oxford, Oxford University Press, 2012) 548–76.

Matthes, CY, 'Judges as Activists: How Polish Judges Mobilise to Defend the Rule of Law' (2022) 38 *East European Politics* 468.

Mayoral, JA and Pérez, AT, 'On Judicial Mobilisation: Entrepreneuring for Policy Change at Time of Crisis' (2018) 40 *Journal of European Integration* 719.

McCann, M, *Rights at Work: Pay Equity Reform and the Politics of Legal Mobilization* (Chicago, University of Chicago Press, 1994).

McCoy, J and Somer, M, 'Toward a Theory of Pernicious Polarization and How It Harms Democracies: Comparative Evidence and Possible Remedies' (2018) 68 *The ANNALS of the American Academy of Political and Social Science* 234.

Mény, Y and Surel, Y, 'The Constitutive Ambiguity of Populism' in Y Mény and Y Surel (eds), *Democracies and the Populist Challenge* (New York, Palgrave, 2002).

Merkel, W, 'Embedded and Defective Democracies' (2004) 11 *Democratization* 33.

Merkel, W and Lührmann, A, 'Resilience of Democracies: Responses to Illiberal and Authoritarian Challenges' (2021) 28 *Democratization*, 871.

Moliterno, JE and Čuroš, P, 'Recent Attacks on Judicial Independence: The Vulgar, the Systemic, and the Insidious' (2021) 22 *German Law Journal* 1159.

Mondon, A, 'I Was Gonna Fight Fascism … The Need for a Critical Approach to Illiberalism' (2024) 4 *Journal of Illiberalism Studies* 9.

Mondon, A, 'Really Existing Liberalism, the Bulwark Fantasy, and the Enabling of Reactionary, Far Right Politics' (2024) *Constellations* (advance online publication).

Mondon, A, and Winter, A, *Reactionary Democracy: How Racism and the Populist Far Right Became Mainstream* (London, Verso, 2020).

Moustafa, T, *The Struggle for Constitutional Power. Law Politics and Economic Development in Egypt* (Cambridge, Cambridge University Press, 2007).

Muller, J-W, *What is Populism?* (Philadelphia, University of Pennsylvania Press, 2016).

Mrowicki, M, *All Rise – Judicial Resistance in Poland* (Washington, D.C., International Center on Nonviolent Conflict 2024).

Norris, P, 'Is Western Democracy Backsliding? Diagnosing the Risks' (2017) *Journal of Democracy*, Online exchange on 'Democratic Deconsolidation'.

Page, S, 'Path dependence' (2006) 1 *Quarterly Journal of Political Science* 87.

Papazoski, Z, 'Major Voter Turn-out in Poland's 2023 Parliamentary Elections' (31 October 2023) National Democracy Institute.

Patterson, M and Renwick Monroe, K, 'Narrative in Political Science' (1998) 1 *Annual Review of Political Science* 315.

Pavone, T, 'Revisiting Judicial Empowerment in the European Union: Limits of Empowerment, Logics of Resistance' (2018) 6 *Journal of Law & Courts* 303.

Pavone, T, 'From Marx to Market: Lawyers, European Law, and the Contentious Transformation of the Port of Genoa' (2019) 53 *Law & Society Review* 851.

Pavone, T, 'Like Oil Floating on Water: Italy's Olive Crisis and the Politics of Backlash against Transnational Legal Orders' (2021) 14 *FIU Law Review* 633.

Pavone, T, '"In this Bureaucratic Silence EU Law Dies": Fieldwork and the (Non)-Practice of EU law in National Courts' in M Rask Madsen, F Nicola and A Vauchez (eds), *Researching the European Court of Justice: Methodological Shifts and Law's Embeddedness* (Cambridge, Cambridge University Press, 2022) 27–48.

Pavone, T, *The Ghostwriters: Lawyers and the Politics Behind the Judicial Construction of Europe* (Cambridge, Cambridge University Press, 2022).

Pavone, T, 'Is the EU's Rule of Law Crisis a Byproduct of Dissensus and Disunion?' (2024) 46 *Journal of European Integration* 963.

Pech, L and Kochenov, D, *Respect for the Rule of Law in the Case Law of the European Court of Justice: A Casebook Overview of Key Judgments since the Portuguese Judges Case* (Stockholm, SIEPS, 2021).

Pech, L and Scheppele, KL, 'Illiberalism Within: Rule of Law Backsliding in the EU' (2017) 19 *Cambridge Yearbook of European Legal Studies* 3.

Pereira, AW, *Political (In)Justice. Authoritarianism and the Rule of Law in Brazil, Chile and Argentina.* (Pittsburgh, University of Pittsburgh Press, 2005).
Pető, A, 'Current Comment: The Illiberal Academic Authority. An Oxymoron?' (2021) 44 *Ber. Wissenschaftsgesch* 461.
Piana, D, *Judicial Accountabilities in New Europe. From Rule of Law to Quality of Justice* (Farnham, Ashgate, 2010).
Piccolino, G and Puleo, L, 'Ideological Drivers of Participatory Democracy in Europe: Disentangling the Different Approaches of Populism and Post-materialist Politics' (2024) 23 *European Political Science* 115.
Pirro, ALP, Stanley, B, 'Forging, Bending, and Breaking: Enacting the "Illiberal Playbook" in Hungary and Poland' (2022) 20 *Perspectives on Politics* 86.
Plattner, M 'From Liberalism to Liberal Democracy' (1999) 10 *Journal of Democracy* 121.
Plattner, M, 'Illiberal Democracy and the Struggle on the Right" (2019) 30 *Journal of Democracy* 5.
Pompeo, M, *Never Give an Inch: Fighting for the America I Love* (New York, Harper Collins, 2023).
Popova, M, 'Can a Leopard Change its Spots? Strategic Behaviour versus Professional Role Conception During Ukraine's 2014 Court Chair Clections' (2020) 42 *Law & Policy* 365.
Posner, RA, 'The Meaning of Judicial Self-Restraint' (1983) 59 *Indiana Law Journal* 59.
Posner, RA, *How Judges Think* (Cambridge, Harvard University Press, 2010).
Posner, RA, 'The Rise and Fall of Judicial Self-Restraint' (2012) 100 *California Law Review* 519.
Przeworski, A, *Democracy and the Market: Political and Economic Reforms in Eastern Europe and Latin America* (Cambridge, Cambridge University Press, 1991).
Puleo, L and Coman, R, 'Explaining Judges' Opposition when Judicial Independence is Undermined: Insights from Poland, Romania, and Hungary' (2024) 31 *Democratization* 47.
Riedl, RB, Friesen, P, McCoy, J and Roberts, K, 'Democratic Backsliding, Resilience, and Resistance' (December) 75 *World Politics* 1.
Robinson, R and Swedlow, B, 'Beyond Liberal and Conservative: Advancing the Study of Judicial Behavior with a Cultural Theory of Political Values' (2018) 6 *Journal of Law and Courts* 263.
Rosenblatt, H, *The Lost History of Liberalism: From Ancient Rome to the Twenty-first Century* (Princeton, Princeton University Press, 2018).
Sadurski, W, 'How Democracy Dies (in Poland): A Case Study of Anti-Constitutional Populist Backsliding' (2018) 18/01 *Sydney Law School Research Paper.*
Sadurski, W, *Poland's Constitutional Breakdown* (Oxford, Oxford University Press 2019).
Sajó, A, *Ruling by Cheating Governance in Illiberal Democracy* (Cambridge, Cambridge University Press, 2020).
Sajó, A and Uitz, R, *Constitution of Freedom. An Introduction to Legal Constitutionalism* (Oxford, Oxford University Press, 2017).
Sallusti, A and Palamara, L, *Il Sistema. Potere, Politica, Affari: Storia Segrata della Magistratura italiana* (Milan, Rizzoli, 2021).
Saurugger, S and Terpan, F, *The Court of Justice of the European Union and the Politics of the Law* (London, Palgrave, 2017).
Schaaf, SD, 'When Do Courts Constrain the Authoritarian State? Judicial Decision-Making in Jordan and Palestine' (2022) 54 *Comparative Politics* 375.
Schacter, JS, 'Putting the Politics of "Judicial Activism" in Historical Perspective' (2018) 2017 *The Supreme Court Review* 209.
Schafer, A and Zurn, M, *Democratic Regression. The Political Causes of Authoritarian Populism* (Cambridge, Polity Press, 2024).
Scheppele, KL, 'Autocratic Legalism' (2018) 85 *University of Chicago Law Review* 545.
Sedelmeier, U, 'Anchoring Democracy from Above? The European Union and Democratic Backsliding in Hungary and Romania after Accession' (2014) 52 *Journal of Common Market Studies* 105.
Sedelmeier, U, 'Is Europeanistion through Conditionality Sustainable? Lock-in of Institutional Change after EU Accession' in T Borzel and T Risse (eds), *From Europeanisation to Diffusion* (London, Routledge 2014) 20–38.
Segal, JA and Spaeth, HJ, *The Supreme Court and the Attitudinal Model* (Cambridge, Cambridge University Press, 1993).
Silbey, S, 'After Legal Consciousness' (2005) 1 *Annual Review of Law and Social Science* 323.

Sillen, J, 'The Concept of "Internal Judicial Independence" in the Case Law of the European Court of Human Rights' (2019) 15 *European Constitutional Law Review* 114.
Šipulová, K, 'The Light and the Dark Side of Judicial Resistance' (2025) 47 *Law & Policy* 1.
Šipulová, K and Kosař, D, 'Purging The Judiciary After a Transition: Between the Rock and the Hard Place' (2025) 17 *Hague Journal on the Rule of Law* 61.
Šipulová, K and Smekal, H, 'Between Human Rights and Transitional Justice: The Dilemma of Constitutional Courts in Post-Communist Central Europe' (2021) 73 *Europa-Asia Studies* 1010.
Šipulová, K and Spáč, S, '(No) Ghost in the Shell: The Role of Values Internalization in Judicial Empowerment in Slovakia' (2023) 24 *German Law Journal* 1412.
Skóra, M, Nonhoff, D and Albrecht, Y, *What Makes the Rule of Law Resilient? Evidence from EU27. RESILIO Monitor Full Report* (Berlin, Institut für Europäische Politik, 2024).
Smilov, D, 'The Judiciary: The Least Dangerous Branch?' in A Sajó and M Rosenfeld (eds), *The Oxford Handbook of Comparative Constitutional Law* (Oxford, Oxford University Press, 2012) 859–73.
Smilova, R, 'The Ideational Core of Democratic Illiberalism' in A Sajó, R Uitz and S Holmes (eds), *Routledge Handbook of Illiberalism* (New York, Routledge, 2021) 177–202.
Somers, MR and Gibson, GD, 'Reclaiming the Epistemological "Other": Narrative and the Social Constitution of Identity', in C Calhoun (ed), *Social Theory and the Politics of Identity* (Oxford, Blackwell 1994) 35–99.
Spano, R, 'The Rule of Law as the Lodestar of the European Convention on Human Rights: The Strasbourg Court and the Independence of the Judiciary' (2021) 27 *European Law Journal* 211.
Staton, JK, *Judicial Power and Strategic Communication in Mexico* (Cambridge: Cambridge University Press, 2010).
Stone Sweet, A, *Governing with Judges: Constitutional Politics in Europe* (Oxford, Oxford University Press, 2000).
Stone Sweet, A, *The Judicial Construction of Europe* (New York, Oxford University Press, 2004).
Stone, DA, 'Causal Stories and the Formation of Policy Agenda' (1989) 104 *Political Science Quarterly* 281.
Szwed, M, 'Protecting the Rights of Judges: the Judgments of the European Court of Human Rights in Juszczyszyn v Poland and Tuleya v. Poland' (2024) 25 *ERA Forum* 141.
Tilly, C and Tarrow, S, *Contentious Politics,* 2nd edn (New York, Oxford University Press, 2015).
Trochev, A and Ellett, R, 'Judges and their Allies: Rethinking Judicial Autonomy through the Prism of Off-Bench Resistance' (2014) 2 *Journal of Law and Courts* 67.
Valentim, V, *The Normalization of the Radical Right: A Norms Theory of Political Supply and Demand* (New York, Oxford University Press, 2024).
Vanhala, L, *Making Rights a Reality? Disability Rights Activists and Legal Mobilization* (Cambridge, Cambridge University Press, 2010).
Vauchez, A (ed), *Brokering Europe. Euro-Lawyers and the Making of a Transnational Polity* (Cambridge, Cambridge University Press, 2015).
Vigour, C, 'Réformer la justice en Europe. Analyse comparée des cas de la Belgique, de la France et de l'Italie' (2004) *Droit et société* 291.
Vile, MJC, *Constitutionalism and the Separation of Powers*, 2nd edn (Indianapolis, Liberty Fund, 1998).
Vink, MP and Graziano, P, 'Challenges of a New Research Agenda' in P Graziano and MP Vink (eds), *Europeanization. New Research Agendas* (New York, Palgrave Macmillan, 2008).
Vittori, D, 'Threat or Corrective? Assessing the Impact of Populist Parties in Government on the Qualities of Democracy: A 19-Country Comparison' (2022) 57 *Government and Opposition* 589.
Wind, M, 'The Nordics, the EU, and the Reluctance Toward Supranational Judicial Review' (2010) 48 *Journal of Common Market Studies* 1039.
Wuttke, A, Gavras, K and Schoen, H, 'Have Europeans Grown Tired of Democracy? New Evidence from Eighteen Consolidated Democracies, 1981–2018' (2020) 52 *British Journal of Political Science* 416.
Wyrzykowski, M, and Ziółkowski, M, 'Illiberal Constitutionalism and the Judiciary' in A Sajó, R Uitz and S Holmes (eds), *Routledge Handbook of Illiberalism* (New York, Routledge, 2021) 517–32.
Yam, J, 'Judging Under Authoritarianism' (2024) 87 *Modern Law Review* 894.
Zakaria, F, 'The Rise of Illiberal Democracy' (1997) 76 *Foreign Affairs* 22.
Zambrano, D, da Silva, LM, Garcia Miron, R and Rodríguez, S, 'How Latin America's Judges are Defending Democracy' (2024) 35 *Journal of Democracy* 118.

INDEX

www.ingramcontent.com/pod-product-compliance
Ingram Content Group UK Ltd.
Pitfield, Milton Keynes, MK11 3LW, UK
UKHW020239290926
15470UKWH00002B/628

9 781509 985005